Teaching Inquiry Science
in Middle and Secondary Schools

Teaching Inquiry Science
in Middle and Secondary Schools

Anton E. Lawson
Arizona State University

SAGE

Los Angeles | London | New Delhi
Singapore | Washington DC

For information:

SAGE Publications, Inc.
2455 Teller Road
Thousand Oaks, California 91320
E-mail: order@sagepub.com

SAGE Publications Ltd.
1 Oliver's Yard
55 City Road
London EC1Y 1SP
United Kingdom

SAGE Publications India Pvt. Ltd.
B 1/I 1 Mohan Cooperative Industrial Area
Mathura Road, New Delhi 110 044
India

SAGE Publications Asia-Pacific Pte. Ltd.
33 Pekin Street #02-01
Far East Square
Singapore 048763

Printed in the United States of America.

Library of Congress Cataloging-in-Publication Data

Lawson, Anton E.
Teaching inquiry science in middle and secondary schools / Anton E. Lawson.
    p. cm.
Includes bibliographical references and index.
ISBN 978-1-4129-6665-8 (pbk.)

  1. Science—Study and teaching (Middle school)   2. Science—Study and teaching (Secondary)
3. Science teachers—Training of. I. Title.

LB1585.L35 2010
507.1'2—dc22   2009015332

Printed on acid-free paper

10   11   12   13   10   9   8   7   6   5   4   3   2

Acquiring Editor:	Diane McDaniel
Associate Editor:	Deya Saoud
Editorial Assistant:	Ashley Conlon
Production Editor:	Sarah K. Quesenberry
Copy Editor:	Melinda Masson
Proofreader:	Gail Fay
Indexer:	Rick Hurd
Typesetter:	C&M Digitals (P) Ltd.
Cover Designer:	Edgar Abarca
Marketing Manager:	Christy Guilbault

Brief Contents

Detailed Contents

Preface

We face several genuine crises in today's world. To remain competitive in that world—indeed, to ensure that humans survive—we must produce both knowledgeable and reflective world citizens capable of making sound decisions now and in the future. This book has been written to that end.

The book is a core textbook for use in courses in middle and high school science teaching methods (i.e., for preservice science teachers who will be teaching Grades 7 through 12). It also will serve as a text for graduate-level instruction in science education for middle and secondary teachers. Additionally it should be of interest to in-service science teachers, university-level science educators, school curriculum personnel, and administrators who wish to update their knowledge of the latest developments in science teaching.

THE APPROACH

What do new science teachers need to know to teach science effectively? My answer to this question is based on answers to these six subordinate questions:

1. What is science?
2. Why teach science?
3. What is the nature of scientific knowledge?
4. How do scientists construct new knowledge?
5. How do children and adolescents learn science concepts and develop scientific reasoning patterns?
6. What teaching methods best help students construct new conceptual knowledge and develop general scientific reasoning patterns?

A primary goal is to answer these questions so that new science teachers not only gain effective science teaching methods but also gain a coherent philosophy of science teaching and a psychologically sound theory of science instruction. A secondary but equally important goal is to include sufficient examples so new teachers can implement the methods in their classrooms with the greatest possible success. The book's main thesis is that students can and should become active, self-directed learners. Truly effective science teaching demands that this self-driven constructive process occur because it is the best way that science instruction can help students construct science concepts *and* develop creative and critical reasoning skills.

The book is unique in at least three ways.

First, it clearly *explicates the nature of the scientific inquiry process.* Experts agree that teachers should teach science as science is practiced. Thus it becomes crucial that teachers develop a sound understanding of scientific inquiry. Unfortunately, in spite of an undergraduate major in the sciences, few students arrive in their science methods courses knowing much about how inquiry works. This book should go a long way in solving that problem.

Second, the book specifically *presents methods for teaching scientific reasoning patterns in the context of inquiry instruction.* In other words, use of the teaching methods not only results in students who better understand key scientific concepts and theories, that is, how science works; the methods also show students how to learn and think scientifically.

Lastly, the book presents a *research-tested theory of instruction complete with cutting-edge work in the field of cognitive psychology.* Thus, the book not only contains useful and practical suggestions for improving science teaching; it also contains the latest in research and pedagogical theory.

ORGANIZATION

The book is organized into five parts.

Part I consists of two chapters on *the nature of science.* **Chapter 1** begins with a brief look at educational purpose and then examines the way science works—that is, the way scientists construct knowledge, the nature of that knowledge, and the reasoning patterns used in knowledge construction. **Chapter 2** continues our look at the nature of science by considering the nature of scientific theories. What are they? What are they for? How are they constructed? And how are they sometimes modified or rejected? Understanding the role theories play in science is invaluable in developing inquiry-based teaching methods, in developing good lesson plans, and in constructing an effective inquiry-based curriculum.

Part II consists of two chapters that *explore student thinking, development, and learning.* Becoming a skilled science teacher requires not only understanding the nature of science but also knowing your students—knowing what they know, what they don't know, and how they reason. Thus **Chapter 3** explores the fascinating topic of student reasoning. The intent is to learn more about how students think so you can help them become more skilled reasoners and better able to learn science concepts and theories. **Chapter 4** introduces the process of self-regulation. Self-regulation is the mental "motor" of learning and intellectual development. The chapter also discusses the important distinction between declarative knowledge (i.e., facts and concepts) and procedural knowledge (i.e., reasoning patterns). Importantly, due to its ability to engage students in self-regulation, inquiry instruction facilitates the construction of both types of knowledge.

Part III consists of four chapters that explore *key elements of inquiry instruction.* **Chapter 5** places the current emphasis on inquiry in its proper historical context by considering some early approaches to science instruction. The chapter then discusses an inquiry approach to physics teaching known as the modeling method. The chapter also discusses how inquiry instruction can improve student creativity, intelligence, and achievement. **Chapter 6** directly confronts the book's central question: What teaching method best helps students learn meaningful science concepts and theories, learn how science works, and develop better reasoning patterns? Based on evidence presented in the previous chapters, we know that self-regulation is involved and that the following events must take place: Students need to explore new phenomena based on present concepts and reasoning patterns. The explorations must produce results that contradict expectations. This produces disequilibrium, which in turn provokes self-regulation and the search for new concepts and/or better reasoning patterns. With this general inquiry-based teaching method in mind, Chapter 7 focuses on lesson planning by identifying key components of inquiry lessons, including student behaviors, teacher behaviors, and questioning techniques. Chapter 8 concludes this part by discussing the current status of technology use in the inquiry classroom and by providing guidelines on how best to incorporate its use. The chapter also discusses the role played by labs and the need for classroom safety guidelines.

Part IV consists of five chapters that introduce several needed *instructional strategies*. To enrich and expand student inquiry, Chapter 9 presents strategies for conducting demonstrations, mini lectures, discussions, and field trips. Good lesson plans help but do not ensure that things run smoothly. Chapter 10, therefore, discusses classroom management problems and the knowledge and skills needed to solve them. Chapter 11 takes up the important topic of student diversity. The chapter begins by considering teaching strategies for English-language learners and then briefly considers ways of avoiding bias in the classroom. Next the chapter discusses strategies for meeting the needs of students with learning disabilities. It then turns to how you can meet the needs of gifted students and concludes with a look at textbook selection and use. Chapter 12 explores curricular approaches that intend not only to teach current knowledge but also to promote the development of reasoning skills. The chapter starts with a closer look at the nature of declarative knowledge—specifically at types of concepts that exist and the order in which they should be taught. The chapter also discusses how to sequence learning cycles and how to integrate technological and societal issues into the curriculum. Chapter 13 begins with a look at types of assessments, how to reduce bias in testing, and how to assign grades. It then considers how to develop effective exams, homework problems, and written assignments.

Part V contains two chapters that address topics of *professional induction and development*. Chapter 14 raises the perplexing question of why more teachers don't use inquiry teaching methods. Teacher interviews suggest several reasons. The chapter confronts these reasons and provides ways of overcoming them. Chapter 15 considers important national standards for professional development and ways in which teachers can become more effective inquiry teachers. It then considers relatively recent research on teacher effectiveness showing that good teaching really matters. The chapter concludes by raising some research questions that teachers can tackle in their own classrooms.

PEDAGOGICAL FEATURES

Chapters begin with engaging activities. Each activity allows readers to begin exploring key issues and/or questions. For example, Chapter 1 begins by posing five alternative approaches to introducing the topic of density. Readers are then challenged to think about each alternative in terms of broader instructional goals. In other words, what do we really want students to know and/or be able to do, and which approach best accomplishes our goals?

Emphasizes scientific reasoning and the nature of science. Many college students who plan to become science teachers lack skill in the use of identifiable and "teachable" reasoning patterns. These reasoning patterns are required not only for doing science but also for acquiring understanding of abstract scientific concepts. And they are most certainly required for teaching inquiry science. Although scientific reasoning is multifaceted, at its core lies an *If/and/then* pattern in which tentative explanations are generated and tested. For example, in response to the question "How do salmon find their home stream to spawn?" one might generate the hypothesis that they do so by smelling dissolved chemicals in the water. Testing this hypothesis can be accomplished with the following reasoning:

If . . . returning salmon smell chemicals in the water to find their home stream (hypothesis),

and . . . the noses of some returning salmon are plugged (planned test),

then . . . these salmon should not be as successful at finding their home stream as some that can smell (prediction).

When this test was later conducted, biologists found that the returning salmon that could smell were significantly more successful than those that could not. *Therefore,* they concluded that the smell hypothesis had been supported. Because skill in use of this sort of hypothetical-predictive reasoning has yet to be acquired by many students, the reasoning pattern is emphasized. This emphasis helps students separate the pattern from the specific contexts in which it is embedded, and thus they become more skilled in its use.

Introduces ideas before terms. Learning new terms is often difficult, particularly in term-rich fields such as science. Consequently, when new terms are introduced, they are introduced only *after* the ideas and examples to which the terms relate have been introduced, discussed, and defined. In this way the new terms have something to connect with in memory; thus they are more easily understood and remembered. For example, before Chapter 4 introduces the term *self-regulation,* students try their hand at mirror drawing. They discover that drawing in a mirror is very difficult as their initial drawing attempts are contracted. Hence, without knowing it, they become engaged in the process of self-regulation. Thus when the term *self-regulation* is later introduced, the students have a direct and recent experience to connect it with.

Makes historical connections. Not only does the text trace the historical roots of inquiry instruction; it also embeds many scientific ideas in their historical contexts. For example, Chapter 2 introduces the Greek four-material theory as a conceptual backdrop for exploring the later "discovery" of oxygen and atomic-molecular theory. Understanding the historical contexts of scientific discoveries is invaluable in designing good inquiry-based lessons because student conceptual development often recapitulates historical development.

Includes concise end-of-chapter reviews. Each chapter concludes with a summary of the chapter's main points and a series of application questions/activities. The summaries allow students to quickly review the main concepts that have been introduced. The application questions/activities are intended to be thought provoking, to encourage students to think beyond what has been discussed, and to explore the concepts' applications and implications. The point is not to narrow students' focus but to broaden it.

Keeps the number of technical terms to a minimum. Many texts introduce hundreds of technical terms. Unnecessary technical terms often hinder meaningful learning because students are unable to separate the important from the trivial. While writing the present text, I carefully considered each term that could be introduced and the number of introduced terms was kept to a minimum.

Includes a complete glossary of key terms. Although the number of technical terms is kept to a minimum, several key terms are introduced using the "ideas first, terms second" approach. These key terms are then defined in a complete glossary.

Includes national standards. The *National Science Education Standards* (National Research Council, 1996) call for teaching science as an inquiry process. For example, Standard A states, "Science teachers plan an inquiry-based program." Standard B states, "Science teachers guide and facilitate learning. In doing so, they focus and support inquiries while interacting with students, and they encourage and model the skills of scientific inquiry." And Standard E states, "Science teachers develop communities of learners that reflect the intellectual rigor of scientific inquiry." Again in the words of the National Research Council (1996, p. 2), "In this way students actively develop their understanding of science by combining scientific knowledge with reasoning and thinking skills." Thus inclusion of the national standards with their emphasis on inquiry teaching aligns perfectly with the book's explication of what scientific inquiry really is, how to embed it into the science curriculum, how to best manage the inquiry classroom, and how to best assess the outcomes of inquiry such as better (a) understanding of science concepts, (b) understanding of the nature of scientific inquiry, (c) reasoning and problem-solving skills, and (d) attitudes toward science. The *National Science Education Standards* are included on the following pages, and each chapter includes a box that indicates which standards correspond to the chapter material. A grid providing an at-a-glance look at how the standards line up with the chapters follows the standards.

OVERVIEW OF TEACHING STANDARDS FROM THE *NATIONAL SCIENCE EDUCATION STANDARDS*

Science Teaching Standards The standards for science teaching are grounded in five assumptions.

- The vision of science education described by the *Standards* requires changes throughout the entire system.
- What students learn is greatly influenced by how they are taught.
- The actions of teachers are deeply influenced by their perceptions of science as an enterprise and as a subject to be taught and learned.

(Continued)

(Continued)

■ Student understanding is actively constructed through individual and social processes.
■ Actions of teachers are deeply influenced by their understanding of and relationships with students.

Teaching Standard A: Teachers of science plan an inquiry-based science program for their students. In doing this, teachers

■ Develop a framework of yearlong and short-term goals for students.
■ Select science content and adapt and design curricula to meet the interest, knowledge, understanding, abilities, and experiences of students.
■ Select teaching and assessment strategies that support the development of student understanding and nurture a community of science learners.
■ Work together as colleagues within and across disciplines and grade levels.

Teaching Standard B: Teachers of science guide and facilitate learning. In doing this, teachers

■ Focus and support inquiries while interacting with students.
■ Orchestrate discourse among students about scientific ideas.
■ Challenge students to accept and share responsibility for their own learning.
■ Recognize and respond to student diversity and encourage all students to participate fully in science learning.
■ Encourage and model the skills of scientific inquiry, as well as the curiosity, openness to new ideas and data, and skepticism that characterize science.

Teaching Standard C: Teachers of science engage in ongoing assessment of their teaching and of student learning. In doing this, teachers

■ Use multiple methods and systematically gather data about student understanding and ability.
■ Analyze assessment data to guide teaching.
■ Guide students in self-assessment.
■ Use student data, observations of teaching, and interactions with colleagues to reflect on and improve teaching practice.

■ Use student data, observations of teaching, and interactions with colleagues to report student achievement and opportunities to learn to students, teachers, parents, policy makers, and the general public.

Teaching Standard D:

Teachers of science design and manage learning environments that provide students with the time, space, and resources needed for learning science. In doing this, teachers

■ Structure the time available so that students are able to engage in extended investigations.
■ Create a setting for student work that is flexible and supportive of science inquiry.
■ Ensure a safe working environment.
■ Make the available science tools, materials, media, and technological resources accessible to students.
■ Identify and use resources outside the school.
■ Engage students in designing the learning environment.

Teaching Standard E:

Teachers of science develop communities of science learners that reflect the intellectual rigor of scientific inquiry and the attitudes and social values conducive to science learning. In doing this, teachers

■ Display and demand respect for the diverse ideas, skills, and experiences of all students.
■ Enable students to have a significant voice in decisions about the content and context of their work and require students to take responsibility for the learning of all members of the community.
■ Nurture collaboration among students.
■ Structure and facilitate ongoing formal and informal discussion based on a shared understanding of rules of scientific discourse.
■ Model and emphasize the skills, attitudes, and values of scientific inquiry.

Teaching Standard F:

Teachers of science actively participate in the ongoing planning and development of the school science program. In doing this, teachers

■ Plan and develop the school science program.
■ Participate in decisions concerning the allocation of time and other resources to the science program.
■ Participate fully in planning and implementing professional growth and development strategies for themselves and their colleagues.

Source: From the *National Science Education Standards*, National Research Council, 1996a, excerpted from pages 27–53.

Chapter	Standard A	Standard B	Standard C	Standard D	Standard E	Standard F
1	■					
2		■			■	
3	■					
4					■	
5	■					
6		■				
7	■					
8				■		
9		■		■		
10		■		■	■	
11	■	■			■	
12						■
13			■			
14			■			
15						■

ANCILLARIES

Instructor Resources are available on a password-protected Web site (www.sagepub.com/lawsoninstr). These include PowerPoint slides for each chapter, a test bank, chapter outlines with notes for the instructor, Internet resources, and example assignments. Qualified instructors may contact Customer Care to receive access to the site.

ACKNOWLEDGMENTS

The late Chester Lawson, Robert Karplus, and Jack Renner were my intellectual fathers. They are missed, but their ideas are alive and well in this book. I thank them for this. Other colleagues who have contributed ideas and advice are John Alcock, Dan Alpert, James Birk, Ken Costenson, David Hestenes, Michael Piburn, Warren Wollman, and several former students who are now successful science teachers. Also a very special thanks is due to Deya

Saoud, Ashley Conlon, Diane McDaniel, Sarah Quesenberry, Melinda Masson, and Leah Mori of SAGE Publications. I would also like to thank the reviewers for their numerous and very helpful comments on the manuscript. They are:

Matthew J. Benus, Purdue University

Joseph Cifelli, St. Joseph's University

Malonne Davies, Emporia State University

Lisa Donnelly, Kent State University

Anuradha Dujari, Delaware State University

James Ealy, Cedar Crest College

Linda M. Easley, Louisiana State University in Shreveport

Bonita Flournoy, Columbus State University

Wendy M. Frazier, George Mason University

Burnette Hamil, Mississippi State University

Carole D. Hillman, Elmhurst College

Ronald A. Johnston, Fayetteville State University

Cynthia E. Ledbetter, University of Texas at Dallas

Jeff Marshall, Clemson University

Sheryl L. McGlamery, University of Nebraska at Omaha

Mark Ness, King's College

John Olson, Metropolitan State University

Carolyn Parker, George Washington University

John Pecore, Georgia State University

Deborah D. Sachs, University of Indianapolis

Meta Van Sickle, College of Charleston

Douglas Zook, Boston University

I acknowledge my debt to these people with pleasure.

Anton E. Lawson
Tempe, Arizona

PART I

The Nature of Science

Chapter 1 EDUCATIONAL GOALS AND THE NATURE OF SCIENTIFIC INQUIRY

There was no doubt that atoms could explain some puzzling phenomena. But in truth they were merely one man's daydreams. Atoms, if they really existed, were far too small to be perceived directly by the senses. How then would it ever be possible to establish their reality? Fortunately, there was a way. The trick was to assume that atoms existed, then deduce a logical consequence of this assumption for the everyday world. If the consequence matched reality, then the idea of atoms was given a boost. If not, then it was time to look for a better idea. (Chown, 2001, p. 6)

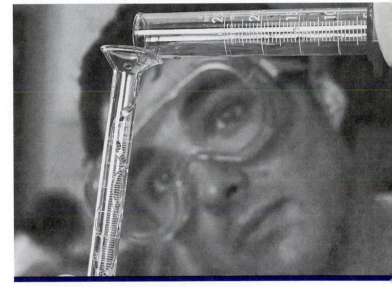

Classroom inquiry begins when students explore nature and make puzzling observations. Why do some liquids change colors when mixed?

Source: Courtesy of the Research Institute in Mathematics and Science Education, Arizona State University.

Is this how people learn? Does learning start with daydreams? Does it involve tricks, assumptions, deductions, and so on? And if so, do teaching methods follow? The goal of this book is to find out. To do so we will first explore how scientists learn. We will then explore how students learn. We will then apply what we discover to developing teaching methods that enable students to learn not only science but also how to learn. After all, great teachers don't just hand students a few fish. They teach them how to fish.

APPLICABLE NSES STANDARDS

Standard A Science teachers plan an inquiry-based program. In doing so, they

- Develop a framework of yearlong and short term goals for students.

Exploring Instructional Alternatives

Let's start with a little exploration. Someday you will be making decisions about how to teach certain science topics. Suppose, for example, you are a general science teacher and next week's topic is density. How will you go about introducing the topic? Rank the following alternatives in terms of how you perceive their effectiveness. Use 1 for the most effective and 5 for the least effective and be prepared to discuss your ranking and reasons with your classmates.

(a) Present a video in which 1-dm^3 blocks of various solid materials are carefully weighed and the volumes of 1-kg blocks are calculated from their dimensions, thus allowing comparison of two density determinations of each material.

(b) Arrange for a laboratory period in which students use rulers, calipers, graduated cylinders, and balances to determine the volumes and masses of solids of widely differing shapes and various materials for plotting on graphs of volume versus mass.

(c) Discuss with students their experiences with floating and sinking objects, including themselves when they swim or play in the water.

(d) Present an explanation and demonstrate ways in which various materials are weighed, their volumes are found by appropriate means, and you finally calculate the density of each material.

(e) Arrange for a laboratory period in which students accurately measure the density of carefully machined blocks and rods of materials whose volumes can be calculated easily from linear measurements.

Regardless of which approach you thought best, to make good instructional decisions you will need to carefully consider the broader goals of education. Why, for instance, are we teaching science in the first place? What do we really want our students to learn and be able to do as a consequence of our instruction?

The Goals of American Education

Freedom of Mind and the Ability to Reason

The acquisition of knowledge, values, attitudes, thinking processes, and creativity has been seen as a worthy educational objectives. But can a common thread be pulled from this diversity? In 1961 the Educational Policies Commission published *The Central Purpose of American Education*. In the commission's view, something it called "freedom of the mind" was of primary importance:

Freedom of the mind is a condition which each individual must develop for himself. To be free, a man must be capable of basing his choices and actions on understandings which he himself achieves and on values which he examines for himself. He must be aware of the basis on which he accepts propositions as true. (pp. 3–4)

In other words, freedom of the mind requires understanding oneself, one's actions, and one's surroundings. How does one come to understand this? The commission's answer was contained in what it called the 10 rational powers—the powers of recalling, imagining, classifying, generalizing, comparing, evaluating, analyzing, synthesizing, deducing, and inferring. In the commission's view, without rational powers, people must accept the ideas, beliefs, and attitudes of others. In short, the commission argued that all of a school's varied objectives depend on the ability to think. But how can instruction be designed and implemented to help students become better thinkers?

Scientific Habits of Mind

In 1966 the Educational Policies Commission, recognizing the key role that science could play in developing the ability to think, published *Education and the Spirit of Science*. That document emphasized science as a way of thinking, a spirit of inquiry driven by a curiosity to understand nature. Although the commission recognized that no scientist may fully exemplify the spirit of science, it nevertheless identified the following scientific habits of mind:

1. Longing to know and to understand

2. Questioning of all things

3. Search for data and their meaning

4. Demand for verification

5. Respect for logic

6. Consideration of premises

7. Consideration of consequences

These habits of mind insist that students are not indoctrinated to think or act in a certain way. Rather, students must acquire the ability to make up their own minds, to develop freedom of the mind, and to learn to make decisions based upon reason and evidence. In this sense, the scientific values are the most complete expression of one of the deepest human values—the belief in human dignity.

Scientific Literacy

More recently the American Association for the Advancement of Science (AAAS, 1989) echoed the importance of effective thinking in terms of achieving scientific literacy. In its words,

Scientific habits of mind can help people in every walk of life to deal sensibly with problems that often involve evidence, quantitative considerations, logical arguments, and uncertainty; without the ability to think critically and independently, citizens are easy prey to dogmatists, flimflam artists, and purveyors of simple solutions to complex problems. (p. 13)

Regrettably, the AAAS concluded that most Americans are not scientifically literate. To achieve scientific literacy the association advocated teaching science as science is practiced. In other words, teaching should (a) start with questions about nature, (b) engage students actively, (c) concentrate on the collection and use of evidence, (d) not separate knowing from finding out, and (e) de-emphasize the memorization of technical vocabulary.

The *National Science Education Standards*

Inquiry teaching is also prominent in the National Research Council's *National Science Education Standards* (NRC, 1996) (see (pp. xx–xxii)) as well as in its guidelines for science teacher education (NRC, 2001). For example, with regard to teaching methods the 1996 document had this to say:

> The Standards call for more than science as a process, in which students learn such skills as observing, inferring, and experimenting. Inquiry is central to science learning. When engaging in inquiry, students describe objects and events, ask questions, construct explanations, test those explanations against current scientific knowledge, and communicate their ideas to others. They identify their assumptions, use critical and logical thinking, and consider alternative explanations. In this way students actively develop their understanding of science by combining scientific knowledge with reasoning and thinking skills. (p. 2)

In summary, these national organizations are advocating teaching science not only as a way to produce more scientists but also as a way to develop citizens who think creatively and critically.

Teaching for Thinking

Thus, the central instructional question is this: *How can we teach science so that students develop scientific thinking skills—freedom of mind—scientific literacy?* The answer proposed in this book is by using teaching methods that allow students to explore nature and advance and test their own ideas. In other words, teaching should allow students to participate in inquiry—that is, in the knowledge construction process. Importantly, as we shall see, thinking skills play a key role in learning science content. Thus, teaching in ways that help students develop their thinking skills will pay off in terms of better content learning and better performance on high-stakes tests such as the SAT (formerly the Scholastic Aptitude Test), the ACT (formerly American College Testing) tests, and the new statewide science tests that have been mandated by the No Child Left Behind Act. This act, passed by Congress in 2002, mandated that by 2007 all students in Grades 10–12 be tested in science.

Consequently, if you want your students to do well on these tests, it behooves you to learn how to teach in ways that help students develop effective thinking skills. And as we shall see, thinking skills do not develop—nor do they function—independent of content. Therefore, we must carefully consider the relationship between content and process. Indeed, as we shall see, lessons in which students truly investigate nature and construct their own knowledge best facilitate both the learning of science content *and* the development of thinking skills.

In short, we do not want to simply give students a few fish. As mentioned, we want to teach them how to fish. To learn how to do this, however, we need to learn how people fish. Consequently, the remainder of this chapter and the next will explore how scientists fish for new knowledge. You may think that you already know quite a bit about how science is practiced. Experience suggests, however, that most prospective teachers, and even many experienced teachers, misunderstand several aspects of how scientific inquiry works. Hopefully you will find the following examples illuminating—perhaps even surprising. You should also find them helpful in setting the stage for the introduction of inquiry-based teaching methods in subsequent chapters.

How Science Is Practiced

Science is often defined as the attempt to explain nature. But how does one do this? Let's tackle this question by traveling to Africa's Serengeti Plain to see how biologists Lue Scheepers and Robert Simmons inquired into why giraffes have long necks.

You have probably heard that giraffes have long necks to feed on leaves in tall trees. This often-repeated explanation even includes the idea that short-necked giraffes can't reach the high-up leaves and starve. So after several generations, only long-necked giraffes have survived. Is this true? If true, where in trees would you expect to find giraffes most often feeding, particularly when food is scarce? Stop reading and generate an answer before reading on.

Now consider the following argument:

If . . . the "feeding-up-high" explanation is correct,

and . . . giraffes are surveyed to find out where they feed,

then . . . they should most often be observed feeding in the upper parts of the trees, particularly during the dry season when food is scarce.

Unfortunately for the feeding-up-high explanation, Scheepers and Simmons observed that giraffes most often feed by bending down (Figure 1.1). Even in the dry season, they spend nearly 40% of their time feeding at relatively low heights. Clearly this isn't the expected result based on the feeding-up-high explanation. Therefore, the explanation is not supported.

Scheepers and Simmons guessed that over several generations, long necks might have been acquired for courtship battles between males. During such battles, two males square off and swing their necks and heads at each other. The male with the longer neck generates

FIGURE 1.1   If the feeding-up-high explanation is correct, what should we see? Is that what we do see? What does this mismatch tell us about the explanation?

more force. So he wins and gets to mate with the female, while the shorter-necked loser is left to die. How might we test this "male-battle" explanation? Consider this argument:

If . . . the feeding-up-high explanation is correct,

and . . . the neck lengths of males and females are compared,

then . . . both males and females should have equally long necks relative to their body size.

Alternatively:

If . . . the male-battle explanation is correct,

then . . . males should have relatively longer necks than females.

When analyzing their data, Simmons and Scheepers found that males do in fact have relatively longer necks than females. Because this is the expected result based on the male-battle explanation, that explanation was supported. Simmons and Scheepers also found that males have relatively larger and heavier heads than females. Although this result was not previously predicted, it does make sense in light of the male-battle explanation because a heavier head, like a longer neck, increases the impact force. Clearly, additional tests would be helpful. Nevertheless, the important point is that scientists use *If/and/then* reasoning to test, and perhaps reject, their proposed explanations.

Notice that the part of the *If/and/then* argument after each *If* is a proposed explanation where the word *explanation* means to make clear the cause or reason of—to account for. Thus, an *explanation* is a tentative *cause* for a puzzling observation. Scientists often refer to proposed explanations as **hypotheses**. The term *hypothesis* sometimes is also used to label tentative descriptive statements—that is, answers to descriptive "who," "what," "when," and "where" questions. However, in this present context, hypotheses will generally refer to possible causes—possible explanations—possible answers to a causal question (e.g., Why do giraffes have long necks?).

The part of *If/and/then* arguments that follows the *and* is sometimes called the **planned test**—or imagined test. In the giraffe example the planned test involved observing giraffes to see where in the trees they most often feed. The part after each *then* is an **expected result** (sometimes called a **prediction**). Expected results are statements of what *should* happen in the future, what one *should* observe in the future, *if* the hypothesis is correct and *if* the test is conducted as planned. In other words, expected results state what reasonably follows from the hypothesis and its planned test.

To make sure that this last point is clear, note that the term *expectation* (or *prediction*) has at least two meanings. For example, suppose during the past few months you have taken 20 math quizzes and earned an A on each one. What grade do you *expect* you will earn on your next math quiz? Based on the past, you could reasonably *expect/predict* that you will earn another A. The statement that the next grade will be an A is an expectation/prediction. But in this case deriving this expectation involves extending (extrapolating) a pattern of past events into the future. This is *not* the sort of expectation involved in hypothesis testing. During hypothesis testing, expectations/predictions are derived not by extrapolation but by a thought process called **deduction**. For example, if giraffes have long necks to feed in tall trees, then it follows (via deduction) that they should feed most often in the upper parts of trees, particularly when food is scarce. That is, it deductively follows that they should feed up high as opposed to the notion that they should feed up high because that is where they have been feeding during the past 20 days. The statement that they should feed up high is an expectation just like the statement that you will earn an A on your next math quiz. However, in one case the expectation comes from extrapolation, and in the other case it comes from deduction.

When we add the observed result and the conclusion to one of Scheepers and Simmons's *If/and/then* arguments, we get something that looks like this:

If . . . the feeding-up-high hypothesis is correct,

and . . . giraffes are surveyed to find out where in trees they most often feed (planned test),

then . . . they should spend most of their time feeding in the upper parts of the trees, particularly during the dry season when food is scarce (expected result).

But . . . giraffes spend most of their time feeding down low, even in the dry season (observed result).

Therefore . . . the hypothesis is contradicted (conclusion).

Notice that the last statement in the argument following the *Therefore* is the **conclusion**. A conclusion is *not* an observed result. Instead, a conclusion tells us about the status of the tested hypothesis. In general, conclusions state whether the hypothesis was supported based on a match between expected and observed results or contradicted based on a mismatch.

In summary, hypothesis testing is a bit odd in the sense that to test a hypothesis you have to suppose, for the time being, that it is correct. You have to do this so you can test it and perhaps find that it is *not* correct!

Avoiding Bias and the Need for Alternative Hypotheses

Let's stay on the Serengeti Plain to take an even closer look at the nature of hypothesis testing. That closer look will consider the potential problem of bias and how to avoid it. We will also consider the source of hypotheses as well as kinds of evidence that can be used in their test.

While watching cheetahs chase gazelles (see Figure 1.2) British biologist Tim Caro noticed that gazelles often leap high in the air with their legs stiffly pointed backward. This puzzling behavior, called *stotting,* led Caro to ask, Why do gazelles stott? Does stotting somehow help them escape? Caro thought that stotting was worth being curious about because it seemed odd that gazelles would jump, slowing themselves down and making themselves more conspicuous while running for their lives. What explanations for stotting can you suggest?

Prior to Caro's research, another biologist proposed an explanation for stotting. He thought that stotting gives gazelles an advantage, despite appearances to the contrary,

FIGURE 1.2   Why do gazelles, such as this one, stott when being chased by cheetahs?

because stotting enables them to better spot cheetahs. Caro knew about this explanation but was unconvinced. Consequently, he generated several additional explanations. One was that a gazelle stotts to warn other gazelles of danger. Another was that an adult gazelle stotts to draw attention from its more vulnerable offspring. Still another was that stotting signals the cheetah that the gazelle is very fit, thus telling the cheetah that the gazelle will be difficult to catch. Consequently, the cheetah should give up the chase.

So Caro didn't generate one explanation. He generated several. Generating several alternatives at the outset is important because it helps one be more open-minded later on. People who fail to consider alternatives often become biased. In other words, they often get stuck believing in an incorrect explanation, particularly if the explanation comes from an authority or obtains initial supporting evidence. Note also that Caro's alternative hypotheses didn't come from direct observation. Instead they came from his prior knowledge of similar situations. For example, he knew that Arctic ground squirrels draw attention to themselves to protect their offspring. So he suspected that gazelles might do the same.

Having used his prior knowledge to generate several hyphotheses, Caro needed to test them. Let's see how he used correlational evidence to test the explanation that stotting signals the cheetah that the gazelle is very fit and hence will be difficult to catch.

The Use of Correlational Evidence

If Caro's "very-fit" hypothesis is correct, what relationship, if any, should exist between stotting and getting caught? Consider this:

If . . . the very-fit hypothesis is correct,

and . . . several chases are observed, some in which stotting takes place and some in which it doesn't,

then . . . stotting gazelles should get caught less often than nonstotting gazelles. Presumably the stotting gazelles won't get caught as often because the cheetahs have received the message that the gazelle is very fit. So they will give up the chase.

Take a look at Caro's observed numbers in Table 1.1. Do the observed numbers support the hypothesis? If the hypothesis is correct, the nonstotters should get caught more often than the stotters. Did this happen? Of the 24 nonstotters, 5 got caught (21%). Of the seven stotters, none got caught (0%). So it looks like the nonstotters got caught about 21% of the time, while the stotters got caught 0% of the time. The stotters always got away! So stotting seems to help. *Therefore,* the very-fit hypothesis is supported. But caution is certainly in order as the data don't rule out alternatives. For example, perhaps stotting confuses the cheetah. How could this alternative be tested?

This present test involves finding a corelationship or correlation between the values of two variables. As you may know, this type of evidence is referred to as correlational evidence. When using correlational evidence, one looks to see if the values of the two variables are "linked." If they are linked as predicted, then the hypothesis is supported—but certainly

TABLE 1.1   Does the Evidence Support the Very-Fit Hypothesis? Caro's Observed
Results

Stott			
	yes	0	7
	no	5	19
		yes	no
			Caught

not proven (more will be said about this in Chapter 2). Suppose, for example, someone hypothesizes that cell phones cause brain tumors. What correlational evidence could you use to test this hypothesis?

Importantly, finding a correlation between two variables in the absence of a prior hypothesis doesn't tell you which variable is the cause and which is the effect, or if a causal relationship even exists. Fortunately, there is another way to test hypotheses that involves "manipulating" nature. Such manipulations are called **experiments,** and they produce **experimental evidence.** Experimental evidence has an advantage over correlational evidence because one can more clearly establish cause and effect.

TESTING HYPOTHESES USING EXPERIMENTS

Let's travel to the Pacific Northwest where biologists used experiments to test hypotheses about the curious homing behavior of silver salmon. Silver salmon are born in the cool, quiet headwaters of freshwater streams in the Pacific Northwest. Young salmon swim downstream to the Pacific Ocean where they grow and mature sexually. They then return to swim upstream, often jumping incredible heights up waterfalls to ultimately lay eggs or deposit sperm in the streams' headwaters before dying. By tagging young salmon, biologists discovered that mature salmon actually return to precisely the same headwaters where they were born some years earlier! The discovery of this descriptive pattern (what scientists would call the **law** of salmon navigation and reproduction) raised a very interesting causal question: How do salmon find their home streams? In other words, what *causes* them to end up in their home streams? Before reading on, take a few minutes and see how many alternative hypotheses you can come up with.

A number of alternative hypotheses can be proposed. For instance, people often navigate by sight. Perhaps salmon do as well. Returning salmon may recall objects, such as large rocks, they saw while swimming downstream. Studies of migratory animals also suggest possibilities. For example, migratory eels are known to be enormously sensitive to dissolved chemicals. Perhaps salmon are as well. Perhaps they swim a short distance into various streams until they find the one that smells right, and they then follow the chemical path home. Also homing pigeons are known to navigate using the Earth's magnetic field. In one experiment, pigeons wearing little magnets (to disrupt the magnetic field) were not as successful at finding their way home as another group of pigeons wearing nonmagnetic metal bars. Perhaps salmon are also sensitive to the magnetic field and use it to find their home streams. Thus, by borrowing explanations from possibly similar contexts—by using **analogies**—we have generated three alternative hypotheses:

1. Salmon use sight.

2. Salmon smell chemicals in their home streams.

3. Salmon use the Earth's magnetic field.

A key point is that the use of analogies, sometimes called analogical transfer, is a creative process. Thus, when trying to explain something, scientists must be creative. They need to brainstorm and generate several alternatives, even if some may seem silly. Scientists can't be afraid of being wrong because that's the way they learn. They often learn from their "mistakes," from their rejected hypotheses.

What Combinations of Hypotheses Exist?

In addition to the three hypotheses listed above, others remain. Indeed none of the three may be correct. Or perhaps salmon use two of the three methods, or perhaps all three. Generating all possible combinations of the hypotheses gives us these possibilities:

1. The sight hypothesis is correct.

2. The smell hypothesis is correct.

3. The magnetic-field hypothesis is correct.

4. Both the sight and the smell hypotheses are correct.

5. Both the sight and the magnetic-field hypotheses are correct.

6. Both the smell and the magnetic-field hypotheses are correct.

7. All three hypotheses are correct.

8. Not one of the three hypotheses is correct. In other words, some other hypothesis is correct.

9. Some combination of other hypotheses is correct.

What Reasoning Guides Experiments?

Having generated all possible combinations of likely explanations, the next task is to test them. But this time we will test the hypotheses by manipulating nature—that is, by doing experiments. However, before we discuss how experiments were conducted on salmon, let's briefly discuss the reasoning that guides experiments in general.

Suppose I have two golf balls, a Titleist and a Top-Flite, and want to find out which is bouncier. Suppose you tell me to drop them to find out. So I drop the Titleist from over my head and the Top-Flite from my waist. To which you reply, "That is not fair. You have to drop them from the same height." "OK," I say. So I drop them from the same height. But this time I drop the Titleist on cement and the Top-Flite on carpet. To which you reply, "That is still not fair. They both have to hit the cement." So I drop them from the same height onto cement. But before letting go, I spin one and not the other. So once again you tell me that the experiment is not fair. And so on. The point is the experiment must be "fair" in the sense that both balls have to be treated the same way for us to discover which ball is bouncier.

Consider a slightly more complicated situation. Take a look at the pendulums shown in Figure 1.3. When the weights hanging on the ends of the pendulums are released, the pendulum on the right swings back and forth much faster than the one on the left. Why does it swing faster? What possibilities can you suggest? You may have noticed that the right pendulum has a shorter string. It also has a heavier weight. And it was pulled out and released from farther out than the left pendulum. So we have at least three possible reasons (causes) for why the right pendulum swings faster:

1. It might swing faster because of its shorter string.

2. It might swing faster because of its heavier weight.

3. It might swing faster because of its more distant release point.

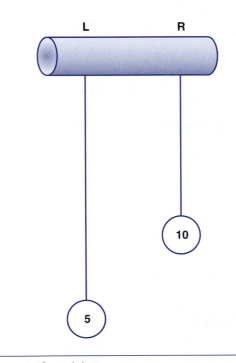

FIGURE 1.3 Diagram of pendulums

Of course, some combination of these three factors (variables) may be the reason. Or perhaps some other variable that we have not thought of may be the reason.

Let's start with hypothesis 1. How could we test the hypothesis that the right pendulum swings faster because it has a shorter string? Let's call it the "string-length" hypothesis. Clearly we would need to swing two pendulums, one with a shorter string and one with a longer string. If we could be certain that the only difference between the two pendulums was string length, and if we do find that the shorter pendulum swings faster, then we could conclude that changing string length causes a difference in swing speed. On the other hand, if we conduct an experiment in which both string length and release point vary and we find a difference in swing speed, then we cannot be sure which variable (string length or release point) caused the difference in swing speed. In other words, we need to conduct an experiment in which we change the values (short vs. long) of one variable (string length) while keeping the values (heavy vs. light weight, near vs. far) of the other variables (weight, release point) the same. Such an experiment is called a **controlled experiment.** So the reasoning guiding the controlled experiment that tests the string-length hypothesis looks like this:

If . . . the string-length hypothesis is correct,

and . . . we change string length while keeping the values of all other potentially causal variables constant (planned test),

then . . . swing speed should vary (prediction).

In this experiment, the string length varies from one trial to the next. So "string length" is the **independent variable** (sometimes called the *input* or *manipulated variable*, the possible *cause*, the *stimulus*, or the variable x in mathematical expressions) because it is being varied independently of the other possible causal variables. And, according to the hypothesis, swing speed should depend on string length. So "swing speed" is called the **dependent variable.** Other terms used to label the dependent variable include the *outcome variable*, the *effect*, the *responding variable*, or simply the *response* (usually designated the variable y in mathematical expressions). Thus, the point of a controlled experiment is to discover if changing the values of one variable (the independent variable) really does cause a change in the values of another variable (the dependent variable). Or said the other way around, the point of a controlled experiment is to discover if the values of one variable (the dependent variable) really do *depend* on the values of another variable (the independent variable). And in this case they do. Therefore the string-length hypothesis is supported. You might want to actually conduct the experiment yourself to see if you get the same result. And what about the other independent variables—pendulum weight and release point? It turns out that these variables don't make a difference. So the weight hypothesis and the release-point hypothesis are not supported. Instead they are contradicted.

Using Controlled Experiments to Test Hypotheses About Salmon Navigation

Let's now consider how American biologist A. D. Hasler conducted controlled experiments to test the hypotheses about salmon navigation. To test the sight hypothesis, Hasler first captured salmon that had just returned to two streams near Seattle, Washington. The streams, shown in Figure 1.4, were the Issaquah and East Fork. Hasler then tagged the captured fish, identifying which had come from the Issaquah and which from the East Fork.

Next, he randomly split the tagged Issaquah fish into two groups and blindfolded all the fish in one group. He then repeated the procedure for the tagged East Fork fish. The blindfolded Issaquah and East Fork fish became the **experimental group**. Hasler then released the blindfolded salmon along with some nonblindfolded salmon from both streams about three quarters of a mile below where the streams join (marked site of release). The nonblindfolded salmon were the **comparison group**—sometimes called the control group. Finally, the tagged fish were recaptured in traps about a mile above the junction as they swam back up the streams (marked recapture site). The following summarizes Hasler's reasoning:

If . . . the sight hypothesis is correct,

and . . . blindfolded salmon and nonblindfolded salmon from the two streams are released below the fork where the two streams join,

then . . . the blindfolded salmon should *not* be recaptured in their home streams as often as the nonblindfolded salmon.

To establish this possible link between the salmon's ability to see and where they are recaptured, all the other ways that the two groups of fish differ must be the same (i.e., held constant). For example, another variable is the amount of time the fish are kept out of water. Clearly it would not be fair to keep the blindfolded salmon out of water longer than the nonblindfolded

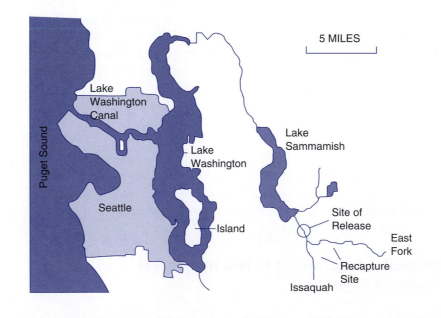

FIGURE 1.4   Issaquah and East Fork streams showing release and recapture sites

salmon because doing so might hurt their homing ability. With this in mind, we can see that a controlled experiment (i.e., a fair test) of the sight hypothesis requires that experimental and comparison groups differ in only one way or be treated differently in only one way.

In Hasler's controlled experiment, the salmon's ability to see varies between the experimental and the control group. So "ability to see" is the independent variable. And, according to the sight hypothesis, where the salmon are recaptured should depend on sight. So "recapture site" is the dependent variable. Thus, as mentioned, the point of a controlled experiment is to discover if changing the values of the independent variable really does *cause* a change in the values of the dependent variable.

Suppose having conducted Hasler's controlled experiment, we discover that the sighted salmon are better at returning home than the blindfolded salmon. This is the predicted result based on the sight hypothesis, so the result would support the hypothesis. However, as mentioned, we need to be careful. Perhaps during the experiment, the blindfolded salmon were hindered in returning, not by lack of sight but by their inability to swim with blindfolds. Or perhaps blindfolding the fish simply shocked them and disrupted their swimming ability. At any rate, one must try to avoid these potential problems (i.e., uncontrolled independent variables) as much as possible. But as you may have guessed, one can never be absolutely certain that all such problems have been eliminated. So caution is needed even when interpreting experimental results.

On the other hand, suppose we conduct the experiment and find that both groups are equally successful at returning home. In this case, the sight hypothesis would be contradicted. In other words, now we can be reasonably sure that salmon navigate some other way. However, again we need to be cautious. Overlooked independent variables might be operating. For example, perhaps the blindfolded salmon could see under their blindfolds. This is how blindfolded magicians see. Or perhaps the blindfolds were not thick enough to block out all the light. Or perhaps the blindfolds were effective and the salmon do use sight when they can, but when they can't, they use some other sense to navigate, such as smell.

In short, the reasoning involved in experimentally testing hypotheses follows the *If/and/then* pattern just like before. But it also involves identifying and attempting to hold constant the values of independent variables. This is crucial. However, because we can never be certain that all of the independent variables have been identified and/or controlled, even after conducting experiments, conclusions must remain somewhat tentative. In sum, scientific arguments and evidence can be convincing *beyond a reasonable doubt* but not *beyond all possible doubt*. As mentioned, we will return to this point in Chapter 2.

As it turned out, when Hasler conducted his experiment, he found that the blindfolded salmon were just as successful as the nonblindfolded salmon at finding their home streams. Therefore, the sight hypothesis was contradicted. So Hasler moved on to test the smell hypothesis.

Testing the Smell Hypothesis

To test the smell hypothesis, Hasler captured and tagged salmon from the two streams and randomly divided the Issaquah fish into two groups. He inserted cotton plugs coated with petroleum jelly in the noses of one group to block their smelling ability (Figure 1.5). These fish became the experimental group. He left the noses of the comparison/control group unplugged. Hasler then randomly split the East Fork fish into two groups and plugged the noses of one group as he had done with the East Fork fish. Finally, he released all the fish to the release point. As the fish returned upstream, they were recaptured in traps above the streams' junction.

Tables 1.2 and 1.3 show Hasler's results. Do they support the smell hypothesis? If so, why? If not, why not? Of course other hypotheses remain. But let's save these for another day.

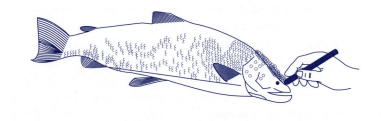

FIGURE 1.5   Will plugging a salmon's nose keep it from finding its home stream?

TABLE 1.2   Observed Results for Comparison Fish With Unplugged Noses

	Recapture Site	
	Issaquah	East Fork
Initial Capture Site		
Issaquah	46	0
East Fork	8	19

TABLE 1.3   Observed Results for Experimental Fish With Plugged Noses

	Recapture Site	
	Issaquah	East Fork
Initial Capture Site		
Issaquah	39	12
East Fork	16	3

BASIC AND APPLIED RESEARCH

Why Do People Test Alternative Explanations?

Why did the scientists go to all the trouble to test alternative hypotheses about long-necked giraffes, stotting gazelles, and navigating salmon? One answer is simply that they were curious. Curiosity often motivates science. The intent is to better understand nature. Such research is called **basic research**.

Sometimes, however, hypotheses are tested with practical purposes in mind. Suppose, for example, that your car is making a strange clicking sound. So you take it to an auto mechanic. The mechanic's task is to discover the cause. To do so, one must generate and test alternative hypotheses. Also, consider what happens when you go to a medical doctor with an illness. The doctor's first task is to answer the **causal question:** What is causing your symptoms? To find the cause, the doctor must generate alternative hypotheses and test them as quickly as possible so that you can be treated and get well. In some cases this may be relatively simple; for example, if the cause is a bacterial infection and antibiotics are prescribed and taken, then you should get well. And after taking the antibiotics, you do get well. Therefore the bacterial infection hypothesis is supported, and everyone is happy. On the other hand, if you do not get well, then perhaps a bacterial infection was not the cause, and the doctor will have to generate and test other hypotheses until you are cured. Medical researchers have generated and tested hypotheses in hopes of finding the causes and possible cures of diseases such as typhoid, syphilis, tuberculosis, polio, cancer, and more recently AIDS. The intent of hypothesis testing in all of these cases from the auto mechanic to the medical researcher is to find a cause so that some practical action can be taken. Hypothesis testing for practical reasons is called **applied research**.

Whether driven by curiosity or practicality, the central issue is finding causes. Generating and testing hypotheses to answer causal questions is central to nearly every aspect of adult life. Unfortunately, however, we seldom have eyewitness accounts to help establish cause-effect relationships. And even when we do, eyewitness accounts are often unreliable. It turns out that people often see what they expect to see, rather than what really happened. You may not have thought of a murder trial as an instance of hypothesis generation and test, but that is exactly what it is. The central causal question is, Who killed the victim (i.e., who caused the death)? If reliable eyewitness testimony is unavailable, the prosecutor's job is to use **circumstantial evidence** and sound reasoning to convince the jury that the "defendant-is-the-killer" hypothesis is correct. On the other hand, the defense's job is to generate and support alternative hypotheses, such as drug dealers killed the victim or a bolt of lightning killed the victim. To get an acquittal, all the defense has to do is get one juror to accept the plausibility of only one of these alternative hypotheses. Doing so would mean that the defendant-is-the-killer hypothesis, in that juror's mind, has not been *proven beyond a reasonable doubt*.

Summary

- The central goal of American education is to teach students how to think. To do so, science must be taught as a process of creative and critical inquiry.

- Basic to science is the generation and test of explanations. The initial generation of several alternative explanations encourages an unbiased test because one is less likely to be committed to any specific explanation. Explanations are tested by supposing that the explanation is correct and by planning some test that allows the deduction of one or more predictions. Data are then gathered and compared with predictions. A good match provides support for the explanation, while a poor match contradicts the explanation and may lead to its rejection.

- Explanations can be tested using circumstantial, correlational, or experimental evidence.

- Although both tentative descriptions and explanations are tested by use of *If/and/then* reasoning, descriptions and explanations are not the same thing. Descriptions (sometimes called laws) tell us about nature in terms of identifiable patterns, while explanations attempt to identify causes for such patterns.

- Generating hypotheses is a creative process based on perceived similarities (analogies) between the present situation and past situations.

- Use of experimental evidence relies on the manipulation of causal variables and is an effective way to test hypotheses because the experimenter can perform controlled experiments.

- People test hypotheses to find out why things happen, to find which of the possible causes is/are the actual cause(s). People want to know the actual causes of things to satisfy their curiosity—basic research—or so that the new knowledge can be put to practical use—applied research.

- Inquiry is open ended as answering one causal question often raises another.

Key Terms

analogies	comparison group
applied research	conclusion
basic research	controlled experiment
biased	correlation
causal question	correlational evidence
circumstantial evidence	deduction

dependent variable   hypotheses

expected result   independent variable

experimental evidence   law

experimental group   planned test

experiments   prediction

Application Questions/Activities

1. During the next day or two, note several objects, events, or situations that raise causal questions. For example, suppose while on the way to class you notice an automobile accident and ask, What caused the accident? Or perhaps you notice a spot of yellow grass in the middle of someone's green lawn and ask, What caused the yellow spot? Make a list of five such causal questions. Pick one of the causal questions listed above. Generate two alternative hypotheses to answer it. How could your hypotheses be tested? Use the pattern of *If/and/then* reasoning to generate expected results based on your hypotheses and some imagined test conditions. Based on your initial observations, generate a list of five descriptive questions. For example, some descriptive questions regarding the auto accident might be, Was anyone hurt? How many people were in the cars? How fast were the cars going?

2. In general, how does a description of an event differ from an explanation? Provide an example.

3. Check the newspaper during the next few days for at least two articles that discuss scientific studies. Identify the causal questions raised. What hypotheses were generated? What sort of evidence (i.e., circumstantial, correlational, experimental) was used to test the hypotheses? Were the hypotheses supported or not supported? Were you convinced by the arguments and evidence? Explain.

4. Given a group of students, name five ways in which the individuals in the group are likely to vary. Name two values for each of the named variables.

5. Fill in the boxes and "clouds" in the following figure to construct a complete argument regarding Scheepers and Simmons's test of the feeding-up-high hypothesis. The boxes represent observations while the "clouds" represent unobservable (imagined) elements of the hypothesis-testing process. Start by writing, "Giraffes have long necks" in the top box. Next, the causal question can be stated like this: "Why do giraffes have long necks?" Write this question in the first "cloud." Now write the hypothesis in the second "cloud." Now complete the figure.

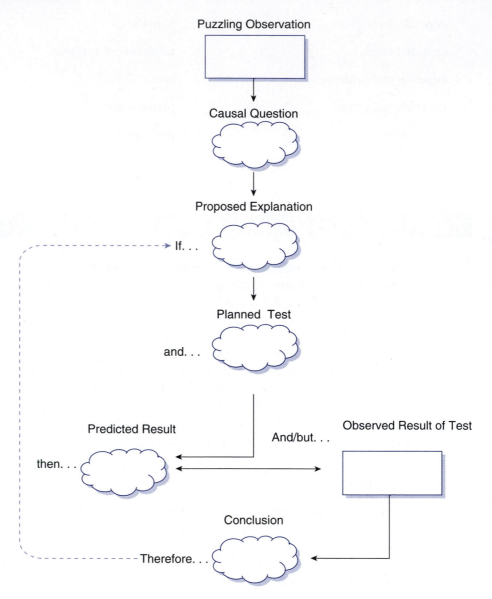

Puzzling Observation

Causal Question

Proposed Explanation

If. . .

Planned Test

and. . .

Predicted Result

And/but. . .

Observed Result of Test

then. . .

Conclusion

Therefore. . .

Chapter 2

THE NATURE OF SCIENTIFIC THEORIES

Chapter 2 continues our exploration into the nature of science by considering the nature of scientific theories. What are theories? What are they for? How are they constructed? And how are they sometimes modified or rejected? Understanding the role theories play in science will be invaluable in developing inquiry-based teaching methods and good lesson plans and in constructing an effective curriculum. Let's start with a quick true/false quiz:

True or false: Science is a process of discovery of the nature of things via observation.

Note your response to this question and compare it to what you think after reading this chapter. The chapter starts with a brief look at what the ancient Greeks believed about the nature of matter. Next, it tells a story about how oxygen was discovered. The chapter then considers an important difference between explanation and description. Lastly the chapter discusses some important limitations of science. The intent is to help you better understand the nature of scientific theories

Do the planets orbit the Sun as indicated by this model? If so, what keeps them in their orbits?

APPLICABLE NSES STANDARDS

Standard B Science teachers guide and facilitate learning. In doing so, they

- Encourage and model the skills of scientific inquiry, as well as curiosity, openness to new ideas and data, and skepticism that characterize science.

Standard E Science teachers develop communities of learners that reflect the intellectual rigor of scientific inquiry and the attitudes and social values conducive to learning.

and scientific reasoning, thus helping you further along the road to becoming a skilled inquiry teacher.

THE GREEK FOUR-MATERIAL THEORY

Suppose I hold a rock in my hand and let go. It will fall to the ground. Why? And why do rocks sink in water while bubbles rise? Why do flames rise from a fire? Why does a hunk of wood float in water? Why can living animals move about while dead ones can't? Why can't rocks move about like living animals?

Would you be impressed if I came up with a simple explanation for all of these puzzling observations? That is just what the ancient Greeks did. The genius of ancient Greece was that, for the first time, people replaced the belief that events were caused by gods with explanations based on natural causes. For example, the prevailing Greek belief about matter from well before the birth of Christ can be summarized in these four statements:

1. All matter consists of four materials in pure form or in various combinations.

2. The four materials are earth, water, air, and fire.

3. Each material has its own "natural" location, earth below water, water below air, and air below fire.

4. Living things differ from nonliving things because they contain a special life-giving *vital force*.

These four statements can explain many observations. For example, rocks (mostly made of earth) fall when released in air or placed in water *because* they seek their natural place below air and water. Bubbles (air) rise in water *because* they seek their natural place above water. Likewise, flames (fire) rise in air *because* they seek their natural place above air. Wood floats in water *because* it is a combination of earth and air. Further, living things move in ways that nonliving things can't *because* they contain a vital force.

In this sense, the statements are like hypotheses. Like hypotheses, they attempt to *explain* puzzling observations: Why do rocks fall? Why do bubbles rise in boiling water? However, together they differ from hypotheses in at least three ways. First, they differ in *complexity*. Here we have four statements. Hypotheses typically consist of a single statement. Second, rather than explaining one puzzling observation, they attempt to explain several observations. In other words, collectively the statements differ in *generality*. And third, the statements claim the existence of nonperceptible forces and/or entities that somehow act to move materials to their natural places and to enable living things to move on their own. Thus, rather than calling the statements hypotheses, collectively they are called a theory. In this case, they are called the *ancient Greek four-material theory*. More specifically, a theory consists of a set of statements (sometimes called postulates) that attempt to explain a broad class of related observations.

The "Discovery" of Oxygen

Chapter 1 explored how hypotheses are generated and tested using *If/and/then* reasoning. Can the same sort of reasoning test theories? Let's answer this question by exploring the how oxygen was "discovered" during the 19th century.

No doubt you have been told that you breathe in oxygen. Most likely, you have also been told that oxygen is needed for combustion. Apparently oxygen is important for humans, for other animals, and for fires. Most likely you also know that plants take in carbon dioxide and expel oxygen. But how do we know all of this? How do we even know that oxygen exists? Certainly, the ancient Greeks knew nothing of oxygen. So who discovered oxygen, and when was it discovered? These may seem like simple questions, yet I assure you they are not. The story of oxygen's discovery teaches an important lesson about the nature of scientific discovery and about the roles theory and observation play in the discovery process.

So who discovered oxygen? If oxygen was discovered through observation, then finding out who did it should be easy. All we need to do is peruse history to find when oxygen was first observed and who did the observing. But wait a minute. How can anyone observe oxygen? Have you ever seen oxygen? Are we not told that oxygen is a type of atom that combines with itself or with other types of atoms such as carbon and hydrogen to produce molecules such as carbon dioxide and water? But have you ever *seen* oxygen atoms? Have you ever *seen* any type of atom? If honest, you will have to answer no. But don't feel bad. No one has ever seen individual atoms. Atoms are just too small to be seen with the naked eye.

Perhaps you have seen photos taken through electron microscopes that presumably show atoms such as those in Figure 2.1. Does the figure really show atoms? What you see are little blobs. Are the blobs really atoms? The point is whether or not the blobs are atoms is a matter of *interpretation,* not observation. So if oxygen can't be observed, how can we find out who discovered it and when it was discovered? Let's consider some early experiments.

Figure 2.1 Are these rows of tiny blobs really gold atoms? Photograph of a very thin leaf of gold taken through an electron microscope (1nm = 1 nanometer).

Phlogiston Theory and the Role of Contradictory Evidence

The ancient Greeks observed that a candle under an inverted jar burns for a short time and then goes out. By the 1700s, this was explained by imagining that candles consist of the ancient Greeks' earth (now called a base) plus their fire, which had become known as **phlogiston**. Consequently, when a candle burns, phlogiston is released, and the base is left behind. Thus, a candle burning inside a jar soon burns out *because* the air becomes filled with phlogiston. When the jar becomes full, burning stops, and the flame goes out. This explanation agrees with observations. Certainly it appears as though flames go from candles into air!

However, phlogiston theory was not free of difficulties. For example, it was known at the time that some metals burn when heated. Presumably phlogiston is released, leaving the base (the ashes) behind. Yet the following reasoning presented a problem:

If . . . phlogiston is released from burning metals,

and . . . the burned metals' ashes are weighed,

then . . . the ashes should weigh less than the original metal—because part of the metal (the phlogiston) has escaped into the air.

But . . . when several metals were burned, their ashes weighed more, not less, than the original metals.

Therefore . . . the claim was contradicted.

What do you suppose the phlogistonists did in the face of this contradictory evidence? Instead of rejecting the claim that phlogiston is released, they simply argued that phlogiston has *negative* weight. Consequently, releasing phlogiston should increase a burned metal's weight! The idea of negative weight may seem too strange to take seriously. However, it makes perfect sense in terms of the ancient Greek four-material theory. After all, fire seeks its natural place above air, and thus fire (phlogiston) should have negative weight!

If you still think this idea of negative weight is too strange, consider the "attractive" and "repulsive" forces of magnets, forces that were well known at the time. If magnets can attract and repel things, why can't phlogiston have negative weight? Little wonder that phlogiston theory was still accepted in the 18th century.

People explored additional aspects of combustion. For example, when the metals' ashes were heated with charcoal in closed jars, the ashes changed back into the metals. Presumably charcoal contains phlogiston, so the explanation was simple. The charcoal's phlogiston combined with the ashes to produce the metal. Interestingly, heating the ashes also changed the jar's air. For example, when a mouse was placed in the jar's air, the mouse quickly died, suggesting that the air had been damaged in some way. Thus, the air was dubbed "damaged" air. However, when a plant was placed in damaged air, the plant did fine. In fact, plants somehow undamaged the damaged air! Phlogiston theory couldn't explain damaged air or, for that matter, undamaged air. Thus, the theory was starting to run into trouble.

Did Bayen Discover Oxygen?

Among the many experiments at the time, one conducted by the Frenchman Pierre Bayen is particularly interesting. Bayen heated mercury's reddish ashes in a bell jar. As you can see in Figure 2.2, the air in the bell jar was exposed to a pool of water, which in turn was exposed to the external air. When Bayen used focused sunlight to heat mercury's reddish ashes, the ashes changed back to the familiar silver liquid. Also the water level inside the bell jar went down. To explain the drop Bayen imagined that a gas had been released from the heated ashes. Unfortunately, Bayen didn't investigate the gases' properties.

In retrospect, we can be rather certain that the released gas was oxygen. Chemists now believe that when mercury burns, the mercury atoms combine with oxygen atoms from the air to produce mercury oxide molecules—the ashes. And, while the mercury oxide ashes are heated, mercury and oxygen atoms separate. The mercury atoms then combine with other mercury atoms to produce the silver liquid, and the oxygen atoms combine to produce oxygen molecules, which end up in the air. Consequently, can we conclude that Bayen discovered oxygen? Because Bayen had no idea what he had found, it hardly seems fair to give him credit. By the same token, we wouldn't conclude that someone who finds a treasure map, only to throw it away, has, in fact, discovered the treasure.

Did Priestley Discover Oxygen?

At the time, Joseph Priestley, an Englishman, was conducting similar experiments. However, unlike Bayen, Priestley explored the properties of the released gas. For example, he observed that a candle produced a "remarkably vigorous" flame when burned in the gas. He also found that mice live much longer enclosed in the gas than in common air. Priestley was soon convinced that the gas was air that was completely free of phlogiston, or so-called dephlogisticated air.

Based on this, you might be tempted to conclude that Priestley discovered oxygen. After all, all we would need to do is change the name from "dephlogisticated air" to "air loaded

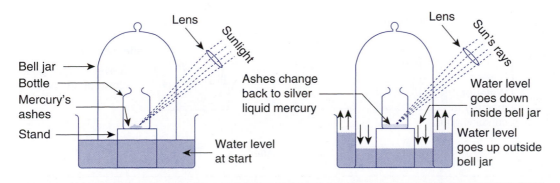

Figure 2.2   Bayen's experimental apparatus for heating mercury's reddish ashes. Why did the water level inside the bell jar go down while the ashes burned?

with oxygen" and we would have it. But this misses an important point. Can we really give Priestley credit when his **concept** of oxygen is so at odds with ours? We conceive of oxygen as a type of atom that combines with other atoms to produce molecules, which in turn can separate to produce smaller molecules and/or the original atoms. This concept would have been completely foreign to Priestley. To Priestley, the released gas was merely normal air without phlogiston. Consequently, it hardly seems right to give him credit.

Viewed in this way, oxygen is not a "thing" to be discovered. Rather, it is a concept to be invented. Did Priestley invent the modern concept of oxygen? No, he didn't; thus, he should not be given credit any more than we should give Bayen credit.

Did Lavoisier Discover Oxygen?

Perhaps the French chemist Antoine Lavoisier deserves credit. Lavoisier read about Priestley's experiments and within a few years presented his own revolutionary theory of combustion. The results of his now classic experiments, depicted in Figure 2.3, can be summarized like this: When liquid mercury (shown at the left) is heated, it turns to reddish ashes, and the water level inside the inverted beaker rises up one fifth of the way (shown at the right). Also, when the ashes are weighed, they weigh more than the original liquid mercury. Next, when the reddish ashes are heated by focusing sunlight on them, the ashes turn back into liquid mercury, which weighs less than the ashes. And the water level in the jar goes down.

Lavoisier explained these observations like this: The ashes weigh more than the original liquid mercury *because* some unseen things left the air and combined with the heated mercury. Further, the water in the inverted beaker rose to replace the things that left the air. To explain what happens when sunlight is then focused on the reddish ashes, Lavoisier imagined a reverse process. According to Lavoisier, heating the ashes causes the unseen things to break away from the ashes, return to the air, and push the water level back down.

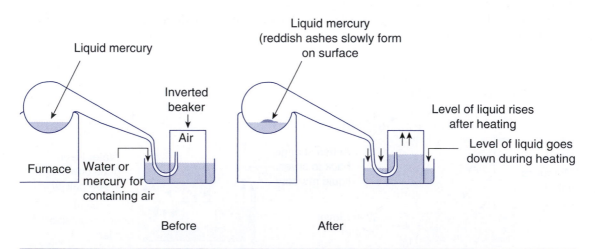

FIGURE 2.3   Lavoisier's experiment investigated weight changes of liquid mercury when heated and converted into reddish ashes. Why did the heated mercury gain weight? And why did the water level rise in the inverted beaker?

So Lavoisier generated a new explanation that included the conception of something new. He called this newly invented something *oxygine* (French for oxygen). With his revolutionary theory of combustion, Lavoisier not only demonstrated no need for phlogiston. Instead he invented a new entity and gave it a name—oxygine. Should we, therefore, conclude that Lavoisier discovered oxygen? Perhaps, but again, this may be giving him too much credit. Up to the end of his life, Lavoisier insisted that he had discovered an atomic "principle of acidity" and that oxygine was formed only when that principle united with the material of heat called the caloric. Thus, just as Priestley and others before him, Lavoisier really did not invent our modern concept of oxygen. Lavoisier's concept of acidity was not banished from chemistry until the early 1800s. And his concept of the caloric did not suffer the same fate until the 1860s.

Did Anyone Discover Oxygen? The Nature of Conceptual Systems

Who then discovered oxygen? Indeed this question can't be answered, except to say that no one did. In fact, no one could have "discovered" oxygen because theoretical entities, such as oxygen, are not discovered—that is, not found, not observed. Instead, they are "invented." Further, these invented/constructed entities gain meaning through their relationships with other concepts within complex **conceptual systems** (theories). The conceptual systems, the theories, change and grow through time and are sometimes overthrown, as in the case of phlogiston theory. All of this implies that the "thing" we conceive of as oxygen may in fact not exist after all. The possibility remains that someday our oxygen concept may go the way of the phlogiston concept. Then again, it may not.

In conclusion, the oxygen concept and the theory detailing oxygen's role in combustion developed over considerable time and generally in three phases. The first phase extended from the days of the ancient Greeks to well into the 18th century. This phase involved *exploration* of a variety of burning materials, such as candles, mercury, and phosphorus, exploring their interactions with living things and explaining what happened in terms of concepts such as phlogiston and dephlogisticated air. The second phase took place when it became clear to Lavoisier that phlogiston theory was wrong. In his view, combustion involved removal of something from the air. He gave that newly imagined something a name—oxygine. The name itself is unimportant. Rather the important point is that Lavoisier had *invented* something new. Thus, he generated a new idea and then gave it a name. The third and final phase extended roughly from the 1770s to the 1860s. This was an *application* phase in which atomic-molecular theory and a modern theory of combustion triumphed. These theories clarified oxygen's role in combustion and put to rest the final vestiges of 18th-century chemical theory, such as the principle of acidity and the caloric.

We don't want to get too far ahead of ourselves. However, when teaching methods are introduced in Chapter 6, you will discover the same three phases of *exploration, invention,* and *application* embedded in science lessons. Thus, by embedding these phases in your lessons, you will be teaching science as science is practiced. Consequently, your students will be constructing/inventing scientific concepts and theories, they will be learning about the nature of science, and they will be developing their scientific reasoning skills.

The phlogiston story reveals that, like hypothesis testing, theory testing requires comparing predictions derived from the theory's basic components with the observed results.

Interestingly, when a mismatch occurs between the theory's predictions and the results, some may reject the theory. However, others may modify one or more of the theory's components or add new ones to keep the predictions in agreement with the evidence. Yet when the necessary modifications become too numerous, most impartial observers abandon the theory. This is especially so when a more plausible and less cumbersome alternative theory exists.

DESCRIPTION VERSUS EXPLANATION: WHY DO OBJECTS FALL?

As mentioned in Chapter 1, descriptions and explanations are not the same thing. To emphasize this point with respect to theories, let's consider the familiar claim that gravity makes things fall. Imagine that you are sitting on the Serengeti Plain under an acacia tree watching the setting Sun. All of a sudden a seedpod drops off the tree and conks you on the head. Like most people, you might say that the seedpod fell *because* of gravity. In other words, gravity *caused* the seedpod to fall. If you have ever taken a physics course you might even be able to tell us that gravity is very general. In other words, gravity exists between any two objects (e.g., the Earth and the seedpod, the Earth and the Sun). Further you might be able to tell us that more massive objects produce more gravitational force and that the gravitational force becomes stronger when the two objects come closer together. In fact, you might even be able to tell us that we have Isaac Newton to thank for these ideas, ideas that are often referred to as Newton's *laws of gravitation*.

Newton's laws of gravitation are very general. But do they really explain? Do they really tell us why the seedpod fell, why the Earth and the seedpod attract each other, why the Earth and the Sun attract each other? According to Newton, the answer is no. Newton's laws of gravitation, like all laws, are *descriptions*. With his famous statement, "I frame no hypotheses," Newton offered no *explanation* for gravity, no cause, no theory. In other words, we know that objects apparently separated by empty space are "attracted" to each other. Yet we do not know why or how. Although Newton offered no explanation for gravity, many others have. It may be helpful to consider one of these explanations. Consideration of this theory, which was first invented shortly after Newton's death, should help further clarify the difference between description and explanation.

Suppose tiny particles blast through space at very high speeds in all directions. Suppose further that the particles are absorbed when they hit objects such as the Earth. When the Earth absorbs particles, the particles give the Earth a push. Now if the particles hit the Earth from all directions, their pushes balance, and the Earth doesn't move. However, with the Sun nearby, the Sun blocks some of the particles blasting toward the Earth from the Sun's direction. Consequently, fewer particles hit the Earth from that direction than from the opposite direction. Thus, the Earth gets a greater push *toward* the Sun than away from it. Likewise, the Earth blocks some of the particles blasting toward the Sun from the Earth's direction. Consequently, fewer particles hit the Sun from the Earth's direction than from the opposite direction. Thus, the Sun gets a greater push *toward* the Earth than away from it. Therefore, the Sun and the Earth are *both* pushed toward each other—they are "attracted" to each other!

Not only does the previous paragraph offer an explanation for the force of gravity; physicists can easily show that the magnitude of the imagined push is just what it should be according to Newton's gravitational laws. In other words, the particle-push theory makes sense. It seems like a perfectly good explanation—a perfectly good theory. Indeed, if you invented the theory, you would be very happy. So what is wrong with it? The problem is that the particle-push theory leads to some predictions that are not observed. Consider the following:

If . . . the Earth absorbs tiny particles from space,

and . . . we measure the Earth's speed,

then . . . over time, the Earth should be slowing down—because more particles will hit the Earth on its front side than on its backside—when you run in the rain, more rain hits your face than the back of your head—thus the Earth should "feel" a resistance to its forward motion and should slow down.

But . . . the Earth is not slowing down at anything near the rate predicted by the particle-push theory.

Therefore . . . the theory is contradicted.

Not only doesn't the particle-push theory work, no theory has ever been invented that explains gravity without leading to a contradicted prediction. So gravity remains an unexplained force—nobody knows *why* seedpods fall. But stay tuned. Someday we may know.

What is the take-home message of this example? Once again, the message is that descriptions (laws) are not explanations (hypotheses/theories). Descriptions may be very helpful, but the task is not over until tested and supported explanations are obtained.

PROOF AND DISPROOF

Explanation testing involves comparing expected and observed results. When there is a match between expectations and observations the explanation has gained support. And when there is a mismatch the explanation has been contradicted. But does a match or mismatch **prove** or **disprove** the explanation? Can we ever be *absolutely certain* about the correctness of any particular explanation? Clearly the answer to this question has to be no. As we have seen, explanations are the product of human imagination (hence potentially unlimited in number), and any two or more explanations may lead to the same predictions. Hence, when observed results match predicted results we can't be certain which explanation is correct. Therefore, scientific proof is not possible.

But can explanations be disproved? Consider the four cards shown in Figure 2.4. Each card has a letter on one side and a number on the other side. A rule states: *Cards with vowels on one side have even numbers on the other side.* Suppose you are allowed to turn over one or more of these cards to see the other

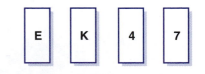

FIGURE 2.4   Which card(s), if turned over, could disprove the following rule? *Cards with vowels on one side have even numbers on the other side.*

side. Which card, or cards, would you turn over to see if the rule is false? Take a few minutes to answer before reading on.

Suppose you turn over the E card and find a 7 on the other side. Would this disprove the rule? I think so. In other words, to disprove the rule, all you need to find is one card with a vowel on one side and an odd number on the other side. Could turning over any of the other cards also disprove the rule? How about the 7 card? Is the rule broken if the other side of the 7 card has a vowel on it? Consider this argument:

If . . . the rule is correct,

and . . . we turn over the 7 card,

then . . . according to the rule, we should find a consonant and *not* a vowel.

But . . . suppose we turn over the 7 card and do find a vowel.

Therefore . . . we would have a vowel on one side and an odd number on the other side, which would break the rule. In other words, the rule would be *disproved*.

So we should turn over both the E and 7 cards because both could disprove the rule. Does this "logic" also work with scientific explanations? Suppose you take a walk in a park and observe the two trees shown in Figure 2.5. Tree A has tall grass growing under it, while tree B has nearly none. How might this puzzling observation be explained? Perhaps tree B provides too much shade for grass growth; tree B drops grass-killing fruit; children trample the grass under tree B; and so on.

Let's test one of these explanations. Suppose tree B's branches are cut off, permitting more sunlight to reach the ground. The too-much-shade explanation leads to the prediction that the grass should now grow. Suppose we conduct the test and after several weeks observe no grass growth. Accordingly,

If . . . the too-much-shade explanation is correct,

and . . . some of tree B's branches are cut off, permitting more sunlight to reach the ground,

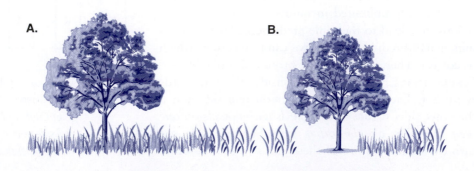

FIGURE 2.5   Why might the grass grow better under tree A than tree B?

then . . . the grass under tree B should grow.

But . . . after the branches are cut off, the grass under tree B does not grow.

Therefore . . . the explanation must be false. It has been disproved.

Would you draw this conclusion? Hopefully you wouldn't. Too much shade may still be the reason that grass did not grow under tree B, but perhaps the grass failed to grow after the branches were cut off because (a) we did not wait long enough; (b) it was now too cold for the grass to grow; (c) the soil now lacked sufficient water; (d) no grass seed remained under tree B; and so on. In other words, because we can't identify and control all of the independent variables that might influence the outcome of the test, some doubt must always remain regarding the falsity of the tested explanation. Therefore, the correct conclusion to draw when a mismatch occurs between predictions and results is that the tested explanation has been contradicted. But it still might be correct. Thus, in science, disproof, like proof, is not possible.

The Elements of Scientific Discovery

Given our look at explanation generation and test, we are now in a position to list the major elements of scientific discovery as follows:

- A puzzling observation is made.
- One or more causal questions are raised.
- Known similar explanations are borrowed and used as tentative explanations. Thus, explanation generation is a creative process using analogies.
- Each tentative explanation is assumed to be correct, and a test is planned. Then using *If/and/then* reasoning, one or more predictions are generated. Generating predictions also requires creativity. Hence, success in testing may also be limited by the scientist's ability to plan a test with clear predictions.
- The planned test is conducted, and its results are observed.
- Observed results are compared with predicted results.
- A good match supports the explanation but doesn't prove it because alternative explanations may give rise to the same prediction(s). Further, a mismatch contradicts but doesn't disprove the explanation because the mismatch may stem from a faulty test or a faulty deduction, rather than from a false explanation.
- The above elements are recycled until one or more of the tentative explanations have gained convincing support and the alternatives have been convincingly contradicted.

Some scientific research doesn't involve all of these elements. Further, sometimes luck plays a role—usually in finding new puzzling observations in need of explanation. And, as mentioned, imagination and creativity are required. Thus, scientific discovery in no way proceeds in a lock-step manner. Rather, the listed elements represent parts of a *general plan* of what needs to be done. In a sense, having a plan helps. Even though you may not know exactly what to do in each case, at least you have a plan of what you are supposed to do.

And, if you don't have a plan, you can't play the game, at least not very well. And, I might add, if you don't know how scientific inquiry happens, you don't stand much of a chance of making it happen in the science classroom!

HOW DO SCIENCE AND RELIGION DIFFER?

Do you suppose that any amount of evidence would have shaken Priestley from his belief in phlogiston? Of course, we can't really answer this question, but suppose the answer is no. In other words, suppose he has taken it as a matter of *faith* that phlogiston exists. Consequently, his task is twofold: (1) to provide evidence consistent with this idea and (2) when anyone else provides counterevidence to the phlogiston claim, to propose new theoretical components that keep the theories' predictions consistent with the evidence.

Compare this approach to one in which (a) several alternative explanations are initially generated, (b) expectations from each alternative are generated, (c) observed results are gathered and compared with the expectations, and (d) the explanation with expectations most in accord with observed results is tentatively accepted, while the others are rejected. These two approaches represent an essential difference between science and religion. Religion asks one to believe at the outset based upon faith. Science asks one to believe at the end based on an unbiased evaluation of the alternatives and evidence. This does not mean that religion is wrong and science is right or that individual scientists may not be deeply religious or free of bias. Rather, what it means is that as collective enterprises, science and religion are fundamentally different.

At the extremes, a religion knows the Truth before nature is consulted. Interestingly, because there are many religions, there are also many Truths. In science, however, the answers must be viewed as only tentative until nature is consulted. Even after nature is consulted and support is found for any particular explanation, science still regards that explanation as only tentatively true. Scientists realize that the possibility exists that in the future someone may invent a better explanation or contradictory evidence may be found. The result of these differences between science and religion is that there are many religions, each claiming the Truth and often not open to change.[1] Ideally, however, there is only one collective body of scientific knowledge, and that body of knowledge must always remain open to change with no claim, or even hope, of ever obtaining truth in any ultimate sense. Rather, scientific knowledge should be accepted as correct only so long as it seems reasonable in light of the alternatives and the evidence and leads to successful predictions about future events. Table 2.1 summarizes key aspects of the nature of the scientific enterprise as identified by the American Association for the Advancement of Science (1989).

Is Intelligent Design Science or Religion?

This might be an opportune time to mention the recent efforts of some religious organizations to introduce the so-called theory of intelligent design into science classrooms. Intelligent design theory argues that because living things are so complex, like well-crafted

TABLE 2.1   Aspects of the Nature of Science

1. The world is understandable.
2. Scientific ideas are subject to change.
3. Scientific knowledge is durable.
4. Science cannot provide complete answers to all questions.
5. Science demands evidence.
6. Science is a blend of logic and imagination.
7. Science explains and predicts.
8. Scientists try to identify and avoid bias.
9. Science is not authoritarian.

watches, they must have been designed by an "intelligent" creator. Science doesn't accept this argument. One reason is that modern theories of evolution and natural selection afford very satisfactory, very testable, and tested and supported explanations for biological complexity and change that don't rely on the supernatural powers of a creator/designer. Perhaps more important, intelligent design theory, with its designer and his unlimited powers, becomes a religion, not a science, in part because its advocates are either unwilling to put their claims to the test or, when their claims are tested and contradicted, unwilling to modify their claims. For example, consider the following test:

If . . . an intelligent designer created all living things,

and . . . we carefully examine the living things that have been designed,

then . . . they should be designed intelligently.

But . . . many living things appear to be designed poorly. For example, millions of poorly adapted species have gone extinct. Kiwi birds have tiny, nonfunctional wings. Cave animals have useless eyes. The human fetus has a transitory coat of hair. Humans have a tiny useless tailbone. And so on . . .

Therefore . . . intelligent design theory is contradicted.

Instead of admitting that this sort of evidence contradicts intelligent design theory, proponents argue that we are simply incapable of understanding the designer's motives. Or they may argue that his motives do not imply the need for physical perfection. In short, the possibility of mutually contradictory and unknowable motives of the designer means that intelligent design theory is not really testable. Therefore it is becomes nonscientific.

Critics further point out that intelligent design doesn't meet the criteria for scientific evidence used by most courts. In its 1993 *Daubert v. Merrell Dow Pharmaceuticals* opinion, the U.S. Supreme Court established a set of criteria for the admissibility of scientific expert testimony. The Daubert criteria, which determine what evidence can be considered scientific in U.S. federal courts and most state courts, are

- The theoretical underpinnings of the methods must yield testable predictions by means of which the theory could be falsified.
- The methods should preferably be published in a peer-reviewed journal.
- There should be a known rate of error that can be used in evaluating the results.
- The methods should be generally accepted within the relevant scientific community.

Intelligent design doesn't meet the legal definition of science on any of these criteria.

Summary

- Like causal hypotheses, theories are explanations of nature. However, causal hypotheses attempt to explain a specific puzzling observation while theories attempt to explain broad classes of related observations and hence are more general, more complex, and more abstract.

- Theories can seldom be tested in their entirety. Rather, typically they are tested component by component, and theory testing often requires the inclusion of a theoretical rationale to link unseen causal agents with predictions.

- Theory testing may be further complicated when an advocate of a contradicted theory decides to modify, rather than reject, the theory. Nevertheless, theories that meet with repeated contradictions are generally replaced, particularly when a reasonable noncontradicted alternative exists.

- Although we often speak as though entities such as oxygen have been discovered in a manner similar to the way someone discovers a lost treasure, this practice is misleading. Instead, entities such as oxygen and phlogiston are better understood as conceptual inventions. The entire discovery process generally includes three phases: exploration, invention, and application. These same three phases should be embedded in classroom instruction.

- Laws describe but do not explain phenomena. Explanation requires knowing causes. When things happen with no apparent cause, people imagine unseen causal agents—they invent theories.

- Any two theoretical claims may lead to the same prediction; hence observation of that predicted result cannot tell us which hypothesis or theoretical claim is correct. Thus, supportive evidence cannot prove an explanation correct.

- Contradictory evidence can arise due either to an incorrect explanation, to a faulty deduction, or to a faulty test. Because it is not possible to be certain one has conducted a controlled test, contradictory evidence cannot disprove an explanation.

- Scientific discovery consists of several elements that serve as a guide, a plan, for scientific research. However, because both explanation generation and prediction generation require creativity, knowledge of the elements does not ensure success in any particular case.

- Typically, a religion asks one to accept a particular explanation based on faith. Alternatively, science asks one to generate alternative explanations and then consult nature as a way of testing the alternatives. Scientific knowledge, which must remain somewhat tentative, comes at the end.

Key Terms

concept

conceptual systems

disprove

phlogiston

prove

theory

Application Questions/Activities

1. Consider this statement: Science is a process of the discovery of the nature of things through observation. In what sense is this statement true? In what sense is it false? Explain. Rewrite the statement so that it more accurately reflects how people do science.

2. In what sense is science both a process and a product?

3. How do hypotheses differ from theories? Provide two examples of each. How do laws differ from theories? In spite of what you may have been told previously, why is it not possible for a hypothesis to become a theory? Why is it not possible for a theory to become a law?

4. How is theory testing similar to, and different from, hypothesis testing?

5. Is a theory that has been rejected by the scientific community still a theory? Explain. Is a theory that has been accepted by the scientific community still a theory? Explain.

6. Name three observations that can be explained by the Greeks' four-material theory. Why do scientists no longer take this theory seriously?

7. If phlogiston is a material, and if all materials weigh something, then a material such as phosphorus should weigh less after it is burned and has lost some of its phlogiston to the air. Yet phosphorous weighs more after burning. Does this result contradict the four-material theory? Explain. How did 18th-century phlogistonists deal with this result?

9. Why is it more accurate to call oxygen, phlogiston, and the vital force conceptual inventions rather than discoveries?

10. Can the scientific way of knowing ever hope to obtain absolute "truth"? Explain.

11. Can the scientific way of knowing provide convincing evidence "beyond a reasonable doubt"? Explain.

12. Both science and religion can be viewed as "ways of knowing." How do the scientific and religious "ways of knowing" differ?

13. Suppose you observe an apple break loose from a tree and fall to the ground. This observation raises the following causal question: After breaking loose from the tree, why did the apple fall to the ground? In other words, why did the apple go down as opposed to up? One theory to explain why objects such as apples fall is called the particle-push theory. A test of the particle-push theory was discussed in this chapter. Use that test to fill in the boxes and "clouds" in a "box/cloud" figure like the one introduced in Chapter 1.

---

1. Some religious knowledge is open to change, but that change typically does not occur in the way scientific knowledge changes. Rather religious change most often occurs by decree of the religious leaders. For example, the leader may experience a "revelation," a message from God that directs a change in religious doctrine.

PART II

Student Thinking, Development, and Learning

Chapter 3 HOW STUDENTS THINK

Have you ever inverted a glass over a burning candle sitting in a pan of water? If you do, you will discover that the flame quickly goes out and the water rushes up into the inverted glass (see Figure 3.1).

Upon seeing the water rise, one high school student generated the hypothesis that the water goes up because the flame consumes the oxygen under the glass and the water gets sucked up to fill the empty space. When then asked to test his hypothesis he replied, *"If the oxygen is consumed and it creates a partial vacuum, then the water level should rise. And the water does rise. Therefore my hypothesis is supported."*

Chapters 1 and 2 provided insight into how science is practiced and how scientists reason. Knowing about the nature of scientific inquiry and scientific reasoning is necessary for becoming a skilled science teacher. However, becoming a skilled teacher also requires knowing your students, knowing what they know and what they don't know, and knowing how, as in the case of the above student, they sometimes don't reason very well.

Helping students become better thinkers is a major goal of science teaching.

APPLICABLE NSES STANDARDS

Standard A Science teachers plan an inquiry-based program. In doing so, they

- Select science content and adapt and design curricula to meet the interests, knowledge, understanding, abilities, and experiences of students.

FIGURE **3.1** Why does water rise in the inverted glass?

The purpose of this chapter is to explore the fascinating topic of student reasoning. The intent will be to learn more about how students think so that you can help them become more skilled reasoners and help them learn science concepts and theories. The next few pages contain three puzzles followed by several typical student responses. First try to solve each puzzle and then compare your solutions and explanations to those of the students. A discussion of student reasoning patterns and instructional implications will follow.

EXPLORING STUDENT REASONING

Puzzle 1: How Do Mealworms Respond to Light and Moisture?

A student tested the response of mealworms to light and moisture by setting four boxes as shown below. He used neon lamps for light and constantly watered pieces of paper for moisture. In the center of each box he placed 20 mealworms. One day later he returned to see where the mealworms ended up (see Figure 3.2).

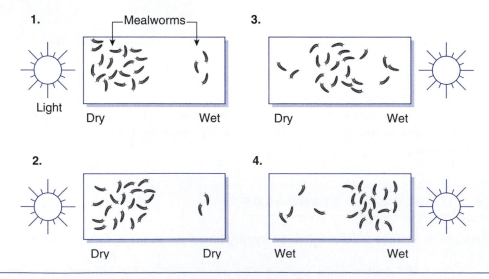

FIGURE **3.2** What factors have the mealworms responded to?

The results show that the mealworms respond to (*respond* means "move toward or away from")

(a) light but not moisture.

(b) moisture but not light.

(c) light and moisture.

(d) neither light nor moisture.

Please explain your choice.

The following are typical student responses to the Mealworms Puzzle. Read the responses and compare them with your own. Note that the responses have been classified into two types—Type A and Type B. Look for similarities among the Type A responses and among the Type B responses. Also look for differences between Type A and Type B responses.

Type A Student Responses

Student A1 (Richard Cripe—Age 18)
Richard chose (d) neither light nor moisture: "Because even though the light was moved in different places the mealworms didn't do the same things."

Student A2 (John Simonds—Age 14)
John chose (a) light but not moisture: "Because there are 17 worms by the light and there are only 3 by moisture."

Student A3 (Ron Gerard—Age 16)
Ron chose (a) light but not moisture: "Because in all situations, the majority goes where there's light. Wetness doesn't seem to make a difference."

Type B Student Responses

Student B1 (Cindy East—Age 15)
Cindy chose (c) light and moisture: "Boxes 1 and 2 show they prefer dry and light to wet and dark, [and] Box 4 eliminates dryness as a factor, so they do respond to light only. Box 3 shows that wetness cancels the effect of the light, so it seems they prefer dry. It would be clearer if one of the boxes was wet-dry with no light."

Student B2 (Pam Stewart—Age 17)
Pam chose (b) moisture but not light: "1, 2, and 3 show that mealworms seem to like the light, but in 3 they seem to be equally spaced. This leads one to believe that mealworms like the dryness and the reason in pictures 3 and 4 they are by the light is because of the heat that the light produces which gives a dryness effect."

Student B3 (Ed Grant—Age 16)
Ed chose (c) light and moisture: "In experiment 3 the mealworms [are] in the middle. So it's safe to assume that light was not the only factor involved."

Questions

1. What similarities did you find among the Type A responses?

2. What similarities did you find among the Type B responses?

3. How do the Type A and Type B responses differ?

Puzzle 2: How High Will the Water Rise?

Below are drawings of two identical cylinders filled to the same level with water (Figure 3.3). Also shown are two marbles, one glass and one steel. The marbles are the same size, but the steel marble is much heavier than the glass marble.

When the glass marble is put into the first cylinder (cylinder 1), it sinks to the bottom, and the water level rises as shown in Figure 3.4.

If the steel marble is put into cylinder 2, will the water level rise to the same level as it did in cylinder 1, to a higher level, or to a lower level? Please explain your prediction.

Read the following student responses and compare them with your own. Look for similarities among the Type A responses and among the Type B responses. Also look for differences between Type A and Type B responses.

Type A Student Responses

Student A1 (Richard Cripe—Age 18)
Prediction: "It will rise. The final water level in cylinder 2 will be 7."
Explanation: "The steel marble is heavier [and] therefore the water will not rise as much."

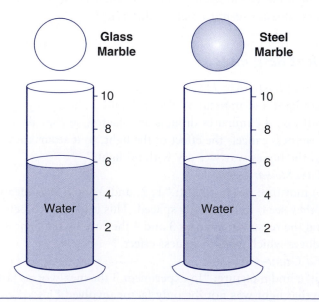

FIGURE 3.3   How high will the water rise?

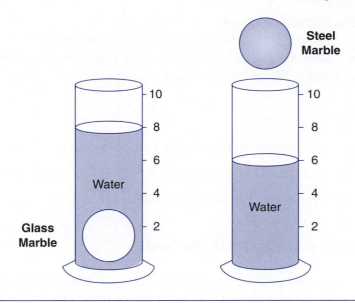

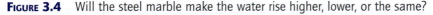

FIGURE 3.4   Will the steel marble make the water rise higher, lower, or the same?

Student A2 (Ron Gerard—Age 16)

Prediction: "The level of water in cylinder 2 will rise to higher than 8—probably 10."

Explanation: "Because the marble in cylinder 2 is heavier than the marble in cylinder 1. It's just like scales; the more weight the higher it goes up."

Student A3 (Cindy East—Age 15)

Prediction: "I think it will stay the same."

Explanation: "I don't really know why. But it would seem the steel marble might have the weight to hold it down. The glass marble is lighter so it pushes the water up."

Student A4 (John Simonds—Age 14)

Prediction: "I think cylinder 2 would be higher to about the number 10 mark."

Explanation: "Because it put more pressure onto the water. This means it would push it upward. The steel ball seems to me like it would be heavier."

Type B Student Responses

Student B1 (Pam Stewart—Age 17)

Prediction: "The water level in cylinder 2 will rise to the same height as in cylinder 1 after the glass marble is put in."

Explanation: "Both marbles had the same volume, [so] therefore the water level, after the marbles were put in, was the same in each cylinder. The weight in no way affected the degree to which the water rose."

Student B2 (Rita Martinez—Age 16)

Prediction: "Rise to 8."

Explanation: "Equal volume spheres displace the same volume of water."

Student B3 (Jean Woods—Age 13)
Prediction: "Cylinder 2's water level will rise to the number 8."
Explanation: "Since the 2 marbles have the same volume they will displace the same amount of water. Eureka! (Weight has nothing to do with it)."

Questions

1. What similarities did you find among the Type A student responses?

2. What similarities did you find among the Type B student responses?

3. How do the Type A and Type B responses differ?

Puzzle 3: How Many Frogs Live in the Pond?

Professor Thistlebush conducted an investigation to discover how many frogs live in a pond near the field station. Because she couldn't catch all the frogs, she caught as many as she could, put a band around their left hind legs, and then put them back in the pond. A week later she returned to the pond and again caught as many frogs as she could. Here are the professor's data.

First trip to the pond: 55 frogs caught and then banded.

Second trip to the pond: 72 frogs caught; 12 of the 72 frogs had previously been banded.

The professor assumed that the banded and unbanded frogs had mixed thoroughly, and from her data she computed an approximate number of frogs in the pond. If you can compute this number, please do so. Then explain in words how you computed your number.

Now read the following student responses and compare them with your own. Look for similarities among the Type A responses and among the Type B responses. Also look for differences between Type A and Type B responses.

Type A Student Responses

Student A1 (Ron Gerard—Age 16)
Answer: 115
Explanation: "55 were caught and banded, 55 with bands. She didn't catch every frog so 55 and 60 would be 115."
Student A2 (Richard Cripe—Age 18)
Answer: 115
Explanation: "There were 55 frogs banded. On the second trip 72 are caught; of those 12 are banded. So 55 plus 60 'new ones' makes 115."
Student A3 (John Simonds—Age 14)
Answer: 115
Explanation: "I say 115 because 55 + 60 = 115 frogs."

Type B Student Responses

Student B1 (Cindy East—Age 15)
Answer: 275
Explanation: "72 – 12 = 60 were not banded. 55/x = 12/60, x = 275 so the number of frogs is 275."
Student B2 (Jim Doyle—Age 16)
Answer: 330
Explanation: "55:x :: 12:72, 12x = 3960, x = 330"
Student B3 (Pam Stewart—Age 17)
Answer: 330
Explanation: "You have to assume that in the week between the first and second sampling none of the banded frogs died or were born. Also the assumption must be made that the frogs mingled thoroughly. This may not be the case but anyway if you make all these assumptions the problem is simple. 12/72 = 1/6 so 1/6th of the frogs have bands: 55 × 6 = 330."

Questions

1. What similarities did you find among the Type A student responses?

2. What similarities did you find among the Type B student responses?

3. How do the Type A and Type B responses differ?

How Do Student Responses Relate to Intellectual Development?

While reading the student responses you undoubtedly recognized that Type A responses were less complete, less consistent, and less systematic; in short, they were not as good as Type B responses. In fact, you may have been surprised to learn that many students gave Type A responses!

According to the late Swiss psychologist Jean Piaget, intellectual development occurs in terms of four major stages. The stages deal primarily with the development of "how to" knowledge, (i.e., **procedural knowledge**) and its importance in the acquisition of "know that" knowledge (i.e., **declarative knowledge**). For example, one needs to know *how to* count to *know that* there are 10 marbles on the table. In biology, one needs to know *how to* sort, classify, and seriate to *know that* species diversity increases from the poles to the equator. And one needs to know *how to* test theories to *know that* evolution has occurred as opposed to special creation.

Piaget's first two developmental stages, called the sensori-motor and preoperational stages respectively, are usually completed before a child is 7 years old; thus they are of little concern to secondary teachers. The third stage, which spans roughly ages 7 to 12, is characterized by reasoning patterns that enable the child to generate and test descriptive hypotheses and thus accurately order and describe perceptible objects, events, and situations within his or her world. The child also generates causal hypotheses but has little interest or expertise in their test. Instead, he or she simply assumes, often mistakenly, that they are true. Piaget called this the **concrete operational stage**.[1]

At about 12 years of age, for some early adolescents, reasoning patterns begin to develop that allow the thinker to test his or her causal hypotheses and thus begin to establish causal relationships for what he or she encounters. Piaget called this the **formal operational stage**. More recent research suggests that there may also be a postformal stage beginning for some young adults at about 18 years of age. More will be said about this possible fifth stage later.

Concrete Operational Reasoning Patterns

The following reasoning patterns characterize the concrete operational (descriptive) stage.

C1 **Class Inclusion:** The individual understands simple classifications and generalizations (e.g., all dogs are animals; only some animals are dogs).

C2 **Conservation Reasoning:** The individual applies conservation reasoning to perceptible objects and properties (e.g., if nothing is added or taken away, the amount, number, length, weight, etc., remains the same—is "conserved"—even though the appearance differs).

C3 **Serial Ordering:** The individual arranges a set of objects or data in serial order and establishes a one-to-one correspondence (e.g., the youngest plants have the smallest leaves).

These reasoning patterns enable individuals to

1. understand terms and statements that make a direct reference to familiar actions and observable objects and can be explained in terms of simple associations (e.g., the plants in this container are taller because they got more fertilizer);

2. follow step-by-step instructions as in a recipe, provided each step is completely specified (e.g., can identify organisms with the use of a taxonomic key or determine the pH of a water sample using an electronic sensor and computer); and

3. relate their viewpoint to that of another in familiar situations (e.g., a girl is aware that she is her sister's sister).

However, individuals whose reasoning has not developed further demonstrate certain limitations. These are evidenced as the individual

4. searches for and identifies some causal variables but does so unsystematically;

5. makes observations and generates hypotheses but in causal contexts doesn't test those hypotheses—doesn't initiate reasoning with the hypothetical—the possible;

6. responds to difficult problems by applying a related but not necessarily correct rule; and

7. processes information but is not aware of his or her own reasoning (e.g., doesn't check his or her own conclusions against the given data or other experience).

The above characteristics typify concrete operational thought previously designated as Type A.

Formal Operational Reasoning Patterns

The following patterns characterize the formal operational (hypothetical) stage—patterns employed in testing alternative causal hypotheses.

F1 Combinatorial Reasoning: The individual systematically considers all possible relations of experimental conditions, even though some may not be realized in nature (e.g., in Chapter 1 we generated all possible combinations of hypotheses to explain salmon navigation).

F2 Identification and the Control of Variables: In testing hypotheses, the individual recognizes the need to consider all the possible causal variables and design a test that controls all but the variable being investigated (e.g., in the Mealworms Puzzle, he or she recognizes the inadequacy of the setup in Box 1).

F3 Proportional Reasoning: The individual recognizes and interprets relationships between relationships described by observable variables (e.g., for every 12 banded frogs there are 72 total frogs; therefore, for every 55 banded frogs there must be 330 total frogs).

F4 Probabilistic Reasoning: The individual recognizes that phenomena are probabilistic in character and that conclusions and explanations must involve probabilistic considerations (e.g., in the Mealworms Puzzle the ability to disregard the few mealworms in the "wrong" ends of Boxes 1, 2, and 3; in the Frogs Puzzle the ability to assess the probability of certain assumptions holding true such as the banded and unbanded frogs mingled thoroughly).

F5 Correlational Reasoning: In spite of random fluctuations, the individual recognizes causes or relations in the phenomenon under study by comparing the relative number of confirming to disconfirming cases (e.g., to test the hypothesis that breast implants cause connective tissue disease one compares the ratio of women with implants and the disease to the ratio of nonimplant women with the disease).

Formal reasoning patterns enable individuals to use causal hypotheses as the starting point for reasoning and to reason in a hypothetical-predictive manner to test them. They can imagine possible causal factors, deduce the consequences of these possibilities, and then empirically verify which of those consequences, in fact, occurs. Previously this was referred to as Type B reasoning.

Classifying Student Responses

Using Table 3.1, reexamine a few student responses to the three puzzles. This time try to apply some of the ideas just discussed to classify these responses into the following more descriptive categories, rather than the superficial A and B designation previously employed.

PC = preconcrete

C = concrete operational

Tr = transitional (mixed concrete and formal characteristics)

F = formal operational

? = not possible to classify without more information

First select one of the students listed in Table 3.1 and reread and classify his or her responses to each puzzle. Record your classification of his or her reasoning patterns in Table 3.1, thus making a reasoning profile for this student. Follow this procedure for at least two students—more if you have time. Then read my analysis of the reasoning involved in each puzzle and my classification of each student's responses. To further assist you in differentiating the reasoning patterns involved in the three puzzles, consider the following general analysis of puzzle responses.

Table 3.1   What Is Your Classification of Student Responses?

	Puzzle Classification		
Student (age)	Mealworms	Water Rise	Frogs
John Simonds (14)			
Cindy East (15)			
Ron Gerard (16)			
Pam Stewart (17)			
Richard Cripe (18)			

Reasoning Patterns in the Mealworms Puzzle

Concrete Reasoning. Individuals will focus on one variable, while ignoring other potentially important variables. They don't understand the idea behind controlled experiments.

   Formal Reasoning. Other variables are controlled while only one is allowed to change. Probabilistic reasoning is also evidenced when students ignore the few mealworms in the "wrong" ends of Boxes 1, 2, and 3. Lastly, students reason correctly with respect to the data in Box 3 (i.e., *If* . . . light is the only factor, *and* . . . we consider the distribution of mealworms in Box 3, *then* . . . they should be near the light. *But* . . . they are in the middle. *Therefore* . . . light must not be the only factor).

Reasoning Patterns in the Water Rise Puzzle

Concrete Reasoning. Common sense suggests that the weight of an immersed object is responsible for the force that lifts the displaced water. Hence the conclusion, given differing weights, is the greater the weight, the higher the water level.

Formal Reasoning. Even though the weight is responsible for lifting the water, the combined volume of water plus marble limits the height of water rise. Because the combined volumes are equal for the two marbles, the water will rise to equal heights if the marbles are fully submerged. The combined or final volume must be introduced by the student.

Reasoning Patterns in the Frogs Puzzle

Concrete Reasoning. Differences rather than ratios are focused on. This student assumes constancy of differences and thus reasons as follows: There were 60 more unbanded than banded frogs in the recapture sample, so there are 60 more frogs in the pond as a whole; $60 + 55 = 115$.

Formal Reasoning. Probabilistic and proportional reasoning are used. Starting with the relative frequency of banded frogs in the recapture sample, this student reasons that the ratio is an estimate of the relative frequency of banded frogs in the pond. After setting $12/72$ equal to $55/x$, the answer follows easily.

Table 3.2 shows one classification of student responses. Notice that not all students responded consistently with concrete or formal reasoning patterns. Many students have been found who respond at varying levels on different tasks. This indicates that students can be at varying levels in various areas. One should not expect a person to be operating at the same level in all contexts. The transition from concrete to formal thought in biology, for example,

TABLE 3.2   What Is My Classification of Student Responses?

	Puzzle Classification		
Student (age)	Mealworms	Water Rise	Frogs
John Simonds (14)	C	C	C
Cindy East (15)	F	Tr	Tr
Ron Gerard (16)	C	C	C
Pam Stewart (17)	F	F	F
Richard Cripe (18)	C	C	C

depends not only on a general change in orientation toward thinking but also on specific experiences in this particular field of study.

IS THERE A FIFTH STAGE?

Do advances in intellectual development continue for some people beyond the formal stage? Read and respond to the following puzzle. We will then discuss how the reasoning may be more advanced than formal stage reasoning.

Why Does Water Rush Up Into the Inverted Glass?

Figure 3.5 shows a drinking glass (open at only one end) and a burning birthday candle stuck in a small piece of clay standing in a pan of water. When the glass is turned upside down, put over the candle, and placed in the water, the candle quickly goes out, and the water rushes up into the glass (as shown at the right).

This puzzling observation raises a question: Why does the water rush up into the inverted glass? Here is a possible explanation:

The flame converts oxygen in the air under the inverted glass to carbon dioxide. Because oxygen molecules do not dissolve rapidly in water but carbon dioxide molecules do, the newly formed carbon dioxide molecules that are now trapped under the inverted glass begin to dissolve in the water under the glass. This movement of CO_2 molecules from the air into the water lowers the air pressure inside the inverted glass. Thus, the relatively greater air pressure outside the glass pushes the water up.

(a) Suppose you have the materials mentioned above plus some matches and some dry ice (dry ice is frozen carbon dioxide). Using these materials, describe a way to test this possible explanation.

(b) What result of your test would show that this explanation is probably wrong?

_____

_____

_____

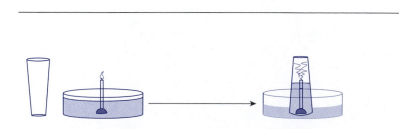

FIGURE 3.5   Why does water rise in the inverted glass?

While responding to this puzzle, did you use the dry ice to saturate the water in one container with CO_2, and did you then generate an argument that goes something like this?

If . . . the water rises because carbon dioxide molecules dissolve rapidly into the water,

and . . . the height of water rise in two containers is compared—one with CO_2-saturated water and one with normal water,

then . . . the water should rise less in the container with the CO_2-saturated water than in the container with the normal water.

But . . . suppose the water rise is the same in both containers.

Therefore . . . the dissolving-CO_2 hypothesis is contradicted and is probably wrong.

If you generated this sort of argument, you would also have reasoned correctly in an *If/then/Therefore* hypothesis-driven manner in a context in which the hypothesized causal agent (dissolving CO_2 molecules) was nonperceptible. Further, to link the imagined causal agent to your experimental manipulation (i.e., the amount of dry ice in the two containers) you would also have generated an additional argument that goes something like this:

Dissolving CO_2 molecules presumably cause a reduction of air pressure in the cylinder. This reduction in turn causes the water to rise. Consequently, when the water is already saturated with CO_2 molecules, the newly created CO_2 molecules cannot escape into the water, and hence the internal pressure will not be reduced and the water will not rise.

This sort of additional argument, sometimes called a *theoretical rationale,* is used to link the imagined causal agent (i.e., dissolved CO_2 molecules) to the manipulated (i.e., independent) variable in the experiment (i.e., the amount of dry ice added to the two containers). Compare the previous argument with a similar argument used to test the hypothesis that the speed at which pendulums swing depends on the amount of weight hanging at their ends:

If . . . the amount of weight causes changes in swing rates,

and . . . the weights are varied while holding other possible causes constant,

then . . . rate of pendulum swing should vary.

But . . . the rates do not vary.

Therefore . . . the weight hypothesis is contradicted and is probably wrong.

Although the *If/then/Therefore* pattern of argumentation is the same as that used to test the dissolving CO_2 hypothesis, a theoretical rationale is not needed here because the test involves an experiment in which the possible cause is directly manipulated. In other words, the proposed cause is the amount of weight, and the experiment's independent variable also is the amount of weight. This variable can be easily manipulated because weight differences can be sensed. Importantly, the ability to generate such arguments begins to develop at roughly 12 years of age and stands as an indicator of formal operational thought (Inhelder & Piaget, 1958).

A. E. Lawson, Drake, Johnson, Kwon, and Scarpone (2000) found in a college biology course that 94% of the students successfully generated *If/then/Therefore* (i.e., hypothetical-predictive) arguments in the pendulum context. But success dropped to 82% on the Mealworms Puzzle and to a dismal 21% on the candle-burning puzzle. Therefore, even though the overall argument pattern is the same, generating *If/then/Therefore* arguments for tasks like the candle-burning task appears more difficult for at least two reasons. First, the hypothesized causal agent in the candle-burning task is no longer perceptible—one cannot directly see carbon dioxide molecules. Second, because the hypothesized causal variable cannot be directly sensed and manipulated, there is a need for a theoretical rationale to link the hypothesized cause(s) to the experimental manipulation. In other words, unlike in the pendulum context where the hypothesized cause and the experiment's independent variable are one and the same (i.e., the amount of weight hanging on the string), this is no longer the case.

Thus, causal hypothesis testing appears to occur on two qualitatively different levels with success at testing hypotheses involving perceptible causal agents as a prerequisite for becoming proficient at testing hypotheses involving nonperceptible theoretical entities. Students may first become generally skilled at testing hypotheses about perceptible causal agents—formal operational skills. And perhaps only then, given the necessary developmental conditions, do they become generally skilled at testing hypotheses about nonperceptible causal agents. Thus we may have a **postformal operational stage** (i.e., a theoretical stage) of development.

By the way, the accepted explanation for the water rise is that the flame transfers kinetic energy (motion) to the inverted glass's trapped gas molecules. The greater kinetic energy causes the gas to expand, which results in some escaping out the bottom. When the flame goes out, the remaining molecules transfer some of their kinetic energy to the cylinder walls and then to the surrounding air and water. This causes a loss of average velocity, fewer collisions, and less gas pressure (a partial vacuum). Water then rises into the cylinder until the total of the water and air pressure inside the cylinder is equal to the total of the atmospheric and water pressure outside the cylinder.

WHY DEVELOPMENTAL STAGES ARE IMPORTANT TO TEACHERS

One of the most frequently quoted statements in educational psychology comes from David Ausubel in his textbook with Novak and Hanesian (1978, p. iv):

> If I had to reduce all of educational psychology to just one principle, it would say this: The most important single factor influencing learning is what the learner already knows. Ascertain this and teach him accordingly.

This statement has been interpreted to imply that the most important "thing" for a teacher to know prior to instruction is what his or her students already know about the subject to be taught. If you intend to teach about evolution, then you need to know your students' prior declarative knowledge of evolution. However, according to D. P. Ausubel (personal communication, September 1989), the word *knows* should not be interpreted so narrowly. Instead *knows* should include both declarative knowledge (specific knowledge about evolution theory) and procedural knowledge—for example, how to test evolution theory. Moreover, procedural knowledge plays the more fundamental role because, in Ausubel's words, "it's involved in everything, while domain-specific knowledge is important to new learning only in the domain of concern and only when prior domain-specific knowledge is made relevant via use of an advance organizer or some other conceptual bridge" (D. P. Ausubel, personal communication, September 1989).

Piaget frequently said much the same thing. According to Piaget, declarative knowledge structures "are the result of a *construction* and are not given in the objects, since they are dependent on action, not in the subject, since the subject must learn how to coordinate his actions" (Piaget, 1976, p. 13), and "to know is to modify, to transform the object, and to understand the process of this transformation and as a consequence to understand the way the object is constructed" (Piaget, 1964, p. 176). Thus to "know" requires the presence of procedural knowledge (reasoning skills). When, for example, do children know the concept of "number"? The developmental answer is that they know it when they "conserve" it—when they recognize that the number of checkers stays the same even though the arrangement changes. This implies the presence of operations that allow thinking back to the start—reversing the action, of rearranging, of counting, of (not) adding to, of (not) taking away. Likewise when do students "know" what an ecosystem is? Again, the answer is that they "know" it when they conserve it—when they recognize that an ecosystem transformed by being stripped of its first-, second-, and higher-order consumers is still an ecosystem. They recognize the key property of ecosystems—an ecosystem's ability to recycle materials. Again procedural operations are implied. As Piaget (1965) stated, "Every notion, whether it be scientific or merely a matter of common sense, presupposes a set of principles of conservation, either explicit or implicit" (p. 2). The point is that a student's operative structures (procedural knowledge) determine what can or cannot be meaningfully known—acted upon either physically or mentally.

Suppose, for example, a biology teacher wants students to understand Gregor Mendel's theory of inheritance. Understanding Mendelian theory requires use of a number of formal or postformal reasoning patterns. First, a general understanding of the nature of theories and their relationship to empirical data is required. Second, the generation of zygote possibilities given certain gamete gene frequencies is required. This involves combinatorial reasoning, as does the generation of gamete possibilities. Application of combinatorial reasoning results in the generation of certain ratios of gene combinations in both zygotes and gametes. These ratios represent probability estimates that certain phenotypes will occur. Thus a variety of higher-order reasoning patterns seem to play roles in "understanding" and applying Mendel's theory.

This analysis suggests that topics such as Mendelian genetics would cause a severe comprehension problem for students with little or no facility with these reasoning patterns. Such students, of course, may be capable of parroting words such as *gene, dominant, recessive,* and *crossing over,* but these words would not be part of their useful bag of conceptual knowledge. A. E. Lawson and Renner (1975) tested this implication in high school biology, chemistry, and physics classes. They first constructed final examinations in all three areas. The final exams tested understanding of the descriptive concepts (those with perceptible exemplars) and theoretical concepts (those without perceptible exemplars) that had been introduced during the school year. They then administered students a variety of tasks that required formal reasoning. Based upon task performance, students were classified into developmental stages and substages ranging from early concrete to fully formal operational. Students were then administered final exams in their respective disciplines.

Results for the combined classes are shown in Figure 3.6. As predicted, the results show that none of the concrete students demonstrated any understanding of theoretical concepts. This provides clear support for the hypothesis that formal and perhaps even postformal reasoning patterns are necessary for understanding theoretical concepts. Notice also that formal reasoning patterns seem to have helped formal students understand the descriptive

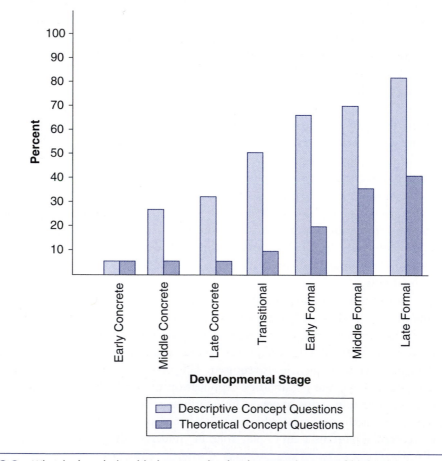

FIGURE 3.6   What is the relationship between the developmental stages of high school science students and their understanding of descriptive and theoretical concepts?

concepts. The fact that the teaching procedures used were largely expository meant that the students were seldom confronted with direct experience into the meaning of any of the terms introduced. This procedure, in effect, may have rendered potentially understandable descriptive concepts meaningless, at least for the concrete students.

This clear link between developmental stage and concept understanding implies that instruction should not overwhelm students' developmental capabilities. Instead, instruction should be designed to improve those capabilities. In other words, it should be designed and implemented so that students develop the reasoning patterns needed to construct scientific concepts and theories. A general principle of instruction then is that the demands that the subject matter places on students' reasoning must be analyzed. Only material that is "developmentally appropriate" should be introduced. But what does "developmentally appropriate" really mean? Surely if the selected concepts place no demands on reasoning, then those topics are not likely to facilitate further development. This result is untenable because, as stated, one of the major objectives of education is to help students become better thinkers. Accordingly, the selection of developmentally appropriate concepts means selecting concepts and activities that challenge but do not overwhelm students' initial reasoning patterns. In this way, science instruction can help students develop their reasoning skills. The good news is that once the problem is understood, there is a lot that teachers can do to help students develop their reasoning skills and construct understanding of the really important scientific concepts and theories. Much more will be said about how this can be done in subsequent chapters.

Summary

- Student responses to problems reveal a wide variety of student reasoning patterns, which can be classified into developmental stages.

- Concrete reasoning patterns allow students to construct descriptions of natural phenomena. Formal reasoning patterns are used in the construction of causal relationships when the hypothesized causal agents are potentially observable. Postformal reasoning is used in the construction of causal relationships when the hypothesized causal agents are nonperceptible. Intellectual development is stage-like because, in addition to probable maturational constraints, the products of previous stages are used in testing the constructions of subsequent stages.

- Developmental stages are important to science teachers because many secondary students have yet to develop formal and postformal reasoning patterns and hence are limited in their ability to construct scientific concepts. This implies that teachers need to teach in ways that provoke the development of higher-order reasoning patterns so that students can become scientifically literate.

- Three important questions are raised: Why have some secondary school students not developed beyond the concrete stage? What problems does this lack of development pose in the science classroom? And what, if anything, can teachers do to help students develop more advanced reasoning patterns?

Key Terms

class inclusion	identification and the control of variables
combinatorial reasoning	
concrete operational stage	postformal operational stage
conservation reasoning	probabilistic reasoning
correlational reasoning	procedural knowledge
declarative knowledge	proportional reasoning
formal operational stage	serial ordering

Application Questions/Activities

1. The data in Figure 3.7 compare representative samples of Japanese and North Carolina students on several tasks requiring use of formal operational thinking patterns. The data suggest a Japanese superiority. Generate several alternative hypotheses to explain this apparent superiority. How might these alternatives be tested? What effect, if any, do you think this has on national competitiveness? Explain.

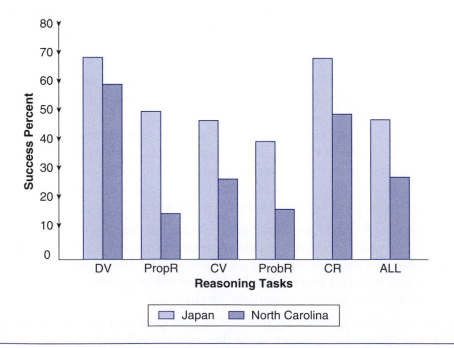

FIGURE 3.7   Comparison of reasoning skills of a representative sample of 4,397 Japanese students with a representative sample of 3,291 North Carolina students (Grades 7, 8, and 9).

Note: DV = Displaced Volume; PropR = Proportional Reasoning; CV = Control of Variables; ProbR = Probabilistic Reasoning; CR = Combinatorial Reasoning; ALL = All Tasks Combined (from Takemura, Matsubara, Manzno, Tadokoro, & Nakayama, 1985).

2. Suppose a rubber balloon hangs by a string from the ceiling of a moving vehicle. Also suppose a floating Mylar balloon is attached by a string to the vehicle's back seat. As the vehicle abruptly stops, the hanging balloon swings forward, and the floating balloon swings backward. This observation raises an interesting question: Why did the hanging balloon swing forward while the floating balloon swung backward? Here is a possible explanation: The hanging balloon is relatively heavy, so its momentum carried it forward when the vehicle stopped. The floating balloon, being lighter than air and having less momentum, went backward because as the vehicle stopped, the heavier air molecules inside the vehicle rushed forward and piled up at the front. Thus, the piled-up air molecules at the front pushed harder on the front side of the balloon than the relatively fewer air molecules on the balloon's backside. Thus, the balloon was pushed backward. Suppose you have two balloons just like those described above, a large airtight chamber on wheels, and a vacuum pump (a pump that can extract air from airtight chambers).

   (a) Describe an experiment using these materials to test the possible explanation.

   (b) What result of your experiment would show that the explanation is probably wrong?

   (c) What level of reasoning (i.e., concrete, formal, or postformal) do you think is required to respond to (a) and (b)? Explain.

3. What sorts of classroom activities might help students develop more advanced reasoning patterns? Explain.

4. Select an excerpt from a middle school or high school science textbook that you think is written entirely at the concrete level. Explain your selection.

5. Select another excerpt that is written entirely at the formal or postformal level. Explain your selection.

6. What, if anything, could be done to make the formal or postformal excerpt understandable to concrete operational students?

7. With a partner, select a few tasks that appear in this chapter. Select two samples of students of various ages. Have your partner administer the tasks to one sample while you administer the tasks to the other sample. Give the tasks to one student at a time so that he or she can explain his or her answers and reasoning. Record student responses and classify the answers and explanations into developmental levels. Exchange the answers and explanations of your sample of students with that of your partner. Both you and your partner should now classify these responses. Compare your new classifications with those initially made by your partner. What is your percentage of agreement? Discuss the disagreements to see if you and your partner can reach agreement. On what percentage of responses are you unable to reach agreement? How could you modify your procedures to reduce this percentage in the future?

---

1. Note that use of Piaget's stage names does not imply acceptance of his theory concerning the underlying structure of mental operations (e.g., combinatorial system and the Inversion, Negation, Reciprocity, and Correlativity, or INRC, group). More recent research indicates that although Piaget's empirical characterization of developmental stages is generally accurate, his theoretical explanations are problematic.

Chapter 4

DEVELOPING AND LEARNING DIFFERENT TYPES OF KNOWLEDGE

Chapter 3 introduced an important distinction between procedural knowledge (e.g., reasoning patterns) and declarative knowledge (e.g., concepts). Psychologists often speak of the *development* of procedural knowledge and the **learning** of declarative knowledge. The development of procedural knowledge is generally a long-term process while the learning of declarative knowledge is often a short-term process. To get a better sense of the two related processes, let's start with a little experiment.

DEVELOPING PROCEDURAL KNOWLEDGE

How good are you at drawing while looking in a mirror? Take a few minutes to try the task presented in Figure 4.1. You will need a mirror. Once you have one, place the figure down in front of it so that you can look into the mirror at the reflected

Students need to use their prior knowledge and their reasoning patterns to figure out why the water rises when a jar is placed over a burning candle.

APPLICABLE NSES STANDARDS

Standard E   Science teachers develop communities of learners that reflect the intellectual rigor of scientific inquiry and the attitudes and social values conducive to learning. In doing so, they

■ Display and demand respect for the diverse ideas, skills, and experiences of all students.

figure. Read and follow the figure's reflected directions. Look only in the mirror—no fair peeking directly at your hand. Try to become conscious of your procedures while drawing. When finished, consider the following questions:

1. Did you improve during the activity?

2. What feedback, if any, was helpful or disruptive?

3. What procedures helped?

4. What errors persisted?

How did you do? If you are like most people, the task proved rather difficult and frustrating. This should come as no surprise. After all, you have spent years writing and drawing without a mirror. So what does this mirror-drawing task reveal?

The task reveals a pattern of how the mind works. Figure 4.2 depicts that pattern, which can be described as follows: First, a reflected image is "recognized" by a specific "mental structure" that is stored in your long-term memory. This recognition process, called **assimilation,** is immediate, automatic, and subconscious. The activated mental structure then drives behavior that, in the past, has been linked to an outcome. Thus, when the structure drives behavior in the present context, the behavior is linked to that outcome. In this sense, the behavior carries with it an expectation (i.e., what you expect to see as a consequence of the behavior). All is well if the behavior is successful—if the outcome matches the expectation. However, if the outcome doesn't match the expectation (e.g., you move

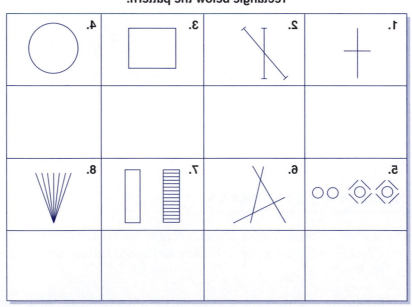

FIGURE 4.1   Can you reproduce these shapes while looking in a mirror? Place this figure in front of a mirror. Read and follow its reflected image.

your hand down and to the right and you expect to see a line drawn up and to the left, but instead you see one drawn up and to the right), contradiction results. The resulting contradiction produces a sort of mental "disruption" that psychologists refer to as **disequilibrium.** Disequilibrium then drives a mental search for another procedure until you come up with one that works, in the sense that it produces noncontradicted behavior. If and when this happens, your behavior has undergone the necessary change (i.e., **accommodation**). Or you may become so frustrated that you quit, in which case your behavior will not undergo the necessary accommodation. In other words, you won't learn to draw in a mirror. The entire process of assimilation and accommodation is called **self-regulation** or sometimes *equilibration*.

Typically mirror drawing doesn't involve language. Nevertheless, if we write down the mental steps involved in drawing a diagonal line, they might go something like this:

If . . . I move my hand down and to the right,

and . . . I watch to see what happens,

then . . . I should see a diagonal line go up to the left.

But . . . the line goes up to the *right*.

Therefore . . . my procedure isn't working, and I need to try something else.

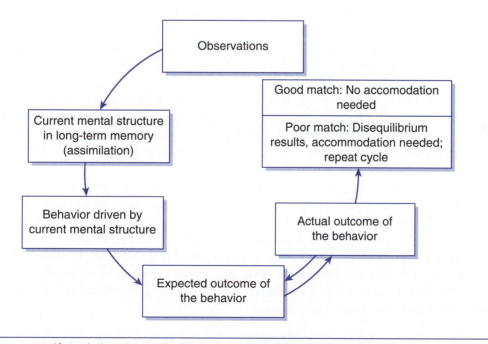

FIGURE 4.2   Self-regulation, or equilibration, begins with spontaneous assimilation of observations by a current mental structure. The structure then drives behavior that, due to past experience, generates an expected outcome. A mismatch of expected and actual outcomes provokes disequilibrium and the need for accommodation.

The important point is that your mind doesn't work the way you might think. You don't look, look again, and look still again until you internalize a successful behavior. Rather, the mind tells you to try something. Importantly, that something, that behavior, carries with it an expectation—a prediction. Hopefully the behavior is successful in the sense that the prediction is matched by the subsequent outcome. But sometimes it's not. So the contradicted behavior then prompts the generation of another idea, and so on until eventually the expectation isn't contradicted. In short, we learn from our mistakes—from what some have called trial and error. As the old saying goes, "You always pass failure on the way to success." In this case success means that you have *developed* new and better *procedures* for mirror drawing. Said the other way around, your procedural knowledge has developed.

A Historical Example of Self-Regulation: Darwin's Contradiction

The self-regulation involved in mirror drawing takes place very much at the sensori-motor level and largely below consciousness. However, self-regulation can also occur consciously at higher conceptual levels. For example, Gruber and Barrett (1974) analyzed Charles Darwin's thinking during a time period when his conceptual thinking underwent self-regulation.

As you may know, as a young man with a religious upbringing Darwin, like many of his contemporaries, believed that God created the Earth and its living things. So when he boarded the *HMS Beagle* in 1831 to begin a trip around the world, he firmly believed that the creator created an unchanging organic world (the world of living organisms), as well as an unchanging physical world. Importantly, as depicted in Figure 4.3, the organic world (O) was perfectly adapted to the physical world (P). In other words, specific kinds of organisms "fit" their physical environments because the creator (C) created them that way.

Although Darwin was a creationist, he was well aware of evolutionary views. In fact, Darwin's own grandfather, Erasmus Darwin, published a book titled *Zoonomia; or, the Laws of Organic Life* that contained speculative ideas about evolution and its possible mechanism. Nevertheless, on that day in 1831 when he boarded the *Beagle*, Darwin was seeking an adventure—not a theory of evolution.

During the first 2 years of the voyage on the *Beagle*, Darwin read some persuasive ideas about the modification of the physical environment through time by Charles Lyell in his two-volume work titled *Principles of Geology*. At each new place Darwin visited, he discovered examples and important extensions of Lyell's ideas. Consequently, Darwin was becoming increasingly convinced that the physical world was not static. Instead, it changed through time. This dynamic conception of the physical world stood in opposition to his earlier beliefs, and it created a serious contradiction (i.e., disequilibrium) as can be seen in Figure 4.3b and by the following argument:

If . . . organisms and their physical world are perfectly adapted to each other,

and . . . the physical world changes,

then . . . organisms must also change to remain adapted to their physical world.

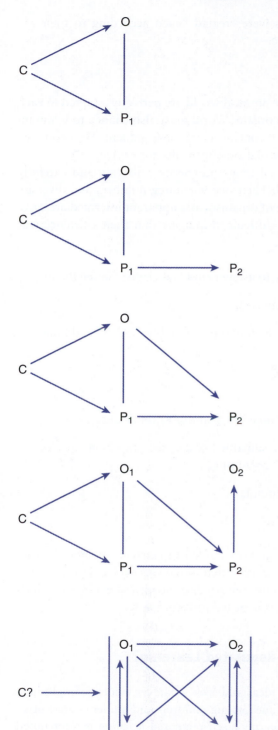

a. 1832 and before: The creator (C) made an organic world (O) and a physical world (P): O was perfectly adapted to P. Mental equilibrium exists.

b. 1832–1834: The physical world undergoes continuous change, governed by natural forces as summarized in Lyell's *Principles of Geology*. A logical contradiction is implied which induces a state of disequilibrium.

c. 1835: Activities of organisms contribute to changes in the physical world (e.g., coral reefs). Disequilibrium persists.

d. 1836–1837: Changes in the physical world imply changes in the organic world if adaptation is to be maintained; the direct action of the physical environment "induces" organic adaptations. Equilibrium is partially restored.

e. 1838 and after: The physical and organic worlds continuously interact and induce reciprocal changes to maintain adaptations. The role of the creator is unclear. He may have set the system into existence yet stands outside. Mental equilibrium is restored at a higher more complex plane.

FIGURE 4.3   How did Darwin's worldview change from 1832 to 1838?

But . . . according to the *Bible,* organisms were created "each according to their own kind" and are not supposed to change.

Therefore . . . a contradiction exists.

In other words, if the organic world and the physical world are perfectly adapted to each other and the physical world changes, then the organic world must also change to maintain their perfect "fit." This, of course, is the logical conclusion of the argument. However, the conclusion contradicted Darwin's original view that organisms do not evolve.

Darwin also spent a considerable amount of time and energy collecting and carefully describing the various life forms that he found. Their overwhelming numbers and diversity profoundly struck Darwin. With each new type of organism and apparent intermediate specimen that he collected, it became increasingly difficult to imagine that their existence was solely the work of a creator. More specifically,

If . . . God created life forms "each according to its own kind" (as claimed in the *Bible*),

and . . . life forms in several places are compared,

then . . . intermediate life forms should *not* be found (presumably God created lions and tigers, but he did not create ligers).

Alternatively:

If . . . life forms evolve through time (as claimed by Darwin's grandfather),

then . . . intermediates should be found (presumably because they represent species in the process of evolving from one "kind" to another).

And . . . intermediate life forms are often found.

Therefore . . . it seems that organisms evolve.

These perplexities and partially grasped arguments added to Darwin's mental disequilibrium as he did not immediately accept the conclusion that organisms evolve. In fact, it was not until 1837, after his return to England, that he converted to the idea of evolution, which allowed the restoration of mental equilibrium as depicted in Figure 4.3e.

What Happens When You Disrupt Self-Regulated Learning?

Of course Darwin was free to pursue his own ideas and seek whatever evidence might help him eventually restore equilibrium. But sometimes young children and students are not so lucky. Considering what can happen when a learner's self-regulated learning is interrupted by well-intentioned but excessive external guidance is useful. The following example captures the essence of the educational issue.

When my son Bobby was 2 years old, he had a set of eight small "nesting" boxes that varied in size so that one would fit within another in a serial order from small to large. The boxes could be "nested" or placed upside-down largest first, next largest next, and so on until each was stacked upon the other to make a tower. Making a tower is an extremely difficult task for a 2-year-old. When we played with the boxes I normally built the tower so he could see the result. Then Bobby would knock the tower down, grab the boxes, and attempt to build it himself. Typically, he would first pick the largest box and perhaps the next largest. However, if left to his own devices, he would err long before completing the tower. He appeared to recognize the correct solution, but he lacked the ability to arrive at it by himself. It was an assumption on my part that he actually was attempting to build the entire tower. His actual motives may have in fact been quite different. Nevertheless his spontaneous effort went on and on.

One day, while he was playing with the boxes, I decided to find out if a concerted effort at teaching him the correct way to build the tower would be successful. When he first grabbed the largest box I let him continue, but instead of letting him proceed when he grabbed an incorrect box, I intervened. "No, Bobby, that's not the correct box. This is the correct one." And so on. I continued this intervention for about 10 minutes until we worked out a successful technique to unerringly build the tower. He would grab a box and then look at me for approval or disapproval. If I approved he would add it to the first. If I disapproved he would grab another box and so on until together we got the tower built.

Unfortunately such a prescription had two rather serious side effects. First, it eliminated all of his spontaneous effort to build the tower. He would not add a box without looking to me for approval. His behavior had changed from spontaneous to dependent in the course of only a few minutes. And second, without me for continual guidance he was not able to build the tower again. Seeing my own child transformed from a curious, ambitious, and energetic builder to a dependent, cautious seeker of approval taught me not to try my heavy-handed teaching methods again.

In short, if adults usurp children's spontaneous and self-directed learning by imposing external procedures or by answering unasked questions, they may be able to solve problems by rote or by parroting words, but they will neither be able to solve novel problems nor be able to understand how those empty words relate to the world they know. The key educational issue raised by this discussion is clearly one of active, spontaneous, self-directed learning versus passive, outer-directed, "reception" learning. Active, spontaneous, self-directed learning is essential if both the development of reasoning skills and meaningful concept acquisition are aims. Unfortunately, the heavy-handed, outer-directed teaching approach is taken far too often in today's elementary and secondary schools. Small wonder so many students arrive at college with only one question on their minds: "What will be on the test?"

PROVOKING SELF-REGULATION IN THE CLASSROOM

So how then can teachers provoke self-regulation and intellectual development in their classrooms? Consider the self-regulation needed by a bright-eyed, conscientious high school sophomore named Karen. When shown one wide and one narrow plastic cylinder of equal height, with equally spaced marks along their heights (see Figure 4.4), she predicted that water that filled the wide one up to the fourth mark would rise higher if poured into the narrow cylinder. When the water in the wide cylinder was poured into the narrow cylinder, it rose to the sixth mark. At seeing this, she predicted the water that rose to six in the wide would rise to eight in the narrow. As she put it, this is because it was two higher before so it would still be two higher. Now of course a problem exists here, but Karen didn't see it. When Karen actually saw the water rise to nine, instead of eight as she predicted, the problem surfaced. Her additive strategy simply didn't work. The result was mental disequilibrium and a search for a new strategy.

Trying to teach Karen to use proportions to solve the problem as well as her inability to do so in other situations (for example, instead of using proportions to triple a recipe she would cook a single recipe three times!) clearly demonstrated the magnitude of the problem. Both theory and experience argue that this isn't an isolated and easily remedied problem. Rather the situation is tied to a whole host of ideas (e.g., probability, correlations, and control of variables) that are a part of a general way of processing information. At this level the required self-regulation will take considerable time and effort on Karen's part. This will take repeated attempts at solving problems until she gives up her inappropriate strategies and develops better ones.

Also consider the case of a seventh grader named Betsy. In Betsy's science class, her teacher presented students with many experiments to perform. For example, they examined the effect of fertilizer on plant growth and the effects of light, temperature, and moisture on

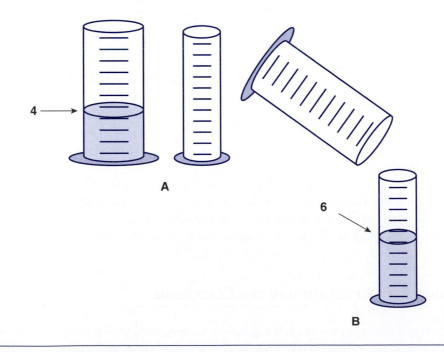

FIGURE 4.4   The pouring water task

the behavior of beetles, snails, and mealworms. Following the experiments, each student wrote up a lab report discussing the question, procedure, data, and conclusions. The reports were straightforward and, in effect, something of a bore—all except for one question the teacher asked repeatedly, "What was the control? Did you perform a controlled experiment?" To these questions Betsy had no ready answer. In spite of the fact that her teacher defined the terms and provided examples, Betsy did not see the relationship between the teacher's explanations and her own ideas and experiments. What did the term *control* really mean? What was a "controlled" experiment? Was the classroom fire extinguisher the control? The teacher's insistence on something being controlled and Betsy's inability to figure out what she meant caused a very real state of disequilibrium.

Fortunately, the teacher continued to bring in a variety of materials for students to experiment with, and after each experiment they were repeatedly asked that penetrating question about controls. With each new experiment, Betsy tried to make sense of those words in terms of her experiments. During this time a great deal of reflecting took place—reflecting about specific activities and about specific terms.

Following some 2 to 3 months of such experimentation, discussion, and reflection, the idea finally dawned on Betsy. To find out if temperature made a difference in plant growth she had to make sure that all the plants were watered the same, had the same amount of fertilizer, and so on; otherwise she couldn't know for sure if the temperature had caused the difference. In other words, *everything* (except the temperature) had to be the same for the experiment to give clear results. Eureka! That was a controlled experiment. Immediately she could apply this idea to any experiment she performed. At last equilibrium was restored.

This example demonstrates that physical experience and social interaction (in this case the teacher's introduction and continued reintroduction of the term *controlled experiment*) clearly have a place in provoking self-regulation and reflective abstraction. The initial experimentation and the introduction of new confusing terms can produce disequilibrium. To the skilled teacher this disequilibrium is an opportunity to provide students with new activities involving the same reasoning pattern(s) in new and varied contexts. This enables students to continue thinking and self-regulate at their individual paces until they reflect sufficiently to disembed the new reasoning pattern from the varied contexts in which it is embedded. *The crucial point here is that the students themselves must do the thinking. Teachers and/or classmates can't do it for them!*

Thus, a key component of self-regulation is thinking back on one's activities and thinking until the "light bulb" finally switches on. Interestingly, Betsy's job might have been easier had her teacher introduced intuitively understandable words like *fair test* as opposed to the more scientific but more confusing phrase *controlled experiment*. In other words, the teacher should have asked, "Did you conduct a fair test?" rather than "Did you conduct a controlled experiment?" Nevertheless, the light bulb finally went on in Betsy's mind thanks to self-regulation and the repeated and patient efforts of a very skilled teacher.

More generally, intellectual development begins with physical experience with objects and with contradictions. The physical experience and/or arguments with others may produce the contradictions, which then force reflection on the procedures, the reasoning, the arguments, and the evidence. By closer inspection and by noting the differences between unsuccessful and successful procedures, learners become aware of what they should and should not do. The introduction of helpful verbal "hints" or "rules" (e.g., make sure your test is fair) also aids in the identification of effective procedures. Finally, additional experiences requiring the same procedure along with the repetition of the hints or rules allow the learner to *reflectively abstract* the procedures from their contexts. Thus, thanks to environmental encounters that provoke self-regulation and reflectivity, the brain constructs and stores abstract (general) rules that can then be applied across a variety of novel domains to facilitate problem solving and learning. Students develop new reasoning patterns—they develop intellectually.

WHY DOES STAGE "RETARDATION" OCCUR?

Knowing about the processes of self-regulation and reflective abstraction helps clarify why stage "retardation" occurs—that is, why some high school and college students fail to develop formal and postformal reasoning patterns. Suppose, for example, that many years ago two identical islands existed in the ocean, each inhabited by 10,000 islanders, each isolated from the outside world, and each ruled by an all-powerful king. Whenever questions arose, the islanders asked their king for answers. Each king provided the answers, and whatever each king said was considered true. But one day, a foreign ship arrived at one of the islands. Over time, a vigorous trading relationship was established between that island and several foreign countries. Importantly, not only did the ships bring many new goods; the sailors brought many new ideas—ideas that spread throughout the island's population. Some of these "foreign" ideas contradicted the "truths" previously handed down by the king. Soon the islanders began wondering which ideas were correct, and more important, they began wondering how they could tell. Eventually, an upheaval took place in which the king was overthrown and replaced by a government run by the people.

Several decades later, an anthropologist arrived on the island to study the island's culture. As part of her study, she administered a reasoning test to the island's teenagers and adults. Soon after, the anthropologist discovered the other island. She was the first outsider to discover this island, which was still controlled by an all-powerful, truth-dispensing king. She administered the reasoning test to the teenagers and adults on this island as well. Question: Which population of islanders do you think did better on the reasoning test? Which population had more formal and postformal reasoners? Why?

I hope you agree that the reasoning patterns of the islanders on the first island should be better developed. Without confrontation with different points of view, no contradiction, no argumentation, and no reflective abstraction take place. Piaget would seem to agree, having stated that the development of advanced reasoning patterns occurs as a consequence of "the shock of our thoughts coming into contact with others, which produces doubt and the desire to prove" (Piaget, 1962). Piaget went on to state,

> The social need to share the thought of others and to communicate our own with success is at the root of our need for verification . . . argument is therefore, the backbone of verification. Logical reasoning is an argument which we have with ourselves, and which produces internally the features of a real argument. (p. 204)

In other words, the growing awareness of and ability to use internalized arguments to guide one's thinking and decision making occurs as a consequence of attempting to engage in arguments of the same sort with others in which alternative claims are put forward and accepted or rejected as the basis of evidence and reason as opposed to authority or emotion. Clearly, if alternatives do not exist, then no external arguments ensue, and no disequilibrium and internalization of patterns of argumentation result.

This position seems consistent with that of Vygotsky (1962) and Luria (1961), who view speech as social in origin and believe that only with time does it become self-directive. According to their view, the process occurs in four steps. First, children learn the meaning of words. Second, language can serve to activate but not limit behavior. Third, language from an external source can activate or limit behavior. And fourth, the internalization of language can serve a self-regulating function through instructions to oneself.

LEARNING DECLARATIVE KNOWLEDGE

Do you know what a table is? Can you find one and show it to someone? Of course you can. You can because you know what tables look and feel like. Thanks to past experiences about tables, you have a "mental representation" of tables. Consequently, when you hear or see the word *table,* your table mental representation is "activated." Hence, you know what the word means, and if asked, you could teach others to know it as well. On the other hand, do you know what a Mellinark is? Can you find one and show one to somebody? You probably can't. That's because you lack a mental representation for the word *Mellinark.* But we can fix that.

Take a look at Figure 4.5. The first row shows several Mellinarks. The "creatures" in row 2 are not Mellinarks. What are the key features of Mellinarks? Can you use the information in Figure 4.4 to find out? If so, which creatures in row 3 are Mellinarks? Take a few minutes to try to answer these questions before reading on.

Perhaps you identified creatures 1, 2, and 6 in row 3 as Mellinarks because they, and only they, have a big "dot," a "tail," and are "shaded." How did you do this? Do you recall the reasoning you used to decide which creatures in row 3 were Mellinarks? Unfortunately, reasoning happens so quickly that it is probably hard for you to recall. Consequently, to gain insight into the reasoning people use to solve the Mellinark task several students tried the task and immediately told us about their reasoning. Consider, for example, the following remarks of a student who identified creatures 1, 2, and 6 in row 3 as Mellinarks:

> Well, the first thing I started looking for was just overall shape, whether it's straight, looks like a dumbbell, but this doesn't really work, because some of these (row 2) are similar in overall body shape. So I ruled that out. Well, then I said, all of these are shaded (row 1). But some of these (row 2) are shaded and these aren't Mellinarks, so that can't be the only thing. So I looked back at these (row 1) and noticed that they all have a tail. But some of these have a tail (row 2), so that can't be the only thing either. And so then I was sort of confused and had to look back, and think about what else it was. Then I saw the big dot. So all of these (row 1) have all three things, but none of these (row 2) have all three.

All of these are Mellinarks.

None of these is a Mellinark.

Which of these are Mellinarks?

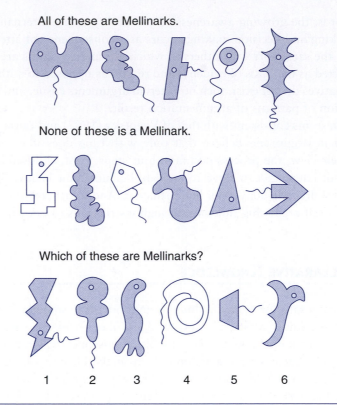

1   2   3   4   5   6

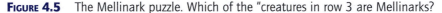

FIGURE 4.5   The Mellinark puzzle. Which of the "creatures in row 3 are Mellinarks?

So this student first generated the idea that overall shape is a critical feature. But as she tells us, this idea was quickly rejected because some of the creatures in row 2 are similar in overall shape to those in row 1. Thus, the student seems to have reasoned like this:

If . . . overall shape is a critical feature of Mellinarks,

and . . . I look closely at the non-Mellinarks in row 2,

then . . . none should be similar in overall shape to the Mellinarks in row 1.

But . . . some of the non-Mellinarks in row 2 are similar in overall shape.

Therefore . . . "I ruled that out" (i.e., I concluded that my initial idea was wrong).

Of course this is the same *If/then/Therefore* reasoning pattern that we found in the mirror drawing task. And as we can see below in the remainder of the student's comments, the pattern is recycled until all contradictions are eliminated. So after rejecting her initial descriptive hypothesis, the student seems to have quickly generated others (e.g., shading is a key feature) and presumably tested them in the same fashion until she eventually found a combination of features (spots, tail, big dot) that led to predictions that were not contradicted—that is,

If . . . Mellinarks are creatures that have spots, a tail, and one big dot,

and . . . I check out all the creatures in rows 1 and 2,

then . . . all those in row 1 should have all three "things" and none in row 2 should have all three "things."

And . . . this is what I see.

Therefore . . . Mellinarks are creatures with all three "things," and creatures 1, 2, and 6 in row 3 have all three "things," so they are Mellinarks.

So learning declarative knowledge (i.e., concept learning), seen in this light, rests on the ability to generate and test alternative hypotheses. In this sense learning declarative knowledge depends in part upon the use of procedural knowledge. So thanks to reasoning and experience, people learn new concepts. Note that saying that one has learned a new concept means that he or she has two things: (1) the appropriate mental representation—the idea—and (2) the related term. Prior to thinking about Figure 4.5 you had the *term* (i.e., Mellinark), but you lacked the *idea*. So you lacked the *concept*. In other words, *ideas* plus *terms* equals *concepts*. This means that terms may exist on paper, but concepts exist only in people's minds. It also means that students can sometimes memorize terms without having the related ideas. Clearly this is not a good thing. Consequently, we need to teach in ways that provoke students to learn concepts, not merely memorize terms. And to do this, they need to engage in cycles of *If/then/Therefore* reasoning.

In summary, we see that concept learning is guided by a pattern of *If/then/Therefore* reasoning. In other words, reasoning "drives" learning. And in a very real sense, active learning provokes reasoning. Therefore, if you want your students to develop procedural knowledge *and* learn declarative knowledge, your instruction needs to allow students to encounter puzzling observations and then attempt to explain them though cycles of *If/then/Therefore* reasoning. Your instruction then needs to provoke students to reflect on the learning process to abstract their successful procedures. In short, students need to engage in scientific inquiry and then think about what they have done. The next section will provide a classroom example of how this can be done.

PROVOKING DEVELOPMENT AND LEARNING IN THE CLASSROOM

The lesson begins with a burning candle held upright in a pan of water using a small piece of clay. Shortly after a glass cylinder is inverted over the burning candle and placed in the water, the candle flame goes out, and water rises in the cylinder. These observations raise two major causal questions: Why did the flame go out? And, why did the water rise? The generally accepted answer to the first question is that the flame converts oxygen in the cylinder to carbon dioxide until too little remains to sustain combustion; thus the flame dies. As mentioned in Chapter 3, the generally accepted answer to the second question is that the flame transfers kinetic energy (motion) to the cylinder's gas molecules. The greater kinetic energy (greater motion) causes some of the now faster-moving molecules to escape out the bottom. When the flame goes out, the remaining molecules transfer some of their kinetic energy to the cylinder walls and then to the surrounding air and water. This causes a loss of velocity, fewer collisions, and less internal gas pressure. Relatively greater external gas pressure then pushes on the external water surface and pushes the water up until the internal and external pressures are equal.

The candle-burning lesson is a particularly good way to provoke disequilibrium because students' initial explanations for the water rise are contradicted and need to be replaced. A common student explanation is that oxygen is "used up" and thus a partial vacuum is created, which "sucks" water into the cylinder. Typically, students fail to understand that when oxygen "burns" it combines with carbon producing CO_2 gas of equal volume (hence no partial vacuum is created). Students also often fail to understand that a vacuum cannot "suck" anything. Rather the force causing the water to rise is a push from the relatively greater number of air molecules hitting the water surface outside the cylinder. Student experiments and discussions provide an opportunity to modify these misconceptions by introducing a more satisfactory explanation based on kinetic-molecular theory.

Exploration

Start the lesson by pointing out the following materials:

- Pie pans
- Candles
- Matches
- Clay
- Jars of various shapes and sizes
- Syringes and rubber tubing
- Baking soda
- Ice
- Dry ice
- Balloons
- pH paper

Next have each student select a partner and pour some water into a pan. Stand a candle in the pan using a small piece of clay for support. Then light the candle and put a cylinder, jar, flask, or beaker over the candle so that it covers the candle and sits in the water. Then observe what happens and repeat the procedure several times, varying several independent variables to determine their possible effects. You should also tell students that they will be challenged to generate several alternative explanations for their puzzling observations and then try to test their alternatives.

Encouraging Alternative Hypothesis Generation—Brainstorming

Allow the initial exploration to proceed as long as students are making good progress. You may need to stop them after about 30–40 minutes to discuss observations, preliminary questions, and possible explanations. During the discussion, observations should be listed on the board, and you should ask students to state the key causal question(s). As mentioned, the most obvious causal questions are, Why did the flame go out? And, why did the water rise? After acknowledging that the flame probably went out due to a lack of oxygen, have students try to generate several possible answers to the second question. This part of the discussion should resemble a brainstorming session in which the class follows specific rules to encourage the open generation of several ideas. Brainstorming rules include (a) *No criticizing allowed.* All ideas that are generated go on the list—no questions asked or comments allowed. (b) *Keep moving.* Don't stop to reflect and consider details. Move on. Go for quantity—not quality. (c) *Piggybacking.* Take ideas already mentioned and extend them with new twists. And (d) *Diversifying.* Try to generate different kinds of explanations. Following these brainstorming rules, students should be able to generate several tentative explanations such as the following:

1. The oxygen is "burned up" creating a partial vacuum. So the water is "sucked" in to replace it.

2. H_2O gas forms by burning. When the H_2O cools, it changes to liquid filling the cylinder.

3. As the candle burns, it consumes O_2 but produces an equal volume of CO_2. The CO_2 dissolves in the water more easily than the original O_2, thus producing a partial vacuum. The water is then "sucked" in.

4. The candle produces smoke, which collects in the cylinder and attracts (pulls) the water up.

5. Burning converts O_2 to CO_2, which is a smaller molecule. Thus it takes up less space and creates a partial vacuum, which "sucks" the water up.

6. The candle's heat causes the air around it to expand. After the candle goes out, air cools, air pressure is reduced, and the water is pushed in by greater air pressure outside. (If no one proposes this explanation you will have to propose it yourself. But make sure that you do not give students the impression that this is the "correct" explanation. Rather it is simply an idea that a student in another class generated, which should be tested along with the others.)

7. Here is an explanation that I like to add to the students' list: A wizard lives on campus and sucks the water up. (You can pick the name of your school sports mascot for the wizard.)

As mentioned, the important point here is that you want students to generate several ideas. Adding a few unlikely hypotheses of your own, such as an invisible wizard, or perhaps suggesting that the flame caused oxygen and hydrogen to combine to produce the water will help students lose their fear and open up their creative "intuitions"—intuitions that play a crucial role in doing science.

Testing the Alternatives

Now that student brainstorming has generated several possible explanations, remind students that their next task is to test the alternatives. Also remind them that to test a possible explanation one must conduct tests with clearly stated expected results (predictions).

You may want to provide an example or simply challenge students to put their heads together to see what they can come up with. This may be an excellent time for the bell to ring so that they can think up experiments as a homework assignment. If you do decide to offer an example, use the *If/and/then* form like this:

If . . . water is sucked in to replace the oxygen,

and . . . the height that water rises with one, two, three, or more candles (all other things being equal) is measured,

then . . . the height of water rise should be the same regardless of the number of burning candles. This result is predicted presumably because there is only so much oxygen in the cylinder to be burned. So more candles will burn up the available oxygen faster than fewer candles, but they will not burn up more oxygen. Hence, the water rise should be the same. Note that the assumption is made that before they go out, more candles do not consume more oxygen than fewer candles.

Now have students conduct their experiments and report results. Results of the example experiment show that the number of burning candles affects the water level (the more candles, the higher the water level). Therefore, the consumed-oxygen explanation is contradicted. Also the water rises after the candles go out, not while they are burning—another observation that contradicts the explanation.

Measuring the total volume of water before and after the water has risen inside can test explanation 2, the water-created-by-burning explanation. If this explanation is correct, then the total volume of water should increase considerably.

Students can test explanation 3, which claims that the CO_2 dissolves in the water, in a couple of ways. One way involves a comparison of the amount of water rise in containers with CO_2-saturated water versus normal water. The explanation leads to the prediction that the water level should rise higher in the cylinder with normal water. One can use dry ice (or sodium bicarbonate and acid) to produce CO_2 gas. Its solubility in water can be tested. The pH of water shaken with CO_2 and the pH of the water below a candle that has just gone out can be compared. Also if the explanation is correct, a cylinder filled with gas from the dry ice (presumably CO_2) when inverted and placed in water should cause water to rise, but water doesn't.

Filling a cylinder with smoke and inverting it in water can test explanation 4, the smoke-attracts-water explanation. If this explanation is correct, then the water should rise. I will leave it to you to figure out a way to test explanation 5, the CO_2-is-a-smaller-molecule explanation.

Explanation 6, the heat-causes-air-expansion explanation, leads to the prediction that bubbles should be seen escaping out the cylinder's bottom (assuming that the cylinder is quickly placed over the candles while the air is still expanding). It also leads to the prediction that more candles should cause more water to rise—presumably because more candles will heat more air; thus, more will escape, which in turn will be replaced by more water. (Although one candle burning over a longer time period releases as much energy as three candles burning for a shorter time, one candle will not raise the cylinder's air temperature as much because energy is dissipated rather quickly.)

Initially students do not take explanation 7, the campus wizard explanation, seriously. So they don't bother to test it. But at my insistence, they soon come up with a way to test the hypothesis with the following thought experiment:

If . . . the water rises because a campus wizard sucks it up,

and . . . the experiment is conducted off campus,

then . . . the water should not rise—presumably because the wizard's powers exist only on campus.

But . . . they surmise that the water does rise off campus.

Therefore . . . the wizard explanation is contradicted and can be rejected.

I reply to this argument that, because they are students, the campus wizard travels with them off campus. Consequently, he can still make the water rise. So the presumed results of their thought experiment do not really contradict the explanation after all. Students then propose telephoning a nonstudent and asking him or her to conduct the experiment off campus. Then when the nonstudent finds that the water still rises, students can conclude that the explanation can be rejected. But the wizard's powers can travel through phone lines, I tell them, so the water should still rise. At this point most students catch on to the game being played, which essentially amounts to giving the wizard ever-expanding powers. And once the wizard's powers become limitless, the explanation can no longer be contradicted—hence it becomes untestable. Thus, continued belief in the explanation becomes a matter of faith, not evidence. In other words, the wizard becomes a religious, godlike entity, not a testable scientific entity in the sense that scientific hypotheses must lead to predictions that may in fact not occur and thus can in principle be contradicted. This discussion is important because it clarifies this essential difference between religion and science for many students for the first time.

Introducing Terms and Applying Concepts

After all the alternatives have been tested and the results discussed, you should carefully summarize and clarify the explanation that is most consistent with the evidence. You can also introduce the term *air pressure* and the major terms associated with kinetic-molecular theory (as listed in Table 4.1) as they pertain to the present phenomenon. You should also discuss the common suction misconception in this context. Kinetic-molecular theory implies that suction (as a force that can pull/suck up water) does not exist (i.e., the water is being pushed into the cylinder by moving particles of air rather than being "sucked" in by some intuitively generated but nonexistent pulling force).

To allow students to apply concepts of kinetic-molecular theory, including the air pressure concept, to a new situation, provide each team with a piece of rubber tubing, a syringe, a beaker, and a pan of water. Instruct the students to invert the beaker in the pan of water and fill it with water in that position with the mouth of the beaker submerged. Some

TABLE 4.1   Some Major Claims of Kinetic-Molecular Theory

1. Matter consists of small particles (atoms and combinations of atoms called molecules).

2. Moving matter can strike other pieces of matter and transfer some/all of its motion (kinetic energy) to the other pieces.

3. Atoms and molecules contain several forms of stored motion (potential energy) such as nuclear, electrical, chemical, and radiant energy.

4. Given enough activation energy, forms of potential energy may be released (e.g., molecular bonds that store potential chemical energy can be broken, causing the atoms to move apart, which in turn can cause collisions and the breaking of more molecular bonds, or perhaps the formation of new molecular bonds).

5. Energy can neither be created nor destroyed; thus energy transfers do not result in changes in energy amounts.

students will make futile efforts to force water through the tube into the beaker before discovering that they must extract air through the tube. Now have them attempt to explain why the water rose without using the word *suction*.

As a homework assignment, challenge students to find a way to insert a peeled, hard-boiled egg into a bottle with an opening that is smaller in diameter than the egg. They must not touch the egg with anything after it has been placed on the opening. After a small amount of water in the bottle has been heated, it is only necessary to place the smaller end of the egg over the opening of the bottle to form a seal. The egg will be forced into the bottle by the greater air pressure outside as the air inside cools. You may also ask students to drink a milkshake with a straw and then challenge them to explain how the milkshake gets into their mouths.

TEACHING FOR DEVELOPMENT AND LEARNING

In conclusion, this chapter has argued that teachers need to design and carry out lessons that provoke students to think. And perhaps the best way to do this is with lessons that raise questions that students cannot answer with their present concepts and/or accustomed ways of thinking. A mismatch of new experiences with expectations provokes student disequilibrium, which in turn can provoke students to rethink what they think they know and why they think they know it. Such continued thinking and self-regulation can then lead not only to new concept learning and perhaps to conceptual change but also to the development of better ways of thinking. In short, not only do such lessons arm students with more scientifically accurate sets of concepts (i.e., declarative knowledge), but they also help students develop improved learning-to-learn skills (i.e., procedural knowledge). As one might expect, however, some students are initially frustrated with disequilibrium and may simply want to be told what to do, how to do it, or what they are supposed to know. But the good news is that for most students, this frustration soon passes as they learn to take control of their own learning. Soon most students cannot imagine trying to learn science any other way. As one former student put it, "If you go back to the old way, it's no longer science!"

Summary

- The development of procedural knowledge occurs via self-regulation in which tasks prompt the brain to spontaneously assimilate input and then generate a procedure that carries with it a specific expectation. Hopefully the expectation is matched by the procedure's outcome. But sometimes it is not, and disequilibrium results. The mismatch may then prompt the generation of another procedure and so on until the resulting behavior is not contradicted. Thus accommodation and intellectual development take place.

- If adults usurp the learner's spontaneous and self-regulated efforts by imposing procedures or by answering unasked questions, learners may be able to solve problems by rote or by parroting words but will neither be able to solve novel problems nor understand how the adults' words relate to their world. Self-regulation is essential if both the development of reasoning skills and meaningful concept understanding are aims.

- Student disequilibrium is an opportunity to provide new activities and "hints" that enable students to continue thinking and self-regulate at their individual rates until they reflect sufficiently to mentally coordinate the new terms with the experiences (via reflective abstraction) to eventually develop new procedures and/or learn new concepts.

- People learn new concepts via reasoning in an *If/then/Therefore* fashion. Thus concept learning is not a purely abstractive process but rests on the ability to generate and test ideas. In this sense, learning new declarative knowledge depends in part on procedural knowledge.

- A new concept has been learned when two or more distinguishable objects, events, or situations are mentally grouped together and set apart on the basis of some common feature(s). Concept learning involves the recognition of the commonality plus the term or terms to refer to that which is common.

- In addition to providing students with opportunities to develop their reasoning skills, the candle-burning lesson provides an opportunity to introduce several new concepts and exemplifies several elements of the nature of science. Nevertheless, developing reasoning skills, learning difficult science concepts, and learning about the nature of science are long-term propositions that require a curriculum that allows students multiple opportunities to participate in the knowledge construction process and self-regulate.

Key Terms

accommodation

assimilation

disequilibrium

learning

self-regulation

Application Questions/Activities

1. Select a theoretical concept that you might wish to teach. Design and describe a lab activity to introduce the concept. Name the key causal question raised. Name at least three alternative hypotheses that students might generate and could test along with the planned tests and their predicted outcomes. What, if any, student misconceptions might you expect to encounter? How should these be dealt with? Describe how the lesson can help students develop better reasoning skills and acquire a better understanding of the nature of science.

2. Teaching is not telling. In what sense is the saying accurate? Can "telling" ever be helpful in the learning process? If so, under what conditions can it be helpful?

3. Read about a scientific discovery in a book or magazine and see if you can identify the scientist's hypotheses, tests, predictions, results, and conclusions. If possible, construct an *If/then/Therefore* argument that the scientist may have used during the "discovery."

4. When in your own experience have you experienced disequilibrium and successfully undergone self-regulation and reflective abstraction? Can you identify aspects of that experience that were important to your success? If so, what were they?

PART III

Elements of Inquiry Instruction

Chapter 5

THE ORIGINS AND OUTCOMES OF INQUIRY INSTRUCTION

Every adult has been a teacher at some time, whether professional or otherwise. Thus, every adult knows something about teaching. Inquiry instruction is consistent with the way people explore their world and learn. Therefore, anyone who has reflected on learning and teaching has no doubt discovered aspects of inquiry instruction. For that reason it is not possible to identify a single inventor of the inquiry method. Indeed, aspects of the method have been invented many times by many people beginning no doubt before Socrates employed his famous Socratic method to provoke his followers to reflect on the inadequacies of their own knowledge. Thus, current advocates of inquiry are part of a long-standing and very rich tradition.

On the other hand, it would be a mistake to think that recent research offers nothing new. The act of teaching involves procedures and thus requires procedural knowledge. And as we have

One outcome of inquiry instruction is that students have fun.

Source: Photo courtesy of Gerry Foster, Desert Vista High School, Phoenix, Arizona.

APPLICABLE NSES STANDARDS

Standard A Science teachers plan an inquiry-based program. In doing so, they

- Develop a framework of yearlong and short term goals for students.
- Select science content and adapt and design curricula to meet the interests, knowledge, understanding, abilities, and experiences of students.

(Continued)

(Continued)

■ Select teaching and assessment strategies that support the development of student understanding and nurture a community of learners.

■ Work together as colleagues within and across disciplines and grade levels.

seen, procedural knowledge develops not through the abrupt invention of new ideas but through gradually increasing awareness of the procedures used in idea invention and test. In a very real sense recent research concerned with improving science instruction represents not a novel departure from past practices but a growing consciousness of how we should teach and why we should teach in a particular way. Increased consciousness leads to a more consistent use of correct procedures and thus leads to more effective learning.

With this in mind this chapter will briefly consider some early approaches to science instruction so that we can place the current emphasis on inquiry in its proper historical context (see also Bybee & DeBoer, 1994). After discussing an inquiry approach to physics instruction known as the modeling method, the chapter will conclude by discussing how inquiry instruction improves student creativity, intelligence, and achievement.

A BRIEF HISTORY OF SCIENCE INSTRUCTION

Early Approaches

Science instruction in American schools initially consisted of daily recitations. Use of the laboratory was unheard of prior to the late 1800s. Physical materials and specimens, if used at all, were a means of verifying book or lecture information. But by the mid to late 1800s, laboratory instruction became popular because it was felt by many that firsthand observation and manipulation were useful in "disciplining" the mind. The idea of mental discipline stemmed from the then-popular theory that mental behavior was compartmentalized into several "faculties" or abilities such as logic, memorization, and observation. Further, "exercising" these faculties would enhance their development so that they would function effectively in all life situations. This so-called **faculty theory** was used to justify the use of abstract, meaningless, laborious tasks during instruction to "exercise" and "strengthen" students' minds.

Largely through the research of psychologists such as E. L. Thorndike, faculty theory soon lost favor. Consequently emphasis shifted away from rote tasks toward efforts to present meaningful information, develop positive attitudes and interests in science, and develop reasoning skills. Indeed by 1898, organizations such as the National Education Association were making modern-sounding recommendations such as "The high school work should confine itself to the elements of the subject . . . full illustration of principles, and methods of thought . . ." (Hall & Committee, 1898).

The sentiment to teach students scientific concepts and reasoning skills was even more apparent in the Central Association of Science and Mathematics Teachers' 1910 committee report on secondary education. The report attempted to identify ways to motivate students, to select appropriate teaching materials, and to teach "the scientific spirit and method" (Galloway, 1910). The committee suggested the following:

1. More emphasis on "reasoning out" rather than memorization.

2. More emphasis on developing a problem-raising and problem-solving attitude among students.

3. More applications of the subject matter to personal and social issues.

4. Less coverage of territory. The course should progress no faster than students can go with understanding.

Although at this time there was considerable criticism of teaching methods that emphasized memorization, no alternative methods were advocated except to suggest that solving problems or conducting projects offered promise for better class discussions, more active student participation, and better opportunities for "research type" learning. John Dewey became a vocal advocate of instruction that emphasized science as a method of inquiry. In an address to the National Education Association, Dewey (1916) argued that

> science is primarily the method of intelligence at work in observation, in inquiry and experimental testing; that, fundamentally, what science means and stands for is simply the best ways yet found out by which human intelligence can do the work it should do, ways that are continuously improved by the very process of use.

In spite of Dewey's urgings, it would take more than 40 years before this view of science would make its way into a large-scale science curriculum movement (Hurd, 1961). The movement was the National Science Foundation–sponsored curriculum development projects of the late 1950s and 1960s. These inquiry-oriented projects, such as the Biological Sciences Curriculum Study (BSCS), the Chemical Education Materials Study (Chem Study), the Science Curriculum Improvement Study (SCIS), the Elementary Science Study (ESS), the Physical Science Study Committee (PSSC Physics), and the Earth Science Curriculum Project (ESCP), sprang up largely as a reaction to the Soviet Union's perceived superiority in science and mathematics education as evidenced by its successful 1957 launch of Sputnik into outer space. Although several of these alphabet soup projects, as they came to be called, developed some excellent inquiry-oriented activities, most of them, with the notable exception of SCIS, failed to generate a systematic method of inquiry teaching. Other projects only alluded to "discovery," "inquiry," or "problem solving" approaches, the steps of which were not always made clear to teachers and thus were difficult to implement.

A survey of various teaching methods advocated in science methods textbooks, just prior to and during this curriculum movement, echoed this emphasis on inquiry. One textbook even included a method called the learning cycle (Heiss, Obourn, & Hoffman, 1950).

The Heiss et al. learning cycle was based on the following sequence of events, which Dewey had previously called a complete act of thought:

1. Sensing the problem or question

2. Analyzing the problem

3. Collecting evidence

4. Interpreting the evidence

5. Drawing and applying conclusions

The corresponding steps in the Heiss et al. (1950) learning cycle were as follows:

1. Exploring the unit—including demonstrations to pose questions, the proposal of hypotheses to answer questions, and cooperative planning for testing

2. Experience getting—including testing hypotheses, collecting and interpreting data, and drawing conclusions

3. Organization of learning—including the preparation of outlines and summaries and taking tests

4. Application of learning—including the application of new information, concepts, and skills to new situations

The Heiss et al. (1950) method involves hypothesis generation and test. However, it does not explicitly include an initial instruction phase where teachers introduce new terminology. Other authors during the 1960s and early 1970s discussed a variation on this teaching method called the problem-solving method (e.g., R. D. Anderson et al., 1970; Van Deventer, 1958; Washton, 1967). For example, Washton listed the following sequence of student behaviors in the problem-solving method:

1. Students explore perplexing phenomena and are asked to state a problem/question.

2. Students are encouraged to propose and screen hypotheses.

3. Students design and conduct experiments to test hypotheses.

4. Students organize and analyze the data obtained.

5. Students are guided to formulate a conclusion, or sometimes they suspend judgment.

Authors such as Collette and Chiappetta (1986), Kuslan and Stone (1968), and Victor (1989) also identified this method but referred to it as the "inquiry" method. Carin and Sund (1980) referred to it as the "guided-discovery" method.

The Role of the Science Curriculum Improvement Study

Identification of three explicit phases of learning cycle instruction can be found in the SCIS program. Indeed, its origin can be traced to the early work of Robert Karplus at the

University of California–Berkeley during the late 1950s and early 1960s (SCIS, 1973). To be more precise, its origin can be traced to a day in 1957 when a second-grade student invited her father, Professor Karplus, a physicist, to talk to her class about the family Wimshurst machine, a device for generating electrical charges. Karplus found the visit enjoyable, and so did the children. During the next few months other talks on electricity and magnetism to both elementary and junior high students followed. Soon Karplus turned his thoughts to developing an elementary school science curriculum.

During the 1959–1960 school year Karplus prepared and taught three units titled "Coordinates," "Force," and "What Am I?" Although the experience proved interesting, analysis of the trial teaching revealed serious student misconceptions and other weaknesses. The experience prompted Karplus to ask, How can teachers create a learning experience that achieves a secure connection between the pupils' intuitive attitudes and the concepts of the modern scientific point of view?

Karplus was helped by a visit to the research institute of Jean Piaget in Switzerland. When Karplus returned to Berkeley in 1961, he developed a plan to stress learning based upon the pupils' own observations and experiences. However, he also planned to help them interpret their observations in a more analytical way. During part of that school year, J. Myron Atkin, then a professor of education at the University of Illinois, visited Berkeley to share his views on teaching with Karplus. Together Atkin and Karplus (1962) formulated a teaching method that was implemented in subsequent trial lessons.

The Atkin and Karplus teaching method was designed to be analogous to the way past scientists invented and used new concepts about nature. In their 1962 paper they offered the example of the ancients' observations and interpretation of the motions of the Sun and planets. The geocentric concept of the solar system was taken to be a conceptual *invention* following initial observations. The heliocentric concept represents an alternative invention. With the help of these inventions, people attempted to *discover* other phenomena besides the ones that led them to propose the inventions in the first place, which could be understood using the invention. These attempts, if successful, led to a reinforcement and refinement of the concepts. If they were unsuccessful, they revealed limits of the concepts or, in some cases, led to their replacement. Recall that this pattern of *exploration—invention—application* was identified in the development of the modern-day conception of combustion recounted in Chapter 2.

Atkin and Karplus (1962) clearly distinguished between the initial introduction of a new term (called *invention*) and its subsequent verification or extension (called *discovery*). They likened the process to the Copernican teacher instructing students that the Sun is at the center of the solar system while almost everyone else *knows* that the Earth is at the center. They did not introduce the terms *exploration* or *learning cycle* in their 1962 paper, but the instructional phases of invention and discovery were clearly evident.

Subsequently it became clear that students need time to explore new phenomena at their own pace with their own preconceptions. Only after this initial exploration is it wise to introduce a more analytical point of view. Armed with this new insight, Karplus tried out the modified approach the following school year in several classes. In 1967 Karplus and Herbert Thier published a book in which the three phases of the teaching approach were first explicitly stated like this: "The plan of a unit may be seen, therefore, to consist of this sequence: preliminary exploration, invention, and discovery" (p. 40). Additional details of this important early work can be found in a collection of papers by Karplus and several of his collaborators called *A Love of Discovery: Science Education—The Second Career of Robert Karplus* (R. G. Fuller, 2002).

Finding Learning Cycles in Early Biology Education

In 1953 the National Academy of Sciences convened a conference to examine biology teaching methods and suggest new alternatives. As a result of that conference, the National Science Foundation funded a project under the direction of Professor Chester Lawson, a geneticist at Michigan State University, which began in 1956 and included 30 high school and university biology teachers from throughout the country. The project resulted in publication of a sourcebook of over 150 laboratory and field activities for use in high school courses (C. A. Lawson & Paulson, 1958). Although no explicit teaching method resulted from that work, it provoked Lawson to begin a search for such a method. The project also served as the precursor to the well-known Biological Sciences Curriculum Study.

Lawson, like Karplus, turned his attention to the history of science for insight into the process of conceptual invention. His 1958 book, *Language, Thought, and the Human Mind,* carefully detailed the nature of scientific invention and identified a general pattern of thought he referred to as *belief—expectation—test.* This pattern is similar to Atkin and Karplus's (1962) pattern of invention and discovery as conceptual invention constitutes a belief (i.e., a hypothesis) that in turn leads to an expectation (i.e., a prediction) to be tested in the real world. If one discovers confirming evidence (finding a good match between expected and observed results), the invention is retained. If not, it is rejected in favor of another belief (i.e., an alternative hypothesis).

Following work on the biology sourcebook, Lawson began a careful review of the psychological research in hopes of developing a comprehensive theory of human learning complete with possible neurological mechanisms and instructional implications. Lawson's theory would not be published until 1967; however, his literature search uncovered the Atkin and Karplus (1962) paper to which he had this to say:

> If we substitute the term "initial unity" for system, "differentiation" for the identification of objects within the system, "pattern or relations" for invention, and "reinforcement" for discovery, we can see the relation of this teaching approach to our theory of learning. (p. 119)

Thus, Atkin and Karplus and Lawson independently invented the same pattern of inquiry instruction. When Karplus, the physicist, needed a biologist to consult in the development of the life sciences half of the SCIS program he called Lawson. What began as a 2-week consultation in the summer of 1965 ended with a 10-year job as director of the SCIS life science curricula. The final product of the SCIS program in the mid 1970s was a K–6 life science and physical science curriculum based on a three-phase learning cycle method.

The SCIS Learning Cycle

Interestingly, the label *learning cycle* does not appear in any of the early SCIS publications although the terms *exploration, invention,* and *discovery* are clearly spelled out (cf., Jacobson & Kondo, 1968; Karplus & Thier, 1967; SCIS, 1973). First mention of learning cycles appears in the Teacher's Guides to the SCIS program units beginning in about 1970 (e.g., SCIS, 1970). Karplus and others continued to use the terms *exploration, invention,* and *discovery* to refer to the three instructional phases through 1975 (e.g., Collea, Fuller, Karplus, Paldy, & Renner, 1975).

However, in 1976 it became apparent that many teachers were having a difficult time understanding what invention and discovery meant in the context of classroom lessons. So, in a series of 1977 publications, the three phases were referred to as *exploration, concept introduction,* and *concept application* (e.g., Karplus et al., 1977).

Still others have modified the labels further. For example, some publications labeled the phases as exploration, *term* introduction, and *concept* application. These terms were used primarily because they intend to convey meanings to teachers (not necessarily to students). Teachers can introduce terms during the second phase of instruction, but they cannot introduce concepts. Students must construct/invent their own concepts. As we shall see below, the SCIS learning cycle method has become the method of choice; however, others have continued to change the names of its instructional phases.

The BSCS Five Es

The BSCS also advocates a learning cycle teaching method. However, the BSCS method divides the exploration phase into *engage* and *explore* "stages." The organization refers to the term introduction phase as the *explain* stage and to the concept application phase as the *elaborate* stage. In addition, BSCS includes another stage called *evaluate.* Of course teachers need to evaluate learning, so the addition of an evaluate stage is not new. Thus the only real change from the SCIS method is the inclusion of an engage stage. Clearly students need to be engaged for learning to take place. Good explorations are engaging as they provoke questioning and the elicitation of connections with past experience. However, some teacher comments to "set the stage" are often worthwhile.

The Modeling Method in Physics Instruction

The currently popular modeling method of physics instruction introduced by Wells, Hestenes, and Swackhammer (1995) is another extension of the learning cycle. The modeling method (as described more fully at http://modeling.asu.edu/) is designed to engage students in understanding the physical world by constructing and using scientific representations (i.e., **models**) that describe, help explain, and predict physical phenomena. The method employs a student-centered approach in which instruction is organized into "modeling cycles" that move students through all phases of model development, evaluation, and application. A key aspect of modeling cycles is the inclusion of activities in which students work in small cooperative groups to explicitly model the phenomena being explored. Typically the models are drawn on whiteboards and presented to the class for comparison, analysis, and debate.

Modeling cycles involve both *model development* and *model deployment.* Model development encompasses the exploration and term introduction phases of learning cycles, while model deployment corresponds to the concept application phase. In high school physics each modeling cycle is 2 or 3 weeks long. Typically there are six cycles each semester. As with all learning cycles, throughout each modeling cycle the teacher has specific objectives, including terms to be introduced, conclusions to be reached, issues to be raised, and misconceptions to be addressed.

The National Research Council's Instructional Guidelines

Based on the successes of learning cycle instruction, as described by programs such as SCIS, BSCS, and the Physics Modeling Method, the National Research Council (NRC, 2001) has recently published guidelines on how science should be taught. In these guidelines, like BSCS the NRC lists the following five key phases of instruction.

Phase 1: Students *engage* with a scientific question, event, or phenomenon. This connects with what they already know, creates dissonance with their own ideas, and/or motivates them to learn more.

Phase 2: Students *explore* ideas through hands-on experience, formulate and test hypotheses, solve problems, and create explanations for what they observe.

Phase 3: Students analyze and interpret data, synthesize their ideas, build models, and clarify concepts and explanations with teachers and other sources of scientific knowledge.

Phase 4: Students *extend* their new understanding and abilities and *apply* what they have learned to new situations.

Phase 5: Students, with their teachers, review and assess what they have learned and how they have learned it (see NRC, 2000a, p. 35).

The main point is that debate among the experts no longer exists about how science should be taught. The clear consensus is that teachers should teach science via inquiry, and by inquiry the experts mean learning cycles.

OUTCOMES OF INQUIRY INSTRUCTION

Does Inquiry Enhance Creativity?

Now that we know a bit more about where inquiry instruction came from, let's see why it has become the method of choice in terms of boosting student creativity, intelligence, and achievement.

Webster's Third New International Dictionary (Grove & the Merriam-Webster Editorial Staff, 1986) defines creativity in terms of "bringing into existence; causing to be; evolving something new from one's own thoughts or imagination." Psychologists think of the creative process in terms of the four sequential phases called *preparation, incubation, illumination,* and *verification.* Consider, for example, the often told story of Archimedes and the "golden" crown.

As Koestler (1964) tells it, King Hiero was given a crown, allegedly made of pure gold. He suspected the crown had been adulterated with silver but couldn't be sure. So he asked Archimedes. Archimedes knew the specific weights of gold and silver—their weights per unit volume. Thus, if he could measure the crown's volume, he could tell whether it had been adulterated. But how could he measure the volume of such an irregularly shaped object? Clearly he couldn't melt the crown and measure the resulting liquid. Nor could he pound it into a measurable rectangular shape. With these easy solutions blocked, Archimedes had a problem. During this time, Archimedes was in the *preparation phase* of creative thought (i.e., the phase when the problem is investigated in several directions).

Having hit numerous dead ends, Archimedes put the problem aside. Nevertheless, his mind was well prepared for progress as several blind alleys had been rejected. In a sense, Archimedes now shunted the problem to his subconscious to let it incubate. This represents the *incubation phase* when the person dismisses the problem from conscious consideration and attends to something else.

The *illumination phase* (i.e., the spontaneous appearance of the new idea) presumably began while Archimedes was about to take a bath. While lowering himself into the tub, he noticed the water level rise. And in a flash it occurred to him that the water rise was an indirect measure of his body's volume. Thus, presumably at that moment, Archimedes "saw" how he could also measure the crown's volume—simply by immersing it in water. And once he knew its volume, he could calculate its specific weight to know if it were made of pure gold. Eureka! Archimedes had a likely solution.

The act of illumination can be understood as one of joining two planes of previously unconnected thought to reach a target solution T. For example, Figure 5.1 depicts the plane of thought P1 that contains the starting point S and several thought paths that have unsuccessfully sought the target. Thus P1 presents the habitual rules that Archimedes used to measure volumes and weights to determine the nature of materials, and so on. But as you can see, the target T is not contained on P1. Instead, it is located on P2—the thought plane associated with taking a bath. Thus, no amount of thinking on P1 can reach T. Archimedes must shift his thinking from P1 to P2. To do this he needs a link L. The link may have been verbal (for example, the sentence "rise in water level in the tub equals melting down of my body"); or it may have been visual in which the water-level rise was seen to correspond to body volume and hence crown volume. Either way, the key notion is that both planes of thought must be active in Archimedes's mind—albeit not both on the conscious level—for the link to occur and for him to consciously "see" the tentative solution.

Once illumination occurs, the *verification phase* can begin (i.e., the phase that involves a conscious and deliberate attempt to test the new idea). To do this, Archimedes presumably thought through the steps of his newly created path from S to T to satisfy himself that no crucial steps had been left out—that the path really led to T. Another aspect of verification involves putting the new strategy to work to discover if Hiero's crown had in fact been adulterated. The following summarizes the key argument:

If . . . the crown is made of pure gold,

and . . . the crown is immersed in water and the displaced water is measured,

then . . . the crown should displace the same volume of water as displaced by a known sample of pure gold of equal weight.

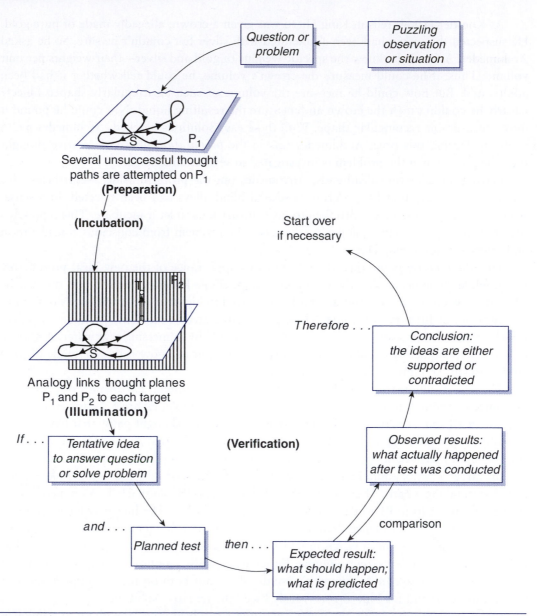

FIGURE 5.1 What are the steps in creative and critical thinking?

Sources: Koestler, 1964; Wallas, 1926; 1970.

Alternatively:

If . . . the crown has been adulterated by silver or by some other less dense metal,

then . . . it should displace a greater volume of water than displaced by a known sample of pure gold of equal weight.

The preparation, incubation, and illumination phases of Archimedes's thinking were creative in the sense that they brought into existence a new piece of procedural knowledge (i.e., a procedure for measuring the volume of irregularly shaped objects). On the other hand, the verification phase can be characterized as critical in the sense that once Archimedes created the new procedure, he used it to analyze the metals in Hiero's crown. This critical thinking produced a new piece of declarative knowledge (i.e., the crown was not pure gold).

Thus, during the creative process, the conscious mind mulls a question or problem only to give up and turn it over to the subconscious. The subconscious then operates until it produces a novel combination of ideas that erupt into consciousness to produce a tentative answer or solution. From here the conscious mind guides a more critical test of the novel idea to discover whether its value is real or illusionary. The similarity of this description of the creative process to the self-regulation process detailed earlier is remarkable. Presumably they are one and the same. If so, creativity can be encouraged by giving students the opportunity to use their own minds in answering questions. While considering the idea of fostering creativity in the classroom, Torrance (1967) had this to say:

> Many complain that we do not yet know enough about the factors affecting creative growth. In my opinion, we have known enough about these factors since the time of Socrates and Plato to do a far better job of creative education than is commonly done. Socrates knew that it was important to ask provocative questions and to encourage natural ways of learning. He knew that it was not enough to ask questions that call only for the reproduction of what has been learned. He knew that thinking is a skill that is developed through practice and that it is important to ask questions that require the learner to do something with what he learns, to evaluate it, produce new ideas from it, and recombine it in new ways. (p. 85)

Therefore, creativity can be enhanced when students are given the opportunity to construct and test their own ideas during inquiry instruction. However, providing the proper climate for this to take place is absolutely crucial. Teachers must become accepting of student ideas. We must become more interested in intellectual invention than in the rightness or wrongness of what is invented. And we must cease to form judgments of students' inventions and instead let the evidence itself be the judge.

Does Inquiry Enhance Intelligence?

The capacity for answering questions, for solving problems, for understanding, for making reasonable decisions, and the like is called **intelligence**. Some people view intelligence as set largely at birth due to the specific set of genes one happens to receive from his or her parents. Clearly, however, one's environment plays a huge role in determining whether or not one reaches his or her full potential. Accordingly, let's consider an intelligence test to see what may be involved in successful performance.

Consider the problem presented in Figure 5.2. The task is to select the correct option from the eight options given below to complete the matrix. Before looking at the answer options, examine the left-hand column of the matrix. Notice that the bottom figure is a

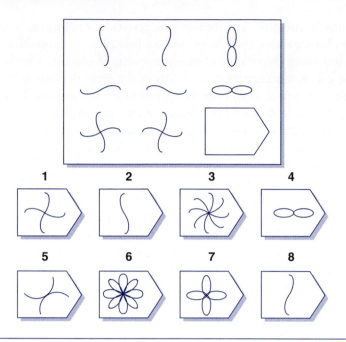

FIGURE 5.2   What reasoning patterns are used to select the correct missing piece?

composite of the top and middle figures. Does this pattern hold for the second column? A quick inspection reveals that it does. Now examine the top row. Notice that the right-hand figure is a combination of the left-hand and middle figures. Does this pattern hold for the second row? Again, it does. Thus the missing figure is most likely a combination of either the first two figures in the third column or a combination of the first two figures in the third row. Either combination will do. And, in fact, both are the same. Thus the correct answer most certainly is option 7. The reasoning pattern just described has been called *additive superimposition* because initial figures are mentally added by superimposing them to produce new figures (Hunt, 1974).

Now consider Figure 5.3. Again the task is to select the correct option to complete the matrix. You will quickly see that the additive superimposition strategy won't work. But if additive superimposition won't work, what will? Consider this strategy: Each figure consists of three parts—a base, sides, and a top. If one considers just the base, it varies in being either present or absent. In all cases when present, the base is straight. Also in each complete row and column there are two figures with bases and one without. If one extrapolates this pattern to the third row or the third column, which contains the missing figure, one can readily conclude that the missing figure must have a base. This follows because both the third row and the third column already contain one figure with a base and one without.

Now consider the sides. In each complete row and column the sides are of one of three types—either one convex and one concave, both straight, or both concave. Again, if one extrapolates this pattern to the row and column with the missing figure, one concludes that the missing figure must have one convex and one concave side because the present figures

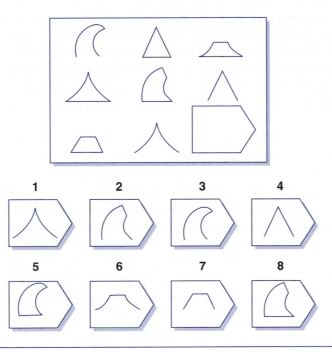

FIGURE 5.3   Can the use of the additive superimposition strategy solve this problem? If not, what else is needed?

have either two straight sides or two concave sides. So all we need to complete the figure is to select the correct top. Notice that in the complete rows and columns, the tops are either pointed or flat. In fact there are two pointed and one flat top in each complete row and column. In the row and column with the missing figures there is one flat and one pointed top; so the missing figure must have a pointed top. Therefore, the missing figure must be option 5.

Such a problem-solving procedure involves identifiable reasoning patterns. First, one needs to divide the figures into their parts—identification of the variables, as it were. Next, there is the need to separate these variables to consider each one by itself in a systematic search for a pattern followed by each. In short the identification, separation, and systematic analysis of variables leads to the correct solution. The less analytical additive superimposition strategy that worked before will not work on this more complex situation.

The two problems just discussed are part of a series of problems collectively known as the Raven Progressive Matrices Test. Raven (1940), its designer, spoke of the test as a measure of a person's innate educative ability. Spearman considered the test to be an appropriate measure of his "g" or general intelligence factor (Spearman & Wynn-Jones, 1951). Indeed, today many psychologists still consider the Raven test to be the best, the purest measure of "g" available. In fact, recent research using positron emission tomography suggests that Spearman's "g" factor (i.e., general intelligence) derives from brain activity in the lateral frontal cortex that controls diverse forms of behavior (Duncan et al., 2000).

Thus, the Raven test may be used with the intent of measuring innate intelligence. For example, a sample of children at a specific age would be tested, and the number of correct items each child selects would be used to classify him or her as bright, average, or dull. A less complex but similar test would be constructed for younger children and administered for the same purpose. More complex but again similar "advanced" tests would be constructed and administered to find out who among older children or adults is bright, average, or dull.

However, there is another way to consider intelligence. That is the way of the developmental psychologist. To the developmental psychologist intelligence need not refer only to innate ability. Intelligence can also refer to how far along in the development of certain reasoning skills one has progressed. Thus, rather than constructing a number of tests of increasing complexity, the same test could be used at varying age levels. Administration of the test in this fashion would then reveal that as children become older they become more intelligent. Taking this alternative view of intelligence to heart, the teacher's job is to teach in a way that facilitates the development of intelligence and make sure that no student fails to complete the developmental process. More specifically, the teacher's job is to help students develop reasoning skills such as those needed to solve problems such as those on Raven's Progressive Matrices. When intelligence is viewed in this way, there is considerable evidence that inquiry instruction helps students become more intelligent.

Does Inquiry Enhance Achievement?

There is also considerable evidence that inquiry instruction provokes general gains in academic achievement. For comprehensive reviews see Alexander and Murphy (1999); Guzzetti, Snyder, Glass, and Gamas (1993); Hake (2000); A. E. Lawson, Abraham, and Renner (1989); Lott (1983); Minstrell and van Zee (2000); the National Research Council (2000a); Shymansky, Kyle, and Alport (1983); and Wenglinsky (2000). Space does not allow for discussion of this vast body of research. Nevertheless, a few studies, such as the one conducted by J. W. Renner, Stafford, Coffia, Kellogg, and Weber (1973), can be mentioned to give you a flavor of the research. Renner et al. used the Stanford Achievement Test to compare two groups of fifth-grade students who were similar except that one group had been taught science for 5 years using learning cycles while the other group learned their science from a textbook. Scores in mathematics concepts, skills, and applications, as well as word meaning and paragraph meaning, were obtained, as were data concerning achievement in social studies skills and content. Analysis of the scores of the two groups on the Stanford Achievement Test showed that the learning cycle group outscored the textbook group on every subtest. A statistical comparison of the seven academic areas revealed significant differences between the two groups in mathematics applications, social studies skills, and paragraph meaning. On the other hand, no significant differences were found in mathematical computations and concepts, social studies content, and word meaning.

Of particular interest was J. W. Renner et al.'s (1973) observation of a thread of commonality in the areas where significant differences were found. In the case of mathematics applications, performance on the instrument was determined by ability to apply mathematical knowledge and to think mathematically in practical situations. The social studies skills test has a stated goal of testing "knowledge in action." The paragraph-meaning test was said to measure the students' ability to understand connected discourse involving varying levels of comprehension. The thread of commonality, then, was that each of these areas requires a level of thought that transcends mere recognition and recall. Apparently, the children who had experience with inquiry tended to utilize higher levels of thinking more effectively than those who did not have such experience.

A similar but more recent study found that a single inquiry science course, called Thinking Science, taught to eighth graders in England improved general academic achievement as evidenced by their superior performance on standardized achievement measures in science, mathematics, and English administered when they had completed the 12th grade (Shayer & Adey, 1993). And Hake (2000) reported results of over 6,000 students, some who experienced traditional physics instruction and others who experienced the modeling method of instruction. In short, Hake's analysis found that the learning cycle students outperformed the tradition students by almost two standard deviations on a mechanics problem-solving test. Importantly, Hake's analysis allowed him to rule out other possible causes of the striking group differences, such as teaching to the test, fraction of course time spent on mechanics, students' post- and pretest motivation, and the Hawthorne effect.

In conclusion, inquiry instruction not only makes great sense from a theoretical perspective; when correctly put into practice it significantly boosts students' creative and critical reasoning and problem-solving skills (i.e., their general intelligence) and their academic achievement. Indeed, less really is more when it comes to teaching and learning science. To make sure that your attempts at implementing inquiry in your classroom will be successful, subsequent chapters will turn to the crucial issues of lesson planning, classroom management, curriculum development, and assessment.

Summary

- Elements of inquiry instruction can be traced to Socrates and his well-known Socratic method. During the early 20th century, theorists such as John Dewey argued that science should be taught as it is practiced—that is, as an inquiry-driven enterprise emphasizing student-generated hypotheses and tests.

- During the 1960s and 1970s several projects systematically tried to embed inquiry instruction into practice in the United States. During that time, the Science Curriculum Improvement Study developed a three-phase learning cycle teaching method. Origins of the learning cycle can also be found in the writings of Chester Lawson and work that led to development of the Biological Sciences Curriculum Study. More recent teaching approaches such as the Physics Modeling Method are derivatives of the learning cycle method. Today inquiry instruction is the preferred mode of science instruction for students in all grades from kindergarten through graduate school.

- Creativity can be fostered if students are given the opportunity to generate and test their own ideas. Providing the proper climate for this to take place is essential.

- Intelligence depends upon creative and critical reasoning skills and an accurate and well-organized body of concepts, facts, and principles. Thus teaching procedures that improve students' reasoning skills and conceptual knowledge can improve students' intelligence and general academic achievement.

Key Terms

creativity   intelligence

faculty theory   models

Application Questions/Activities

1. What is faculty theory, and why did it contribute to the use of rote memorization in the classroom? Do you have any evidence that rote memorization still occurs? What is your evidence? Should students still be asked to memorize some things? If so, what and why? If not, why not?

2. How do the Atkin and Karplus (1962) phases of exploration, invention, and discovery relate to scientific discovery? How do they relate to classroom instruction? Provide examples.

3. How is the Physics Modeling Method similar to and different from SCIS learning cycles?

4. Explain how the use of inquiry can make students better creative and critical thinkers. How can it make them more intelligent?

5. Look up one or more of the review articles cited earlier concerning the outcomes of inquiry use in the classroom (e.g., Alexander & Murphy, 1999; Guzzetti et al., 1993; Hake, 2000). Select and discuss one or more of the research articles cited in the review(s) in terms of how they support or fail to support the claim that inquiry instruction improves academic achievement.

6. Although inquiry is the experts' teaching method of choice, many science teachers in the United States and in other countries still spend most of their time teaching in more traditional didactic ways. Generate at least four alternative hypotheses to explain this gap between what teachers should be doing and what they are doing. How could your hypotheses be tested? Assuming that one or more of your hypotheses is supported, what do you think should be done to close the gap?

Chapter **6** INQUIRY INSTRUCTION

We now come to the central question of this book: What teaching methods help students develop advanced reasoning patterns, learn how science works, and learn meaningful science concepts and theories? Previous chapters have argued that self-regulation is involved and that the following events need to take place:

Students explore new phenomena based on present reasoning patterns and concepts.

Explorations produce results that contradict present expectations. This produces disequilibrium, which in turn provokes self-regulation and the search for new concepts and/or better reasoning patterns.

Teachers then introduce new terms and/or better reasoning patterns, which students then attempt to assimilate and apply in both old and new contexts to eventually restore equilibrium.

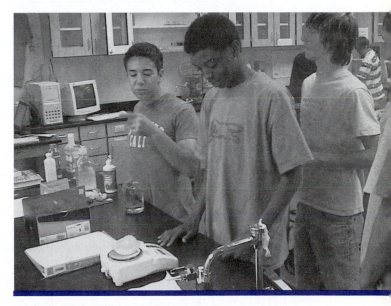

After discovering that eggs in various solutions change weight, these biology students will have to generate and test hypotheses to figure out why.

APPLICABLE NSES STANDARDS

Standard B Science teachers guide and facilitate learning. In doing so, they

- Focus and support inquiries while interacting with students.
- Orchestrate discourse among students about scientific ideas.

(Continued)

(Continued)

■ Challenge students to accept and share responsibility for their own learning.

■ Recognize and respond to student diversity and encourage all students to participate fully in learning.

■ Encourage and model the skills of scientific inquiry, as well as curiosity, openness to new ideas and data, and skepticism that characterize science.

EXPLORING INSTRUCTIONAL ALTERNATIVES

Given the above necessary events, which of the following alternative approaches would you choose to begin teaching about the metabolism of water fleas (*Daphnia*)?

(a) Provide students with live *Daphnia*, thermometers, depression slides, and microscopes. Have them count and record *Daphnia* heartbeats per minute at three different temperatures: 5°, 20°, and 35°C. Ask students to graph the number of heartbeats versus temperature.

(b) Provide students with live *Daphnia*, thermometers, depression slides, and microscopes, and ask them to find out if temperature influences heart rate.

(c) Explain to students that temperature has a general effect on the metabolism of invertebrates. Higher temperature produces a faster rate, and lower temperature produces a slower rate. Thus, environmental temperature influences a "cold-blooded" animal like the *Daphnia*. A rule states that metabolic rate doubles for every 10 degrees of increase in temperature. Now have students go to the laboratory and use the heart rate of live *Daphnia* to verify that what you have said is correct.

(d) Provide students with live *Daphnia*, a hot plate, Dexedrine solution, 5% alcohol solution, a light source, rulers, thermometers, slides, pH paper, balances, graph paper, microscopes, a stirring device, and ice cubes. Ask them to investigate the influence of environmental changes on the heart rate of *Daphnia* and to search for and try to explain quantitative relationships among the variables.

Certainly your resources and your students' preparation will influence your choice. Compare your selection with the following comments:

(a) This approach may be effective for students who are inexperienced with inquiry, as it is fairly directive yet does not spoil student motivation by telling them what they will find. However, for more experienced students, it may be too restrictive as it limits the scope of inquiry to only one variable (temperature) and fails to justify the selection of three specific values. In other words, why were 5°, 20°, and 35°C selected?

(b) This approach is very much like the previous one as it focuses on a single variable, although it does so without specifying which temperatures to use. This increased openness is a plus because students are more apt to think about what they are doing and make their own decisions. If improved reasoning skill is a goal, then some nondirectedness is essential.

(c) There is little to recommend in this approach as it tells students what they will find. This has two unfortunate consequences. First, it shifts student motivation away from satisfying one's curiosity about nature to satisfying the teacher. Second, it shifts authority about what is correct or incorrect from its natural place in data to an authority figure, namely, the teacher. Regrettably, most teachers take this approach.

(d) This is the most indirect, open-ended approach. It does what approaches (1) and (2) do, only more so. For inexperienced students, this openness would be difficult to cope with without helpful procedural hints. If frustration becomes a problem, these hints can be provided to small student groups; or the entire class can be stopped to discuss ways to get started. This approach is highly recommended for experienced students as it provides a variety of paths of inquiry that in turn provide considerable opportunity to think and make decisions about what to investigate and how best to investigate it.

The recommended approach in (d) and the somewhat more direct approaches in (a) and (b) are activities upon which subsequent understandings can be built. They represent an initial instructional phase called **exploration.** During exploration, students learn through their own actions and reactions as they explore new materials and new ideas. The new experiences should raise questions that cannot be answered with accustomed ways of thinking. Exploration also allows students to voice potentially conflicting or at least partially inadequate ideas, which can spark debate and an analysis of students' reasons and reasoning. The analysis also allows for a careful examination of the procedures used and can lead to a discussion of ways of testing alternative ideas. In addition, students may identify patterns of regularity (e.g., heart rate increases with temperature). Approaches (a) and (b) are also considered explorations although for many students they are not as likely to encourage self-regulation as approach (d).

A second instructional phase starts with the introduction of a new term or terms such as *metabolism, cold-blooded,* or *poikilotherm* that refer to the pattern or patterns discovered during exploration. The teacher, the textbook, a video, or another student may introduce the term(s). This phase, called **term introduction**, follows exploration and relates directly to the discovered pattern(s) or idea. The lecture in alternative (c) could be part of a term introduction session following lab activities like (d). Ideally, students should discover as much of a new pattern or construct as much of a new idea as possible before it is introduced to the class; but expecting students to discover all of the patterns and to construct all of the concepts of modern science is unrealistic.

During a third instructional phase, students attempt to assimilate and apply the new terms and/or reasoning patterns to additional contexts. For example, after the introduction of the term *cold-bloodedness*, students might be asked to determine the type of metabolism of other organisms such as mice or humans. This third phase is called **concept application**. This phase is necessary to extend the range of applicability of new concepts and reasoning patterns. Without a number and variety of applications, meanings may remain restricted to the examples used at the time they were initially introduced. In other words, many students may fail to generalize them to other situations. In addition, concept application activities aid students whose conceptual reorganization takes place more slowly than average or who did not adequately relate the teacher's original comments to their experiences.

Note that this third phase is called *concept* application while the second phase is called *term* introduction. A concept has been defined as an idea in one's mind that is linked to a term. Thus, a concept is the pattern/idea plus the term. Teachers can introduce new terms, but students must construct the concepts themselves. Therefore, term introduction seems a better label for the second phase than concept introduction.

In summary, exploration allows students to discover new patterns and propose new ideas. Term introduction allows teachers to introduce new terms and students to initially try to link the patterns, the ideas, and the new terms. Finally, concept application enables students to apply the concepts and/or reasoning patterns in new contexts and acquire deeper understanding. Collectively, this three-phase inquiry approach to instruction is called the **learning cycle**, sometimes referred to as **inquiry instruction**.[1]

The learning cycle constitutes a very flexible approach to instruction that integrates student inquiry with teacher guidance and input at just the right times. For young children and for anyone who lacks direct physical experiences with particular phenomena, the exploration phase should provide that direct experience (several excellent examples can be found in Marek & Cavallo, 1997). However, not all explorations must be hands-on. Indeed, during graduate school, I had the pleasure of taking a history of science course taught using learning cycles where the explorations consisted of slide presentations, lectures, and discussions. The class explored various scientists' ideas and activities in this way and only later "invented" the concept of science. Thus, the format of each instructional phase may vary; but if the sequence is changed or if a phase is deleted, one no longer has a learning cycle.

The main instructional point is that allowing students to examine prior concepts forces them to argue about and test those concepts. This in turn provokes disequilibrium and the need for self-regulation when prior concepts are contradicted and provides the opportunity to construct new concepts and become increasingly conscious of and skilled in use of the reasoning patterns used in concept construction. The central instructional claim is that correct use of learning cycles accomplishes this end.

When learning cycles are linked together to produce a curriculum, the curriculum takes on a spiral shape. Explorations frequently require the application of prior concepts. Term introduction frequently raises new questions best answered through concept applications. And concept applications allow students to apply concepts while exploring new phenomena. So in a sense, learning "cycles" are really learning "spirals" in that students do not return to the same place they were at the outset as in a true cycle. Instead they end up on a different higher plane.

TYPES OF LEARNING CYCLES

Descriptive Learning Cycles

Suppose that during exploration students try to answer this question: How do characteristics vary within species? To find out, they select large samples of various kinds of seashells. They then select one or more ways in which the shells vary and measure and graph frequency distributions.

For example, they may plot shell length versus frequency of a scallop-shaped species. When posted on the board, student graphs reveal that most distributions have few shells at either extreme of the range and many shells near the middle. When this pattern is pointed out, the teacher introduces the terms *normal distribution* and *bell-shaped distribution* to label the pattern. This is term introduction. Students now select several other characteristics from other species (e.g., the length of pine needles, the weights of students, the heights of corn plants) and discover the same normal distribution among these characteristics. This is concept application.

Such a lesson constitutes a **descriptive learning cycle** because students discover and describe a pattern within a specific context (exploration). The teacher gives it a name (term introduction), and the pattern is identified in additional contexts (concept application). Hence students are describing what they observe without attempting to explain their observations. Descriptive learning cycles answer descriptive "who," "what," "when," and "where" questions but do not raise or attempt to answer causal "why" or "how" questions (e.g., Why do characteristics distribute themselves normally?). Descriptive cycles seldom provoke much argumentation among students because possible cause-effect relationships are not generated and tested.

Empirical-Abductive Learning Cycles

Next consider a learning cycle called "What Causes the Breakdown of Dead Organisms?" which is designed to teach about biological decomposition. At the outset students are asked, What factors affect the breakdown rate of dead organisms? To find out, they design experiments to test the effects of a variety of factors such as temperature, amount of water, amount of light, and amounts of chemicals such as salt, sugar, alcohol, and antiseptic solution. Following student experimentation (exploration), results are displayed on the board. The results reveal that increased temperature and increased amounts of water speed up breakdown, while chemicals such as salt, sugar, and alcohol slow or stop breakdown.

The teacher then poses a causal question: What might actually be causing the breakdown? In spite of the fact that the students have just observed the growth of large quantities and varieties of molds, they invariably respond by saying that heat and water *caused* the breakdown. Typically, some student will generate the hypothesis that molds and/or bacteria caused the breakdown but only after considerable prodding with questions: What do you suppose caused the bad odor? What is that fuzzy black stuff all over the bread? What do you suspect the black stuff is doing? Nevertheless, once the hypothesis is finally generated (a reasoning process sometimes called abduction), the students can then return to their data to see if the hypothesis "works" in the sense that it explains already gathered data. In other words,

If . . . molds and/or bacteria *cause* the breakdown,

and . . . dead organisms are placed in containers with harsh environments known to kill molds and bacteria (e.g., no water, extreme temperatures, toxic substances),

then . . . the dead organisms should not break down.

And . . . the dead organisms in such harsh environments did not break down nearly as much as those in less harsh environments.

Therefore . . . the mold/bacteria hypothesis has been supported.

In other words, because molds and bacteria are living things and because all living things presumably require water and a proper temperature for survival, it makes sense that the containers with no water or at freezing temperatures would show no breakdown because the growth of molds and bacteria would be slowed or stopped. Likewise, the containers with salt and alcohol might kill the molds and bacteria. Therefore, the molds/bacteria hypothesis is supported by the prior data, and the teacher can then introduce the term *biological decomposition* to label the process just discussed (term introduction). Additional phenomena can next be explored that allow the biological decomposition concept to be applied in other contexts (concept application). This sort of learning cycle in which causal hypotheses are tested using data previously gathered during the exploration phase is called an **empirical-abductive learning cycle**.

Let's think more about this type of learning cycle to see why it's called empirical-abductive. First, the learning cycle begins with an exploration into the empirical world. However, student explorations and their subsequent experiments are seldom designed with well-formulated causal hypotheses in mind. Students may have a hunch that increased temperature will speed breakdown. But this idea, more than likely, comes from past experience (e.g., with refrigeration) and extrapolation rather than from a theory about biological decomposition and hypothetical-predictive reasoning. Second, when asked about the actual causes of the breakdown, students initially use their experimental results to report that both water and heat *caused* the breakdown. To go beyond this restricted view, students need hints and encouragement to think more deeply until one of them "hits" on the idea the molds and/or bacteria are the actual causal agents. Because this "hitting" on the right idea involves the use of analogy to borrow ideas from past experience, not extrapolation, and because the process is necessary to arrive at the desired theory of biological decomposition, the term *empirical-abductive* has been chosen to label learning cycles of this sort. In short, learning cycles that begin with a "What factors affect?" question and follow experimental results with the generation of causal hypotheses are empirical-abductive.

Hypothetical-Predictive Learning Cycles

Now consider the candle-burning lab discussed in Chapter 4. As you recall, students inverted a cylinder over a candle burning in a pan of water. They observed that the flame went out and water rushed into the cylinder. Thus two causal questions were raised: Why did the flame go out? And, why did the water rise? The typical student answer to the first question was that the flame used up the cylinder's oxygen and left a partial vacuum, which then "sucked" the water up. As we have seen, testing this explanation requires hypothetical-predictive reasoning and the identification and control of variables:

If . . . water rises because the oxygen has been "consumed,"

and . . . we vary the number of burning candles while holding all other variables constant,

then . . . the water should rise the same regardless of the number of burning candles.

But . . . the water rises considerably higher with additional burning candles.

Therefore . . . the consumed-oxygen hypothesis is contradicted.

Given this contradictory result, students then generate and test several additional hypotheses. This third type of learning cycle is called a **hypothetical-predictive learning cycle** because it initially raises one or more causal questions to which the students generate alternative hypotheses. Student time is then devoted to explicitly designing and conducting tests of their hypotheses (exploration) by deducing one or more predictions. The analysis of results then allows for some hypotheses to be rejected (i.e., those whose predictions did not match results), for some to be retained (i.e., those whose predictions did match results), and for new terms to be introduced (term introduction). Finally, the relevant concepts and reasoning patterns that are involved and discussed may be applied in other situations at a later time (concept application). The explicit generation and test of alternative hypotheses through a comparison of predictions with observed results is required in this type of learning cycle, hence the name *hypothetical-predictive*.

Like empirical-abductive learning cycles, hypothetical-predictive learning cycles require students to do more than describe phenomena. Explanations are required. In the burning candle learning cycle, finding an explanation opens the door to a multitude of alternative hypotheses—some of which constitute scientific misconceptions. The resulting arguments and analysis of evidence constitute an excellent example of how hypothetical-predictive learning cycles can promote disequilibrium, the construction of conceptual knowledge, and the development of improved reasoning skills.

Also consider water rise in plants. Objects are attracted toward the center of the Earth by a force called gravity. Yet water rises in tall trees to the uppermost leaves to allow photosynthesis to take place. What causes the water to rise in spite of the downward gravitational force? The following alternative hypotheses (alternative conceptions/misconceptions) were proposed in a recent biology lab:

1. Water evaporates from the leaves to create a vacuum, which sucks water up.

2. Roots squeeze to push water up through one-way valves in the stem tubes.

3. Capillary action pulls water up like water soaking up in a paper towel.

4. Osmosis pulls water up.

Equipment limitations keep some ideas from being tested. Nevertheless, comparing water rise in plants with and without leaves can test the leaf-evaporation hypothesis. The experiment also requires the identification and control of variables:

If . . . water rises in plants due to evaporation from leaves (leaf-evaporation hypothesis),

and . . . the amount of water rise in several plants, some with and some without leaves, is measured over a period of time—all other variables held constant,

then . . . water should rise higher in the plants with leaves than in those without leaves.

Comparing water rise in plants with and without roots can test the root-squeeze hypothesis. Comparing water rise in right-side-up and upside-down stems can test the one-way-valve hypothesis. Results then allow for rejection of some of the hypotheses and not others. The survivors are considered "correct," for the time being at least, just as is the case in doing real science. Following student experimentation, terms such as *transpiration* can be introduced and applied elsewhere as is the case for all types of learning cycles.

The question of water rise in plants may involve misconceptions, but few students are strongly committed to any particular explanation. But consider the case of evolution. Here commitments often run deep. Consequently, a hypothetical-predictive learning cycle into the question "Where did present-day life forms come from?" often stirs up considerable controversy, argumentation, and thinking. To explore the origins of present-day species diversity, students can first explore several fossils embedded in the fossil record including several present-day organisms and attempt to explain what they find. At least three alternative theories can be offered:

1. Present-day species were created during a brief period of time by an act of God. Further, God created species in virtually the same forms as we see today (special-creation theory).

2. Throughout time, species have arisen spontaneously from dead materials. For example, dead, rotting meat produces fly larvae. Old rags in damp places produce baby rats (spontaneous-generation theory).

3. Present-day species evolved from simpler organisms over vast periods of time (evolution theory).

Students may propose other explanations, but at least these three should be advanced. Notice that what represents the revealed truth for some people, namely, the idea of special creation, is treated not as truth but simply as one of three alternative theories. The recognition that alternative theories exist, as opposed to revealed truths, represents a crucial first step.

Once alternative theories have been proposed, they can then be tested through prediction, data gathering, and data analysis. Consideration of spontaneous generation theory may lead to replication or discussion of the classic experiments of John Needham, Lazzaro Spallanzani, and Louis Pasteur and to its rejection. The theories of special creation and evolution lead to consideration of the processes of geologic sedimentation and fossil formation and to a closer look at the fossil record. Importantly, the *predicted* fossil records for the two theories differ—for example,

If . . . species were created during a brief period of time and have not changed since (special-creation theory),

and . . . we examine the fossil record,

then . . . fossils from the lower, older layers should look the same as present organisms.

Alternatively:

If . . . species have evolved over time (evolution theory),

then . . . fossils from the lower, older layers should look different from present organisms.

In addition, special-creation theory predicts a pattern with no fossils in the deepest, oldest sedimentary layers (before special creation) and fossils of all forms of simple and complex life in the layer immediately following creation, with the remaining layers up to the surface showing fewer and fewer life forms as some become extinct. Evolution theory also predicts no life in the deepest, oldest layers (before evolution began), but the next layers should contain very few and only the simplest life forms (e.g., single-cell bacteria, blue-green algae), with the progressively higher, younger layers showing gradually more complex, larger, and more varied life forms:

If . . . special-creation theory is correct,

and . . . we examine the fossil record,

then . . . the lower, older rock layers as well as the higher, younger ones should contain fossils of virtually all the complex and diverse species present today, with the possible exception of those lost during the flood.

Alternatively:

If . . . evolution theory is correct,

then . . . the lower, older rock layers should contain only fossils of relatively simple organisms, and the higher, younger layers should contain fossils of progressively more complex and more diverse forms.

Which predicted results are observed? To find out, the students simulate a hike in the Grand Canyon and observe fossils collected from six sedimentary layers in the canyon walls. The fossils reveal a pattern like that predicted by evolution theory and very unlike that predicted by special-creation theory. Therefore, evidence in favor of evolution theory has been obtained. Subsequent activities allow evolution theory to be applied in other contexts. One such activity should be a learning cycle into the process of natural selection.

How Do Learning Cycles Relate to Doing Science?

As we have seen, learning cycles can be classified as one of three types: descriptive, empirical-abductive, and hypothetical-predictive. The essential difference among the three types is the degree to which students describe nature or explicitly generate and test alternative causal hypotheses. Thus, the three types represent segments along a continuum from descriptive to experimental science. As such, they place differing demands on student initiative, knowledge, and reasoning skill. In terms of student reasoning, descriptive learning cycles generally require only concrete reasoning patterns (e.g., seriation, classification, conservation) while hypothetical-predictive learning cycles demand use of formal or postformal patterns (e.g., controlling variables, correlational reasoning). Empirical-abductive learning cycles are intermediate and require concrete patterns but generally involve some higher-order patterns as well. Figure 6.1 summarizes the major differences among the three types of learning cycles.

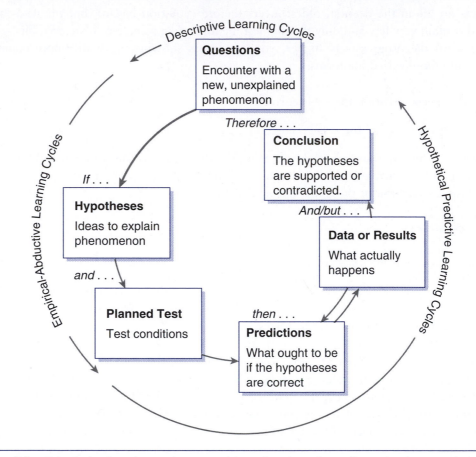

FIGURE 6.1 Descriptive learning cycles start with explorations that tell us what happens in specific contexts. They represent descriptive science. Empirical-abductive learning cycles include the descriptive part but go further and call for causal questions and hypotheses. Hypothetical-predictive learning cycles generally start with a causal question and move to the generation of alternative hypotheses and their test.

USING TEXTBOOKS TO INTRODUCE NEW TERMS

Next consider the two textbook passages that follow (from Musheno & Lawson, 1999, pp. 28–29). Take a few minutes to read each passage before reading on. While reading, ask yourself what new terms are being introduced and what similarities and differences exist between the two passages in the way those new terms are introduced. In short, which passage should be pedagogically more effective, and why?

Passage 1

Does Cooperation Ever Replace Competition in Nature?

Organisms compete for food, water, and space, and defend themselves from others who might want to make a meal of them. Is life always competitive or do two species sometimes cooperate? Consider two examples:

In the lowlands of Mexico and Central America, the bull's horn acacia tree grows. To protect itself from being eaten, the tree grows large thorns at the base of its leaves. At the very tip of each leaflet, the tree produces small orange bead-like structures, which are filled with oils and proteins. Scientists could find no purpose for the orange beads until they made an interesting observation. They found that a certain type of ant uses the acacia tree for its home. The ants, which live in the thorns of the tree, use the mysterious orange beads for food.

The ants do not harm the tree, but they do aggressively attack anything that touches it. They attack other insects that land on the leaves or branches and if a large animal even brushes against the tree, they swarm and attack with painful, burning bites. The ants even chew up and destroy plants that grow near their tree. If the ants are removed animals will eat the acacia's tender leaves and neighboring plants will quickly outgrow the damaged trees. So the acacia tree and ants depend on each other. Both benefit; neither is harmed. Teaming up affords both species an advantage. This kind of cooperation is known as mutualism. Is the next example also mutualism?

In Africa, a bird known as the oxpecker eats ticks as the main part of its diet. But the oxpecker has a very interesting manner of collecting its meals. Each bird will choose a large grazing animal, such as a zebra, and set up house on the zebra's back. The bird picks off all the ticks it can find, and the zebra allows the oxpecker to hitch a ride as long as it chooses. In this relationship, the bird has a steady food supply, and the zebra is kept tick free.

In both examples, the species have a close, long-term, cooperative relationship. Thus they are both examples of mutualism. Consider another example: In Tanzania, a heron-like bird called the cattle egret follows cape buffaloes and other large grass-eating mammals. The birds gather at the buffaloes' feet, sometimes even perching on the grazers' back. As the buffaloes walk and graze, they scare up small mice and insects, which become the egrets' food supply. Egrets that follow the buffaloes find a better food supply than they could on their own. The buffaloes do not benefit from the egrets' presence, but do not seem to be bothered by the egrets, either. The egret and buffalo have a close, long-term relationship. However, in this case only the egret benefits. The buffalo is not affected. This type of association, which benefits one species and does not affect the other, is called commensalism.

Does the next example represent mutualism, commensalism, or something different? Mistletoe, the leafy green plant that many Americans traditionally hang in doorways during the Christmas season, does not grow on the ground like most plants. Mistletoe grows only on the branches of trees such as oaks, or mesquite trees in Arizona. The mistletoe has a special type of root that burrows into the tree and taps into the tree's sap supply. The sap provides nutrition for the mistletoe, which can then grow larger, sinking new "roots" into the tree branches as its need for food grows. As the mesquite tree gives up more of its sap to support the mistletoe, it will be harmed because it loses valuable water and nutrients. Thus this example shows a close, long-term relationship between two species. But here the mistletoe benefits and the mesquite trees are harmed. When one species benefits while the other is harmed, the relationship is known as parasitism. In this example, the mistletoe is the parasite.

Mutualism, commensalism, and parasitism all involve close, long-term relationships between two species. The relationship can be between plants, between animals, or between plants and animals. Collectively, the close, long-term relationships are called symbiosis. This word comes from the Greek language: *bios* means life and *sym* means together, so the word symbiosis translates into life together.

Passage 2

Symbiosis

Symbiosis is a term that means a close, long-term relationship between organisms of two different species. The relationship can be between plants, between animals, or between plants and animals. The word "symbiosis" comes from the Greek language: *bios* means life and *sym* means together, so the word symbiosis translates into life together.

In nature, relationships between species are usually competitive, with plants and animals battling for food, water and space to live, as well as defending themselves from other species that might want to make a meal of them. Symbiosis represents a different, noncompetitive type of relationship between two species, which involves cooperation and dependence and is found in three distinct forms called mutualism, commensalism and parasitism. In mutualism, the close, long-term relationship is beneficial to both species. In commensalism, the relationship benefits one species and the other species neither is harmed nor benefits. In the third form, parasitism, one species benefits at the expense of the other species, which is harmed in the process.

A good example of mutualism between a plant and an animal species can be found in the lowlands of Mexico and Central America, where the bull's horn acacia tree grows. To help protect itself from being eaten, the tree grows large thorns at the base of its leaves. At the very tip of each leaflet, the tree produces small orange bead-like structures, which are filled with oils and proteins. Scientists could find no purpose for the orange beads until they made an interesting observation. They found that a certain type of ant uses the acacia tree for its home. The ants, which live in the thorns of the tree, use the mysterious orange beads for food.

The ants do not harm the tree, but they do aggressively attack anything that touches it. They attack other insects that land on the leaves or branches and if a large animal even brushes against the tree, they swarm and attack with painful, burning bites. The ants even chew up and destroy plants that grow near their tree. If the ants are removed animals eat the acacia's tender leaves and neighboring plants quickly outgrow the damaged trees. Thus the acacia tree and ants depend on each other for food and protection. The relationship is long term and benefits both species.

In another example of mutualism, in this case between two species of animals, an African bird known as the oxpecker eats ticks as the main part of its diet. But the oxpecker has a very interesting manner of collecting its meals. Each bird will choose a large grazing animal, such as a zebra, and set up house on the zebra's back. The bird picks off all the ticks it can find, and the zebra allows the oxpecker to hitch a ride as long as it chooses. In this relationship, the bird has a steady food supply, and the zebra is kept tick free.

Commensalism is much less common than mutualism or parasitism as it is hard to find cases where one of the species is not affected at all by the relationship. One good example of commensalism, again between two species of animals, is found in Tanzania, where a heron-like bird called the cattle egret follows cape buffaloes and other large grass-eating mammals. The birds gather at the buffaloes' feet, sometimes even perching on the grazer's back. As the buffaloes walk and graze, they scare up small mice and insects, which become the egret's food supply. Egrets that follow the buffaloes find a better food supply than they could on their own. The buffaloes do not benefit from the egrets' presence, but do not seem to be bothered by the egrets, either.

Parasitism is the final form of symbiosis. There are many examples of this type of relationship found in nature. For example, mistletoe, the leafy green plant that many Americans traditionally hang in doorways during the Christmas season, does not grow on the ground like most plants. Mistletoe grows only on the branches of trees such as oaks, or mesquite trees in Arizona. The mistletoe has a special type of root that burrows into the tree and taps into the tree's sap supply. The sap provides nutrition for the mistletoe, which can then grow larger, sinking new "roots" into the tree branches as its need for food grows. As the mesquite tree gives up more of its sap to support the mistletoe, it will be harmed because it loses valuable water and nutrients.

How Do the Passages Differ?

As you discovered, both passages introduce four new biological terms: *symbiosis, mutualism, commensalism,* and *parasitism.* Passage 1 discusses examples first and then introduces the new terms. Also the new terms are introduced in a "bottom-up" manner. In other words, in terms of the conceptual hierarchy, the less inclusive (subordinate) concepts of mutualism, commensalism, and parasitism are introduced before the more inclusive superordinate symbiosis concept. On the other hand, in passage 2 the new terms are introduced prior to the examples—terms first, examples second. The passage also introduces the new terms in a more "traditional" top-down manner with symbiosis coming first.

In theory, passage 1 should work better because the prior examples give the new terms something to connect with. However, in passage 2 learning should not take place easily because new terms come before the examples and thus have nowhere to connect. As expected, the 9th- and 10th-grade students who read passage 1 scored significantly higher on a posttest of concept comprehension than those who read passage 2 (Musheno & Lawson, 1999). More generally, all learning contexts (e.g., labs, lectures, discussions) that employ the learning cycle's examples-first, bottom-up approach should be more effective than the more traditional term-first, top-down approaches. For example, who among us has not suffered through the occasional lecture in which the speaker strung together several unfamiliar words that, although easy to hear, were, nevertheless, meaningless. Consequently, we quickly become "lost"—some of us even fall asleep.

Summary

- Inquiry instruction allows students to examine prior concepts and to argue about and test those concepts. This in turn provokes disequilibrium and provides the opportunity to construct new concepts and become increasingly conscious of and skilled in use of the reasoning patterns used in concept construction. Learning cycles integrate student inquiry with teacher guidance and input. Exploration provides students with the opportunity to discover patterns and construct ideas. Term introduction allows teachers to introduce new terms and provides students with the opportunity to initially link the new terms with patterns and ideas. Concept application allows students to apply concepts and/or reasoning patterns to new contexts and acquire deeper understanding.

- The three types of learning cycles represent segments along a continuum from descriptive to experimental science and place differing demands on student initiative, knowledge, and reasoning skills.

- Textbook passages can be written following the pattern of scientific inquiry and the learning cycle. Such passages promote better and longer-lasting learning.

Key Terms

concept application

descriptive learning cycle

empirical-abductive learning cycle

exploration

hypothetical-predictive learning cycle

inquiry instruction

learning cycle

term introduction

Application Questions/Activities

1. Teachers are urged to teach science as science is practiced. Describe how learning cycles allow teachers to do this.

2. Select a concept or set of closely related concepts that you intend to teach. Design a descriptive learning cycle to teach the concept or concepts. Describe the exploration activity. What term(s) will be introduced? How and when will you introduce them? Design a concept application activity to follow.

3. Select a concept or set of closely related concepts that you intend to teach. Design an empirical-abductive learning cycle to teach the concept or concepts. Describe the exploration activity. What term(s) will be introduced? How and when will you introduce them? Design a concept application activity to follow.

4. Select a concept or set of closely related concepts that you intend to teach. Design a hypothetical-predictive learning cycle to teach the concept or concepts. Describe the exploration activity. What term(s) will be introduced? How and when will you introduce them? Design a concept application activity to follow.

1. Some authors do not regard learning cycle and inquiry instruction as synonymous. Instead they include so-called discovery instruction as a type of inquiry instruction. Although the meaning of the phrase *discovery instruction* may vary, if it refers to an approach where students explore new phenomena and then try to discover, on their own, what happens and why it happens, then such instruction would qualify as inquiry but not leaning cycle. Learning cycle instruction certainly allows students to openly explore new phenomena. But due to its inclusion of the term introduction phase, students are given guidance in generating and testing explanations. Learning cycle teachers also introduce key scientific terms at appropriate times and help students identify important applications during the concept application phase.

Chapter 7 PLANNING FOR INQUIRY

One of my previous ideas about inquiry was that it consisted mainly of doing laboratory activities. I discovered that, although labs can aid in the process of sense-making, they often don't because they are either "cookbook" (they don't allow the students to make choices or judgments) or are "confirmatory" (they follow lectures or students' reading). What I have realized is that the essence of inquiry does not lie in any elaborate, equipment-intensive laboratory exercise. It lies, rather, in the interactions between the student and the materials, as well as in the teacher-student and student-student interactions that occur dozens of times each and every class period. (Reflection of a high school physics teacher, National Research Council, 2000b, p. 90)

Calls for educational reform emphasize the need to teach science in a "hands-on," "minds-on," investigative way that actively engages students. For example, a National Science Foundation–sponsored

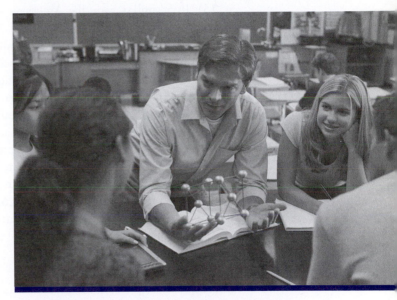

Good planning is needed to know what questions can be raised and answered though student inquiries.

(Continued)

■ Select teaching and assessment strategies that support the development of student understanding and nurture a community of learners.

■ Work together as colleagues within and across disciplines and grade levels.

panel recommended that the focus of science courses should be " . . . on open-ended activities that enhance skills of observation and discovery, hypothesis formation, testing, and evaluation" (Division of Undergraduate Science, Engineering, and Mathematics Education, 1989, p. 15). In a similar vein, the American Association for the Advancement of Science (1990) stated, "Science taught as it is practiced would be presented as open-ended rather than closed and investigative rather than merely confirmatory. Science progresses through creativity and innovation—asking pertinent and impertinent questions—but science students are seldom expected to do more than answer questions and follow instructions" (p. 30).

Although many school districts strive for curriculum reform that embodies the goal of teaching science as science is practiced, many teachers lack experience and expertise in inquiry teaching. Consequently, when attempting to teach using inquiry they often fail to incorporate key lesson characteristics and fail to employ key teaching strategies. Thus they encounter difficulties. To help eliminate such difficulties, this chapter begins by identifying key components of inquiry lessons, including student behaviors, teacher behaviors, and questioning techniques. We will then consider how to prepare good lesson plans including the use of technology and the consideration of important safety and animal use procedures.

QUESTIONS TO CONSIDER

Here are 25 questions to consider when planning for inquiry:

Lesson Characteristics

1. *Does the lesson involve concepts fundamental to understanding the discipline's embedded theories?* In the past, understanding has been gained via the generation and test of major theories. Students gain understanding through inquiries that allow for the construction of such theories, not through the cookbook activities and the memorization of facts.

2. *Is the lesson appropriate in terms of the students' developmental stages?* Knowledge of developmental stages is extremely important in selecting what and how to teach. Instruction must challenge but not overwhelm student reasoning. Successful teachers know both their students' developmental stages *and* the intellectual demands of their lessons.

3. *Does the lesson involve materials and activities that interest diverse students?* Lessons must include materials and activities that appeal to diverse students and provoke interest and curiosity.

4. *Do lesson materials and/or activities provoke student thinking, questioning, and discussion of meanings?* Students must be confronted with puzzling observations and alternative views that lead them to question and otherwise challenge their understanding and/or reasoning skills.

5. *Are there provisions within the lesson for a variety of levels and paths of investigation?* Not all students have the same background knowledge, work at the same pace, are equally interested, or are at the same developmental stage. Therefore, lessons should involve some flexibility. When students are free to interact with a variety of materials they will automatically do so at their own levels and in their own directions.

6. *Does the amount of reading impede the success of students with limited reading ability?* Although reading is extremely important, lesson success should not depend on reading ability. Generally, assigned readings should come *after* the exploration and term introduction phases, not before. This is particularly important for non-English language learners.

7. *Are visual and technical aids such as demonstrations, diagrams, slides, videos, and computers used as effective aids or supplements?* Once initial understandings have been obtained through firsthand experience, slides, videos, computer animations, and other technical devices can serve as effective means of expanding student understanding, eliminating misconceptions, and closing gender gaps.

Student Behaviors

8. *Are students making observations that raise questions?* A clearest indication that inquiry is taking place is that students are actively engaged in explorations that confront them with puzzling observations in need of explanation.

9. *Are students generating hypotheses and theories and deducing predictions that aid in answering the questions?* Suppose that during the exploration of seed growth, students discover differences in seed germination and growth rates. In response to the resulting causal questions, student hypotheses may include "Some seeds didn't grow because they got too much or too little water, sunlight, space, or fertilizer." After generating such hypotheses, students should test them by planning and conducting experiments with clearly stated predictions.

10. *Are students analyzing and interpreting data and reflecting on their meaning singly, in groups, or as a class with the teacher's guidance?* A useful technique is to first have student groups display their data on the board. Then the entire class can look for patterns and discuss the data and their meanings.

11. *Are class conclusions based on the evidence rather than on teacher authority?* Class conclusions must be based on data, not on teacher authority. If an investigation produces inconsistent results (or incorrect results from the point of view of modern science), a further

investigation should be proposed that might clarify the situation. If inconsistency remains, the best course of action may be to conduct the investigation once again. Indeed, this is how science is often done.

Teacher Behaviors

12. *Is the teacher a fellow investigator?* During exploration, walk about the room finding out what students are doing and what results they are obtaining. Be prepared to pose individual questions to provoke further investigation. Also be alert for students who might be having difficulty and need assistance in getting started or in keeping the inquiry going. Because students are conducting investigations that you most likely have already conducted, the temptation may exist to sit back and ignore what the class is doing or, worse yet, to tell the students the "right" answers. This must be avoided! In short, you need to become an enthusiastic and convincing actor—an actor who facilitates inquiry by raising probing questions and by providing helpful hints.

13. *Does the teacher act as a classroom secretary when data need to be collected and analyzed?* A primary job of the inquiry teacher is guide and organizer. By suggesting ways in which data can be recorded and displayed, the teacher not only helps students organize their results but also focuses attention on aspects of the data to help in their analysis and interpretation.

14. *Are new terms introduced only after students have had direct experience with materials, events, or situations that enable students to assimilate the verbal presentation?* New terms must be mentally linked to some pattern and/or idea grounded in firsthand experience. Introducing new terms prior to such experience generally leads to memorization, incomprehension, and poor retention.

15. *Does the teacher provide additional materials, experiences, or events that enlarge, refine, and reinforce the meaning of the introduced terms?* Once initial comprehension has been acquired, students should seek applications in new contexts. Suppose, for example, students have simulated the process of natural selection with colored toothpicks on a lawn and the teacher has subsequently introduced the term *natural selection* to label the process. Clearly, the natural selection concept is not very useful if it applies only to this particular situation. If, however, students are provided with other examples (e.g., the increasing resistance of bacteria to antibiotics and insects to pesticides), the concept's meaning and importance are extended.

16. *Does the teacher handle classroom interruptions by calmly walking over to the offending student and addressing him or her personally?* A common mistake made by many teachers is to raise their voices to reprimand disruptive students. This behavior, while perhaps initially successful, seldom has lasting effects and generally leads to loss of teacher respect and classroom control. Instead, personally addressing offending students in a calm and deliberate manner generally solves the problem.

17. *Does the teacher appear confident, calm, and friendly?* These traits as well as understanding, patience, and a good sense of humor often make the difference between a successful and an unsuccessful lesson, be it inquiry or otherwise.

Questioning Techniques

18. *Does the teacher pose a majority of open-ended or evaluative questions?* Questions such as "What have you observed?" "What are some possible causes?" and "How might you test your idea?" have multiple answers and thus are called **divergent questions**. Divergent questions stimulate discussion and allow for divergent, creative, and critical thinking.

19. *Are convergent questions used to focus students' attention on particular aspects of a difficult investigation?* Questions such as "Which liquid evaporated first?" and "How many *Daphnia* were eaten?" that require predetermined answers are called **convergent questions**. Convergent questions narrow thinking and center attention on specific details. They can help students analyze a situation or find and correct a possible error or point of confusion. However, following use of convergent questions, the teacher should ask divergent questions to once again stimulate students to think more widely.

20. *Are teacher questions phrased directly and simply?* To maximize student response, keep questions direct and to the point. Remember, if students don't understand the question, they can't respond in a productive way. To become a good teacher, one must have the right questions and know when and how to pose them. This point can't be emphasized too strongly.

21. *Does the teacher call on a student after posing a question?* Calling on a specific student *before* asking a question encourages the rest of the class to disregard the question. If you ask the question first and only then call on a student to respond, the entire class is stimulated to think. Another problem arises when the teacher asks a question and fails to call on a specific student for a response. This procedure often leads to a chorus of responses that can get out of hand and lead to control problems.

22. *Does the teacher wait at least 4 to 5 seconds for a response?* The length of time a teacher allows for a student response is called **wait-time I**. Extending wait-time I greatly increases the quality of student thinking and increases the eventual number and quality of student responses (Rowe, 1973, 2003). The teacher can also, and often should, increase the time they wait following a student response. Increasing this second wait-time (so-called **wait-time II**) also increases the quality and quantity of student thinking and responses.

23. *Does the teacher listen to and accept all sincere student answers as valuable contributions?* Accepting all student responses as valuable contributions, even if you know them to be wrong, not only opens up the classroom to free discussion and meaningful inquiry but also puts the authority for correctness and incorrectness where it belongs in the data.

24. *When answering student questions, does the teacher respond by providing additional information or asking leading questions that enable students to continue thinking?* Any time teachers supply answers that students could have gained through further thinking or inquiry, student thinking stops. Thus, teachers need to respond to student questions with additional questions and/or with suggestions for further inquiry that enable them to continue their thinking. This does not mean, however, that student questions should never receive direct answers. For example, either a question such as "What kind of tree is this?" should be answered directly, or the student should be provided with means of obtaining the answer.

25. Did the students and teacher enjoy the lesson? People become scientists because they are curious and enjoy exploring nature and seeking explanations. Teaching science as something other than an interesting and enjoyable enterprise is unnecessary and, in fact, is a misrepresentation of the discipline.

PREPARING GOOD LESSON PLANS

Steps to Follow—Backward Design

The first step in lesson planning is to carefully review national, state, and district standards and select appropriate unit objectives and how they might be assessed. In other words, the steps for developing good lesson plans should incorporate key elements of what Wiggins and McTighe (2005) call backward design—backward because objectives and assessments drive lesson planning rather than the other way around. Stage 1 in their design scheme involves identifying desired results—that is, what do you want students to know and/or be able to do? Stage 2 requires identification of acceptable evidence that your desired results have been attained. This step makes student assessment (the topic of Chapter 13) an integral part of lesson planning. Lastly Stage 3 involves the planning of learning experiences and instruction.

Thus, as mentioned, you need to start by considering lesson objectives. When selecting and writing lesson objectives, keep in mind that they should point the way—but not provide answers. Also you need to make sure that your objectives do not include terms that have not yet been introduced. For example, a lesson called "What Can Be Learned From Skulls?" might explore skull structure and function and allow you to introduce the terms *omnivore, carnivore,* and *herbivore.* Consequently, it would be inappropriate to state an objective such as "In this lesson you will learn the concepts of omnivore, carnivore, and herbivore." Instead, the lesson's stated objectives should focus on what students should learn to do. Appropriate action-oriented objectives for this lesson and a similar inquiry-based lesson on evaporation rates called "Why Do Liquids Evaporate at Different Rates?" include the following:

LESSON: What Can Be Learned From Skulls?

Objectives

- Observe characteristics of a variety of vertebrate skulls and preserved specimens and generate hypotheses about what they ate and where they lived.
- Test your hypotheses using additional skull characteristics.
- During a discussion report your puzzling observations, hypotheses, evidence, and arguments for at least one skull.

> **LESSON: Why Do Liquids Evaporate at Different Rates?**
>
> **Objectives**
>
> - Measure the evaporation rates of four colorless liquids.
> - Generate alternative hypotheses to explain differences in the observed evaporation rates.
> - Plan and conduct tests of your hypotheses.

Preparing Individual Lessons

Preparing individual lesson plans is the next step. You should be forewarned that good lesson planning and good teaching require lots of practice and effort. Do not expect things to go smoothly without careful planning. This includes thinking through each lesson and knowing precisely what questions will be raised and just how students can "tackle" them. The following steps will help you prepare lesson plans for each type of learning cycle:

1. Descriptive Learning Cycles

(a) The teacher selects some concept(s) to be taught.

(b) The teacher selects some phenomenon incorporating the pattern upon which the concept(s) is based.

(c) *Exploration:* Students explore the phenomenon and attempt to discover and describe the pattern.

(d) *Term Introduction:* Students report data gathered and describe the pattern; the teacher then introduces a term(s) to label the pattern.

(e) *Concept Application:* Additional phenomena are discussed and/or explored involving the same concept(s).

For example, during a descriptive learning cycle called "How Were Alien Monoliths Sorted?" students use a variety of procedures to measure and compare the mass and volume of several monoliths that were discovered on a recent archaeological expedition to Burma. They then attempt to discover a method for sorting the monoliths and saving young Indiana Smith from the wrath of the expedition leader. By constructing graphs, students discover that only one property can be used to distinguish the monoliths. That property is labeled with the term *density*. Subsequent activities and learning cycles allow students to apply the density concept in additional contexts.

2. Empirical-Abductive Learning Cycles

(a) The teacher selects some concept(s) to be taught.

(b) The teacher selects some phenomenon incorporating the pattern upon which the concept(s) is based.

(c) *Exploration:* The teacher and/or students raise the descriptive question.

(d) Students gather data to answer the descriptive question.

(e) Data to answer the descriptive question are displayed on the board.

(f) The descriptive question is answered, and a causal question is raised.

(g) Alternative hypotheses are advanced to answer the causal question, and the already gathered data are examined to allow for an initial test of the alternatives.

(h) *Term Introduction:* Terms are introduced that relate to the explored phenomenon and to the hypothesized explanation(s).

(i) *Concept Application:* Additional phenomena are discussed or explored involving the same concept(s).

For example, during an empirical-abductive learning cycle called "What Is Energy?" students experiment with Newton spheres, pendulums, and several additional systems that illustrate different sources of energy and energy transfer. After initial explorations, the students generate causal questions and alternative hypotheses to explain the storage and transfer of motion from one object and/or system to another. The term *energy* is introduced and defined in the context of stored motion and the transfer of motion and in terms of energy sources, energy transfers, and energy receivers.

3. Hypothetical-Predictive Learning Cycles

(a) The teacher selects some concept(s) to be taught.

(b) The teacher selects some phenomenon incorporating the pattern upon which the concept(s) is based.

(c) *Exploration:* Students explore a phenomenon that raises the causal question, or the teacher raises the casual question.

(d) During class discussion, hypotheses are advanced, and students design tests of their hypotheses.

(e) Students conduct tests of their hypotheses.

(f) *Term Introduction:* Data are compared and analyzed, terms are introduced, and conclusions are drawn.

(g) *Concept Application:* Additional phenomena are discussed or explored involving the same concept(s).

For example, during a hypothetical-predictive learning cycle called "Is Water a Pure Substance?" students test the postulate of ancient Greek theory claiming that water is a "pure" substance by passing electricity through water to see if it decomposes. The electricity causes the water to bubble, and the bubbles are collected in test tubes. Students then use flame tests to determine that the collected gases are not identical, indicating that water is not a pure substance but instead consists of at least two different substances in a 2-to-1 ratio. Thus, evidence is obtained that allows for introduction of the *law of definite proportions* and *atomic theory*.

Although steps for preparing learning cycles have been suggested, you need to try out your plan in the classroom. These initial trials will provide important feedback that will help you improve the lesson. Having another teacher in the classroom to provide feedback is also helpful. Unfortunately, you may discover that your initial lesson was ineffective and should be discarded. But assuming that successful revisions are made, you should write up a detailed lesson plan to share with colleagues. Additional feedback from their trials will further improve the lesson. In this way, new learning cycles will be developed so that you and other teachers will have a wide variety to choose from. Also students can periodically provide important feedback. After a series of lessons, students can anonymously report which lessons they liked best, which lessons they liked least, and why.

This might be a good time to remind you of the Biological Sciences Curriculum Study's Five E (BSCS) teaching method, which was discussed briefly in Chapter 5. As mentioned, the Five E method is learning cycle based. However, the BSCS divides exploration into the *engage* and *explore* "stages." The organization refers to term introduction as the *explain* stage and to concept application as the *elaborate* stage. In addition, the BSCS includes an *evaluate* stage. Of course teachers need to evaluate learning, so the addition of a "stage" for evaluation is useful in terms of your planning. Also when planning, you will need to think about whether or not you will need a separate stage/phase for student engagement. Although students need to be engaged for learning to take place, good explorations are engaging and often need to be preceded by only the briefest teacher comments. In fact, experience observing beginning teachers is that they often say too much, not too little, at the start of lessons.

Components of Good Lesson Plans

Lesson plans are written by and for teachers to list how they will help students attain lesson objectives. Lesson plans should include not only what the teacher and students will do during each phase of instruction but also why they will do it. Good lesson plans typically include the following components:

1. Lesson Synopsis

The lesson synopsis should be a very brief overview of the lesson's primary objective(s) and concepts to be introduced, as well as how the lesson will be conducted. For example, the following synopses summarize the previous lessons on skull structure/function and evaporation rates:

Synopsis. Students observe a variety of vertebrate skulls and preserved specimens and use circumstantial evidence to test hypotheses about each animal's habitat and what it eats. Through class discussion the relationships among skull characteristics and implied functions are explored and the terms *herbivore, omnivore, carnivore, nocturnal, diurnal, habitat,* and *niche* are introduced. This is a hypothetical-predictive learning cycle.

Synopsis. Students use molecular models and structural drawings as the basis for generating hypotheses and predicting the order in which four colorless chemicals will evaporate. They then measure evaporation rates and use experimental evidence to test their hypotheses. Following an analysis of results, which generally contradict their initial hypotheses, the terms *volatility* and *polarity* are introduced. This is a hypothetical-predictive learning cycle.

2. Background Information

Lesson plans should contain a section containing the conceptual background embedded in the lesson. The primary goal here is to bring others who may want to use the lesson "up to speed" regarding the lesson's content. In a sense, this section should read like a textbook to explicate the lesson's concepts. The section should also include misconceptions that students may bring with them. For example, with respect to the previously described candle-burning lesson, most students come to class holding two major and instruction-resistant misconceptions: (a) Combustion consumes (i.e., gets rid of oxygen from the air), and (b) a partial vacuum creates a pulling (i.e., sucking) force, which in this case causes the water to rise in the cylinder. Also, if the lesson engages students in generating and testing hypotheses, the hypotheses that students can be expected to generate, along with ways of testing them, should be included.

Once you have taught a lesson several times, this background information section becomes unnecessary. However, the section is crucial for new teachers. For new teachers to be successful they need (a) a good understanding of the scientific concepts they intend to teach, (b) a good sense of what students know coming in, and (c) a good idea of what hypotheses and predictions students are likely to generate during the lesson. As mentioned, knowing common student misconceptions and how to tackle them is also extremely helpful.

3. Advanced Preparation

This section is generally brief and at times may be omitted all together. The purpose is simply to remind you what must be done prior to the lesson and/or what materials must be gathered and distributed. For example, for the skull lab, teachers are reminded to place a specimen at each of 15 numbered stations.

4. Engagement Strategies

Make sure that you have everyone's attention (i.e., students are quiet and looking toward you) before introducing the lesson. As mentioned, you will need to signal students that you are ready to begin (e.g., by politely asking for their attention, by tuning the lights off and on, or by raising your hand and by having students do the same). Once you have everyone's attention, briefly review what was learned in the previous lesson and discuss, in general terms, what the current lesson is about. For example, you may want to say something like "During the last lesson, we obtained evidence that species change across time. But how does this change take place? How do species change? The primary purpose of today's lesson is to explore how species change across time."

During your introductory remarks, make sure not to "give away the punch line." More specifically, don't tell students what terms they are expected to learn, as this violates the spirit of inquiry. In short, the goal of engagement should be to help students connect past learning to the current lesson and to motivate the current lesson—to make it sound interesting, fun, and important.

Also keep in mind that your remarks should be relatively brief. If they take more than about 5 minutes, you have taken too long and will bore students, rather than engage them. In fact, many lessons can begin very effectively without your saying much at all. For example, when introducing the candle-burning lesson all you need to do is tell students to use a piece of clay to sit a candle in a pan of water. Then light the candle, place an inverted beaker over it, and see what happens. Once they see the candle go out and the water rise, you have them "hooked" (i.e., engaged), and they can proceed with hypothesis generation and test from there. The point is that good explorations can be very engaging. Thus planning for a separate engagement phase may often be unnecessary.

5. Exploration Strategies

The main strategy during exploration is to let students investigate as long as they are making progress. In general, you want to let students inquire in different directions based on their own interests and levels of expertise. Thus, it helps considerably to have enough diversity of materials available so that diverse students can take alternative routes. Having all students do the same thing will underwhelm some students and overwhelm others. For example, a lesson that explores isopod behavior should allow some students to use the materials to make relatively "simple" tests, such as seeing if isopods react to light differences or to the presence of smelly substances such as perfume. And the lesson should also allow other students to design more difficult experiments, such as one that will determine whether or not isopods can communicate. During exploration, you should walk about the classroom, closely watching and listening to student groups to check progress, to offer helpful hints to those having difficulty getting started, and to offer challenges to those who are finished quickly or who are losing interest.

To exemplify these points, let's consider the candle-burning lesson in some detail. As mentioned, you can start by simply letting students obtain the materials and see what happens when the cylinder is placed over a burning candle. Once they see the candle burn out and the water rise, challenge them to see what happens when the values of several independent variables are varied. For example, what happens when more candles are used, when a large jar is used instead of the cylinder, or when a jar is placed over the candle more slowly? You will probably want to stop student exploration after about 20 to 30 minutes for a discussion of their observations and initial questions. During the discussion, observations and/or questions should be listed on the board. The most obvious questions are as follows: Why did the flame go out? And, why did the water rise? If one or more student groups have tried to answer these questions, the most likely answer is that the candle went out because it "burned up" all the oxygen and because once the oxygen was gone, the water was "sucked" up to replace it.

At this time you should use "brainstorming" techniques to encourage the generation of several alternative explanations—the more the better. Recall that generating several alternatives at the outset not only increases one's chances of finding the right cause; it also reduces possible bias later on. Keep in mind that hypotheses should not be critiqued at this time as doing so discourages free thinking. Also feel free to generate an idea or two yourself—preferably "wrong" ones (i.e., hypotheses that when tested will not be supported). This also encourages free thinking. You should then challenge students to test as many of the alternative hypotheses as they can. For example, you may want to lead students to realize that the consumed-oxygen hypothesis predicts that varying the number of burning candles will *not* affect the level of water rise. Four candles, for instance, would burn up the available oxygen faster and go out sooner than one candle. But four candles would not burn up more oxygen; hence the water should rise to the same level.

Ask students to conduct this experiment and any additional experiments that they can think up and report results. The results of the experiment will show that the number of candles does affect the water level—the more candles, the higher the water level. The consumed-oxygen hypothesis, therefore, has been contradicted. At this point you can reemphasize the need to test the alternative explanations or perhaps generate some additional ones. This may be an excellent time for the bell to ring as no one may have good tests of the alternatives. Thus, you can challenge students to think up some tests as their homework assignment.

If and when someone does propose the "correct" explanation (i.e., the heated air escaped out the bottom) do not tell the class it is correct. Rather treat it as just another hypothesis to be tested. Ask students to try to think of a way to test the hypothesis. They should eventually realize that the hypothesis leads to the prediction that bubbles should be seen escaping out the bottom of the cylinder. The hypothesis also leads to the prediction that the number of candles should affect the level of water rise because more candles will heat more air; therefore, more will escape and in turn will be replaced by more water. Have students observe closely to see if bubbles can be seen. However, if no one proposes the hypothesis you will have to propose it yourself. But make sure not to give students the impression that this is the correct explanation. Rather, it is simply an idea you had that should be tested along with the other ideas that were generated. The conclusion that it is correct should come only *after* data have been gathered that are consistent with its predictions.

6. Term Introduction Strategies

Properly introducing new terms is no simple matter. In general, one should first discuss students' observations that "embody" the relevant concept(s), then define the related term(s), and lastly introduce the term(s) (i.e., observations—> definitions—> terms). For example, with respect to the skull lesson, students observe that a particular skull has sharp pointed teeth and eye sockets pointing forward. Both characteristics imply that the animal eats other animals (i.e., *If* . . . the animal has sharp teeth to rip the flesh of captured animals, *and* . . . we check the positioning of its eye sockets, *then* . . . the eye sockets should be pointing forward to afford good depth perception needed to capture other animals). After acknowledging that the animal most likely ate other animals, you can tell students that "animals that eat other animals" (the definition) are called *carnivores* (the term). Similarly, a skull with flat teeth and eyes to the side most likely is that of a plant eater. And "animals that eat plants" (the definition) are called *herbivores* (the term). As you can see, in this way, the terms come *after* the ideas to which they relate. This means that students can easily link the new terms to those ideas and more easily "construct" the concepts. Recall that the more traditional approach of terms first and ideas second does not work as well because the new terms have nothing to link with in students' minds.

In theoretical contexts such as the candle-burning lab, term introduction follows the same sequence but is somewhat more complicated. For example, after evidence has been found that supports the expanding-air hypothesis, you should draw a diagram on the board complete with lots of dots (to represent moving air molecules). Once the dots have been drawn and their motion has been discussed, including their ability to bump into and push on other things, such as the water surface and the cylinder walls, and once some of their motion has been transferred to such surfaces (the definition), the term *air pressure* can be introduced to label this theoretical force (i.e., the force presumably caused by moving/pushing molecules). Note how this concept of air pressure is part of a general theory of gases that postulates that air is composed of moving particles that have weight and can bounce into objects (such as water) and push them out of the way. Thus, relevant aspects of *kinetic-molecular theory* will also have to be introduced.

A common mistake made by teachers new to the inquiry approach is to introduce new terms without their proper foundation. As mentioned, ideas must come first and terms second. Thus, the exploration phase must allow for the relevant ideas to "emerge." If they do not, then you should introduce the related terms. Suppose, for example, that students have conducted fruit fly crosses and found a 3-to-1 ratio of red- to brown-eyed flies in the third generation. Gregor Mendel's theory of inheritance would explain this ratio by postulating the existence of *dominant* and *recessive genes* that pass unchanged from one generation to the next. In this sense, you could use the data to introduce these aspects of Mendel's theory (i.e., these terms). We now know that genes consist of deoxyribonucleic acid. However, there is nothing in the fruit fly data to suggest what genes are made up of (i.e., for all Mendel knew, genes could have been made of practically any type of molecule). Therefore, you cannot use these data to introduce the term *deoxyribonucleic acid (DNA)*. Not until the 1950s, nearly 100 years after Mendel's work, did James Watson and Francis Crick have evidence that genes were made of DNA.

7. Concept Application Strategies

The point of the concept application phase is to allow students to discover applications of the introduced concepts and thus extend their range of applicability and clarify their meanings. Each lesson plan should contain suggestions for one or more concept application activities. These may include subsequent learning cycles that not only allow for the application of previously introduced concepts but also allow for the introduction of new terms.

To enable students to apply the air pressure concept and kinetic-molecular theory introduced in the candle-burning lesson, students can be given a piece of rubber tubing, a syringe, a beaker, and a pan of water. They can then be challenged to invert the beaker in the pan of water and fill it with water in that position with the mouth of the beaker submerged. Making this a contest to see which student group can fill the beaker first is a fun way to challenge students to apply the concepts to new contexts. Some students will make futile efforts to force water through the tube into the beaker before discovering that they must extract air through the tube. When each group has at last been successful, have a student attempt to explain why the water rose in his or her group's beaker. Typically the student will use the word *suction* (e.g., "We used the syringe to *suck* the air out of the cylinder—the empty cylinder then *sucked* the water up"). At this point it may be helpful to have the student draw a picture of the syringe and beaker on the board, including some of the molecules presumably present in the apparatus. Have the student then try to show where the molecules move and just why they move in that direction. This should eventually lead to the realization that molecular "pulls" are not possible—only "pushes" (i.e., bumps from the rear) are possible. Hence, suction, as a pulling force, cannot exist. However, do not expect many students to understand this right away. After all, we are talking about unseen theoretical molecules, and most secondary school students (perhaps even most 12th graders) have yet to develop the postformal reasoning skills that may be necessary for their complete construction. Presumably thinking about just such theoretical issues will provoke students to begin to develop postformal thinking skills.

Additional application activities include challenging students to insert a peeled, hard-boiled egg into a bottle with an opening that is smaller in diameter than the egg without touching the egg and having students drink a milkshake with a straw and then explain how the milkshake gets into their mouths—without using the word *suction*. Also unobserved by students, you can place water in a metal can to a depth of about 1 cm and boil the water vigorously. Then screw the cap on tightly to form a seal. Place the can on your desk in full view of the students and allow them to witness the can being crushed. Challenge them to explain their observations using kinetic-molecular theory and the concept of air pressure.

8. Assessing Student Understanding

Because Chapter 13 will be devoted to assessment, little will be said about it at this time. Nevertheless, a good lesson plan should include an assessment plan along with some sample assessment items. Keep in mind that you will need to assess not only the extent to which students understand the introduced concepts (i.e., the declarative knowledge) but also the extent to which they can "do" science and think scientifically (i.e., the procedural knowledge). To help you do this Chapter 13 will introduce a taxonomy called Bloom's taxonomy of educational objectives (L. W. Anderson & Krathwohl, 2001; Bloom, 1956).

Bloom's taxonomy consists of six increasingly demanding and educationally important levels of assessment. The levels are called Knowledge, Comprehension, Application, Analysis, Synthesis, and Evaluation. Items written at the Knowledge level only require students to recall specific bits of declarative knowledge. These sorts of items are very easy to write and to administer. For example, What is the first phase of mitosis? In what year was Isaac Newton born? Unfortunately teachers often use these sorts of "low level" items for assessment instead of increasingly higher Bloom levels that require a mix of both declarative and procedural knowledge. For example, an item written at the Analysis level may require students to recognize unstated assumptions, distinguish facts from hypotheses, and check the consistency of hypotheses with given information. The key point is that although such "higher level" items are more difficult to write and more difficult for students to respond to, they must become part of your assessment plan for students to take inquiry seriously and for your lessons to provoke meaningful learning and continued intellectual development.

Summary

- Major educational objectives include developing reasoning skills, constructing concepts, and developing confidence. Instructional elements can be grouped into lesson characteristics, student behaviors, teacher behaviors, and questioning techniques.

- Once national and state standards have been reviewed and appropriate action-oriented objectives have been selected, lesson plans can be prepared. Plans should include a lesson synopsis, background information, tips for advanced preparation, engagement/exploration strategies, term introduction strategies, application components, and sample evaluation components.

- New terms should not be introduced without their proper foundation during exploration. Ideas must come first and terms second. Thus, exploration must allow for the relevant patterns and ideas to "emerge."

- Assessment should include measures of the extent to which students understand the introduced concepts (declarative knowledge) as well as measures of the extent to which they can do science and think scientifically (procedural knowledge).

Key Terms

convergent questions

divergent questions

wait-time I

wait-time II

Application Questions/Activities

1. Select one of the example lessons presented in this book or online. Review the 25 characteristics of effective science instruction and describe specifically how they will be incorporated into the lesson. Prepare a set of notes that you can use to teach it (do not modify the prepared lesson plan unless you are very sure that your modification[s] will improve the lesson—this is no time to be creative—you will have plenty of time for that later). What safety precautions should be taken before and during the lesson? How will you alert students to these precautions? Now teach the lesson to a group of peers, a small group of high school students, or an entire class. At the conclusion of the lesson have your peers offer feedback and suggestions for improvement. Or if you teach the lesson to high school students make sure that one or more of your peers attended the lesson so that he, she, or they can offer feedback. While listening to the feedback, make sure not to be too "thin skinned." Remember that we all make mistakes and that it takes lots of practice and reflectivity to develop teaching expertise.

Chapter 8

TECHNOLOGY, LABS, AND SAFETY IN THE INQUIRY CLASSROOM

In the words of Intel Corporation Chairman Craig Barrett (2006), "Teachers are the magic in the classroom—it's not the computers, it's not anything else." In spite of Barrett's sage words, whenever a new technology has been developed (from radios to calculators to computers), developers have championed its use in the classroom. Yet, in virtually all cases, the developers have had little knowledge of effective pedagogy. Their primary motive, not surprisingly, has been profit. Fortunately, in spite of the frequent intense corporate pressure to infuse new technologies in classrooms, most educators, like Barrett, believe that at best technology can support, but not supplant, classroom inquiry. With this in mind, this chapter will discuss the current status of technology use in the classroom and will provide guidelines on how to best incorporate its use. The chapter will then turn to the role played by labs in inquiry, and it will conclude with a look at the important topic of classroom safety.

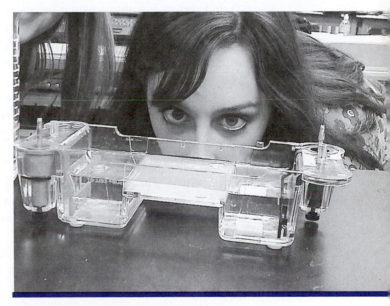

The high school biology students are trying to solve a mystery using DNA fingerprinting technology.

APPLICABLE NSES STANDARDS

Standard D Science teachers design and manage learning environments that provide students with the time, space, and resources needed for learning. In doing so, they

- Ensure a safe working environment.
- Make science tools, materials, media, and technological resources available to students.
- Engage students in designing the learning environment.

CLASSROOM TECHNOLOGY

The Current Status

It may come as a surprise, but research often finds that incorporating technology into classroom activities results in less student learning. For example, among fourth and eighth graders, Wenglinsky (1998) reported that using computers to teach low-order thinking skills, such as drill and practice, had a negative impact on achievement as measured by the National Assessment of Educational Progress mathematics test. Similarly Hiebert (1999) found that overpracticing procedures before understanding them made it more difficult for students to make sense of them later. On the other hand, Hiebert found that using computers to solve simulations improved student math scores. Thus, perhaps not surprisingly, researchers have concluded that it is not computer use itself that has a positive or negative effect on achievement. Rather it is the way computers are used (e.g., Papanastasiou, Zemblyas, & Vrasidas, 2003).

A key, according to Roschelle, Pea, Hoadley, Gordin, and Means (2000), is that technology (generally meaning computer use) can help students develop higher-order thinking skills when their use engages students in authentic, complex tasks within collaborative learning contexts. As Flick and Bell (2000, p. 16) put it, "Use of technology should support student understanding of scientific inquiry and how scientific investigations are conceived and conducted." Similarly, Bell, Gess-Newsome, and Luft (2007) caution that even with all of the promising new technologies available, the teacher is still the most important part of the equation. Hence, before using a new technology, a teacher needs to ask, "Will this actually help students learn the material better?" Further, the use of simulations of experiments that would otherwise be impossible in school classrooms may be an excellent use of technology. But before simulations are selected, one always needs to ask, "Could my students actually do the experiment themselves?"

Others have reported useful additions to and extensions of the inquiry process using technology (e.g., Berger, Lu, Belzer, & Voss, 1994; Edelson, 2001; Linn, Davis, & Bell, 2004; Sandholtz, Ringstaff, & Dwyer, 1997). For example, Edelson describes how a modified learning cycle approach, which incorporates both computer visualizations and hands-on labs, can be used to teach middle school students about physical geography and its influence on global climatic patterns. And having students take part in engineering design projects such as building bridges or constructing hot-air balloons not only helps them learn design principles (e.g., consideration of constraints, trade-offs, failure, overdesign); such projects also provide opportunities to learn and apply science concepts (e.g., Cajas, 2001).

In summary, four factors seem to be involved in the successful use of technology to enhance both what and how students learn. They are (1) active engagement, (2) participation in groups, (3) frequent interaction and feedback, and (4) connections to real-world contexts. Further, it seems that the use of technology is more effective as a learning tool when embedded in a broader education reform movement that includes improvements in teacher training, curriculum, student assessment, and a school's capacity for change.

Guidelines for Effective Technology Use

Influential national reform documents such as the National Research Council's *Inquiry and the National Science Education Standards: A Guide for Teaching and Learning* (NRC,

1996) include technological standards. For example, with respect to Grades 9–12 they urge the use of technology and mathematics to improve inquiries and communications:

> A variety of technologies, such as hand tools, measuring instruments, and calculators, should be an integral component of scientific investigations. The use of computers for the collection, analysis, and display of data is also a part of this standard. Mathematics plays an essential role in all aspects of an inquiry. For example, measurement is used for posing questions, formulas are used for developing explanations, and charts and graphs are used for communicating results. (p. 166)

With this in mind, there are at least five ways in which new technologies, if used thoughtfully, can help:

1. Finding Out

Students can look up stored information by using the Internet and by using reference software. They can use distributed information sources such as real-time data, online databases, peer groups, and mentors/experts in many locations to investigate scientific questions. They can use Web-based photo journals and virtual field trips to explore remote geographic locations. They can use geographic information systems (GIS) to visualize, manipulate, analyze, and display spatial data. Also they can detect, record, and graph new data during microcomputer-based labs (MBLs) and calculator-based labs (CBLs). For example, using sensory probes connected to handheld devices and computer software developed by Vernier Software and Technology (www.vernier.com), several variables can be detected, recorded, and graphed including acceleration, barometric pressure, conductivity, carbon dioxide gas, dissolved oxygen, electrical current, force, heart rate, ion concentration, light intensity, magnetic field, motion, pH, relative humidity, solution concentration, sound intensity, temperature, turbidity, and voltage. However, if you decide to use MBLs and/or CBLs, caution is advised on at least two accounts. First, few lab and field activities that have been developed using these technologies are inquiry based (those developed by the Modeling Instruction Program in physics are notable exceptions—see http://modeling.asu.edu/). Second, many students lack skill in measuring, recording, and graphing data. Therefore, allowing technology to do the job for them robs them of valuable opportunities to develop these important skills. The implication is that the technologies should not be used until students have first developed the necessary understanding and skills by performing the needed recordings and calculations and constructing graphs by hand.

2. Composing

Students can compose lab reports and other sorts of papers using word processing software, multimedia authoring systems, and concept mapping and webbing programs. Word processing is a standard computer application available in almost every school. In addition to lab reports and papers, word processing programs can be used for students to create newsletters and magazines, advertisements, and flyers. The drawing tools included in most word processing programs allow students to create pictures, graphs, data tables, and more. Using HTML conversion utilities, students can create Web pages and interactive documents using hyperlinks, and the word processing features, such as tracking and commenting, facilitate collaborative projects. The educational value of organizing ideas cannot be overstated. Composing can do much more than demonstrate one's knowledge. The right sorts of writing assignments can provoke reflection, which can in turn identify gaps and even contradictions in one's thinking and knowledge. In short, writing can encourage and facilitate self-regulation. Thus, although writing most often is a slow and painstaking process, it can be one of the most educationally beneficial activities in which students can engage.

3. Analyzing

Once data are gathered, computer-based graphing software, databases, spreadsheets, and statistical programs exist to help students organize and analyze their data. Although these sorts of programs are exceptionally fast and powerful, caution is again advised to ensure that the technology does not overshadow student inquiry and to ensure that the programs are not used blindly—that is, with little or no understanding of the programs' operations and limitations.

4. Communicating

Students can communicate their findings and conclusions using presentation software (e.g., PowerPoint), e-mail, electronic mailing lists, and the World Wide Web. These technologies open up extraordinary communication possibilities. Students can now communicate with other students literally on the other side of the world virtually instantaneously. But once again, caution is in order to make sure that the technology tail does not wag the educational dog. For example, the use of PowerPoint to prepare and give presentations has recently drawn serious criticism because its format seems to force oversimplification and shallow thinking. Perhaps its harshest critic, Edward Tufte, the well-known Yale theorist of information presentation, had this to say about what he called the PowerPoint cognitive style:

> Particularly disturbing is introduction of the PowerPoint cognitive style into schools. Instead of writing a report using sentences, children learn how to make client pitches and info-mercials, which is better than encouraging children to smoke. Elementary school PP exercises (as seen in teacher's guides, and in student work posted on the internet) typically show 10 to 20 words and a piece of clip art on each side in a presentation consisting of 3 to 6 slides—a total of perhaps 80 words (15 seconds of silent reading) for a week of work. Rather than being trained as mini-bureaucrats in PPPhluff and foreshortening of thought, students would be better off if schools simply closed down on those days and everyone went to The Exploratorium—or wrote an illustrated essay explaining something. (Tufte, 2003, p. 11)

5. Visualizing and Simulating

New computer-based visualizations and simulations are being produced and introduced virtually every month. The visualizations can be particularly effective at showing students what microscopic objects and processes presumably look like or what happens in nature over extended periods of time. The use of computer-based simulations during concept application can greatly extend and refine the usefulness of concepts previously introduced. For example, the simulation of genetic crosses over numerous generations or the simulation of ecological trends over many years, even centuries, can be easily accomplished with computers. Simulations can also be used during exploration when the phenomena of interest cannot be directly experienced given normal classroom constraints.

Thomas and Hooper (1991) classify the use of simulations into three categories called experiencing, informing, and reinforcing/integrating. During exploration, experiencing simulations can be used to provide motivation, provide an organizing structure, serve as examples, or expose misconceptions and areas of knowledge deficiency. During term introduction, informing simulations can serve as the initial formal exposure to a topic. And during concept application, reinforcing/integrating simulations allow students to apply new knowledge to new contexts.

More recently, Yezierski and Birk (2006) found that including computer animations that depicted the atomic nature of water in high school chemistry lessons helped students overcome some of their misconceptions related to phases of matter and phase changes. Importantly, the animations were more effective for females than for males, so much so that the achievement difference favoring males was virtually wiped out. Nevertheless, visual aids should not substitute for firsthand experiences. Likewise, computers can help gather, organize, and present data, but they should not be used to replace firsthand experiences with natural phenomena.

In conclusion, technologies, if used properly, can enhance but not supplant student inquiry and learning. Technology cannot take the place of an experienced and expert teacher. As Craig Barrett said, "Teachers are the magic in the classroom." And most likely, teachers will remain the magic, regardless of what new technologies might come along. So become a technology expert if doing so suits your teaching needs and your students' learning needs. But keep your eye on the bigger picture, which is to provoke your students to think. And this means that they must pose questions, generate possible explanations, test their explanations, and argue and debate what those tests might mean. For this to happen, well-designed laboratory activities are essential. Consequently, the next section turns to the use of labs during classroom inquiry.

LABS IN THE INQUIRY CLASSROOM

Unlike the use of technology, which may hinder or help classroom inquiry, labs play a critical and central role in the inquiry classroom. In short, inquiry means that labs become the core of your classroom instruction. Labs provide the means for student exploration. They provide the primary context in which new terms are introduced. They often provide the contexts in which new concepts can be applied to broaden and deepen their meanings. And importantly, labs *precede,* not follow, textbook and other supplemental readings.

With this in mind, what follows is an example inquiry lab called "Why Do Liquids Evaporate at Different Rates?" The lab consists of a Teacher Guide and a Student Guide. As you read the guides, you may wish to evaluate the lab in terms of the 25 lesson characteristics presented in Chapter 7. Also you should pay particular attention to how the lab is designed as a learning cycle, thus including instructional phases of exploration, term introduction, and concept application.

Why Do Liquids Evaporate at Different Rates?—Teacher Guide

Background Information for the Teacher

This lab investigates variables that affect evaporation rates of acetone, methanol, propanol, and water. Evaporation is the change of phase from a liquid to a gas as molecules at the liquid's surface acquire sufficient kinetic energy to escape into the gaseous state. The energy required for evaporation comes from the surrounding environment. All other things being equal, the more energy it takes to separate molecules and send them into the gaseous state, the lower their evaporation rate.

The tendency for a liquid to evaporate, known as *volatility,* is determined by two "internal" factors—molecular weight and intermolecular forces. Heavy molecules require more energy to evaporate than do light ones. Thus, methane (CH_4, molecular weight 18 amu) is so volatile that it is a gas at room temperature, while octane (C_8H_{18}, molecular weight 114 amu) is a liquid at room temperature.

The molecular weight (or size) hypothesis is among the first generated by students and is at least partially supported (i.e., methanol is lighter/smaller than propanol, and it evaporates faster). However, water (molecular weight 18 amu) is lighter/smaller but evaporates more slowly than the heavier molecules. This result contradicts the molecular weight hypothesis and indicates that some other variable(s) must play a role.

The other variable(s) is a class of interactions collectively referred to as *intermolecular forces.* Ionic attraction, van der Waals forces, and hydrogen bonding are examples of intermolecular forces. In this activity, intermolecular forces are exemplified by *polarity.* Polarity is the existence of a separation of positive and negative electrical charge within a molecule due to an unequal sharing of electrons in one or more covalent bond(s). Polar molecules are attracted to one another because of electromagnetic forces acting among these positive and negative "poles." The net effect is that liquids comprising polar molecules have low volatility owing to the "stickiness" of their molecules.

Molecular polarity occurs due to the tendency of an atom to attract electrons when in a covalent bond with another atom, a property called electronegativity. For example, oxygen atoms have a relatively high electronegativity. Thus, when an oxygen atom covalently bonds with a hydrogen atom, which has a relatively low electronegativity, an unequal sharing of negatively charged electrons occurs. However, when an oxygen atom bonds with a carbon atom, with electronegativity much closer to its own, a far more equal electron sharing occurs. When electron sharing is unequal, a molecule has polar character. When electron sharing is equal (or when the inequality is perfectly symmetrical), a molecule is nonpolar.

The data from this lab (i.e., the observed order of evaporation is acetone, methanol, propanol, and water) can be interpreted in light of the above discussion. Water, while small in size, contains two oxygen–hydrogen bonds. These bonds, in which electron sharing is unequal owing to a large difference in electronegativity, result in a highly polar molecule. Therefore, water molecules must gain a lot of energy before they separate from one another and evaporate. Water has an extremely low volatility. Acetone, on the other hand, contains no oxygen–hydrogen bonds and is, therefore, quite nonpolar. Far less energy is needed to evaporate acetone molecules; thus acetone is extremely volatile. The two alcohols each contain a single oxygen–hydrogen bond. Therefore, their polarities are equal and are intermediate between water and acetone. Because of the equivalence in polarity, the smaller alcohol and methanol molecules have a higher volatility than the larger propanol molecules.

The concept of polarity can be extended in subsequent labs (i.e., concept application) to include its effects on boiling point temperature, equilibrium vapor pressure, and solubility.

LESSON PLAN: Why Do Liquids Evaporate at Different Rates?

Advance Preparation

Before class, draw the molecular structures on the board.

Engagement

The introduction in the Student Guide can be summarized in your own words. You might ask students to identify liquids that, in their experience, evaporate quickly. Responses may include nail polish remover (acetone), paint thinner, and gasoline. Pose the causal question: Why might liquids evaporate at different rates?

Exploration

1. Have each student copy the molecular structures onto his or her data sheet. Have students form teams of two or three to build the models. They should compare their models with those of other groups to check accuracy.

2. Upon completion of the model building, have the students predict the order of liquids in terms of evaporation rates. The most common prediction (based on the molecular size/weight hypothesis) will be that water will evaporate fastest, while propanol will evaporate slowest.

3. Write some of the predictions on the board, but do not evaluate them at this time.

4. For each prediction, ask students to provide a reason, if possible, why they made that prediction. When a reason is given, point out that this is their hypothesis.

5. Have students perform the evaporation experiment and record results. Monitor students to help them conduct controlled experiments (e.g., not blowing or fanning liquids, controlling the size of drops). Do not use white ceramic spot plates for evaporation because it is extremely difficult to tell exactly when evaporation is complete. Note any major differences in the procedures used from group to group, as procedural differences can have a profound effect on measured evaporation rate for a given liquid. These differences can form the basis of an interesting discussion after student data are posted and compared. When unexpected group differences appear, ask students to try to explain such differences. This will cause them to reflect on their procedures and hopefully discover procedural differences from one group to the next. The discovery of such differences will allow you to again stress the importance of controlling extraneous variables.

6. Have students record their three trial times for each liquid on the board. Draw a table on the board to organize the large amounts of data.

Term Introduction

1. Initiate a discussion to arrive at a consensus about the rankings. Point out any differences in the rankings and discuss procedures that may have led to these differences. For instance, a group that consistently (or even inconsistently) fanned its drops will have shorter evaporation times. As mentioned, this is a good opportunity to review the ideas of controlling variables, experimental error, between-group variation, and within-group variation. Nevertheless, the pattern in the data should be clear, and it should not be necessary to redo the experiment.

(Continued)

(Continued)

2. Encourage the class to evaluate its alternative hypotheses in light of the data using hypothetical-predictive arguments. For example:

If...it takes more energy to vaporize larger molecules because they weigh more than smaller molecules,

and...the same volume of acetone, propanol, methanol, and water molecules is evaporated under controlled conditions,

then...the order of evaporation should be as follows: water, methanol, acetone, and propanol.

But...the observed order of evaporation is acetone, methanol, propanol, and water.

Therefore...the size/weight hypothesis is at least partially contradicted. Something else must make a difference.

Hypotheses and results that contradict them are

Hypotheses	*Contradicting Data*
Molecular size	Smallest evaporates at the lowest rate.
Presence of a double bond	No data contradict this hypothesis.
Molecular weight	Higher weight (acetone) evaporates most quickly, lowest weight (water) most slowly.
Alphabetized ranking	No data contradict this hypothesis, but names of substances are arbitrary.
Straight chain versus bent chain structure	Acetone has "straight chain" form and evaporates quickly; propanol has same form and evaporates relatively slowly.
Amount of hydrogen around the molecule	Acetone has more hydrogen than methanol but evaporates faster; acetone has more hydrogen than water but evaporates faster.
Only liquids with carbon atoms evaporate	Water eventually does evaporate.
Intermolecular forces	Not contradicted but requires elaboration.

3. Begin the discussion by introducing the term *volatility* as follows: Some molecules have the tendency to go from the liquid state to the gaseous state more easily than others, which is to say that they evaporate more easily. Those that evaporate more easily (more quickly) are said to be more *volatile* than those that evaporate more slowly. Throughout the rest of the discussion, use the term *volatile* whenever appropriate.

4. Two hypotheses are supported by at least some of the data. The molecular size hypothesis is supported by the observation that methanol, a smaller molecule, evaporates more quickly than does propanol. This comparison is "controlled" in the sense that the polarity of these two molecules is equivalent. Results of comparing the evaporation rates of propanol and acetone support the intermolecular-forces hypothesis. This comparison is also controlled because the molecular size of propanol and acetone is substantially similar, but their evaporation rates are quite different; thus some other force (in this case, polarity) is at work.

5. If students have previously been introduced to electronegativity, the term *polarity* should be relatively easy to introduce as follows: Atoms with a higher electronegativity tend to pull shared electrons toward them, causing an unequal distribution of electrons around the molecule. This unequal distribution gives the molecule a positive end and a negative end (or "pole"). This aspect of a molecule is called *polarity*. The more the distribution is unequal, the more polar the molecule. You can use the idea of a magnet to help the students visualize this.

6. Tell the students that O-H bonds are very polar, while C-O bonds are only somewhat polar and C-H bonds are not polar. Have the students use this information to determine the relative polarities of the four types of molecules. Then have them combine this ranking, with the ranking based on molecular size, to try to explain the observed evaporation rates.

Concept Application

1. Provide students with drawings and/or models of new liquids and have them predict the evaporation ranking of these liquids. Following this, have the students perform an experiment to test their predictions. Space is provided in the table in the Student Guide for these new data. Other possible liquids include ethanol, diethyl ether, 1-butanol, and methylethyl ketone.

LESSON: Why Do Liquids Evaporate at Different Rates?—Student Guide

Have you ever had a sunburn or high fever? To cool your skin, you may have used rubbing alcohol. The alcohol works because it evaporates quickly and lowers skin temperature. Putting water on your skin will also work—but not as well. Both liquids look the same, yet there must be some difference between them to explain the difference in evaporation rates. In this investigation we will attempt to discover why liquids evaporate at different rates.

Objectives

1. To measure the evaporation rates of four colorless liquids.
2. To generate and test hypotheses to explain differences in the evaporation rates.

Materials

Distilled water, H_2O	Spot plates/watch glasses
Acetone, C_3H_6O	Droppers
Methanol, CH_3OH	Watch/clock with second hand
Propanol, C_3H_7OH	Molecular model kits

Additional liquids will be supplied later.

(Continued)

(Continued)

Procedure

1. Copy each of the molecular structures from the board. Using the molecular model kits, build three-dimensional models of water, acetone, propanol, and methanol.

2. Based on the properties of the model molecules, predict the order of evaporation of the four liquids. Be prepared to share the reasons for your predictions in a class discussion. These reasons are your initial hypotheses.

3. Conduct controlled experiments to test your hypotheses. Do at least three trials for each hypothesis and record your results in a data table.

4. Rank the rates of evaporation of the liquids on a scale of 1 through 4 (1 = fastest) and record your ranks on a class data table.

5. Is your observed ranking the same as your predicted ranking? If so, you have obtained support for your initial hypotheses. If your initial hypotheses were not supported, generate at least two alternative hypotheses to account for your results. Be prepared to present your data and discuss your alternative hypotheses with the class.

6. Following the class discussion, you will be given some additional liquids. Knowing what you now know about variables that affect evaporation rates, predict the order in which these liquids will evaporate. Conduct controlled experiments with sufficient replicates to test your prediction.

As will be discussed in Chapter 14, the development and widespread distribution of good inquiry-based labs remains a problem for some disciplines at some grade levels. Nevertheless, many good labs have been developed, and more are being developed and distributed each year. While the curriculum at some schools may not readily support inquiry, there are a number of resources available to you to add inquiry into your teaching. Ask experienced teachers can share their lessons with you. Turn to the variety of publishers and scientific organizations that prepare and distribute inquiry labs. There are resources available to you that can be found with a little research.

LAB SAFETY AND ORGANISM USE

Regardless of the extent to which you embed technology and inquiry into your instruction, lab safety is not optional. Safety precautions and guidelines simply must be followed for the benefit of you and your students. For example, consider what happened when a mischievous student named Joe swiped a hunk of potassium from the chemistry stockroom. After wrapping the potassium in a paper towel, he stuck it in his pants pocket and headed home. Unfortunately for Joe, and for his chemistry teacher, along the way the potassium spontaneously ignited and caught Joe's pants on fire. The result was third-degree burns along with a lawsuit filed by Joe's parents against his teacher.

Chapter 8 ■ Technology, Labs, and Safety in the Inquiry Classroom

General Safety Guidelines

Who is likely to be held responsible in this case—the teacher, the school, Joe, or perhaps even Joe's parents? If the chemistry teacher or the school could have "reasonably foreseen the consequences" of what they had done, or not done, they may be held responsible. Consequently, it becomes imperative that teachers become knowledgeable of school safety issues and procedures. Basically there are five things you can do to establish that you have acted "reasonably" and "responsibly" and are not seen as "negligent" (i.e., guilty of conduct that falls below a standard established by law or profession to protect others from harm). The five things, as suggested by Flinn Scientific Inc. on its Web site (www.flinnsci.com), follow

1. Have each student and his or her parents or guardians sign a written safety contract at the beginning of the school year. Sample contracts can be found on the Flinn Web site. Although such contracts do not carry legal weight, they do help establish that you are a reasonable and responsible teacher.

2. Keep a record of safety discussions that you hold with students in your lesson plan book. Such a record will also provide evidence that you have acted responsibly.

3. Hang safety posters with listed safety procedures in prominent locations in the classroom.

4. Adopt a firm goggle policy (e.g., when chemicals, glassware, or heat is used, students must wear lab goggles).

5. Give students who break lab rules safety "tickets." Keep a record of each ticket date and type of infraction. Also establish consequences for too many tickets.

Additionally, Table 8.1 lists general safety guidelines established by the Council of State Science Supervisors (CSSS, n.d.) in its document *Science & Safety: Making the Connection* (available at http://www.csss-science.org/downloads/scisafe.pdf).

TABLE 8.1   General Science Safety Guidelines

- Have and use appropriate protective equipment such as goggles, chemical aprons, nonallergenic gloves, dust masks, eyewash, showers, ABC fire extinguishers, sand buckets, and fire blankets in easily assessable locations (generally within 15 seconds or 30 steps from any location in the room).
- Notify supervisors immediately of hazardous or potentially hazardous conditions, such as lack of Ground-Fault Interrupters (GFIs) near sinks or inadequate ventilation, or potential hazards such as study halls scheduled in lab rooms or tile floors not waxed with nonskid wax.
- Check the fume hoods regularly for efficiency and do not use hoods for storage. Make sure that hoods are properly vented through the roof.
- Use only equipment in good condition and in good working order.
- Have a goggle sanitation plan for goggles used by multiple classes during the day.
- Have separate disposal containers for broken glassware and flammables.

(Continued)

TABLE 8.1 (Continued)

- Discuss and post emergency and escape plans. Clearly mark fire exits and keep them unobstructed.
- Have and enforce a safety contract with students and parents.
- Identify medical and allergy problems for each student and anticipate potential hazards.
- Model, post, and enforce all safety procedures. Display safety posters.
- Keep the lab uncluttered and keep it locked when not in use.
- Know the district and state policies concerning administering first aid and have an adequately stocked first-aid kit accessible at all time.
- Know district and state policies/guidelines regarding the use of hazardous chemicals, live animals, and animal and plant specimens.
- Report all injuries, including animal scratches, bites, and allergic reactions, immediately to appropriate supervisors.
- Keep a record of safety training and laboratory incidents.
- Provide sufficient workspace per student (60 square feet per student); provide 5-ft-wide aisles and low lab tables for wheelchair accessibility. For details of physical layout/specifications see the cited CSSS Web site.
- Provide a sufficient number of qualified teachers/aides (no less than 1 teacher/aide per 24 students).
- Have easily accessible master cut-off switches/valves within each laboratory; know how to use them; keep water, gas, and electricity turned off when not in use.
- Maintain up-to-date chemical and equipment inventories, including Materials Safety Data Sheet (MSDS) files.
- Label chemicals and equipment properly with respect to hazards and other needed information.
- Post the National Fire Protection Association (NFPA) "diamond" at all chemical storeroom entrances denoting the most hazardous chemical in each category within. Regularly send an updated copy of the inventory to the local fire department.
- Arrange chemicals by National Institute for Occupational Safety and Health (NIOSH)/Occupational Safety and Health Administration (OSHA) compatibility classes, with special storage availability for oxidizers, nonflammable compressed gases, acids, and flammables.
- Store chemicals in appropriate places—for example, below eye level, large containers no higher than 2 ft above the floor, acids in corrosive cabinets, and solvents in OSHA-/NFPA-approved flammables cabinets—with acids separated from bases and oxidizers separated from organics within secure, limited-access, adequately ventilated storerooms. Chemical shelving should be wooded, with a front lip and without metal supports.
- Provide in a readily accessible location appropriate materials and procedures for cleanup of hazardous spills and accidents (e.g., aspirator or kit for mercury spills, vermiculite and baking soda for acids, 10% Clorox bleach solution or 5% Lysol solution for body fluids, and appropriate procedures for disposal of chemo- and biohazardous materials).
- Prohibit the use of pathogens or any procedures or materials in any school laboratory above Biosafety Level 1 as outlined by Centers for Disease Control and Prevention/National Institutes of Health protocols.
- Keep live animals and students adequately protected from one another.

Source: From *Science & Safety: Making the Connection*, by the Council of State Science Supervisors (n.d.), available at http://www.csss-science.org/downloads/scisafe.pdf.

Legal Duties

Teachers have three primary legal duties with regard to student safety—the duty of instruction, the duty of supervision, and the duty of maintenance.

1. Duty of instruction means that teachers must inform students before the lesson (preferably in writing) of potential dangers and appropriate lab or field trip procedures.

2. Duty of supervision means that teachers must oversee the lesson to make sure that students behave properly in light of potential dangers. Several things need to be kept in mind, including the following: Misbehavior should not be tolerated; failure to take proper action is grounds for liability; the greater the danger, the more supervision required; the younger the students or the greater the degree of inclusion of "special" population students, the more supervision required; students should not be left unattended except when the potential harm of not leaving the classroom is greater than the perceived risk; if you must leave, the potential risk should be minimized by transferring supervision to another authorized person.

3. Duty of maintenance means that you have the responsibility to maintain a safe classroom. This includes not using defective equipment; filing written reports of corrections of hazardous conditions and replacements of defective equipment with the administration; regularly inspecting safety and first-aid equipment and documenting such inspections; following safety guidelines concerning chemical purchase, labeling, and storage as detailed in Table 8.2; and following safety and environmental guidelines concerning chemical disposal.

TABLE 8.2   How Should You Purchase, Label, and Store Chemicals?

Purchasing Chemicals—questions to consider before purchase:
- Will the amount purchased be used within a reasonable time period?
- Can the chemical be properly stored?
- Can the chemical be properly disposed of?
- Does the classroom have proper personal protective equipment?
- Are personnel aware of potential hazards associated with the chemical?
- Are personnel properly trained in the use and handling of the chemical?

Labeling Chemicals
- Identify manufacturer or supplier including address and telephone number.
- Identify chemical name and/or trade name.
- Identify date received or replaced.
- List chemical strength.
- List handling and/or mixing precautions.
- Include hazard symbol and National Fire Protection Association rating.

(Continued)

TABLE 8.2 (Continued)

Storing Chemicals

- Use separate storage area.
- Use appropriate warning symbols to mark storage area.
- Make sure that storage area is properly ventilated.
- Make sure that adequate exits are provided.
- Provide adequate fire extinguishers or extinguishing systems.
- Make sure that shelves are properly attached to wall and that they have a 1-in. or 2.5-cm lip to prevent bottles from sliding off.
- Separate organic and inorganic chemicals.
- Use a reputable guide (e.g., NIOSH/OSHA) to help to separate incompatible chemicals.
- Do not store chemicals past listed shelf life.
- Use appropriate containers.
- Store flammables and corrosives separately.

For safe chemical disposal you will need to consult the relevant Materials Safety Data Sheet (MSDS). If your school doesn't have one, you can request one from the manufacturer or obtain one online at www.msdsonline.com. The Environmental Protection Agency (EPA) and the American Chemical Society list the following possible disposal sites/methods: (a) sanitary landfills, (b) hazardous waste landfills, (c) sewer systems, (d) incineration, (e) recycle/reuse, and (f) chemical, physical, or biological treatment, including neutralization, oxidation, precipitation, and solidification. If you are unsure if a waste is hazardous, contact a local/state or regional EPA office, fire marshal's office, or state department of education.

What to Do in Case of an Accident

Although you may have put the proper precautions in place, accidents may still happen. In case of an accident you will need to act quickly and decisively. This means that you need to plan your actions ahead of time. Here are some general suggestions: If possible remove the hazard to prevent further injury; check the injured person to determine the severity of the injury; notify the principal and school nurse and if necessary call 911 or other appropriate medical personnel; have a properly trained person care for the injured person; make sure that a parent or guardian and/or a family physician has been notified; after the emergency has passed, record the relevant facts and obtain witness reports; and provide copies to the school principal and keep copies in your files.

If the accident involves a chemical in the eye, while holding the eyelids apart, flush the eye immediately and continuously with water for at least 15 minutes or until medical personnel arrive. If a contact lens is being worn, the water should flush it out. However, if the lens adheres to the eye, do not try to remove it. That is a job better left to a professional.

If the accident involves a person on fire, you may need assistance in getting the victim under the drench shower to douse the flames. If a shower is not available, drop and roll the victim and smother the flames in a flame-retardant blanket. But never wrap a standing victim in a blanket because this creates a "chimney" effect. For material fires, using an approved ABC fire extinguisher, remove the pin and approach the fire. When you are 5 to 6 feet away, start discharging the retardant making sure to smother, not scatter, the fire. Keep in mind that the extinguisher will operate at maximum effectiveness for only about 8–10 seconds. Use sand from a sand bucket to smother burning alkali metals.

Neutralize acid spills with baking soda (i.e., powered sodium hydrogen carbonate, sodium bicarbonate) and bases with vinegar (i.e., 5% acetic acid solution). Spread diatomaceous earth to absorb the neutralized spills. Then sweep up and dispose properly. For acid spills on skin, flush the skin with cold water from a faucet or a drench shower for at least 5 minutes. For base spills on skin, daub the skin with vinegar and obtain medical attention as soon as possible. For spills on clothing, drench with water and cut/remove the affected area of clothing as soon as possible to keep the chemical from reaching and/or staying in contact with the skin. Do not cover affected skin with bandages.

Wear gloves to clean up released body fluids, spilled pathogenic bacteria, or spilled DNA samples. A disinfectant, such as 5% Lysol or 10% Clorox bleach solution, should be poured on the spill area and worked toward the center with paper towels. The paper towels should then be placed in a biohazard bag for disposal. Contaminated glassware should be sterilized in an autoclave. In case of a mercury spill, cover droplets with sulfur to reduce volatility and then retrieve with an aspirator bulb or a mercury vacuum device.

Effective and Ethical Use of Organisms

Organizations such as the National Science Teachers Association (NSTA), the National Association of Biology Teachers (NABT), and the CSSS strongly support the use of organisms, both living and preserved, for educational purposes, and they caution against using less effective alternatives. Nevertheless, when using living organisms, some guidelines need to be kept in mind. Specifically on its Web site the NSTA recommends that teachers

- learn how to acquire, care for, and use animals so that both students and the animals stay safe and healthy during all activities.
- follow local, state, and national laws, policies, and regulations when using live organisms.
- integrate live organisms into the curriculum using sound pedagogy.
- develop activities that promote observation and comparison skills that instill in students an appreciation for the value of life and the importance of caring for animals responsibly.
- instruct students on safety precautions for handling live organisms and establish a plan for addressing such issues as allergies and fear of animals.
- develop and implement a plan for future care or disposition of animals at the conclusion of the study as well as during school breaks and summer vacations.
- espouse the importance of conducting procedures on animals that are not likely to cause pain, induce nutritional deficiencies, or expose them to parasites, hazardous/toxic chemicals, or radiation.

- shelter animals when the classroom is being cleaned with chemical cleaners or sprayed with pesticides and during other times when potentially harmful chemicals are being used.
- refrain from releasing animals into a nonindigenous environment.

In addition to these general recommendations, Table 8.3 lists specific precautions to be taken in the classroom for using and handling both live animals and plants. Field trip safety precautions will be discussed in the next chapter when we take up the use of classroom demonstrations, lectures, and discussions along with field trips to enhance student inquiry.

TABLE 8.3   *Precautions When Using Organisms*

Before and/or while living animals are used in the classroom:
- Inquire beforehand about student allergies to specific animals.
- Allow students to touch/handle animals only after they receive proper directions and/or demonstrations.
- Immediately report animal bites or scratches to the principal and school nurse.
- Have a veterinarian evaluate any animal that dies unexpectedly.
- Do not depose of fecal matter in sinks or with commonly used equipment.
- Do not use wild mammals. Instead, use mammals from pet suppliers.
- Do not bring poisonous animals to the classroom.
- Do not allow students to tease animals or touch animals to their mouths.

Before and/or while living plants are used in the classroom:
- Inquire beforehand about student allergies to specific plants.
- Do not bring poisonous or allergy-producing plants to the classroom.
- Do not burn plants that contain allergy-causing oils (e.g., poison ivy).
- Make a clear distinction between edible and non-edible plants.

Summary

- Corporate pressure exists to infuse new technologies in the classroom based largely on the profit motive. In spite of this pressure, most science educators believe that at best technology can support, but not supplant, classroom inquiry. There are at least five ways in which new technologies can help in (1) finding out, (2) composing, (3) analyzing, (4) communicating, and (5) visualizing/simulating.

- Labs play a central role in classroom inquiry. They provide the means for student exploration. They provide the primary context in which new terms are introduced. They often provide the contexts in which new concepts can be applied to broaden and deepen their meanings. And they should precede, not follow, textbook and supplemental readings.

- It is imperative that students are knowledgeable of school safety issues and procedures. You need to establish that you have acted reasonably and responsibly by (a) having each student and his or her parents or guardians sign a safety contract; (b) keeping a record of safety discussions with your students; (c) hanging safety posters; (d) adopting a firm goggle policy; and (e) giving students who break lab rules safety "tickets."

- Professional organizations strongly support the use of organisms, both living and preserved, for educational purposes, and they caution against using less effective alternatives. Nevertheless, when using organisms, precautions need to be taken, such as avoidance of poisonous animals and plants and demonstration of proper handling and disposal.

Application Questions/Activities

1. Select an example lesson. Review the 25 characteristics of effective science instruction listed in Chapter 7 and describe specifically how they will be incorporated into the lesson. Prepare a set of notes that you can use to teach it (do not modify the prepared lesson plan unless you are very sure that your modification(s) will improve the lesson—this is no time to be creative—you will have plenty of time for that later). What safety precautions should be taken before and during the lesson? How will you alert students to these precautions? Now teach the lesson to a group of peers, a small group of high school students, or an entire class. At the conclusion of the lesson have your peers offer feedback and suggestions for improvement. Or if you teach the lesson to high school students make sure that one or more of your peers attend the lesson so that he, she, or they can offer feedback. While listening to the feedback, make sure not to be too "thin skinned." Remember that we all make mistakes and that it takes lots of practice and reflectivity to develop teaching expertise.

2. Select a technological device for classroom use. Describe how it will be used to support classroom inquiry, rather than replace it. What, if anything, can you do to make sure that teaching students how to use the technology does not detract from the presumed value of its use?

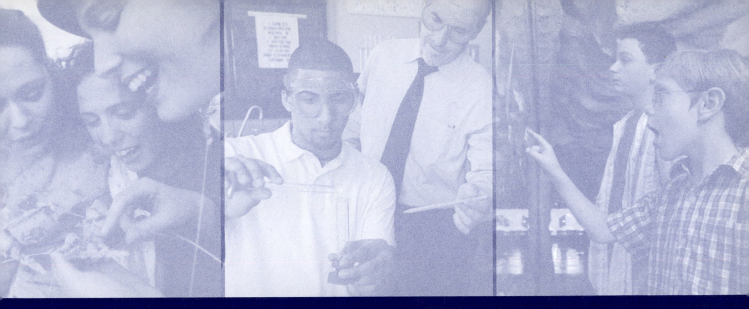

PART IV
Instructional Strategies

Chapter 9

DEMONSTRATIONS, LECTURES, DISCUSSIONS, AND FIELD TRIPS

Hands-on, minds-on laboratory activities lie at the heart of classroom inquiry. Nevertheless, if properly designed, demonstrations, mini lectures, discussions, and field trips can be used to enrich and expand student inquiry. The purpose of this chapter is to help you design and carry out these activities effectively. We will start with demonstrations.

DEMONSTRATIONS

Some Options

Consider some demonstration options that you might use to begin a unit on air pressure. For each option you first place two thick books on a table about 5 inches apart. You then lay an 8.5- by 11-inch

During field trips several puzzling observations can be made, and several hypotheses can be generated.

APPLICABLE NSES STANDARDS

Standard B Science teachers guide and facilitate learning. In doing so, they

- Orchestrate discourse among students about scientific ideas.

- Challenge students to accept and share responsibility for their own learning.

- Recognize and respond to student diversity and encourage all students to participate fully in learning.

(Continued)

(Continued)

Standard D Science teachers design and manage learning environments that provide students with the time, space, and resources needed for learning. In doing so, they

■ Identify and use resources outside of the school.

piece of paper on the books so that it spans the space between them. Please rank the following four options in terms of their effectiveness in engaging the students in the topic. Also provide reasons for your ranking:

(a) Rapidly blow air under the paper and note that the paper bends down between the two books. Then ask students for some alternative explanations for why the paper bent down.

(b) Tell students that you are going to rapidly blow air under the paper and ask them to predict what they think will happen. Once students have made some predictions, ask them why they made those predictions. Then blow under the paper and observe what happens. Next have students discuss the results in terms of their predictions and reasons.

(c) Tell students that you are going to rapidly blow air under the paper and ask them to predict what they think will happen. Once students have made some predictions, you then blow under the paper and observe what happens. Then explain that the paper bent down because blowing reduced the lower air pressure so the greater upper air pressure pushed down.

(d) Rapidly blow air under the paper and note that the paper bends down between the two books. Then explain that the paper bent down because blowing reduced the lower air pressure so the greater upper air pressure pushed down.

Crouch, Fagen, Callen, and Mazur (2004) conducted a study that compared the effectiveness of similar options in a physics course. Demonstrations included colliding a rubber ball and a putty ball with a bowling pin to see which ball knocked the pin over, comparing tension on a string when fixed to a wall at one end versus when attached to weights at both ends, and comparing the time of travel for balls on two tracks that have the same starting and end points but only one of which has a dip in the middle. Interestingly, they found that option (b) was the most effective. Option (d) was the worst. In fact, students who experienced option (d) did no better in terms of understanding than control students who saw none of the demonstrations. How would you rank options (a) and (c)? Why?

Selecting Demonstrations

Demonstrations can contribute to student inquiry if used at the right time in the right way. For example, as suggested above, they can be used during the engagement phase of learning cycles to raise questions and spark student interest, particularly if they present unexpected results. Demonstrations can also be used during term introduction to help explicate new concepts. And they can be used during concept application to extend student understanding to new contexts. Demonstrations can even be used to help assess student understanding.

Experienced teachers have developed and published several excellent demonstrations. Unfortunately, many of these published demonstrations merely describe without explaining the concepts behind them or suggesting effective ways of presentation. Consequently many do little more than entertain. To help make demonstrations more effective Simanek (2003) suggests asking the following six questions prior to selecting a demonstration: (1) Does the demonstration fit into your course story line? (2) Is the demonstration important enough to justify building a story line around it? (3) Does the demonstration clearly illustrate a phenomenon or help explicate new concepts? (If too many interacting concepts affect the outcome you should select a "cleaner" demonstration.) (4) Can the demonstrated concepts be understood at the level of the course? (If not, don't use them.) (5) Do you fully understand the demonstration? (If not, don't use it.) And (6) Is the demonstration being conducted for entertainment or because the concepts behind it need demonstrating? Also keep in mind that demonstrations should not take the place of student explorations. Obviously conducting a demonstration requires only one "setup" while explorations require enough materials for each group of students. Nevertheless, in most cases the added cost of getting materials into students' hands is well worth the price in terms of increased motivation and learning.

Practicing the Demonstration

Simanek (2003) also suggests practicing the demonstration until you have it perfected. You can even present it to a critical observer who can tell you what points are not clear and what details of explanation you have omitted. Also make sure that you know what the demonstration demonstrates—not what you intend it to demonstrate. Next prepare your students. Show them the apparatus, describe what you intend to do before you do it, and indicate what they should watch for. Ask students to predict in advance what will happen. And don't proceed until at least some students have provided explanations (i.e., hypotheses) for their predictions. Only when you have made the situation clear and have the students' attention should you conduct the demonstration. Then analyze the results. Discuss which student predictions and hypotheses were supported and which were contradicted. Repeat the demonstration again during the discussion and be prepared to test additional student hypotheses by varying the demonstration or by making some additional measurements.

Showmanship Tips

Lastly, Simanek (2003) offers several showmanship tips that will help you effectively pull off the demonstration. These include using an apparatus large enough for students to see clearly. When something can be seen only in a narrow range of angles, stand to one side so the audience subtends a smaller angle from your position or show it from different angles if necessary so no one is cheated. If necessary, stand back in the classroom to judge the effect. And don't ask students to trust a measurement that they can't see. For electrical experiments you might consider projection analog scales or projection digital meters. Avoid using electronic balances. Instead use visible mechanical ones. Often a visual indication of which direction something moves is all that is needed.

The use of colors and plenty of light can enhance visibility and help distinguish one thing from another. Use paper sheets that come in many bright colors as do ping-pong balls and golf balls. Use a selection of unpatterned tablecloths in attractive colors. Equipment stands out much better against them. White or black string can be replaced with colored kite string, mason's cord (a hardware store item), or rug maker's cord. You may want to add food coloring to water to make it more visible. Make sure, however, to tell students that you have added food coloring so they won't think it is something other than water. Lastly, conduct the demonstration in a well-lighted classroom and use sensory clues. For example, to indicate that something is rigid, tap it on the table so students can hear it or yank a string to show it doesn't stretch.

LECTURES

Although lectures are a frequent means of college instruction, evidence indicates that they are a poor way to teach. For example, when students are interviewed a day or two after a lecture, they often recall only insignificant details. Interviewing students periodically during lectures suggests why this is so. Interviews reveal that after an initial settling-in period of about 5 minutes, students pay attention well for only the next 5 minutes or so. Then confusion and boredom set in, and attention falls off rapidly, only to pick up again near the end of the lecture when students are somewhat revived by the thought that the lecture will soon be over. Even lectures in medical schools have a poor reputation. For example, Edlich (1993) concluded that medical lectures are outdated and ineffective. Similarly, McIntosh (1996) noted that most are frequently a one-way process unaccompanied by discussion, questioning, or immediate practice.

Why then are lectures so commonly used in higher education? The answer is simple. They are relatively inexpensive because one professor can "teach" as many as 350 tuition-paying students all at once. Fortunately, economics do not compel secondary school teachers to do the same. Nevertheless, some secondary teachers, perhaps thinking that they should do unto their students what their professors did unto them, lecture longer and far more often than they should.

This is not to say that lectures, at least relatively brief interactive ones, can never be useful. In fact, if redefined as "brief occasions in which you address the entire class at the appropriate time using interactive techniques," then lectures can become an effective component of inquiry instruction. More specifically, brief interactive lectures can help arouse interest in a topic, or they can provide needed background information during the engagement phase. They can introduce new concepts during concept introduction. And they can extend introduced concepts to new contexts during concept application.

Characteristics of Effective Lectures

Effective lectures are characterized by teacher and student questions, a shared responsibility for sense making, small-group problem-solving activities, a variety of supporting media, and limited note taking. In contrast, ineffective lectures are typically characterized by little or no interaction and few, if any, teacher or student questions. Instead, students depend on teachers for all information, and typically there are no student activities, no supporting media, and extensive note taking. In short, during ineffective lectures teachers stand behind a lectern and talk.

Sullivan and McIntosh (1996) suggest several techniques to make lectures more interactive and effective. These include beginning with an introduction that captures students' interest and attention, communicating on a personal level, and maintaining eye contact to provide you with feedback on how well students understand. You should also communicate a caring attitude and exhibit enthusiasm by smiling, by moving around the room, and by gesturing with your hands and arms. And try to display a sense of humor, using humorous transparencies or slides and/or topic-related stories. Also make sure to avoid the use of slang or repetitive words, phrases, or gestures that become distracting. Avoid the use of fillers (e.g., "and um," "you know").

As mentioned, you should use a variety of audiovisuals and ask a number of well-thought-out questions targeting a divergent question to specific students. Use students' names when asking and answering questions, if possible, as name recognition is a powerful motivator. And don't forget to encourage student questions by providing positive feedback when students ask questions, answer questions, or make comments. Praise creates a positive climate and encourages student participation. Repeat students' questions and answers to ensure that all students hear the discussion. You can answer student questions directly, ask students a different related question, or offer the question to another student. But make sure to avoid a questioning pattern. Always asking and answering questions in the same way undermines effectiveness. Lastly, make smooth transitions between parts of the lecture (e.g., a brief overview of the next topic, a review of the agenda between topics, a change of media, a summary before a new topic, or an activity).

Planning Interactive Lectures

Now that you have some idea what is involved in delivering good interactive lectures, let's briefly consider how they should be planned. You will need to consider a number of factors including lecture notes, lecture length, room configuration, media use, and small-group discussions and activities.

Prepare careful lecture notes in outline form. You can prepare your outline on sheets of paper, note cards, overhead transparencies, flipchart pages, slides, or computer-based projections (e.g., PowerPoint). Using text rather than an outline encourages you to read the text, which quickly results in student disinterest, boredom, and even disruptiveness. The outline will help you stay on topic, introduce the main points, glance at a specific point, and quickly return attention to the students. Most important, relax and focus on delivery instead of worrying about what point to make next.

How long should you lecture? By analyzing videotaped medical school lectures, Arredondo, Busch, Douglas, and Petrelli (1994) set the recommended lecture time at no more than 45 minutes, including approximately 15 minutes devoted to audience interaction—and they are talking about medical students! After analyzing medical lectures, P. Renner (1993) recommended that lectures last no longer than 30 minutes. Consequently, when working with secondary school students you should limit your lecture time even more. For example, your remarks during the engagement phase of learning cycles should last no longer than 5 minutes. Remarks during term introduction can last up to about 20 minutes, but they should include considerable questioning and student interaction.

With regard to room configuration, a room with tables arranged in a U shape and chairs for 20–24 students is ideal as it allows you to interact extensively with students and use a variety of small-group methods and media. If you ever have to lecture to a considerably larger group, a room with 100 seats arranged theater-style with an aisle down the middle allows you to move up and down the aisle and interact with students. You can also ask students to turn their chairs around to form small discussion groups. A lecture room with a sloped floor and 200 anchored seats makes it difficult to divide students into small groups. You can still, however, ask students to turn to their neighbor to discuss a question, generate some hypotheses, or solve a problem. Most large lecture rooms are equipped for the use of slides, overhead transparencies, video, and computer-based projections. To develop an effective lecture, you will need to learn to use these media effectively.

What to Do During Each Part of the Lecture

A key to delivering an effective lecture is to divide it into parts and use a variety of techniques in each part. The three main parts of a lecture are the introduction, the body, and the summary. The introduction should capture student attention and interest. Sullivan and Wircenski (1996) suggest a number of ways of spicing up your introduction, including asking for a show of hands in response to a general question, using an interesting or a famous quote, relating the topic to previously introduced content or to a real-life experience, using a case study or problem-solving activity, using videotape or other media, showing an appropriate cartoon, making a provocative statement to encourage discussion, conducting a demonstration, using a game or role play, or sharing a personal experience.

Once you have the students' attention and interest, make a smooth transition to the lecture body, which contains the core of the lecture information. Here the use of brainstorming, discussions, problem-solving activities, case studies, and games can be effective. Make sure to ask and encourage lots of questions. Finally move on to the lecture summary. The summary should briefly address only the main points. You may ask students for questions, which gives them a chance to clarify their understanding. Or you can ask them questions, which gives you a check on their understanding. You may also use a transparency, slide, or flipchart to briefly review the main points.

Table 9.1 contains a checklist to help plan, evaluate, and improve your lectures. The checklist can also be used to evaluate up to five of your own videotaped lectures or for a colleague to observe and evaluate your lectures.

TABLE 9.1   Lecture Skills Checklist

Lecture Skills	Lecture Number				
	1	2	3	4	5
Preparation Skills					
Selected lecture methods in advance.					
Prepared lecture notes in advance.					
Prepared audiovisuals in advance.					
Planned effective techniques to introduce the lecture.					
Arranged room appropriately.					
Verbal Presentation Skills					
Projected voice (changed pitch, tone and volume).					
Avoided fillers ("and um," "you know," etc.).					
Used many examples.					
Provided praise and reinforcement.					
Accepted student ideas and suggestions.					
Used appropriate humor.					
Nonverbal Presentation Skills					
Maintained eye contact.					
Maintained positive facial expressions.					
Gestured with hands and arms.					
Maintained good posture.					
Moved around the room with energy.					
Followed lecture notes.					

For each skill, use the following rating scale to indicate the level of performance:

NO: Skill not observed in this lecture.

NA: Skill not applicable to this lecture.

1: Cannot perform this skill and requires extensive practice.

2: Can perform this skill but requires additional practice.

3: Competent at this skill and requires no additional practice.

(Continued)

TABLE 9.1 (Continued)

Lecture Skills	Lecture Number				
	1	2	3	4	5
Questioning Skills					
Asked questions at varying levels of difficulty.					
Asked questions to group.					
Asked questions to individual students.					
Involved all students (if possible).					
Repeated student responses and questions.					
Provided positive reinforcement.					
Audiovisual Skills					
Used presentation media correctly.					
Summarizing Skills					
Asked for questions.					
Asked questions.					
Used media to review main points.					

For each skill, use the following rating scale to indicate the level of performance:

NO: Skill not observed in this lecture.

NA: Skill not applicable to this lecture.

1: Cannot perform this skill and requires extensive practice.

2: Can perform this skill but requires additional practice.

3: Competent at this skill and requires no additional practice.

DISCUSSIONS

Virtues of Good Discussions

When I first started teaching I had an intuitive sense that discussions were worthwhile. In fact Cavanaugh (2001) cites several virtues of good classroom discussions. These include sharing observations and ideas, gaining insights from diverse points of view, increasing student communication and argumentative skills, increasing topic connection and student ownership, increasing awareness of and tolerance for ambiguity and complexity, increasing awareness of hidden and sometimes incorrect assumptions, encouraging attentive respectful listening, encouraging respect for diverse opinions, developing the capacity for clear communication of ideas and meanings, developing habits of collaborative learning, developing skills of synthesis and evaluation, and affirming students' role as cocreators of knowledge.

Keys to Good Discussions

In spite of these considerable virtues, as a new teacher I had difficulty getting students to pay much attention to me—not to mention to discuss anything worthwhile. No matter how hard or what I tried, nothing seemed to work. Fortunately at that time I had the habit of leaving my classroom door open, and so did the experienced teacher across the hall. So periodically I would look into his classroom to see what was going on. Amazingly, whenever he was holding a discussion, his students all seemed engaged and paying attention to what he or to what each other were saying. How in the world did he get his students so involved? Surely his students were no different from mine, yet somehow his students were sharing ideas, listening to each other, and participating while mine were simply giving me blank stares and silence. What was his secret?

After reading about inquiry instruction in the previous chapters you may already have figured out the answer. It turned out that his secret was that he never asked his students to discuss a topic or listen to him until *after* they had participated in a hands-on exploration of the topic to be discussed. It turns out that once students have explored a topic and have shared an experience, they are more than willing to share their thoughts and listen to those of others about what has been discovered and what it might mean. So his secret was this: *Explore first; discuss second!*

In addition to holding discussions only *after* student explorations, discussions can be improved by making certain that students know at the outset that they are expected to be full participants. For example, Cavanaugh (2001) introduces the following discussion guidelines given to each student on the first day of class:

You are expected to contribute to the quality of classroom discussions. Among other things, participation will allow you to test and improve your ability to convince peers that you have approached questions and problems thoughtfully and that your approach will help achieve the desired result. Criteria used to measure effective class participation include:

1. Is your comment clear and relevant?
2. Do you support your comment with evidence and a well-reasoned argument?
3. Do you explore the implications and importance of your comment and those of others?
4. Is your comment insightful? Does it broaden the discussion and/or clarify an issue?
5. Is your comment complete and concise?

An average comment satisfies 1 and some of 2. A good comment satisfies 1–3. An excellent comment satisfies 1–5. Class participation represents a significant component of your grade (30%). When asked a question, you are not allowed to say "I don't know." You are not required to know, but you are expected to think. So if asked a question and you don't know the answer, you are responsible to think of a possibility, to guess, to speculate, and to wonder aloud.

Thus, it helps to make sure that the students know in advance that they all need to be involved. And to keep them all involved you should resist responding to student comments yourself. Instead, randomly ask students, by name, to respond. And keep in mind that a good discussion is based on thoughtful, deliberative, and well-reasoned responses, rather than on intuitive, instantaneous, and gut-level reactions. So become comfortable with silences and be willing to pause for several seconds while students formulate thoughtful responses. In other words, make sure to use wait-time I and wait-time II. Also remember to express interest in their comments by encouraging them to elaborate on their comments, by asking students to respond to each other's comments, by explaining a link between the comments of two students, by making a contribution that builds on a student's comment, by paraphrasing a student's comment, and lastly by summarizing several comments.

Establishing eye contact is also important as it opens a communication channel and selects a specific student for a turn to speak. Breaking eye contact during a student's turn and scanning the class helps distribute the student's comments throughout the class. Your scanning eyes also signal students that they should be paying attention to the speaker. Regular scanning keeps students engaged and can provide you with important feedback. In short, scanning is a surveillance tool. If you are making eye contact with *all* the students, they are more likely to stay involved—and if they are not involved, you will know it immediately.

Lastly, you might want to try assigning the following conversational roles to specific students to improve discussions:

1. *Problem, dilemma, or theme poser:* Introduces the topic of conversation

2. *Reflective analyst:* Records the conversation's flow, offering a periodic summary

3. *Scrounger:* Listens for suggestions and needs, records them, and reviews them at the end of the discussion so the group may decide on an action plan

4. *Devil's advocate:* Expresses a contrary view to group consensus

5. *Detective:* Listens for unexplored biases and brings attention to them

6. *Theme spotter:* Identifies themes needing time at the next session

7. *Umpire:* Listens for personal judgments in order to enforce ground rules (see below)

Classroom arrangement is also important when planning discussions. For example, arranging desks in a circle or horseshoe prevents students from hiding in corners or behind others. These arrangements also improve communication by allowing students to see each other's faces and hear each other's responses. They also allow you easier access to students. Decreasing the distance between you and your students is important as it establishes and narrows a communication channel. Moving toward the speaker is a clear signal that you are interested in what a student is saying and that others should be listening too. Moving away from a speaker widens the communication channel. As you back up, the audience grows as more students can move into the speaker's gaze. Also working from among or even behind students can lessen the threat from the teacher. And sitting in a student desk as part of the circle signals that you want to be *a part of* the discussion rather than *apart from* it.

Discussion Formats

Cavanaugh (2001) and Johnson and Johnson (2003) list several formats that are available for discussions and small-group work. Those listed by Johnson and Johnson are called **cooperative learning** formats as they explicitly include an element of peer teaching and both personal and group accountability. Cooperative learning formats include

Think-Pair-Share. The teacher poses questions and/or problems. Students are then given a set time period to individually think of a response. They then pair up to discuss their thoughts and perhaps reach consensus. Lastly, the teacher asks student pairs to share their thoughts with the entire class.

Brainstorming. Student groups are given time to generate alternative hypotheses to a posed causal question. Students then offer hypotheses one at a time, and the teacher (or another leader) records all hypotheses on a chalkboard or poster. No criticism or elaboration is allowed until the brainstorming period ends.

Circle of Voices. Students form groups of five. Students then have 3 minutes of silent time to consider the topic. Next each student has 3 minutes to discuss the topic with others in the group. Group members may react to the comments expressed.

Posted Dialogues. Groups summarize their conversations on large sheets of newsprint, transparencies, or whiteboards. Students then walk about the room reading all the responses and adding comments.

Rotating Stations. Each group starts at a station where students have 10 minutes to discuss a provocative issue and record their ideas on newsprint or a whiteboard. When time is up, the groups move to new stations where they continue their discussion based on ideas recorded by the previous group. Rotations continue every 10 minutes until each group has visited each station.

Snowballing. Students individually respond to a question or an issue. They then create progressively larger conversational groups by doubling the group every few minutes until everyone reconvenes in one large group.

Three-Step Interviews. The class is divided into four-member groups, each with an A-B pair and a C-D pair. During step 1, A interviews B, and C interviews D. During step 2, B interviews A, and D interviews C. During step 3, each student shares information with others in the group of four.

Numbered Heads Together. Each student in a four-person group is numbered from 1 to 4. The teacher poses a question, an issue, or a problem. Students discuss within the group and prepare a response. The teacher then calls on students by number to represent their group.

Roundtable. The teacher poses a divergent question or gives each group a worksheet. The group has only one piece of paper or worksheet and perhaps only one pen. A student writes down one response, says it aloud, and then passes the paper or worksheet to the person on the left. The process continues in this way.

Generating Truth Statements. Groups of four students create three endings to open-ended statements (e.g., "It is true of energy that . . ."). They then choose one or more to share with the class.

Workshops. Workshops are typically used to introduce and discuss new skills. Time is allotted for students to work on and/or prepare for a specific task. You can answer questions or work with students during that time.

Critical Debate. Identify a contentious issue and frame the issue as a debate motion. Ask students to select a group to draft either supporting or opposing arguments. Once students have selected the group they wish to join, announce that those who have selected the supporting group will draft arguments to oppose the motion, and vice versa. After argument preparation, both groups choose a student to present their case. After these initial presentations, both groups reconvene to draft rebuttal arguments and again choose a student to present them. Following the debate, the teacher holds a discussion focusing on the quality of student arguments and how it felt to argue against positions students were committed to. If you like, students can be asked to write a follow-up paper reflecting on the debate.

Jigsaw. Generate a short list of topics. Each student then becomes an "expert" on one topic, first by him- or herself and then in discussion with other experts. Next, each expert helps non-experts become experts. For example, a class of 25 students works on five topics. Each student selects one topic and develops the required expertise before and/or during class time. Students who have selected the same topic gather in groups of five to discuss and compare what they have learned. When these discussions are over, new groups of five are formed including an expert for each of the five topics. The experts then lead a discussion of their topic. These discussions end when all group members think they understand all of the topics. The jigsaw may end there, or it may end following a whole-class summary.

Concluding and Evaluating Discussions

Regardless of the discussion format, at the end of a discussion you should ask for final comments, summarize progress, and/or ask for ideas about how students could continue the inquiry. Summary questions might include the following: Have students debated and refuted a particular statement or position? Have they effectively tackled and exposed "what's wrong" speeches, articles, or stories that include incorrect science content and/or faulty arguments? Have they taken the role of teacher in which they present their ideas and arguments on a whiteboard, on the class board, on an overhead, or perhaps using a PowerPoint presentation? These sorts of activities build accountability and foster a student-centered class.

You might also have students write reflections or exit journal notes to process their experience. And don't forget to evaluate the discussion by asking whether or not (a) the discussion was effectively initiated, (b) the educational objectives were achieved, (c) there was equitable student participation, and (d) there were high-quality student responses. The bottom line is that regardless of the particular format used, you want discussions to foster higher-order thinking and reflectivity.

FIELD TRIPS

In addition to demonstrations, brief interactive lectures, and discussions, field trips can foster inquiry. Student motivation and excitement are usually high during field trips. Therefore students are apt to learn and retain more than they will in the classroom. Likewise many phenomena can be explored in the field that simply can't be brought into the classroom. In terms of learning cycles, fieldwork can serve as the exploration phase with term introduction and application taking place back in the classroom. In some instances the first two phases, or perhaps even the initial applications, can take place in the field.

Some Alternative Approaches to Fieldwork

To obtain a better sense of how fieldwork can promote student inquiry, here are four alternative approaches to initiating fieldwork. Start by ranking them in terms of how you perceive their effectiveness at provoking student thinking and self-regulation. Use 1 for most effective and 4 for least effective. My comments will follow.

(a) Provide students with rulers. Have them run a transect from the upper to the lower zone in the intertidal area and measure and record shell sizes of *Tegula funebralis* snails (a common West Coast snail) found along the transect. Ask them to plot size-versus-frequency graphs for all the snails measured.

(b) Provide students with rulers, quadrats, and a map of the intertidal area. Ask them to measure and record *Tegula* shell sizes and determine the density of the snails from three locations in the intertidal area—the lower, middle, and upper zones. Then ask them to search for quantitative relationships among the variables and to explain these relationships in light of other observations and ecological concepts.

(c) Explain to students that interspecific competition affects population characteristics of many species. For example, the snail *Tegula funebralis* is common in the intertidal area. The older snails (larger ones) are found in the lower zone while the younger snails (smaller ones) live in the upper zone. Tell students this is because their food source (algae) is more abundant in the lower zone. However, the starfish *Pisaster* that preys upon them lives in the lower zone. Because the smaller snails are too slow to escape the starfish, they must remain in the upper zone. Now have your students go to the intertidal area and collect data to verify that what you have explained is correct.

(d) Provide students with rulers, thermometers, identification keys, quadrats, and a map of the intertidal area. Ask them to select an abundant population in the area, identify interesting variables with respect to individual organisms and the population's distribution, and search for quantitative relationships among these variables.

Because of their openness procedures (b) and (d) are the most likely ways to initiate student thinking and self-regulation. Procedure (d) may be more effective than (b) for the more advanced students in that it is more open and allows students an opportunity to examine interesting phenomena that you may not have anticipated. However, this procedure affords little guidance and may not be as effective as the somewhat more structured approach in

(b) for concrete operational students. The choice of openness or structure depends on the reasoning skills of your students and their past experiences with inquiry-based instruction.

Procedure (a) provides firsthand experience. However, as presented, it is not likely to initiate student reasoning and self-regulation due to its directive and "cookbook" nature. Self-regulation could, however, be initiated if the plotted data raised some questions relative to previous partial understandings. Procedure (c) unfortunately is very much like the kind of labs and fieldwork many teachers conduct. Because students already know what the data are supposed to show, no reasoning, no self-regulation, and no intellectual development is likely to occur. Further, procedure (c) encourages reliance on authority rather than on evidence and self-initiative; thus it is contradictory to the nature of science.

A Field Trip Checklist and Some Precautions

As mentioned, field trips can serve a vital purpose in the curriculum in terms of both motivation and lasting learning. Just think back on your own experiences. Do you remember the field trips you took? Most likely you do. Do you remember the lectures you sat through? Most likely you do not. Nevertheless, to make the most of fieldwork, you will not only need a well-thought-out field trip plan, but you will also need to take care of some vital administrative details. To help make sure that nothing is overlooked, read through and check off each item listed in Table 9.2 before each and every trip. Also Table 9.3 lists some important field trip precautions that should not be overlooked.

TABLE 9.2   A Checklist of Important Items Prior to Taking a Field Trip

———— Permission granted by school administration

———— Arrangements made with field site personnel

———— Field site fees determined and method of payment determined

———— Departure and return dates/times and locations set

———— Transportation arranged

———— Parent/guardian consent forms prepared and signed

———— Qualified chaperones obtained

———— List of participating students made (one left with principal)

———— Emergency medical forms for students who require them obtained

———— Cellular/emergency phone obtained

———— Lunch and/or snacks prepared

———— Special clothing obtained (e.g., hats, shoes)

———— Special equipment obtained (e.g., pencils/pens, binoculars, thermometers, paper, clipboards)

———— Location of lavatory facilities determined

Source: Chiappetta & Koballa, 2002.

TABLE 9.3   Field Trip Precautions

- Inform students of any hazardous areas they should avoid or near which they should exhibit extra caution.
- Inform students of appropriate water and clothing to bring and to wear—including footwear and hats.
- Caution students about any possible poisonous or hazardous plants (e.g., cacti) and instruct them in plant identification.
- Warn students not to stick hands into crevasses or to pick up reptiles and/or dead organisms.
- Warn students about eating plants or plant parts unless identified as edible by an expert.

Source: From *Science & Safety: Making the Connection*, by the Council of State Science Supervisors (n.d.), available at http://www.csss-science.org/downloads/scisafe.pdf.

Summary

- Demonstrations can contribute to student inquiry and learning if used during the engagement phase of learning cycles. They can also be used during term introduction to help explicate new concepts. And they can be used during concept application to extend student understanding. Several techniques exist to help you plan and carry out effective demonstrations.

- Standard lectures are a poor way to teach. Nevertheless, relatively brief interactive "lectures" can become an effective component of inquiry instruction to help arouse interest in a topic or provide needed background information, to introduce new concepts, or to extend introduced concepts to new contexts.

- Several techniques exist to help you plan and carry out brief lectures in a more interactive and effective way.

- Classroom discussions have many virtues. The secret to good discussions is explore first; discuss second.

- Several formats exist for holding effective discussions. Regardless of the format used, you should evaluate discussions by asking for final comments or for student-written reflections.

- Field trips can also foster inquiry where student motivation is usually high and students are apt to learn and retain more than in the classroom. Good field trips, like good classroom inquiries, should allow for a variety of paths of inquiry.

Key Term

cooperative learning

Application Questions/Activities

1. Consult a recent publication such as *Journal of Chemical Education, The Physics Teacher, The American Biology Teacher,* or *Journal of Geoscience Education* for an article describing a classroom demonstration. Briefly describe the demonstration and answer the following questions:

   (a) What puzzling observation(s) will be demonstrated?

   (b) What causal question(s) will be raised?

   (c) What predictions and hypotheses are students likely to generate?

   (d) How can student hypotheses be tested?

   (e) What concept(s) is demonstrated, and how/when will you introduce the related scientific term(s)?

2. Select an inquiry-based lesson and then select a discussion format that can be used during the term introduction or application phase. What format did you select, and how will it be used? Why did you select that particular format? How will you try to ensure all students will be involved in the discussion?

3. Select an inquiry-based lesson and plan a brief interactive "lecture" that you can use during the term introduction phase. What specific divergent and/or convergent questions will you raise, and in what order will you raise them? What student answers do you expect? How will you respond to each student answer? What new terms will you introduce? Explain how the term or terms introduced relate to the preceding exploration activity.

4. Suppose you are taking students on a field trip to explore an out-of-doors location. Tell us where you will go. Describe the location and how you will use it to provoke student inquiry. What exploration activity will students engage in? What term introduction and application activities will follow (in the field or later in the classroom)? What modifications will you make for students in wheelchairs, for students with visual impairments, for students with hearing impairments, and for gifted students? What specific rules and procedures will you propose to help ensure student safety while on the field trip? How and when will you inform students of those rules/procedures? What, if any, other precautions will you take in case of an accident?

Chapter 10

MANAGING THE INQUIRY CLASSROOM

Good lesson plans help but do not ensure that things run smoothly. Effective teaching requires classroom management skills that take time and practice to develop. Invariably, problems arise along the way. After considering general classroom rules, this chapter addresses classroom management problems and how with practice and experience they can be eliminated altogether or at least reduced to minor irritants. Lastly, an instrument called the Science Management Scale is introduced. Use of this scale will allow you to measure and improve your management skills.

As before, let's start by considering some options. Suppose your students have dissected various types of flowers and have just posted their dissection drawings on the board for discussion.

Good inquiry teachers provide helpful hints and pose challenging questions.

APPLICABLE NSES STANDARDS

Standard B Science teachers guide and facilitate learning. In doing so, they

■ Focus and support inquiries while interacting with students.

■ Orchestrate discourse among students about scientific ideas.

■ Challenge students to accept and share responsibility for their own learning.

(Continued)

(Continued)

- Recognize and respond to student diversity and encourage all students to participate fully in learning.

- Encourage and model the skills of scientific inquiry, as well as curiosity, openness to new ideas and data, and skepticism that characterize science.

Standard D Science teachers design and manage learning environments that provide students with the time, space, and resources needed for learning. In doing so, they

- Structure the time available so that students are able to engage in extended investigations.

- Create a flexible and supportive setting for student inquiry.

- Make science tools, materials, media, and technological resources available to students.

- Engage students in designing the learning environment.

Standard E Science teachers develop communities of learners that reflect the intellectual rigor of scientific inquiry and the attitudes and social values conducive to learning. In doing so, they

- Display and demand respect for the diverse ideas, skills, and experiences of all students.

- Enable students to have a significant voice in decisions about the content and context of their work and require students to take responsibility for the learning of all members of the community.

- Nurture collaboration among students.

- Structure and facilitate ongoing formal and informal discussion based on a shared understanding of the rules of scientific discourse.

- Model and emphasize the skills, attitudes, and values of scientific inquiry.

Please rank the following options in terms of the most effective way to proceed. Also provide reasons for your ranking:

(a) Ask students to look at the drawings and try to identify common structures. Then call on a specific student by name to report what he or she has found.

(b) Call on a specific student by name and ask him or her to look at the drawings and identify common structures.

(c) Ask students to look at all of the drawings and try to identify common structures. Then ask students to raise their hands when they have something to report. Call on a student who has raised his or her hand.

(d) Look over the drawings and point out common structures to the class.

If possible, discuss your ranking and reasons with your classmates and/or your instructor; then read on.

Classroom Rules and Procedures

General Rules

You can always ease up as the school year progresses, but it is nearly impossible to enforce new rules after the first few weeks have passed. Thus, before classes start you need to give careful thought to which rules you really need. Consistency is a key. So do not set any rule that you do not intend to enforce. In general, rules should be few in number and should be fair, understandable, and workable. For example, here are six that should work:

1. Bring all needed materials to class.

2. Be seated and ready to work when the bell rings.

3. Respect and be polite to others.

4. Listen and remain seated while someone else is addressing the class.

5. Respect other people's property.

6. Obey all school rules.

Inquiry lessons often involve lab materials, so you also need to have a cleanup policy in place. You might want to add a rule stating that students will not be dismissed until all lab materials are back in their proper place and the lab tables and desks are clean and arranged properly.

Management Problems

Regardless of having good rules in place, some classroom management problems are inevitable. For example, during a recent semester, several new biology teachers taught several inquiry lessons. At the semester's end, the teachers were asked to generate a list of problems they experienced and to rank them in terms of their severity. The problems and their severity appear in Table 10.1. As you can see, 14 problems were identified ranging from lack of student motivation and participation, which ranked as a serious problem, to student tardiness, which ranked as a slight problem. The next several sections discuss ways of solving these problems.

TABLE 10.1   Some Classroom Management Problems

Serious Problem

1. Some students lack motivation and do not participate enough.

Serious to Moderate Problems

2. Some students do not know how to get the inquiry started.

3. Some students do not care and do not see the inquiry as relevant to their lives.

Moderate Problems

4. Some students do not listen.

5. Some students lack background knowledge for inquiries.

6. Some students talk at inappropriate times.

7. Some students have bad attitudes and are disruptive.

8. Some students do poorly and want extra credit.

9. Some students do not want to think for themselves.

Moderate to Slight Problems

10. Some students socialize during class.

11. Some students participate too much.

12. Some students do not clean up after themselves.

13. Some students plagiarize the work of others.

Slight Problem

14. Some students are tardy.

SOLVING MANAGEMENT PROBLEMS

Increasing Student Motivation and Participation

Problem 1. Some students lack motivation and do not participate enough (serious problem). There are several points to keep in mind while trying to engage students in inquiry. Perhaps the most important is to make certain that the materials and tasks chosen for exploration are numerous and diverse enough to allow for multiple paths of investigation. There may be no way to engage all students all of the time. However, explorations with interesting materials and alternative routes of investigation help a great deal by provoking student curiosity and by enabling students with diverse interests, skills, and backgrounds to find something of interest.

Having said this, there may be more to solving the lack-of-participation problem. Developing skill at catching fish takes practice. Likewise, hooking and reeling in students takes practice. Scientific inquiry starts with puzzling observations that raise questions. Consequently, the key to hooking and reeling in students is having the right bait (the right puzzling observations) and helping students raise questions that they understand and want to answer. The bottom line is that you need to have a clear idea which questions should be raised and pursued, which ones you should just answer, and which ones have to be postponed.

During class discussions, the best way to encourage participation is to use effective questioning techniques. As mentioned, this takes careful planning and involves identifying in advance *exactly* what questions you will need to raise and when to raise them. The key is to raise appropriate, well-phrased, divergent questions because they provoke student thinking. Convergent questions do not encourage thinking and student participation because students either know or do not know the answers and thus either respond or keep quiet. Although specific questions will vary, the following questions lie at the core of scientific and classroom inquiry:

1. What did you observe?

2. What patterns did you find?

3. What questions are raised?

4. What might be the cause?

5. What are some other possibilities?

6. How could you test each possibility?

7. What evidence would you need?

8. What does each hypothesis and planned test lead you to expect?

9. What are the predicted results?

10. How do your results compare with your predictions?

11. Which hypothesis was supported and/or contradicted?

12. What conclusions should be drawn?

Once you have raised a well-phrased divergent question, you should pause briefly (4 to 5 seconds will do) to allow students time to think about possible answers. In other words, as discussed in Chapter 7, use wait-time I even though it may seem like an eternity. Following wait-time I, you might also try using a shuffled deck of cards, each with a student's name, to randomly call on a student to respond. Once a student responds, pause again for a period of time (i.e., wait-time II). Wait-time II signals the class that you are giving the response careful consideration—even if you have heard it before or if it doesn't make sense. Following your moment of careful consideration, reply by saying something like "That's an interesting idea." Or "That is a possibility. I hadn't thought of that." Make sure not to tell the student that he or she is "right" or "wrong" because doing so signals that you are hunting for one "right" answer rather than trying to provoke students to think of alternative possibilities.

If the student you call on is unable or unwilling to provide an answer, respond by saying something like "That's OK. I'll get back to you later when you have had more time to think." This strategy generally works well. Such students often come up with a good answer in a short time and have their hands in the air begging to be called on. When they do raise their hands, call on them and welcome their input. Next, randomly select another student to respond to the initial question or to comment on the first student's idea, and so on. Continue this procedure until several comments have been made. At this point you can allow students with additional ideas to offer them. These six steps, as summarized below, typically result in several excellent student-to-student exchanges:

1. Raise a well-phrased divergent question.

2. Use wait-time I.

3. Randomly call on a student by name.

4. Listen carefully to the student's response.

5. Use wait-time II.

6. Randomly call on another student to comment on the first student's response, and so on . . .

Another factor that helps increase student motivation is making sure that working groups are as small as possible given the available materials and the nature of the tasks. Generally, students should work in teams of two because larger groups provide too much opportunity for nonparticipation. Also you need to decide ahead of time how much time students will need to complete specific tasks (e.g., conduct initial explorations, design an experiment) and inform them of these time constraints before they start. When students know how long they have to complete a task, they are better able to pace their work and stay on task.

Unfortunately, making effective time-management decisions requires experience. Nevertheless, strive to master classroom timing as soon as possible. Generally, plan a variety of activities and plan more than you expect to complete as this avoids having students with no work to do while instructional time remains. And you should always monitor student progress by walking about the classroom watching and listening. If a particular student group is having difficulty getting started, offer helpful hints/suggestions—but no directives as these limit thinking. Also, if one or more groups finish early, have additional questions or tasks up your sleeve so the faster groups stay busy until the slower ones catch up. It also helps when students have a specific to-be-graded assignment that they must complete and hand in before leaving the classroom.

Proper scheduling of learning cycles is also important. Because some learning cycles require extended time periods for data gathering, which on any one day may only require a few minutes, you will often need to initiate new learning cycles prior to finishing others. Running two or three learning cycles at any one time is common. To ensure that class time is utilized fully, list the day's activities on a corner of the board. When students become familiar with this approach they will often come to class, read the list, and get right to work.

Helping Students Get Started

Problem 2. Some students do not know how to get the inquiry started (serious to moderate problem). This problem may stem from unclear and/or incomplete introductory teacher remarks. Because students are not given "cookbook" instructions in how to inquire, you must be clear on the objectives before asking students to start a particular task (e.g., explore the materials and raise five descriptive questions and five causal questions; generate at least three hypotheses to answer causal question X). A failure to make objectives clear often results in confusion, hence producing the need to "get around to all student groups." Nevertheless, after having made your best attempt at clear introductory remarks and asking students to begin, if several groups are still struggling you should stop the entire class and hold a discussion. During the discussion have the few groups that are making progress share their ideas with others, and/or you can offer collective assistance.

Keeping Students Interested and Motivated

Problem 3. Some students do not care and do not see the inquiry as relevant to their lives (serious to moderate problem). The key here is to admit that many questions raised by the inquiries are, in fact, not directly relevant to students' lives (e.g., How do organisms evolve? What colors of light do plants use for photosynthesis?). But most, if not all, of the concepts embedded in the inquiries are relevant (e.g., the natural selection of bacteria to some drugs has resulted in resistant bacterial stains that can cause death; photosynthesis directly or indirectly provides all our food and oxygen). Point out these connections when it is appropriate to do so—typically during concept application.

Surprisingly, whether or not students see the relevancy of specific inquiries has little to do with motivation. Instead, most students are motivated by lessons that raise challenging, but not overwhelming, questions. For example, most students like the candle-burning inquiry (discussed in Chapter 4) because it raises a very obvious yet challenging question: Why does the water rise in the inverted cylinder? The question is challenging because students soon discover that it cannot be answered with what initially seemed like the obvious answer (i.e., the flame consumed the oxygen and created a partial vacuum). Consequently, the candle-burning inquiry provides a very real intellectual mystery, and students, just like professional scientists, are "turned on" by such mysteries. Thus, as mentioned, the key is to make sure students experience some puzzling phenomenon, understand the question(s), generate a variety of plausible answers, and have some ideas about how to test them. It also helps to frequently remind students that the reasoning patterns employed in answering scientific questions are also employed in answering questions in everyday life, as well as in the professional fields in which they may someday participate.

Also keep in mind that students who know that the teacher randomly calls on them are more likely to stay engaged and alert. Also a boring teacher produces bored students. So act and sound enthusiastic, even when you are not. As mentioned, a major role of the teacher in an inquiry setting is that of fellow investigator. You need to be an *enthusiastic* fellow investigator. A little humor also helps. Studies have found that humor not only improves the classroom climate; it also promotes creative thinking (Isen, Means, Patrick, & Nowicki, 1982).

Getting Students to Listen

Problem 4. Some students do not listen (moderate problem). The attention span of most students is surprisingly short. So your introductory remarks should be brief and to the point. Don't spend excessive time taking roll, making general announcements, and/or going over previous assignments. Students are much better at paying attention *after* an exploration activity because the discussion can center on common experiences, questions, and hypotheses. Remember that the exploration phase of learning cycles *precedes* term introduction.

Making Sure Students Have Needed Background Knowledge

Problem 5. Some students lack background knowledge (moderate problem). The solution here lies to some extent in lesson sequencing. Ideally, knowledge acquired from one inquiry serves as background for subsequent inquiries. For example, in the inquiry titled "What variables affect the passage of molecules through cell membranes?" students learn about osmosis. Consequently, in a subsequent inquiry titled "How does water rise in vascular plants?" students borrow the osmosis concept to generate a hypothesis for water rise.

Another strategy for solving this problem is to use your introductory remarks to provide needed background knowledge—provided the background knowledge is relatively easy for students to grasp. For example, the polarity of water molecules plays an important role in water rise in vascular plants. So if molecular polarity has not been previously introduced, you may be able to introduce it during your introductory remarks.

Also when you arrive at the point during the inquiry when you need to elicit student hypotheses, you must send the message that you are *not* looking for a single "right" answer. Rather you want students to be creative and to generate a variety of possible answers. So make sure to ask divergent questions such as "What *might be* the cause of such and such?" or "What other possibilities can you think of?" rather than asking a convergent question such as "What *is* the cause of such and such?" And when a student generates a partial hypothesis—that is, when he or she suggests part of an explanation but is unclear on its details—use this as an opportunity to provide those details or to invite other students to do so. Such details will become important later when students attempt to test their hypotheses. Testing an ambiguous hypothesis is difficult at best. However, be careful not to be critical of student hypotheses at this point and do not let other students criticize as well. In other words, do not allow comments such as "Your idea can't be right because of such and such." The time for a careful critique comes only after a variety of hypotheses have been generated. Critiquing hypotheses during hypothesis generation not only causes the process to bog down; it also makes students far less willing to generate additional hypotheses for fear of being criticized. Also keep in mind that you may generate one or more hypotheses yourself. This is particularly important when students fail to generate the "correct" hypothesis. However, if you do find it necessary to generate the "correct" hypothesis, make sure that you offer one or more "incorrect" ones as well. At all costs, you need to avoid giving students the impression that your hypothesis will ultimately turn out to be correct.

Another excellent strategy when students are struggling to come up with hypotheses is to stop the class discussion and have them take 5 minutes or so to convene small-group discussions to generate some hypotheses to be shared with the entire class. Asking students to brainstorm in small groups works well in many other situations as well (e.g., identifying key causal questions, designing experiments, deriving predictions), so be prepared to call for such discussions whenever students need more time to think.

At the end of an inquiry avoid the temptation to tell students the correct answer because doing so undermines the inquiry process. Hence, students will become unwilling future participants. Instead, they will merely wait for you to tell them the correct answer. Telling students the correct answer also gives them the false notion that scientific knowledge comes from authorities, rather than from long and often difficult periods of testing and retesting. It also stops their thinking. In general, leaving students with open questions that they can continue to ponder is far better than giving them dogmatic answers.

On the other hand, students may become frustrated with the inquiry process if they feel that inadequate progress is being made. If you sense too much student frustration, you might try concluding an inquiry by saying something like "Although our data do not allow us to draw a firm conclusion, data gathered by others [e.g., other students, scientists X and Y] strongly support hypothesis such and such." Also keep in mind that time spent conducting replications and conducting tests of ad hoc hypotheses is often time well spent.

Keeping Students From Talking at Inappropriate Times

Problem 6. Some students talk at inappropriate times (moderate problem). No teacher likes to have students talk while he or she is talking. To avoid this problem, don't start talking until everyone is quiet and you have everyone's attention. A polite request such as "May I have your attention please?" is very appropriate. Once everyone is quiet, you can begin. Now if an impolite student starts talking, it will be obvious to everyone that he or she is interrupting you. A glance at the offending student should be sufficient. If not, calmly walk over and stand next to the student while continuing to address the class. If this doesn't work, you will need to ask the student to be quiet. But remember to speak calmly and in a low voice. You don't want students to know that they can make you lose your "cool."

Avoiding Bad Attitudes and Disruptiveness

Problem 7. Some students have bad attitudes and are disruptive (moderate problem). Bad attitudes and disruptiveness can have several causes. Typically, problems occur when you have been talking too much or when the activities are either too challenging or too simple. As mentioned, keep your introductory remarks brief and make sure that explorations precede discussions. And keep in mind that more directed and less abstract inquires should precede those that require more student initiative and more advanced, abstract reasoning. Also, given the emphasis on scientific reasoning in inquiry instruction and given the typically wide range of students' initial stages of intellectual development, it is particularly important to offer appropriately challenging tasks to students at each developmental stage. For example, during an inquiry titled "How smart are animals?" concrete operational students will be appropriately challenged by trying to conduct a controlled experiment to test isopods' response to light. However, formal operational students find this too easy and boring. Thus, as mentioned previously, they need to be challenged by a more difficult task, such as designing and conducting an experiment to find out if isopods can communicate.

Consequently, you should use student scores on a reasoning pretest to alert yourself to student differences in reasoning skill and use this knowledge to pose appropriate challenges for individual students. You can also pair more and less advanced reasoners and appeal to the more advanced reasoners to become "peer" instructors. Peers can then help others better understand the reasoning behind the inquiries. The less advanced reasoners will not be the only ones who benefit from such peer instruction as trying to teach something to others is an excellent way to clarify one's own thinking and improve one's attitude. Additionally, Table 10.2 (after Watson, 1998) lists several ways of avoiding or dealing with a variety of discipline problems. More suggestions for problems ranging all the way from gum chewing to violence and extortion can be found in Sprick and Howard (1995).

TABLE 10.2   How to Avoid or Deal With Discipline Problems

1. Start the year with a well-thought-out discipline plan.

2. Organize classroom seating to avoid problems. Have a seating plan that separates "buddies." Seat problem students near your desk. Do not allow grouping of desks in corners and do not place students in the hall where they are out of sight.

3. Make your classroom a "junk-food-free" zone as junk food often contains excessive sugar and/or chemicals that can provoke hyperactivity.

4. Respect all students. Written rules cannot take the place of mutual respect.

5. Do not ignore poor behavior.

6. Do not favor one student over others. Do not create a "teacher's pet."

7. Use your voice to control behavior. Develop a strong resolute tone.

8. Do not tolerate put-downs, abusive behavior, note passing, swearing, water pistols, spitball shooters, and the like.

9. Do not speak over student talking. Make sure students are quiet before you speak.

10. Do not spend excessive time passing out or collecting papers as this provides off-task time when students can be disruptive.

11. Do not hand back corrected tests while students are still taking the test as this can be disruptive.

12. To avoid "downtime," always plan more activities than you think you will have time for.

13. Discipline students when they are not with other students. People act and react differently when they are in a group and when they are alone.

14. Become sensitive to the customs and cultural diversity of students and their families. You may need to adjust disciplinary procedures accordingly.

15. Make sure that you have extra adult supervision on field trips.

16. Seek interactive support from the administrative office.

Getting Students to Think for Themselves

Problem 8. Some students don't want to think for themselves (moderate problem). In their pasts, many students have been rewarded only for knowing correct answers—not for thinking and knowing how to derive correct answers. Their teachers just gave them the correct answers, and the students just gave the answers back on quizzes and exams. So many students assume that knowing the correct answers is all that matters. To send a different message, make sure that your quizzes and exams require reasoning. In other words, you need to write good thought-provoking quizzes and exams and to make sure that students are aware of two key points early on. First, students need to learn that your job is *not* to dispense answers. Rather, your job is to help raise interesting and challenging questions and to provide students with materials and suggestions of how to seek answers. And second, students need to know that their job is not merely to recite answers. Rather, they must become good at generating possible answers, designing and conducting ways of testing the possible answers, and using evidence to construct convincing arguments for some of the possibilities and against the others. It also helps when you show students that such intellectual pursuits are far more fun, and far more useful, than the more common practice of "in one ear and out the other."

Keeping Students From Asking for Extra Credit

Problem 9. Some students do poorly and want extra credit (moderate problem). In general, offering extra credit simply provides students with a way of avoiding major course objectives. Extra credit also necessitates additional grading. For these reasons, extra credit should typically not be an option. If you tell students at the outset that extra credit is not an option, the problem will be reduced considerably.

Keeping Students From Socializing

Problem 10. Some students socialize during class (moderate to slight problem). Some socializing is inevitable and even worthwhile as it contributes to positive working relationships. Problems arise when students socialize when they should be working. So walk about the classroom and watch and listen to what students are doing and saying. This not only provides an opportunity to politely tell students to stay "on task" or pose challenging questions to help focus their activities; it also sends the signal that you are monitoring their activities, so they had better get to work.

Keeping Students From Participating Too Much

Problem 11. Some students participate too much (moderate to slight problem). Although overparticipation is not as common as underparticipation, it too can be detrimental. Not surprisingly, the solution is much the same as the solution to the underparticipation problem. Instead of calling only on students who raise their hands, randomly call on students. This does not mean that you should never call on students who raise their hands. But it does mean that you need not keep hearing the ideas of overeager students at the exclusion of others.

Getting Students to Clean Up

Problem 12. Some students do not clean up after themselves (moderate to slight problem). To solve this problem make sure to announce a cleanup policy at the start of the school year and stick with it. For example, you may decide to allow students to work up until a set time and then require them all to participate in cleanup with one or two students assigned to erasing the boards. Then don't excuse anyone until the classroom is cleaned to your satisfaction.

Keeping Students From Cheating

Problem 13. Some students cheat and plagiarize the work of others (moderate to slight problem). Copying on exams and quizzes can be reduced by asking open-ended essay questions and/or by creating and using alternate test forms. Unfortunately, grading essay questions and creating alternate test forms is time consuming. A more significant problem arises when students are allowed, indeed encouraged, to work together to complete in-class assignments, homework assignments, and lab reports yet are asked to submit such assignments "in their own words." No easy solution exists for this problem. Perhaps the best thing is to make your policy clear at the outset and remind students of it frequently. When plagiarism seems likely, talk to each student about the problem as soon as possible and inform him or her of your concern. You may ask such students to rewrite and resubmit the assignment for credit. If the problem persists, award their papers zero points. If the problem still persists, the students should be dealt with more severely.

Getting Students to Arrive on Time

Problem 14. Some students are tardy (slight problem). The key here is announcing your class policies at the outset and sticking with them. Offenses should be recorded, and the offending student(s) should be made aware that a problem exists and that it has/will cost them. Initially students should be given some leeway as unforeseen events occur that may necessitate an occasional tardiness. However, recurring offenses should have increasingly serious consequences.

In summary, the intent of the foregoing suggestions is to help teachers new to inquiry deal with the inevitable problems that arise. Developing the classroom management skills needed to successfully guide student inquiry takes considerable practice and commitment. But once those skills have been acquired, the inquiry classroom becomes a very exciting and rewarding place. Table 10.3 summarizes the classroom management tips just discussed.

TABLE 10.3   Tips on Managing the Inquiry Classroom

Preparation

- Use a pretest to alert yourself to varying levels of student reasoning skill.
- Prepare for extra activities.
- Plan key questions to raise and plan how/when to raise them.
- Make sure that the materials allow for a variety of tasks of varying difficulty levels.

Introduction

- Do not start talking until the class is quiet.
- Announce safety, cleanup, and attendance polices and stick with them.
- Keep your introductory remarks clear and concise.
- Use your introductory remarks to provide key background knowledge.

Exploration

- Keep working groups as small as possible.
- Mix reasoning skill levels to form effective working groups.
- Tell students about how much time they have to complete each clearly specified task (but no "cookbook" procedures).
- Carefully time brief transitions from one activity to the next and make sure that your directions are clear and concise.
- Be an enthusiastic fellow investigator.

Discussion/Concept Introduction

- Hold discussions *after* exploration activities.
- When necessary, provide time for small-group discussions that utilize cooperative strategies such as think-pair-share.
- Hold class discussions when groups are struggling.
- Phrase questions clearly.
- Randomly call on students to respond.
- Use wait-time I and wait-time II.
- Accept all sincere student responses.
- Raise a well-phrased divergent question to initiate student hypothesis generation.
- Do not allow hypotheses to be critiqued during their generation.
- Generate some hypotheses yourself.
- Do not tell students which hypotheses are "correct."

Application

- Introduce relevant concept applications.
- Remind students of the importance of the reasoning patterns involved in inquiry.
- Sequence learning cycles so that subsequent explorations serve as concept applications.

Assessment

- Make sure that quizzes and exams require thinking and concept understanding (not memorization).
- Use essay questions and/or alternate test forms.
- Do not allow extra credit.

THE CLASSROOM MANAGEMENT SCALE

As a way of summarizing many of the management ideas presented in this chapter, this last section presents a simple way to measure classroom management skills. The measure, called the Classroom Management Scale, consists of 16 items. The items, listed in Table 10.4, enable teachers to rate, and hopefully improve, their classroom management skills. As you can see, the skills are grouped into (a) classroom timing, (b) supervision, (c) collaboration, (d) materials care and use, and (e) safety.

TABLE 10.4   The Classroom Management Scale

Timing

1. The teacher has an effective means of quickly getting students' attention.*
2. The teacher's introductory remarks and those between transitions are brief, clear, and concise.
3. For each activity the teacher informs students of the main objective(s) and about how much time they have to accomplish it.
4. The majority of class time is devoted to academic tasks.

Supervision

5. The teacher effectively enforces classroom rules based on reasonable consequences.
6. The teacher does not try to "talk over" the students.
7. The teacher circulates around the room keeping students on task, listening, and, if necessary, challenging students with thoughtful questions.

Collaboration

8. Working groups are small and strategies are used to ensure that each student participates effectively.
9. Each student is personally accountable for the activity objective(s).

Materials care and use

10. Students are responsible for keeping materials clean and in working condition.
11. An effective routine exists for obtaining and returning supplies (e.g., separate stations exist so students do not congregate in any one place).
12. When necessary a procedure is used to quickly inventory materials before and after lab activities.
13. Cleanup duties are assigned and enforced.

Safety

14. Safety rules are posted and enforced during lab activities.
15. Students know where to find safety equipment and how to use it.
16. There are consequences and documentation of unsafe lab behavior.

*Each item is scored on a 0 to 3 scale: 0 = not observed, 1 = sometimes observed, 2 = often observed, 3 = very descriptive. Thus total management scores may range from 0 to 48.

There are several ways to improve one's ratings. For example, item 1 states that "The teacher has an effective means of quickly getting students' attention." Some teachers may do this by briefly flipping the lights off or by ringing a bell. Others may raise an arm to signal each student to raise his or her arm in turn until all students have raised an arm and are quiet. Although the specific method employed is one of personal preference, teachers need to have some consistently used and effective method. Application Question 2 at the end of the chapter suggests a way to become familiar with the 16 items and to begin to develop your own classroom rules and management skills.

Once you begin teaching, you should periodically rate and remind yourself of what you should be doing. Use of the measure will also provide a way of documenting your progress. Becoming a first-rate inquiry teacher, like developing many other aspects of procedural knowledge, will take considerable practice and reflection. Hopefully use of the scale will aid in this process.

Summary

- Before classes start, develop classroom rules and procedures. Rules should be few in number, and they should be fair, understandable, workable, and consistently enforced throughout the school year.

- Several classroom management problems arise when inexperienced teachers first use inquiry. Problems, which range from serious to slight, include lack of student motivation and participation; inability to get the inquiries started; lack of attention or needed background knowledge; excess talking and socializing; poor attitudes; too much participation; plagiarizing; and tardiness. Suggestions for solving each of these problems were provided.

- The Classroom Management Scale consists of criteria grouped into five categories. Continued review and use of the criteria should help you improve your classroom management skills.

Application Questions/Activities

1. Select an inquiry lesson from this book or from elsewhere in which students will be generating and testing hypotheses or theories. Briefly describe the exploration activity. What descriptive and/or causal questions will be raised during exploration? State these questions *exactly* as they will be posed during the lesson. List at least three hypotheses that students are likely to generate and describe how they can be tested. Construct *If/and/then* arguments showing how each hypothesis and planned test leads deductively to one or more predictions. In terms of specific classroom management strategies, describe what you will do to make sure that

   (a) all students understand the central causal question.

   (b) several alternative hypotheses are generated, including the "correct" one.

(c) all students know how to test the alternatives.

(d) student data/results are shared so that all students know what each group has done.

(e) all students understand which hypotheses have been supported and which have been contradicted by the data.

(f) new terms are introduced at the right time in the right way.

2. With a fellow student from your teacher-preparation program, observe a classroom during a lab activity and use the Classroom Management Scale to independently rate the classroom and teacher. Then compare and discuss ratings, particularly those that differ substantially. Use your observations, discussions, and prior readings to develop a set of general classroom rules and procedures that you might use when you start teaching. Have one or more other fellow students read and critique them. Make any changes that you think are reasonable in light of their comments. If you are fortunate enough to locate an experienced inquiry teacher in a nearby school, you should also share and discuss your proposed rules and procedures with that teacher.

Chapter 11 INQUIRY INSTRUCTION AND DIVERSE LEARNERS

A few years ago a teacher from a local high school invited me to visit her third-period biology class. This in itself was not unusual, but her challenge to me was. As she explained it, there were several gang members in the class, a healthy mix of African Americans, Whites, Hispanics, a few students with learning disabilities, and even a few gifted students—just to make things interesting. Her challenge to me was to spend the period observing to see if I could tell which students were which. Needless to say, the visit turned out to be unforgettable, but not because of the expected chaos. What I observed that day was a classroom filled with active, artistic, creative, and very enthusiastic students totally engaged in scientific inquiry. The teacher won her challenge as I certainly had no way of telling a gang member from an honors student, and so on. All I could tell was that I had just witnessed education at its very best.

Inquiry is the best way to meet the needs of diverse learners.

APPLICABLE NSES STANDARDS

Standard A Science teachers plan an inquiry-based program. In doing so, they

- Develop a framework of yearlong and short term goals for students.
- Select science content and adapt and design curricula to meet the interests, knowledge, understanding, abilities, and experiences of students.

(Continued)

(Continued)

Standard B Science teachers guide and facilitate learning. In doing so, they

■ Recognize and respond to student diversity and encourage all students to participate fully in learning.

Standard E Science teachers develop communities of learners that reflect the intellectual rigor of scientific inquiry and the attitudes and social values conducive to learning. In doing so, they

■ Display and demand respect for the diverse ideas, skills, and experiences of all students.

■ Enable students to have a significant voice in decisions about the content and context of their work and require students to take responsibility for the learning of all members of the community.

■ Nurture collaboration among students.

This chapter takes up the important topic of student diversity. The key question is how can you optimally teach science in classrooms filled with increasingly diverse student groups? Or to put it more plainly, how did the biology teacher mentioned above pull it off? The chapter begins by considering teaching strategies for English-language learners and then briefly considers ways of avoiding bias in the classroom. Next the chapter discusses strategies for meeting the needs of students with a variety of learning disabilities. It then discusses how you can meet the needs of gifted students. Lastly the chapter takes a look at textbook selection and use. When dealing with diverse learners, extra care must be taken to make sure that your textbook supports inquiry and doesn't overwhelm students with unnecessary terminology.

STRATEGIES FOR ENGLISH-LANGUAGE LEARNERS

Classroom inquiry provides the foundation for effective instruction for virtually all students, not just those from the dominant American culture who speak English as their native language. Indeed, incorporation of inquiry into lessons may be even more important for English-language learners because some may be less extrinsically motivated to please the teacher or to achieve a high grade. Inquiry lessons are intrinsically motivating, and thus for such students inquiry is not just a good way to teach; it becomes a necessary way to teach.

With this in mind, take a few minutes to compare the 25 characteristics of inquiry instruction introduced in Chapter 7 to the characteristics of effective instruction for English-language learners listed in Table 11.1. When you do, you will discover many similarities— as well as some important additions. Because inquiry teaching places exploration and explanation on center stage and vocabulary learning on the side, experts in teaching science to culturally diverse students and to English-language learners are virtually unanimous in their support of inquiry (e.g., Atwater, 1994; Diller & Moule, 2005; Echevarria, Vogt, & Short, 2004; Marshall, 2002; Matsumoto-Grah, 1992). Note in particular how learning cycle instruction with its exploration and term introduction phases respectively incorporates Item 7 of Table 11.1 (i.e., explicitly link concepts to students' background) and Item 8 (i.e., emphasize key terms), while the concept application phase incorporates Item 16 (i.e., provide activities to clarify and apply new content).

TABLE 11.1   Characteristics of Effective Instruction for English-Language Learners

Preparation

1. Select content objectives that are appropriate to students' age and background.
2. Clearly state content objectives.
3. Clearly state language objectives.
4. Select and use effective supplementary materials.
5. Adapt content to all student levels.
6. Integrate activities and concepts with language practice (e.g., reading, writing, listening, speaking).

Instruction

7. Explicitly link concepts to students' background.
8. Emphasize key terms.
9. Speak slowly and enunciate clearly.
10. Clearly explicate learning tasks.
11. Use a variety of instructional techniques (e.g., hands-on, demonstrations, gestures, body language).
12. Provide opportunities for students to use new strategies.
13. Use appropriate wait time and use a variety of question types, including those that provoke higher-order thinking.
14. Provide frequent opportunities for teacher/student and student/student discussion.
15. Configure groups to support language and content objectives.
16. Provide activities to clarify and apply new content.
17. Make sure that students are engaged approximately 90% to 100% of the period.
18. Pace the lesson to students' ability levels.

Review/Assessment

19. Review key concepts and vocabulary.
20. Provide frequent feedback and assessment on student progress during lesson (e.g., spot checking, group response).

AVOIDING GENDER BIAS

Few beginning teachers are aware of possible unconscious bias against certain types of students. For example, gender bias, typically against females, may occur without male teachers even knowing it. Such bias may involve calling on males more often, asking males more higher-order questions, giving males more encouragement and praise, giving males more access to materials, and providing exemplars of concepts and posing test items in masculine contexts (Baker & Leary, 1995; Baker & Piburn, 1997; Brickhouse, 2001; Kahle & Meece, 1994). Accordingly, here are 12 strategies to keep in mind to help motivate both male and female students in culturally diverse classrooms:

1. Use gender-neutral language.

2. Use an equitable system for calling on all students.

3. Be careful not to prejudice student participation and performance based on cultural differences, socioeconomic status, and gender.

4. Promote self-esteem by ensuring that all students experience some successes.

5. Encourage students to respect the feelings of others, especially those who differ culturally.

6. Avoid placing value on having money, spending money, or major consumer products.

7. Learn and use some words from the home languages of limited-English-proficient students.

8. Actively confront instances of stereotyping, bias, and discrimination if and when they occur by students.

9. Build a supportive, cooperative, and noncompetitive classroom environment.

10. Choose text and readings that show both male and female and multicultural contributions.

11. Choose text and readings that include historical and social perspectives as well as career opportunities.

12. Invite women scientists and college women who are majoring in the sciences to visit your classroom and discuss their experiences.

STUDENTS WITH LEARNING DISABILITIES

Students with average or above-average intelligence with some type of impairment of the central nervous system that makes learning more difficult are said to have a learning disability. The Individuals with Disabilities Education Act (IDEA) passed in 1990 and amended in 1997 requires that schools place students with physical or behavioral learning disabilities in the least educationally restrictive environments possible. Practically speaking, this means that you will occasionally have students with learning disabilities in your classroom. Many types of learning disabilities exist such as hearing impairments, vision impairments, motor impairments/orthopedic disabilities (e.g., spinal cord injury, muscular dystrophy, cerebral palsy, epilepsy, cardiovascular disease, respiratory disorders, diabetes, and amputation), and behavioral disabilities such as attention deficit disorder.

According to IDEA, each disabled student placed in a general education classroom must have a specific educational program (called an Individualized Education Program) developed and agreed to by specialists, administrators, and teachers. The program includes information such as (a) the results of assessments used to place the student; (b) statements regarding general health, disability, and/or behavioral problems and how to deal with them; (c) educational goals for the student in your classroom; (d) special services that need to be provided; (e) assessment procedures and time tables; and (f) recommended instructional activities.

One of the first considerations when teaching students with learning disabilities is learning about the specific impairment and the likely degree of educational limitation. Fortunately, most school systems have specialists trained to help both you and the student. You should consult your school specialist when the need arises. In the meantime Table 11.2 provides some general teaching strategies including tips on lab work, fieldwork, and assessment for dealing with students with disabilities. After considering the more general strategies listed in Table 11.2, the next few sections will discuss in a bit more detail how to deal with some specific and common disabilities.

Table 11.2   Strategies for Teaching Students With Disabilities

General Strategies

- Consult with the special education specialist regarding the specific nature of the learning disability. Then talk with the disabled student during the first week of classes to discuss his or her difficulties, needs, and ways to compensate.

- Acknowledge when a disability exists. Not acknowledging this fact is not acknowledging the person.

- When it appears that the student needs help, ask if you can help. Accept a "no, thank you" graciously.

- Speak directly to the disabled student as you would with other students.

- Allow use of a tape recorder when necessary.

- Remove potential obstacles to students in wheelchairs.

- Use table-type desks with enough clearance for wheelchairs.

- Don't lean on a student's wheelchair as it is part of his or her body space.

- Don't patronize students in wheelchairs by patting them on the head.

- Push a wheelchair only when asked.

- To place yourself at his or her eye level, sit down or kneel when talking to a student in a wheelchair.

- Words like *walking* and *running* are appropriate. Sensitivity to these words is not necessary as students in wheelchairs use the same words.

- Have custodians use nonskid floor polish for students who use crutches and wheelchairs.

(Continued)

TABLE 11.2 (Continued)

Laboratory Strategies

- If possible increase size of screens, wheels, dials, handles, and buttons on lab equipment.
- If possible select nonmanual types of lab equipment (e.g., electronic probes vs. pipette bulbs).
- Label lab supplies and equipment with regular print, large print, and/or Braille and always try to keep supplies and equipment in the same places.
- Lower supplies and equipment for easier access or simply give them to the student as needed.
- Assign a nondisabled lab partner who can help reach, describe, and/or manipulate objects as needed. But be sensitive when making lab pairings so that both students are satisfied with the pairing.

Fieldwork Strategies

- When the activity involves fieldwork, students using wheelchairs may need you to make special travel arrangements as they often rely on attendants, ramp-adapted vans, or power-lift vans.
- Make sure that the field site is accessible. Are nearby parking spaces reserved for persons with disabilities? Is there a ramp or a step-free entrance? Are there accessible rest rooms? If the site is not on the ground level, does the building have an elevator? Are water fountains low enough for students in wheelchairs?
- Anticipate areas of difficulty and ask the disabled student to do the same.
- Consider alternative activities/exercises with similar learning objectives that can be accomplished with less difficulty. You may be able to arrange with curators of museums, science centers, and so on for alternative activities.
- Use a peer-buddy system.
- Provide assistance. But also provide positive reinforcement when the student does something unaided.

Assessment Strategies

- Consider alternative forms of assessment (e.g., oral, hands-on demonstration, open-book, portfolio).
- Stay on top of student progress through informal assessment. Don't wait until it's too late to solve a problem.
- Present exams in a form that will be unbiased to visually impaired students. Ask such students for the approach they find to be most accessible (e.g., record exam items on tape and have the students record their responses).
- Provide study questions that demonstrate exam format and content.
- Avoid overly complicated language in exam items.
- Clearly separate items when spacing them on the exam.
- Consider the use of illustrations and large print.
- Avoid answer sheets. Allow students to write answers (check or circle) on the exam (or even dictate their responses).
- Eliminate distractions during exams.
- Permit use of a dictionary and/or thesaurus and a calculator.
- Permit time extensions when there are significant demands on reading and writing skills.
- Permit students to take exams in a separate quiet room, with a proctor, and/or with a writer. But do not compromise the integrity of the testing situation.

Strategies for Students With Hearing Impairment

There are two main categories of students with hearing impairment: hard of hearing and deaf. IDEA defines students who are hard of hearing as "those with a hearing impairment, whether permanent or fluctuating, which adversely affects a student's educational performance, but which is not included under the definition of deaf." IDEA defines students who are deaf as "those with a hearing impairment so severe that a student is impaired in processing linguistic information through hearing, with or without amplification, which adversely affects educational performance."

With advancing age, the typical student with hearing impairment, as compared to the student with normal hearing, shows an increasing lag in vocabulary growth, in sentence comprehension, in sentence construction, and in concept formation. To make matters worse, students with hearing impairment often learn to feign comprehension, which masks problems and often contributes to poor communication and learning. Therefore, the following teaching strategies for students with hearing impairment are primarily concerned with improving communication:

1. Ask where the student would like to sit to communicate in an optimal manner. Avoid seating in heavy-traffic areas.

2. Because expressions, gestures, and other body language help convey information, get the student's attention before speaking and communicate facing the student.

3. Don't stand in front of a window or light source that may silhouette you and hinder visual cues.

4. If necessary, use written notes and visual aids to communicate.

5. When possible, use captioned films, videos, and laser disks.

6. Write all new terms, assignments, class instructions, and procedural changes on the board.

7. Make board notes legible and don't talk while writing on the board.

8. Eliminate background noise. Sounds taken for granted and normally ignored by hearing students are amplified by a hearing aid and interfere with communication.

9. If the student lip-reads, keep your hands away from your mouth and speak slowly and clearly. But don't exaggerate your lip movements or shout.

10. Lip-reading students may need note takers as it is difficult to take notes while lip-reading. Carbonless note paper can be used. The note taker takes notes and then gives the student with hearing impairment a copy.

11. If the student uses an interpreter, speak directly to the student rather than the interpreter. During presentations, the interpreter should stand near the section of the board that you are using, allowing the student to see both the signs and the writing on the board.

12. If possible give the student and the interpreter outlines of the lecture or written material in advance so they can become familiar with new technical vocabulary.

13. Establish emergency procedures. For example, agree that for a fire drill (or fire) you will write on the board, "Fire drill FIRE—go out back door." Also, if you have a signing student, learn the signs for *emergency, fire, go,* and so forth.

14. If ambiguities or difficulties arise concerning homework assignments, have the parents note these difficulties and follow up in writing.

Strategies for Students With Vision Impairment

There are also two main categories of visual impairments: low vision and blind. Students with low vision usually can read but may require special equipment and materials. The definition of legal blindness covers a broad range of visual impairments. The extent of visual disability depends upon the physical sensory impairment of the student's eyes, the student's age at the onset of vision impairment, and the cause of the impairment. Vision may also fluctuate daily and may be influenced by poor lighting, light glare, or fatigue. Due to the fact that a vast amount of learning materials are visual in nature (e.g., textbooks, class outlines, films, videos, board notes, computer screens), overcoming a student's visual limitation requires unique and individual strategies based on that student's particular visual impairment and his or her other communication skills. Here are some specific things to try:

1. Speak to the class upon entering and leaving the room or site.

2. Describe and tactually familiarize the student to the classroom, laboratory, equipment, materials, field sites, and so forth.

3. Call the student by name if you want his or her attention.

4. Use descriptive words such as *straight, forward, left,* and so forth in relation to the student's body orientation.

5. Give specific directions and avoid the use of vague terms with unusable information, such as *over there, here, this,* and so forth.

6. Describe, in detail, pertinent visual aspects of the learning activities.

7. Verbally tell the student when you need to move or to end a conversation.

8. Offer to read, or arrange to have read, written information.

9. Various Braille devices can be used to assist reading.

10. Paid or volunteer readers or writers can assist with texts, materials, and library readings.

11. If asked to guide a student with a visual impairment, identify yourself. Offer your assistance and, if accepted, offer your arm to the student's hand. Verbalize steps up or down, doorways to the left or right, and possible hazards.

12. Don't touch or pet a guide dog as this may distract the dog from its duties.

Strategies for Students With Attention Deficit Disorder

Attention deficit disorder (ADD) is an increasingly common behavioral disorder characterized by serious and persistent difficulties in attention span, impulse control, and hyperactivity. ADD is a chronic disorder that can begin in infancy and extend throughout adulthood with a significant negative impact on one's life at home, in school, and in the community.

There are two types of attention deficit disorders: undifferentiated attention deficit disorder and attention deficit hyperactivity disorder. In the undifferentiated form, the primary and most significant characteristic is inattentiveness. Hyperactivity is not present. However, these students still manifest problems with organization and distractibility, even though they may seem quiet and passive. They also tend to be overlooked more easily in the classroom and may be at a higher risk for academic failure than those with hyperactivity. To be diagnosed as the more severe form of ADD that includes hyperactivity, a student must display, for 6 months or more, at least eight of the following characteristics prior to the age of 7 (American Psychiatric Association, 1987):

1. Fidgets, squirms

2. Has difficulty remaining seated

3. Is easily distracted

4. Has difficulty waiting for his or her turn

5. Blurts out answers

6. Has difficulty following instructions

7. Has difficulty sustaining attention

8. Shifts from one uncompleted task to another

9. Has difficulty playing quietly

10. Talks excessively

11. Interrupts or is rude to others

12. Does not appear to listen

13. Often loses things necessary for tasks

14. Frequently engages in dangerous actions

There are several things you can do to help students with both forms of ADD. These include the following:

1. Seat the student at the front of the class facing forward to keep other students out of view.

2. Don't place the student near distracting stimuli such as air conditioners, high-traffic areas, heaters, doors, or windows.

3. Avoid physical relocations, changes in schedule, and disruptions.

4. Avoid publicly reminding students on medication to "take their medicine."

5. Reduce the amount of materials present during work time by having the student put away unnecessary items.

6. Have a place for tools, materials, and books.

7. Surround the student with good role models.

8. Encourage peer tutoring and cooperative learning.

9. Maintain eye contact during verbal instructions.

10. Make rules and instructions clear, concise, and consistent.

11. If needed, repeat instructions in a calm, positive manner.

12. When asking a question, first say the student's name and then pause for a few seconds as a signal to pay attention.

13. Provide clear and consistent transitions between activities or warn the student a few minutes ahead of time before changing activities.

14. Frequently monitor behavior.

15. Provide encouragement by praising good behavior and by rewarding more than punishing.

16. Have a preestablished consequence for misbehavior, remain calm, state the infraction of the rule, and avoid arguing with the student.

17. Encourage the use of attention self-monitoring techniques. These include self-cueing so that the student can determine how well he or she is attending to the task at hand. Cueing may also be aided by providing an audio tone.

18. Encourage positive self-talk (e.g., "I did very well remaining in my seat today"). This promotes self-confidence.

19. Boost the student's confidence by starting assignments with a few questions or activities that he or she can successfully complete.

20. Require a daily assignment log as necessary and make sure the student writes down all assignments. Initial the log daily to signify completion of homework assignments. Parents should also sign.

21. Encourage parents to set up appropriate study space at home with set study times and routines, with parental review of completed homework, and with periodic notebook and/or book bag organization.

Note that all of these strategies, which have been collected over the past several decades, have been found to assist students with disabilities in their academic pursuits. They have been collected primarily from science teachers, special educators, and teachers in schools for the deaf and blind. The collection is based not on rigorous statistical assessments but rather on the craft of teachers' knowledge about what works with their disabled students. What works well for one student may or may not work for another, even if both students are classified as having the same disability.

MEETING THE NEEDS OF GIFTED STUDENTS

You may also be challenged to meet the needs of exceptionally able or so-called gifted students. Gifted students are found in all cultures and across all economic levels. Today, the term *gifted* reflects a multifaceted perspective and is defined by aptitude, traits, and behaviors rather than by a presumably changeless IQ test performance. In short, gifted students are those who exhibit one or more of the following attributes: (a) a high degree of intellectual, creative, and/or artistic ability; (b) exceptional leadership abilities; (c) the ability to grasp concepts rapidly; (d) intense curiosity about how things work; (e) the ability to generate and test alternative hypotheses and theories; and (f) the ability to produce products that express insight, creativity, and/or excellence. Importantly, students gifted in some areas (art, math) may be very average in others.

To meet the needs of gifted students, schools and teachers can differentiate the curriculum by making adjustments in terms of *acceleration, enrichment,* and/or *grouping* (e.g., Association for Supervision and Curriculum Development, 1994; Reis, Burns, & Renzulli, 1992). Acceleration refers to grade skipping or increasing the pace of instruction to enable gifted students to complete the curriculum in less time than usual. Acceleration can occur in one or more subject areas. Ways of accelerating the curriculum include the following (based in part on the *New Jersey Science Curriculum Framework,* New Jersey Department of Education, 1998, available online at www.state.nj.us/njded/frameworks/science/chap9c.pdf):

Flexible Pacing. Gifted students can be assigned to specific advanced classes or be placed in higher grades based on their ability regardless of age.

Multiage Classes. Two or more grade levels can be combined in multiage classes. Gifted students can differentially accelerate through self-pacing.

Compacting. Compacting, also known as telescoping, refers to a form of acceleration in which part of the curriculum is taught during a shorter-than-usual time period. Previously mastered content can be determined through pretesting.

College Course Work. Gifted students can take college courses for college credits while completing high school requirements (i.e., concurrent enrollment). College courses may be taken in the summer.

Early College Entrance. Once the standards for high school courses are met, early admission to college may be an option for some.

Advanced Placement. The Advanced Placement Program (APP), administered by the College Entrance Examination Board, enables gifted high school students to obtain both high school and college credit for demanding course work offered as part of the high school curriculum.

Enrichment is a second way to help meet the needs of gifted students. The following are ways to enrich the curriculum:

Alternative Learning Activities. Alternative learning activities permit gifted students to engage in new learning and avoid the boredom of repeating instruction or engaging in unnecessary practice of skills already mastered.

Independent Study. Gifted students can conduct planned, self-directed research projects carefully monitored by the teacher. Prerequisites include instruction in field-based and library research skills, the scientific method, and other authentic types of inquiry.

Advanced Thinking Processes. Teachers can provide assignments in several curriculum areas emphasizing higher-level thinking processes such as synthesis, analysis, and evaluation.

Guest Speakers. Guest speakers can provide information on topics beyond your expertise. University faculty, parents, business and industry leaders, or other teachers in specific areas may be used as resources.

Mentors/Internships. Gifted students can interact with adult experts in fields of mutual interest. Mentors can act as role models and students' career awareness can be enhanced.

Alternative Resources. Materials from higher grade levels can be used. Access to business, university, and community resources such as laboratories, libraries, and computer facilities is appropriate.

Exchange Programs. Gifted students can attend schools in different communities and/or countries to enrich educational experiences.

Lastly, grouping gifted students together in special classes or clustering them in the same classroom is a third way to differentiate instruction. Grouping allows for more appropriate, rapid, and advanced instruction. Examples include:

Self-Contained Classes. Grouping gifted students in self-contained classes allows them (a) to be challenged in every area throughout the day, (b) to be stimulated by their intellectual peers, and (c) to have guidance from teachers with expertise in sequential, integrated, and accelerated curricula.

Pullout Programs. In pullout programs, gifted students spend part of their time in regular classes from which they are regularly "pulled out" to spend time in sessions in which they receive instruction with other gifted students. Pullout programs require careful coordination and communication between the teachers of both classes.

Cluster Grouping. Gifted students can be grouped or "clustered" with other gifted students in regular classrooms. Clustering permits homogeneous grouping according to interests and achievement.

Cluster Scheduling. To enhance rapid pacing, less drill, and greater depth, the schedules of gifted students can be arranged, or "clustered," so that they take their required core courses together.

Honors Classes. Special advanced or so-called honors classes can be provided to enable gifted students to practice higher-level thinking, creativity, and exploration of in-depth course content.

Seminars. Seminars can be aimed at research, interdisciplinary studies, visual and performing arts, academic subjects, or other areas of interest. These seminars provide interaction with specialists who can give guidance in specific areas.

Resource Centers. Districts can establish resource centers that are available to all students. Times can then be reserved in which the centers are open only for use by gifted students from broad geographical areas (e.g., interdistrict or countywide).

SELECTING AND USING A TEXTBOOK FOR DIVERSE LEARNERS

The textbook, for many teachers, is an integral part of the science curriculum. Textbook selection and use is particularly critical when dealing with diverse student groups. Unfortunately, most textbooks do a poor job of meeting the needs of diverse students, particularly English-language learners and students with disabilities, as they often (a) take insufficient account of students' prior knowledge, (b) lack sufficient exemplars of key concepts, (c) are very term dense, (d) do not help students develop their reasoning skills, and (e) do not adequately address the nature of science (e.g., Stern & Roseman, 2004). For example, with respect to too many terms, Yager (1983) found that a very popular high school biology text called *Modern Biology* includes 17,130 special biological terms with an average of 23 special terms per page. Needless to say this is far too many terms for high school students to meaningfully learn. The inevitable result is rote memorization and/or outright intellectual dropout.

Text Selection Guidelines—What to Beware

So what sort of textbook should you look for? Mayer and Barufaldi (1988), through the National Center for Science Education, suggest several factors to be wary of when selecting a textbook (reprinted with permission):

1. Beware the encyclopedic text, the one that purports to "cover" the discipline. No textbook can do so and no student should be asked to memorize such wealth of detail.

2. Beware any text that emphasizes memorization of vocabulary. Students are expected to learn new words when confronted by a new discipline, but page after page containing bold-faced or italicized words to be defined and memorized constitute a dull exercise not exemplifying either disciplinary concepts or the nature of science.

3. Beware the text that does not read well. One written in short choppy sentences that develops detail but not ideas is quite likely to be used by the student to uncover only a snippet of information. The text should provide a narrative of inquiry, rather than a collection of conclusions.

4. Beware the dogmatic textbook. Science is an ever-changing body of data constantly refined on the basis of new evidence. Texts that present the corpus of science as a fixed and unchanging mass of evidence do not prepare students to live in a world where change may be the only constant.

5. Beware the text as the sole source of information. The textbook must be regarded as an introduction to science that provides alternative avenues for learning.

6. Beware the text that does not explicate the nature of science. The processes of science should permeate the textbook and not be confined to an isolated chapter or paragraph.

7. Beware the text that does not clearly elucidate the role of controlled experiment, hypothesis formulation, and theory in science.

8. Beware the bland textbook, the one written is such a way as to eliminate controversial or contentious issues and the one that presents science simply as a fixed body of non-applicable data. Students should be encouraged to analyze, synthesize and evaluate evidence for and against a given hypothesis.

9. Beware the textbook that emphasizes only one aspect of the discipline. Further, the interrelationships of science with social and technological aspects should permeate the text.

10. Beware the classical textbook, one that leaves the student with an impression that science is a retrospective exercise. A textbook that does not deal in some measure with current problems is not preparing students for the future they will face.

To emphasize Mayer and Barufaldi's (1988) point that too many terms not only dulls the mind but also dulls the spirit, consider the following passage from *Human Biology* (Chiras, 1999, p. 345). Note that whenever a new biological term appears, it has been replaced with an unfamiliar italicized term. This should help you better appreciate what students feel when they first encounter a new topic by reading a typical textbook.

Sisotim Is Divided Into Four Stages

The four stages of sisotim are <u>orpphase, atemphase, anaphase,</u> and <u>oletphase.</u>

Orpphase

<u>Orpphase</u> begins immediately after <u>retniphase,</u> a time during which the <u>emosomorhcs</u> replicate. During <u>orpphase,</u> the replicated <u>emosomorhcs</u> shorten and thicken considerably, forming compact structures. In addition, the <u>iloelcun,</u> regions of active <u>ANRr</u> synthesis, gradually disappear.

Two events of great importance occur in the <u>msalpotyc</u> during <u>orpphase.</u> The first is the division of the <u>llec's</u> <u>eloirtnecs.</u> Each <u>eloirtnecs</u> consists of two small cylindrical structures identical to the <u>lasab</u> bodies (Chapter 3). Like other <u>ellenagros, eloirtnecs</u> replicate during <u>retniphase.</u> During <u>orpphase,</u> the <u>eloirtnecs</u> separate, migrating to opposite ends of the *suelcun.*

The second <u>cimsalpotyc</u> event of importance is the formation of the *citotim* <u>lldnips.</u> The *citotim* <u>lldnips</u> is an elaborate array of <u>elubutorcims</u> responsible for subsequent movement of the <u>emosomorhcs.</u>

Did you understand the passage? Now your task is to memorize the underlined terms so that you can recognize them on a recall-based exam. Are you motivated to memorize the terms? Are you surprised that such textbook passages turn many students away from science?

What Does Inquiry Look Like in a Textbook?

Unfortunately, few textbooks are written with inquiry in mind. Nevertheless, some are. To provide a sense of what inquiry looks like in a textbook and what to look for, consider the following passages that use a learning cycle "exploration first–terms second" approach to introduce *embryonic induction* (from A. E. Lawson, 2004, pp. 128–130).

Exploring the phenomena *before* introducing the related terms makes it much easier for students to assimilate and retain the terms because, when introduced, the terms have something to connect to in the students' minds. Importantly, the phrase *embryonic induction* is introduced in the context of the experiments and reasoning that lead to its "invention" in the first place. Thus the passages reinforce the reasoning patterns involved in that conceptual invention.

Does One Embryo Part Influence Development of Another?

The nervous system is the first system to develop in frog embryos. Not only is it first, but its initial development involves outer-layer (ectoderm) cells. So, not surprisingly, the nervous system was the first system studied in detail. Embryologists found that a flattened area appears on the frog embryo's upper surface. Folds then appear along the area's sides. The folds then grow upward and fuse in the center to form a tube (Figure a). This tube, called the *neural tube,* eventually becomes the brain and the spinal cord. The ectoderm cells on either side of the flattened area eventually become skin. When they first appear, all ectoderm cells look the same. So a key

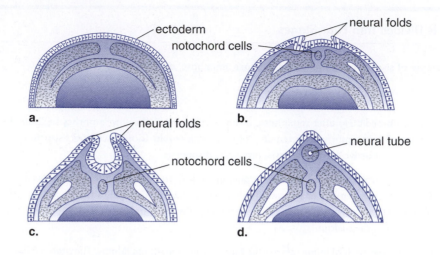

causal question can be raised: What causes some ectoderm cells to develop into the neural tube and eventually into the nervous system, while others develop into skin?

When embryos at the neural-tube stage are preserved, thinly sliced, stained, and then observed under a microscope, a group of cells called *notochord* cells (which come from the mesoderm) can be seen just under the neural tube (shown in Figures b, c, and d as a group of cells below in the neural tube). Could notochord cells somehow cause (i.e., induce/influence) the ectoderm cells above them to differentiate into the neural tube? Or do these specific ectoderm cells develop into the neural tube because they somehow differ internally from others that become skin?

In the 1920s, German embryologist Johannes Holtfreter tested these alternative hypotheses with an experiment that involved removing the ectoderm cells that were destined to become the neural tube and growing them by themselves. Holtfreter's experiment can be summarized like this:

If . . . the notochord-induction hypothesis is correct,

and . . . the ectoderm cells that will eventually become the neural tube are removed before the notochord cells appear below them,

then . . . when grown by themselves, the removed ectoderm cells should *not* develop into a neural tube. They should not develop into a neural tube because the inducer notochord cells are no longer nearby.

Alternatively,

if . . . neural-tube development is controlled by something inside the ectoderm cells (internal-control hypothesis),

then . . . the removed ectoderm cells should still develop into a neural tube.

When Holtfreter conducted his experiment, he found that the removed ectoderm cells did not develop into a neural tube. Therefore, he found support for the notochord-induction hypothesis. Apparently neural tube development is somehow influenced by nearby notochord cells. In a subsequent experiment, Holtfreter extracted both ectoderm and notochord cells and grew them next to each other. In this experiment the ectoderm cells also developed into a neural tube. Therefore, Holtfreter found additional evidence that notochord cells induce nearby cells to develop in specific ways, a process later referred to as **embryonic induction**. Holtfreter also removed ectoderm cells after the notochord cells had appeared below them. In this experiment, he found that the removed ectoderm cells still developed into a neural tube. Apparently the notochord cells had already exerted their influence.

Do Other Embryonic Parts Develop Due to Induction?

Following Holtfreter's work, his colleague Hans Spemann conducted an amazing experiment with a frog embryo (a gastrula). Spemann cut the top half off, rotated it 180 degrees, and then stuck it back on the bottom half. Incredibly the embryo continued to develop normally just as though the rotation had not been made! In other words, the front end of the embryo did not turn into the back end as one might expect. Spemann's result suggested that the embryo's bottom half might somehow control the top half. Could the entire bottom half be an inducer?

Spemann suspected not. Knowing about Holtfreter's findings, Spemann had his eye on the dorsal lip cells from the upper half. In Holtfreter's experiment, these were the cells that had moved inside and induced neural tube development. Consequently, Spemann suspected that the dorsal lip cells might be the inducer. How could such a hypothesis be tested? In 1924, Hilda Mangold, a student of Spemann's, conducted the difficult test. The test consisted of cutting the dorsal lip cells out of one embryo and grafting them into another. Mangold's and Spemann's reasoning can be summarized like this:

> *If . . .* induction of the neural tube is caused by notochord cells that come from the dorsal lip region (dorsal-lip-induction hypothesis),
>
> *and . . .* the dorsal lip cells are grafted into another embryo that already has dorsal lip cells,
>
> *then . . .* both sets of dorsal lip cells should move into the embryo and two neural tubes should develop.
>
> On the other hand,
>
> *if . . .* the bottom half is the inducer (bottom-half-induction hypothesis),
>
> *then . . .* only one neural tube should develop.

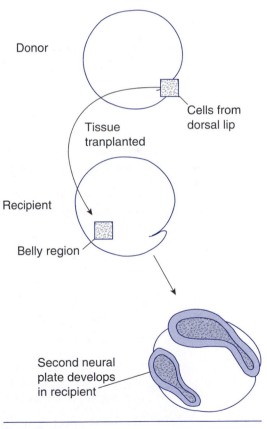

Figure B

As predicted by the dorsal-lip-induction hypothesis, Figure B shows that two neural tubes developed. Therefore, Mangold and Spemann concluded that notochord cells, which had come from the upper half of the embryo's dorsal lip, had indeed caused the ectoderm cells to differentiate into neural tubes. Thus, in response to the question, what causes neural tube cells to differentiate? Mangold and Spemann could confidently answer that the notochord cells from the dorsal lip region are the cause. However, this answer is limited to just one embryonic system. Mangold and Spemann were after much more. They were after an answer to the more general question: What causes *all* embryonic cells to differentiate? Certainly their experiment was noteworthy, enough so that in 1935 it won them a Nobel Prize. However, concluding that all embryonic cells differentiate because they are induced to do so by nearby cells would require finding induction of still other embryo parts and in other kinds of embryos.

Note how the passages not only contain separate exploration, term introduction, and concept application phases, but they also explicitly state alternative hypotheses and predictions. For English-language learners and/or for students who have not yet become fully conscious of this hypothetical-predictive reasoning pattern and are not aware of the difference between hypotheses and predictions or between results and conclusions, this treatment can be very helpful.

In conclusion, just like inquiry-based classroom instruction, inquiry-based textbooks are better at meeting the needs of diverse learners. Consequently, when selecting a text, select a good inquiry-based text and use it to support, not supplant, student inquiry. This means that text readings should come *after* the exploration and term introduction phases of classroom instruction. In other words, text readings become part of the concept application phase.

So how did the biology teacher mentioned at the outset pull it off? How did she teach her class so that a classroom observer such as I could not tell her gifted students from her gang-member students from her students with learning disabilities? In short, she taught using the inquiry process.

Summary

- Classroom inquiry provides the foundation for effective instruction for virtually all students, not just those from the dominant American culture and those who speak English as their native language. Inquiry lessons are intrinsically motivating, and thus they are not just a good way to teach; they become a necessary way to teach to reach diverse student groups.

- Gender bias, typically against females, may occur in science classrooms. However, several strategies exist to motivate both male and female students in culturally diverse classrooms.

- The Individuals with Disabilities Education Act (IDEA) requires that schools place students with learning disabilities in the least educationally restrictive environments possible. Thus you are likely to occasionally have students with learning disabilities in your classroom. Many types of learning disabilities exist, and you must help develop an Individualized Education Program for each learning disabled student in your classroom.

- Gifted students are found in all cultures and across all economic levels. To meet the needs of gifted students, schools and teachers can differentiate the curriculum by making adjustments in terms of acceleration, enrichment, and/or grouping.

- Textbook selection and use is particularly critical when dealing with diverse student groups. Because inquiry-based textbooks provide a narrative of the inquiry process and use a learning cycle–based "examples first–terms second" approach, they are better than traditional textbooks at meeting the needs of diverse learners. Consequently, when selecting a text, select an inquiry-based text and use it during the concept application phase of instruction *after* students have explored the related phenomena in the classroom or field.

Application Questions/Activities

1. Select a lesson and describe how you will make sure that it will sufficiently challenge gifted students while not overwhelming your concrete operational students. What modifications/additions, if any, will be needed to meet the needs of English-language learners, to avoid gender or cultural bias, and to make sure that students with disabilities can effectively participate?

2. It makes no sense to introduce all 17,130 of the special biological terms that Yager (1983) found in *Modern Biology* to your students. But some terms should be introduced. How will you decide which terms to introduce and which ones to ignore? What selection criteria does the Educational Policies Commission recommend?

3. Select a textbook and use the National Center for Science Education guidelines to evaluate its appropriateness for use.

Chapter 12

CURRICULUM DEVELOPMENT

No society can be certain that its present knowledge is adequate to deal with an ever-changing world. Thus, there must be means of constructing new knowledge and modifying or replacing mistakes unknowingly embedded in that knowledge. For this, the ability to reason well is necessary. Accordingly, this chapter will explore curricular approaches that intend to not only teach current knowledge but also promote the development of the reasoning skills needed for the construction of new knowledge. We will start with a closer look at the nature of declarative knowledge—specifically at types of concepts that exist as this will provide the key to knowing which concepts need to be taught and in what order they should be taught. The chapter will also discuss how to best schedule learning cycles and how to integrate technological and societal issues, some of which may be controversial, into the curriculum.

This aquarium represents an "undifferentiated whole" that a biology curriculum can "differentiate."

APPLICABLE NSES STANDARDS

Standard F Science teachers actively participate in the ongoing planning and development of the school science program. In doing so, they

- Plan and develop the school science program.
- Participate in decisions concerning the allocation of time and other resources to the science program.
- Participate fully in planning and implementing professional growth and development strategies for themselves and their colleagues.

TYPES OF CONCEPTS

Concepts are generally seen as the central units of instruction. They can be classified into different types depending on their sources of meaning. For example, consider the following list of terms and try to decide whether students can acquire understanding through (a) internal sensory stimuli, (b) external stimuli and the classification and seriation of observable phenomena, or (c) inferences from experience and assumptions about imaginary but not directly perceptible objects, events, or situations:

gene

environment

hunger

light wave

solution

pain

electrical conductor

interaction

ideal gas

Meanings of the terms *hunger* and *pain* come directly from internal senses, as do the meanings of terms such as *thirsty, tiredness,* and so on. Only if you have been hungry can you know what the term *hunger* means. External senses can also provide direct meanings. For example, the meanings of terms such as *green, red, hot/cold,* and *bitter/sweet* come directly from external stimuli. If you want to know how coffee tastes, you have to taste some coffee! In other words, the complete meaning of such terms is apprehended directly from internal or external stimuli. Thus this first type of concept is called a **concept by apprehension**. Such concepts are well understood before children enter kindergarten; hence they are not objects of school instruction.

The terms *environment, solution, electrical conductor,* and *interaction* can be understood by reference to familiar actions, perceptions, and examples. Their meanings come from external stimuli. However, unlike concepts by apprehension, as we discovered way back in Chapter 4 when we learned what Mellinarks are, their meanings are not immediately apprehended in their totality. For example, consider terms such as *table, chair,* and *book*. In reality these terms refer to abstractions. For example, not all tables look alike, but they are still tables. Thus such terms refer to "idealized" objects that have been hypothesized to exist in the "world out there" and have subsequently been unconsciously verified through their implied consequences. In other words, even though properties of tables, chairs, and books are perceptible, the ideas themselves are mental constructions. Conceptualizing and labeling such mental constructions serve to organize, summarize, and describe; hence such concepts are called **descriptive concepts**. Descriptive concepts also refer to perceived relations of objects and events. *Taller, heavier, wider, older, on top of, before,* and *under* are all terms that derive meaning from a comparison of properties of objects, events, or situations. To understand the meaning of such terms, people must also mentally construct order from environmental encounters.

The terms *gene, light wave,* and *ideal gas* must be understood in terms of complex interrelationships with other concepts (heredity, pressure, volume), functional relationships (ideal gas law, wave function), or inferences from experience. These understandings are not the result of direct experiences with perceptible properties. Rather the properties of such imagined entities are themselves imagined. As such, these concepts are called **theoretical concepts**. Said another way, theoretical concepts differ from descriptive concepts in that their defining properties are not perceptible. Theoretical concepts function as explanations for events that need causes but for which no causal agent can be directly perceived. Fairies, poltergeists, and ghosts fall into this category. Common examples from science are atoms, molecules, electrons, genes, and natural selection. The reason for the existence of theoretical concepts lies in a basic assumption we make about nature—that is, events do not occur without a cause. Thus, if we perceive certain events but cannot perceive objects or processes that cause such events, we do not conclude that the events are spontaneous and without cause. Instead we invent imaginary objects and interactions to explain the events in analogous perceptible causal terms. Because theoretical concepts are imagined and function to explain the otherwise unexplainable, they can be given whatever properties or qualities are necessary in terms of the theory in which they reside. That is, they derive their meaning in terms of the postulates of the theory of which they are a part.

Some terms have more than one meaning and thus may represent a descriptive or a theoretical concept depending upon their definition. *Temperature,* as read on a thermometer, represents a descriptive concept. However, *temperature,* as a measure of the average kinetic molecular energy, is a theoretical concept. Likewise, the term *habitat,* if defined as a place where an organism lives, is a descriptive concept. Indeed this meaning has been successfully taught to first graders. However, if the term *habitat* is defined as ecologists sometimes do as "an n-dimensional hyper-volume, every point of which corresponds to an environmental state permitting the species in question to maintain a steady state," the concept is clearly theoretical, and it even causes some graduate students difficulty. Thus, before being classified, a term must be clearly defined.

Importantly, both descriptive and theoretical concepts are "abstract" in the sense that their meanings come from multiple experiences and examples. *Interaction* is abstract in that it is very general, applicable to all objects that influence one another regardless of whether they exchange energy or momentum, modify the chemical composition, or (if living) infect one another with a disease. Because numerous experiences are readily available to illustrate the meaning of *interaction,* the concept is descriptive and has been taught successfully to second graders. The *light wave* concept is also abstract, though more restricted in applicability than *interaction.* Yet the meaning of *light wave* depends essentially on Maxwell's electromagnetic theory, which can be understood only through the use of functional relationships, abstract variables, idealized models, and other formal and/or postformal reasoning patterns. Hence, *light wave* is a theoretical concept.

In biology the *environment* concept is very abstract and general because it applies to individual cells, to entire multicellular organisms, to populations of organisms, and so on. Nonetheless, numerous direct experiences are readily available to demonstrate its meaning. The *gene* concept is also abstract. However, it is a different kind of abstraction than *environment*. Mendel hypothesized the existence of "factors" with specific imagined properties to explain ratios of observable characteristics obtained through crosses of pea plants. The factors, or genes, themselves did not give rise to direct experience. Thus, the *gene* concept has to be understood in terms of other concepts (heredity, trait), the possible combinations of genes that produce observable effects, and a theory relating the theoretical concept of genotype to the descriptive concept of phenotype. Hence, the *gene* concept is theoretical.

Of significance to the teacher attempting to teach theoretical concepts such as the electron, very young students can imagine tiny particles and can call them electrons, if the teacher wishes, but with little or no awareness or understanding of (a) the theory in which electrons reside and from which they derive their meaning and importance, (b) the puzzling observations that led to the postulation of these "tiny particles" in the first place, and (c) the evidence that supports their postulated existence. To the concrete operational student with little or no understanding of what theories are and their relationships to empirical data, the idea of the electron and other theoretical concepts must seem to have been derived as if by magic or perhaps by decree of some omniscient scientist. In short, one cannot fully comprehend the meaning of any single theoretical concept without some understanding of the theory of which it is a part and the empirical data upon which that theory is based. This is why lecturing about theoretical concepts to less than formal operational students—perhaps even less than postformal operational students—is typically met with blank stares, boredom, and in some cases disruptive behavior. The next section will discuss the nature of conceptual systems.

CONCEPTUAL SYSTEMS

How Are Concepts Organized?

Read the following six statements to see if you can identify the most "inclusive" concept.

1. Biological communities consist of interacting populations in which energy enters and exits the community and inorganic molecules are cycled between the community and its abiotic environment.

2. An ecosystem consists of the biological community, its abiotic environment, and all their interactions in a particular area.

3. The communities' producers absorb small inorganic molecules from the environment and with the use of solar energy synthesize complex organic molecules that are then used as a food energy (chemical energy) source during plant respiration.

4. Food energy is distributed to other populations in the community (the consumers and decomposers) through links in food chains and food webs.

5. Respiration of individuals at each feeding level converts useable food energy into nonuseable heat energy; thus less and less useable food energy is available at progressively higher levels, limiting the length of food chains.

6. Excretion and decomposition return inorganic molecules to the environment for absorption and reuse by producers.

The statements contain several biological terms (e.g., *biological communities, energy, ecosystem, abiotic environment*). If you understand each statement, you not only understand several concepts; you understand a conceptual system—in this case the ecosystem conceptual system. Importantly, the concepts embedded within this and other conceptual systems have an internal order in which each concept is related to others in a necessary way. Presumably this internal order reflects a similar order in the natural world.

Some of the descriptive concepts within any conceptual system are fundamental. They represent the system's descriptive foundation. Other concepts, though necessary, represent second- or third-order concepts and can be derived from the fundamental descriptive concepts. For example, to teach the higher-order ecosystem concept, lower-order descriptive concepts such as plants, animals, molds, bacteria, and yeasts need to be taught first. From these lower-order concepts are derived higher-order descriptive concepts such as producers, consumers, and decomposers. The producer concept refers to all the populations that produce food. The consumer concept refers to all the populations that eat producers or eat other consumers. And decomposers are organisms that ingest and break down the complex molecules contained in dead organisms and then deposit simpler inorganic molecules back into the environment. A third-order descriptive concept is that of the biological community, which includes all the producer, consumer, and decomposer populations in a given area. Finally, the most inclusive ecosystem concept is a fourth-order concept because ecosystems consist of the biological community plus the abiotic environmental factors in a given area. Thus, the ecosystem conceptual system, like other conceptual systems, has a hierarchical structure of subordinate and superordinate concepts (i.e., more inclusive concepts) as depicted in Figure 12.1.

A useful way to identify the key concepts in any conceptual system is to identify its basic claims (i.e., postulates), which is what the previous list of six statements comprises. That is, the statements are the basic postulates of ecosystem theory. The postulates of three additional conceptual systems (kinetic-molecular theory, Mendel's theory of inheritance, and natural selection theory) appear in Table 12.1. The postulates of these systems, when taken together, constitute the explanations of how atoms and molecules behave, how traits are passed from parent to offspring, and how organisms evolve. Concepts such as atom, molecule, gene, and dominant and recessive derive their meaning from postulates of the theories. When the theories become convincingly supported and widely accepted, they are referred to as "embedded" theories, and their postulates may take on the status of "facts." Thus, conceptual systems constitute our knowledge of the world and universe. They make up the laws of the land, the philosophies and religions that guide human lives—in short, the contents of human minds.

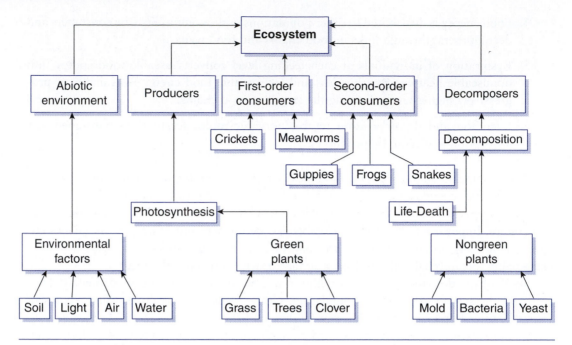

Figure 12.1 The hierarchical structure of some of the concepts within the ecosystem conceptual system.

Table 12.1 Postulates of Three Scientific Conceptual Systems

Kinetic-Molecular Theory

1. Matter consists of small particles (atoms and combinations of bonded atoms called molecules) and light, which consists of still smaller particles called photons.

2. Matter moves and can strike other matter and transfer some/all of its motion (kinetic energy) to the other piece of matter.

3. Photons can interact with electrons and cause them to move more rapidly. Photons may also be "released" from electrons, which causes light to be emitted and results in a reduction in the motion of the electrons.

4. Atoms differ from one another due to the different numbers of protons, neutrons, and electrons contained in each.

5. Attractive forces between atoms (i.e., molecular bonds) can "break," causing the atoms to move apart, which in turn can cause collisions and transfers of energy.

6. Molecular bonds can be formed between atoms when they strike one another.

Mendel's Theory of Inheritance

1. Inherited characteristics are determined by tiny particles called genes (Mendel called them factors).

2. Genes are passed from parent to offspring in the gametes.

3. Individuals have at least one pair of genes for each characteristic in all cells except the gametes.

4. During gamete formation, paired genes separate. Each gamete receives one gene of each pair with an equal chance of receiving either one.

5. When considering two or more pairs of genes, the genes of each pair assort independently to the gametes.

6. Genes of a pair separated in the gametes recombine randomly during fertilization.

7. Sometimes one gene of a pair dominates the other so that it alone controls the characteristic (dominant/recessive).

Natural Selection Theory

1. Populations have the potential to rapidly increase in numbers across generations.
2. In the short run, the number of individuals within populations remains fairly constant because environments limit population growth.
3. Individuals within populations exhibit variations in characteristics.
4. There is a struggle for survival so that individuals having favorable variations will survive to produce more offspring than those with unfavorable variations.
5. Some of the variations responsible for differential survival and reproduction are passed from parent to offspring (i.e., are heritable).
6. The environments of many organisms have been changing throughout geologic time.
7. Natural selection causes the accumulation of favorable variations and the loss of unfavorable variations.

The Role of Chunking

Importantly, the mind at any one moment can process only a limited amount of information. Miller (1956) introduced the term *chunk* to refer to the discrete units of information that could be consciously held in working memory and processed. He and others have found considerable evidence suggesting that the maximum number of these discrete units/chunks is about seven. However, as depicted in Figure 12.1, we clearly construct complex concepts that consist of far more information than seven units. For example, the ecosystem concept subsumes a far greater number of discrete units or chunks than seven. Yet the ecosystem concept probably consists of but one "chunk" in memory. This implies that a mental process must occur in which previously unrelated parts—that is, chunks of information (a maximum of about seven)—are assembled by the mind into one higher-order chunk or unit of thought. This implied process is known as **chunking.**

The result of chunking is extremely important. Chunking reduces the load on mental capacity and simultaneously opens up additional capacity that can then be occupied by additional concepts. This in turn allows one to form still more complex and inclusive concepts—concepts that subsume greater numbers of subordinate concepts. Turning back to our initial example, once we all know what an ecosystem is we no longer have to refer to an ecosystem as a biological community (including producers, consumers, and decomposers) plus the abiotic (i.e., nonliving) environment and so on. Use of the term *ecosystem* to subsume all of this information greatly facilitates thinking *and* communication when all parties have chunked/constructed the same concept.

INITIATING AND SEQUENCING UNITS

Any conceptual system can be meaningful to students only to the extent that it relates to their personal experiences. Thus, the beginning of any specific unit that intends to teach new concepts must provide students with experiences with the empirical world, either by direct sensory contact with physical and/or biological examples or by secondary experiences such as videos or descriptions of events or situations that the students can relate to their personal experiences. In teaching a conceptual system, an important task is to identify the basic concepts of the system. Each basic concept relates either perceptibly (i.e., descriptive concepts) or imperceptibly (i.e., theoretical concepts) to some phenomena. Because both types of concepts derive meaning from phenomena, either directly or indirectly, students cannot be expected to comprehend a concept's meaning without first experiencing the phenomena in question. In other words, because conceptual systems are constructed first upon a basic description of perceptible phenomena and only later upon imperceptible theoretical concepts, students must begin their conceptual construction with perceptible experience. Introduction of first-order descriptive concepts should precede introduction of second-order concepts so that the first-order concepts can be "chunked" into second-order concepts. Then the second-order descriptive concepts can be chunked into third-order descriptive concepts and so on. Once this descriptive base is formed, the groundwork has been laid for the introduction of the system's theoretical concepts, if there are any.

When the perceptible experiences are presented to introduce the descriptive concepts, they should be presented in a way that integrates the material to be learned, albeit in an undifferentiated way. Or, if students already understand the descriptive concepts, then the theoretical concepts can also be initially presented in an integrated yet undifferentiated fashion. The basic instructional sequence is as follows:

1. Perceptible phenomena presented

2. First-order descriptive concepts

3. Second-order descriptive concepts

4. Higher-order descriptive concepts

5. Theoretical concepts

Starting With an Undifferentiated "Whole"

At the start of any curriculum, students need to know, at least in a general way, what the curriculum is about and what it is not about. For example, consider a middle school curriculum to teach the ecosystem concept. Instruction might start with students exploring a plastic box divided into two sections with an aquarium in one section and a terrarium in the other. The aquarium contains sand, water, fish, snails, and various aquatic plants. The terrarium contains soil in which the students plant several types of seeds. The choice of an aquarium/terrarium system as a starting place is deliberate. The aquarium/terrarium is a miniature ecosystem with several parts that students will eventually learn about. The parts will then be conceptually integrated to eventually produce the ecosystem conceptual system. In this sense, the aquarium/terrarium represents an **undifferentiated whole.**

The idea of an undifferentiated whole may be vague and elusive, but it plays an essential role in meaningful learning—as opposed to the memorization of unrelated items. An undifferentiated whole spontaneously results from an interaction of the mind with new sensory input. The undifferentiated whole becomes differentiated and its resulting parts become integrated as a result of continued interaction with the experience. Perhaps an analogy will help clarify the concept. Consider a fertilized egg cell—a zygote. A zygote is a single relatively undifferentiated cell that has the potential to develop into a mature organism. Embryological development involves repeated cell divisions, cell differentiations, and their integration into a living, functioning organism. Likewise, an undifferentiated conceptual whole becomes conceptually differentiated through mental integration of the parts of the initial phenomenon.

Types of Undifferentiated Wholes

There are two types of undifferentiated wholes that are of interest. The aquarium/terrarium system mentioned above is an example of the first type—a whole of perceptible objects. The aquarium/terrarium system whole eventually becomes differentiated and integrated into the ecosystem concept at the end of the unit. Students can initially differentiate some parts of the system. But they are blind to many other parts and to practically all of the interrelations among those parts. For these students, the aquarium/terrarium system created in their minds a whole that was largely undifferentiated but that could be differentiated and eventually integrated into a complex conceptual system. Nevertheless, at the beginning, the whole was at the perceptible level because the students' initial reactions are primarily naming the parts they see, such as the fish, the water, and the sand, and asking for names of other parts, such as the duckweed and *Daphnia*.

An example of the second type of undifferentiated whole appears in Figure 12.2. The figure is from a textbook called *Biology: An Inquiry Approach* (A. E. Lawson, 2008). The figure represents both the puzzling observations and the basic components of a theory that attempts to explain them; hence it represents a theoretical symbolic whole. The figure includes both descriptive and theoretical concepts. In the text, the author introduces the basic descriptive concepts. He describes patterns of heredity in pea plants in which plants with purple flowers are mated with those with white flowers. All of the second-generation offspring plants have purple flowers. When these second-generation plants are next mated with themselves, the resulting third-generation plants have either purple or white flowers. Further, the ratio of purple- to white-flowered plants in the third generation turns out to be 3 to 1. Several causal questions are raised by these observations. For example: Why do all the second-generation plants have purple flowers? In other words, why did the white flowers disappear? Why do the third-generation plants have both purple and white flowers? Why did the white flowers reappear? And why do the flower colors appear in a 3-to-1 ratio?

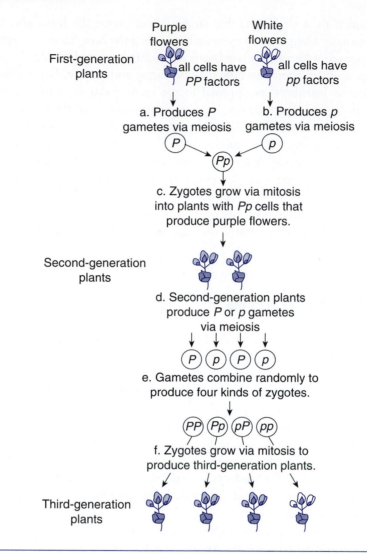

FIGURE 12.2   What does a theoretical symbolic whole look like? Descriptive concepts introduced and defined in relation to the diagram are gamete, zygote, and phenotype. Theoretical concepts introduced and defined are gene, genotype, heterozygous, homozygous, dominant, and recessive.

Thus, in the beginning, the descriptive foundation is laid for the introduction of the theoretical conceptual system that attempts to explain the descriptive foundation. Importantly, the entire explanatory system is not introduced at the start. Instead, only the basic descriptive and theoretical concepts are introduced. These basic concepts are part of Gregor Mendel's inheritance theory. The basic postulates of that theory, first published in 1866, were listed in Table 12.1. Those basic postulates lay the foundation that is later developed into a refined conceptual system by the dual processes of differentiation and integration.

Another example of a theoretical symbolic whole appears in Figure 12.3. The figure comes from a geology course taught by geologist Steven Semken for Native Americans,

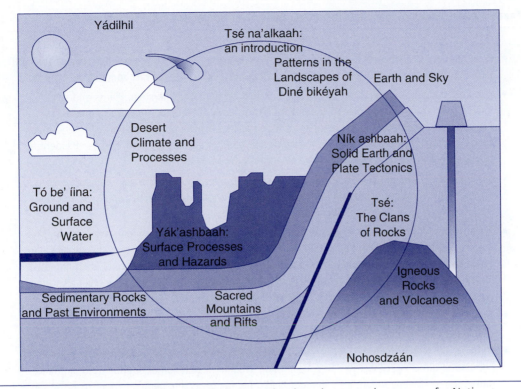

Yádilhil

Tsé na'alkaah:
an introduction
Patterns in the
Landscapes of
Diné bikéyah

Earth and Sky

Desert
Climate and
Processes

Ník ashbaah:
Solid Earth and
Plate Tectonics

Tó be' íina:
Ground and
Surface
Water

Tsé:
The Clans
of Rocks

Yák'ashbaah:
Surface Processes
and Hazards

Igneous
Rocks
and Volcanoes

Sedimentary Rocks
and Past Environments

Sacred
Mountains
and Rifts

Nohosdzáán

FIGURE 12.3   A symbolic undifferentiated whole used to introduce a geology course for Native Americans, Navajos, living on the Colorado Plateau.

Navajos, living on the Colorado Plateau in northeastern Arizona. The figure, which is presented on the first day of class and depicts the entire course scope and sequence, is designed to evoke a sense of Colorado Plateau geology and to illustrate the physical and spatial relationships among the 12 major subject areas presented in the course. Each of the subject areas is directly relevant to the homeland environment and interests of the Navajo people.

TEACHING THE ECOSYSTEM CONCEPTUAL SYSTEM

Let's now consider an example to illustrate how the curriculum construction principles can be applied to construct "units" of instruction (i.e., series of learning cycles to teach specific concepts and conceptual systems). The example is that of the ecosystem. This is a reasonable topic to consider as student understanding of ecosystem dynamics is included in both national and state standards (see Table 12.2). In developing units, teachers and curriculum developers should begin with a careful review of such standards.

As mentioned, ecosystem theory derives its meaning from an analysis of the relationships among the various *classes* of objects within the system. First, observable objects and organisms such as water, frogs, and grass must be organized into classes such as producers and consumers, and then relationships among these classes must be examined. It is the

TABLE 12.2 National Standards Regarding Biological Populations and Ecosystems

- A population consists of all individuals of a species that occur together at a given place and time. All populations living together and the physical factors with which they interact compose an ecosystem.

- Populations can be categorized by the function they serve in an ecosystem. Plants and some microorganisms are producers—they make their own food. All animals, including humans, are consumers, which obtain food by eating other organisms. Decomposers, primarily bacteria and fungi, are consumers that use waste materials and dead organisms for food. Food webs identify the relationships among producers, consumers, and decomposers.

- For ecosystems, the major source of energy is sunlight. Energy entering ecosystems as sunlight is transferred by producers into chemical energy through photosynthesis. That energy then passes from organism to organism in food webs.

- The number of organisms an ecosystem can support depends on the resources available and abiotic factors, such as quantity of light and water, range of temperatures, and soil composition. Given biotic and abiotic resources and no disease or predators, populations (including humans) increase at rapid rates. Lack of resources and other factors, such as predation and climate, limit the growth of populations in specific niches in the ecosystem.

- Organisms both cooperate and compete in ecosystems. The interrelationships and interdependencies may generate ecosystems that remain stable for hundreds or thousands of years.

- Humans live within the world's ecosystems. Increasingly, humans modify ecosystems as a result of population growth, technology, and consumption. Human destruction of habitats through direct harvesting, pollution, atmospheric changes, and other factors is threatening current global stability, and if not addressed, ecosystems will be irreversibly affected.

pattern, or form, of the relationships among these related classes that constitutes an ecosystem; hence the ecosystem concept requires understanding higher-order relationships. How can students understand these higher-order relationships? Let's examine some of the learning cycle lessons that have been designed to do just this.

Introducing the Undifferentiated Whole

As described earlier, to initiate exploration, students start with a complete but simple ecosystem—an undifferentiated perceptual whole. The assumption is made that the introduction of a complete but simplified ecosystem in this way is sufficient to capitalize on students' intuitive and partial understandings of living and nonliving systems. In other words, students realize that we need food, water, and air; they realize that cows eat grass, that too much heat kills plants, and so on. These are the types of intuitive and partial understandings that subsequent inquiries will differentiate and integrate into an understanding of ecosystems.

First, students are grouped into teams to build their own systems. They plant a variety of seeds in the terrarium and add *Anacharis*, green algae culture, duckweed, and other green plants to the aquarium. In a week or so, after the plants have begun to grow and the algae population has increased, *Daphnia*, mealworms, isopods, snails, crickets, tadpoles, or other plant eaters are added to the systems. During this time students observe and record the feeding relationships and behavior patterns of the organisms. Animal eaters are then added to the systems. Guppies, frogs, or chameleons can be used for this purpose. Again, feeding relationships are observed. The guppies will eat the *Daphnia,* which ate the algae. The frogs will eat the mealworms; and the chameleons will eat the crickets, which ate the grass, and so on.

Introducing Basic Descriptive Concepts

During a class discussion, the terms *environmental factors* and *environment* are introduced. To do so, students compare the various systems in the classroom and name all the living or nonliving "things" that they think may affect the organisms in their systems. Students suggest factors such as soil, water, light, air, temperature, the plastic box itself, and so forth. When each factor is mentioned, it is listed on the board. At the top of the list the teacher then writes the term *environmental factors* and points out that all of these environmental factors taken together make up an organism's *environment.* This represents term introduction.

While the plant eaters and animal eaters are being added to the systems, a number of specific experiments are initiated to examine relationships among the plants and animals of the systems and their environmental factors. These experiments are considered concept application activities with the descriptive concept of environmental factors. The response of isopods to water, heat, and light is explored, as is the effect of various concentrations of salt on the hatching of brine shrimp eggs. Experiments examining the effect of a number of factors such as light, heat, soil, sand, water, and antiseptic solutions on the rate of decomposition of various types of plants and animals present are other interesting ways to examine environmental relationships.

Following a number of these experiments and observations of the aquarium/terrarium systems, students again gather together for a discussion of what they have done and observed. A blank chart such as that shown in Figure 12.4 is drawn on the board.

The teacher then asks students to report the names of the plant types in their systems. As the name of each plant type is mentioned, it is placed on the chart in the appropriate box. The teacher then asks students to report on which animals ate which plants. The names of the plant eaters are then written on the chart with an arrow drawn from the plant to the animal indicating the feeding relationship. Students then name the animals that ate other animals. Once the names of all the organism types are written on the chart and the arrows are drawn (as shown in Figure 12.5), the teacher focuses students' attention on sequences of feeding relationships and introduces the term *food chain* to refer to each such sequence. The term *food chain* labels this second-order descriptive concept. The terms *producers, first-* and *second-order consumers,* and *decomposers* are also introduced. These terms correspond to sections of the chart; thus classes of organisms with specific feeding relationships are differentiated within the system.

Terms that refer to the third-order descriptive concepts of *aquarium community* and *terrarium community* are then written on the board below the chart to indicate that the sum of all such feeding relationships among the classes or organisms in an area (in this case in the aquarium/terrarium system) is called a *biological community.*

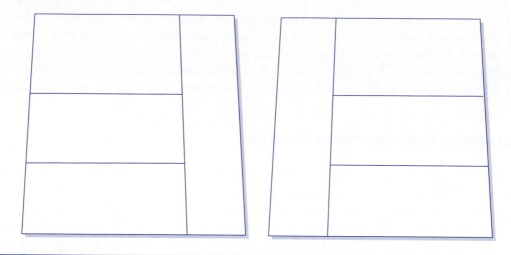

FIGURE 12.4   A blank chart used to record feeding relationships.

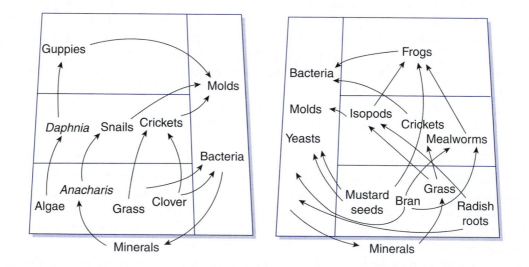

FIGURE 12.5   The chart showing observed feeding relationships within the classroom systems.

Introducing the Higher-Order Ecosystem Concept

All of these lessons pave the way for introduction of the term *ecosystem*. Once the chart of the aquarium and terrarium communities is completed, all that remains to be added is the abiotic environment. To do this, the teacher asks the students what things, other than food, the populations in the community require in order to live. Students suggest environmental factors such as those studied previously and perhaps others not already mentioned. All of these factors are then listed on the board with arrows indicating which populations each factor influences. This is shown in Figure 12.6. The teacher adds the word *environment* to the bottom

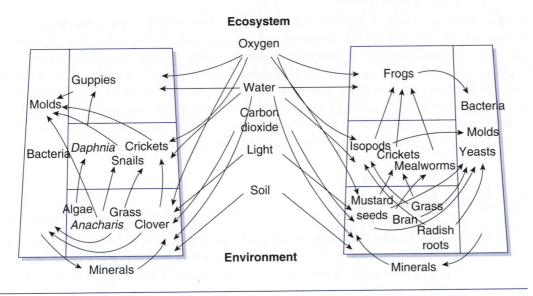

FIGURE 12.6   The chart is a symbolic representation (i.e., a model) of the aquarium/terrarium systems used to introduce the higher-order term *ecosystem.* Symbolization of familiar objects and familiar events is a necessary step in concept construction.

of the list and explains that a biological community interacting with its abiotic (nonliving) environment is called an *ecosystem*. The term *ecosystem* is then written at the top of the chart, and term introduction is complete. The subordinate concepts can then be mentally "chunked" (i.e., integrated) to produce a single higher-order concept—the ecosystem concept.

At this point, most students will have an initial grasp of the meaning of the term *ecosystem* and its use but relative only to the experienced phenomena—that is, relative to the classroom aquarium/terrarium systems. If instruction ended here, the more general aspects of the ecosystem concept would probably be lost. In other words, biologists realize that human beings are a part of ecosystems, and they conceptualize ponds, forests, grasslands, seashores, the ocean floor, and so on all as ecosystems. These ecosystems are interconnected, but at the same time they can be conceptually isolated. However, it is extremely unlikely that students will construct these more abstract understandings unless additional activities involving the ecosystem concept are initiated. These additional activities constitute the concept application phase of instruction, and they are essential for students to construct a more general and useful understanding.

Generalizing the Ecosystem Concept

According to the suggested instructional pattern, to generalize the ecosystem concept, students need a series of additional activities all involving the same concepts and the same symbolic notation but in varying contexts. In other words, students need to explore other ecosystems such as forests, rivers, ponds, sandy beaches, rocky intertidal areas, deserts, lawns, and so on. These ecosystems can be explored through field trips to the actual areas be they 50 miles away or on the school grounds, through videos, slides, the Internet, trips to museums, or perhaps zoos. The language (symbolic notation) used throughout all of these explorations must stay the same. That language of course includes terms such as *environment, producers, consumers, decomposers, population, food chain, food web, community,* and *ecosystem*. The exploration of a variety of ecosystems and the continued reintroduction of the terms allows the students to use the terms in a variety of contexts and to eventually abstract the more general "form" of the concepts from their "concrete" exemplars.

SCHEDULING LEARNING CYCLES

As we have seen, an inquiry curriculum consists of a series of carefully chosen and sequenced learning cycles. But how can the learning cycles be scheduled to best facilitate student involvement and achievement? Because some learning cycles require extended periods of time for data gathering, which on any one day may only require a few minutes of class time, you will often need to initiate one learning cycle before finishing others. In fact, it is common to have several learning cycles simultaneously in progress. Instead of this leading to student confusion, it is actually an opportunity for synthesis of related subject matter.

To ensure that class time is used fully, reserve a place on the board to list the day's activities. For example, on any one day your list may look like this: (a) gather data for lesson 5 (about 10 minutes); (b) post graphs from lesson 4 on board and discuss (about 20 minutes); (c) introduce and begin lesson 6 (about 20 minutes). When students become familiar with this approach, they will arrive in the classroom, read the board, and often go straight to work without your having to say anything at all.

Now that we have introduced some of the basic principles for designing and teaching an inquiry-based curriculum, the chapter concludes by briefly considering how to integrate technological and societal issues into the curriculum.

INTEGRATING TECHNOLOGICAL AND SOCIETAL ISSUES

During the past few decades, an influential movement called the "Science-Technology-Society" (STS) movement has argued for the integration of technological and societal issues into the science classroom. Some science educators have even taken the STS movement so to heart that they appear to be advocating curriculum reform in which key technological and societal issues provide the primary focus of instruction. For example, units of instruction could be developed around the energy crisis, the greenhouse effect, oil spills, and so forth. In such a curriculum, science concepts are introduced when needed to understand aspects of the relevant technological and/or societal issues.

Developing science units around technological and societal issues may be appropriate on occasion and highly motivating. For example, Arwood (2004) developed and taught a cell biology course in which students learned how to use fingerprinting and DNA typing.

Students then held a mock murder trial in which these and other techniques were used to gather key evidence. The course not only was highly motivating; it significantly increased both student reasoning skills and their attitudes toward science. Similarly, Sadler (2004) reviewed considerable evidence suggesting that the STS approach can provide an important forum for developing students' reasoning/argumentation skills, their understanding of the nature of science, and their understanding of fundamental science concepts.

As a general strategy for curriculum development, however, the STS approach may lead to difficulties for essentially three reasons. First, few teachers are expert and knowledgeable enough to be able to "pull off" this sort of integration. Second, the curriculum would have to be modified whenever a new crisis arises, and third, there is another way. That other way is to integrate relevant technological and societal issues into the curriculum as part of the concept application phase of learning cycles—cycles that have the primary objective of exploring and explaining nature. This inquiry approach puts the motivation for science instruction where it naturally resides—in one's natural curiosity to explore and explain nature. Once such explanations have been obtained in the sense of basic science, they can then be applied to technological and/or societal issues, in the sense of applied science. Indeed this is the normal historical relationship.

For example, the suggested inquiry approach would be to *explore* patterns of inheritance, *introduce* concepts of Mendelian genetics, *explore* the molecular nature of the genetic "material," *introduce* concepts of DNA structure/function, and then discover how these concepts *apply* to issues such as genetic engineering, DNA fingerprinting, cancer research, and so on. Or, in a chemistry class, students can *explore* the question: What's in water? The teacher could then *introduce* terms such as *hardness, polarity,* and *solubility* and other concepts of solution chemistry. These concepts could then be *applied* to issues of water pollution. Thus, a beauty of constructing a curriculum based on sequenced learning cycles is that each cycle contains a built-in application phase. Consequently, linking (i.e., applying) newly introduced concepts to technological and societal issues is relatively easy when the teacher or curriculum developer knows ahead of time what those links are. However, even when teachers or developers do not provide explicit links, students can often find such links on their own. Of course, teachers can encourage this by asking students to sift through recent newspaper and magazine articles and the like for applications/links.

Advocating the inquiry approach to linking technological and societal issues to the basic science does not imply that such issues do not influence basic science. Indeed they do; however, these influences, outside of the obvious influences that microscopes and telescopes have on biology and astronomy, are generally very subtle and beyond the experience of most secondary school students. Thus these subtle issues are better left for graduate-level college courses in the history and/or philosophy of science. In short, using inquiry, teachers can link technological and societal issues to the science rather than the other way around.

The Committee on High School Biology Education advocates a similar approach and similar objection to courses offered under the STS banner (National Research Council, 1990). In the committee's words:

> We are concerned that courses offered as "science, technology, and society" (STS) usually do not follow a study of basic sciences. Instead, they typically replace basic

science courses, and that results in both a dilution of fundamental knowledge of basic sciences and a lack of scientific breadth needed to study interdisciplinary topics more than superficially. (p. 88)

So instead of running the risk of creating an STS curriculum in which students fail to acquire the needed scientific declarative and procedural knowledge for application to technological and societal issues, the council takes the position, like that stated above, that the basic science should be taught as the core and then applied in relevant social contexts. More specifically, it proposes an interdisciplinary "capstone" course offered during the last year of high school that would consider current STS issues.

Summary

- Concepts by apprehension derive meaning from internal or external sensory stimuli. Descriptive concepts derive meaning from postulation and test. Descriptive concepts have directly perceptible properties. Theoretical concepts derive meaning from analogies and from their positions within conceptual systems.

- Chunking occurs in which previously unrelated chunks are assembled into higher-order chunks. Chunking reduces the load on working memory and simultaneously opens up additional capacity that can then be occupied by additional concepts, thus allowing for the construction of more complex and inclusive concepts.

- Conceptual systems are based on a description of perceptible phenomena and later on imperceptible theoretical concepts. Thus, curricula should begin with perceptible experience and the introduction of descriptive concepts followed by the introduction of theoretical concepts. Both perceptible experiences and theoretical concepts should be initially presented as integrated yet undifferentiated wholes.

- An example of curriculum development details how inquiries are used to eventually allow for introduction of ecosystem theory.

- Inquiry instruction puts the motivation for instruction in one's natural curiosity to explore and explain nature. Once such explanations have been obtained in the sense of basic science, they can be applied to technological and/or societal issues as part of the concept application phase.

Key Terms

chunking

concept by apprehension

descriptive concepts

theoretical concepts

undifferentiated whole

Application Questions/Activities

1. Identify the basic theories (conceptual systems) that you think should be taught in your course (e.g., high school biology, eighth-grade physical science, high school physics). On a large sheet of paper create a diagram (i.e., a concept map) showing the primary relationships among the major concepts.

2. What relationship, if any, does your diagram have with the levels of organization (i.e., atom → molecule → cell → organ → organism → population → community → ecosystem → biosphere → planet → solar system → galaxy → universe)?

3. In what way(s) does your diagram reflect hierarchical relationships?

4. In what order should the basic concepts/theories be taught in your course? Why?

Chapter 13

ASSESSING STUDENT PROGRESS

The Educational Policies Commission (1961) offered two criteria for selecting the knowledge students should learn. In its words, "One is the potential of the knowledge for the development of rational powers, and the other is the relative importance of the knowledge in the life of the pupil and of society" (p. 19). Although these criteria are helpful in selecting topics to teach, they are even more helpful in selecting topics to assess. This chapter begins with a look at types of assessments, how to reduce bias in testing, and how to assign grades. It then considers how to develop effective exams, homework problems, and written assignments.

To get started thinking critically about assessment, try to answer both of the following exam items and then think about what facts and/or reasoning patterns you needed to answer them correctly. If possible compare your thoughts with those of other students and/or your course instructor.

Tests are only one way to assess student progress.

APPLICABLE NSES STANDARDS

Standard C Science teachers engage in ongoing assessment of their teaching and of student learning. In doing so, they

- Use multiple methods and systematically gather data about student understanding and ability.
- Guide students in self-assessment.

(Continued)

(Continued)

■ Use student data, teaching observations, and interactions with colleagues to reflect on and improve teaching practice.

■ Use student data, teaching observations, and interactions with colleagues to report student achievement and learning opportunities to students, teachers, parents, policy makers, and the general public.

Item 1. Which type of bond is most often found in carbon compounds?

    a. metallic bond
    b. covalent bond
    c. ionic bond
    d. hydrogen bond
    e. cohesive bond

Item 2. The following two hypotheses have been advanced to explain neural tube development on the dorsal (upper) surface of a frog embryo.

Hypothesis I: Notochord cells under the dorsal ectoderm induce the ectoderm cells to differentiate into a neural tube.

Hypothesis II: Something internal to the ectoderm cells causes them to differentiate into a neural tube.

Which of the following results would contradict Hypothesis I?

    a. Notochord cells are removed, and the ectoderm cells differentiate into a neural tube.
    b. Notochord cells are removed, and the ectoderm cells do not differentiate into a neural tube.
    c. Ectoderm cells cultured by themselves do not differentiate into a neural tube.

TYPES OF ASSESSMENT

Authentic Assessment

Consider scientists. How would you find out how good they are as scientists? Perhaps you would attend a presentation of theirs on their latest research. You might also read one or more of their recent publications. You might then assess the quality of their presentation and/or publications based on some well-thought-out criteria. Based on how their "performance" stacks up, you give them high marks. You might even judge their performance as exceptional, perhaps even worthy of a Nobel Prize.

In a similar manner one could ask science students to conduct some research of their own, present it to their classmates, and write it up as a report. You could then use some well-thought-out criteria to assess their performance. Likewise an English teacher might assess students' short stories, a drama teacher might assess students' performances in a play, an art teacher might assess students' paintings, an engineering teacher might assess students' inventions, and a music teacher might assess students' performances at a recital or a concert.

Although such "performance" assessments are time consuming and more difficult to grade than standard pencil-paper exams, they are strongly encouraged for several reasons, not the least of which is that they become part of the learning experience. If we were to conduct such assessments, we would be using what is referred to as **authentic assessment**. According to Wiggins and McTighe (2005), an assessment task, a problem, or a project is authentic if it (a) is realistically contextualized, (b) requires student judgment and innovation, (c) asks students to "do" the subject, (d) replicates a situation in which adults are "tested" in the workplace, (e) assesses students' ability to use skills and concepts, and (f) provides opportunities for students to rehearse, practice, consult resources, get feedback, and refine their performance and/or product. Clearly, developing authentic assessments is a goal to strive for.

Formative and Summative Assessment

With the goal of making our assessments authentic, we should note that assessment data and procedures have two mutually supportive components. First, we would like to know where students stand at the start of instruction and the extent to which they are progressing toward course goals as the curriculum unfolds. For example, you may want to administer a test of reasoning skills prior to the start of instruction. Knowing how students reason at the outset can be very helpful not only in making sure that you pitch initial instruction at their level but also in knowing which students need extra help and which need an extra challenge. Prior assessments of this sort are often referred to as **formative assessment**. Formative assessment can help us make initial curricular decisions as well as midcourse corrections to improve the curriculum and/or our teaching methods. It may also help us know what specific concepts, or misconceptions, students have prior to instruction. You can develop and administer formative assessments to find out. Classroom discussions can also do the trick. Whenever a good causal question is raised and students are asked to brainstorm alternative hypotheses, they reveal prior conceptions and misconceptions.

When we reach the end of instruction, we need to know how successful the curriculum and our methods were in terms of students' attainment of course goals. This second type of assessment is called **summative assessment** and is often reflected in a course grade for each student.

ANTICIPATING AND REDUCING BIAS

It goes without saying that our assessments should be unbiased. With this in mind, consider the following research results:

1. Expectations affect performance. For example, when tests are preceded by statements such as "Females tend to outperform males on this test," they do, and vice versa. This sort of expectation effect is also likely to extend to students from minority cultures.

2. Past interests and experiences affect performance. For example, when test items are written in female contexts, females tend outperform males, and vice versa. De-contextualized items tend to favor males.

3. Test formats affect performance. Male performance superiority found on some pencil-paper measures is reduced or eliminated in oral versions of the same measures. On multiple-choice items that include an "I don't know" response option, females select it more often than males. Although females may know less than males about such items, they may know more than males; hence they see hidden complexities and become more cautious. Perhaps you can suggest other possibilities and how they might be tested.

4. The test administrator's gender, race, and cultural background affect performance. For example, female performance is enhanced when the test administrator is female. Black student performance is enhanced when the test administrator is Black.

5. Test anxiety adversely affects performance. Some minority student groups have been adversely affected by one or more of the previously mentioned factors. Hence when they are about to take another test, especially a test that is perceived to be difficult and/or one with limited time to complete, test anxiety is further increased, which further reduces performance.

What then can teachers do to reduce or eliminate gender and cultural bias when designing and administering assessments? Here are some suggestions:

1. Avoid saying or doing anything that suggests to any student group that it is likely to perform worse than another group or groups.

2. Construct assessment items that are contextualized. For example, a de-contextualized item looks like this:

   What are ways that DDT can still enter the food chains of birds?

   A contextualized item looks like this:

   Biologists have found that eggs of fish-eating birds often have very thin shells that crack open before hatching. This is puzzling because DDT, a chemical linked to fragile bird eggs, has not been used in the United States for over 20 years. What are some ways that the birds might still be being exposed to DDT? (Baker & Piburn, 1997)

3. Balance items in terms of formats, contexts, and past student experiences so that you do not favor particular student groups. Keep in mind that just changing a few male pronouns to female pronouns or a few Roberts to Robertos makes little or no difference.

4. Look at past performance patterns on specific items that might suggest hidden gender or cultural bias. Remove or change any such items.

5. Try to avoid high-stress testing conditions whenever possible. For example, teach students how to prepare for tests. Make sure they have sufficient time to prepare for and to take tests. Use a variety of assessment procedures (e.g., take-home tests typically provoke little stress). Make sure that no one assessment counts for an inordinate amount of students' grades. And provide students with timely and adequate feedback so they are better prepared for and more confident to take the next test.

ASSIGNING GRADES

Good inquiry instruction raises questions that students are naturally curious about and intrinsically motivated to answer. In contrast, motivation to earn a good grade represents extrinsic motivation. And when people do something solely for extrinsic reward, they often stop doing so whenever the extrinsic reward is eliminated. In this sense assigning grades can be counterproductive as it may discourage students from future learning. Nevertheless, grading is necessary as a means of providing valuable feedback to students, to their parents, and to other interested parties; hence it must be carried out thoughtfully and fairly.

After reviewing the available but sparse literature on grading practices, Stiggins, Frisbie, and Griswold (1989) offer the following recommendations and reasons:

1. Students should be informed of the policies, procedures, and components (including relative weighting of each component) used to arrive at final grades at the outset of instruction. Reason: Teachers have a professional and ethical obligation to be open and fair to students.

2. Grades should be awarded based on the acquisition of both procedural and declarative knowledge. Reason: Both types of knowledge allow for clear and measurable means of assigning grades.

3. Attitude, motivation, interest, and personality should not be used as a basis for grading. Reason: Not only are these aspects too subjective to define and difficult to measure; they do not necessarily reflect academic achievement.

4. Learning ability should not be used as the sole basis for assigning grades. Reason: Although learning ability (typically measured by reasoning ability—see Chapter 3) often correlates highly with achievement, it alone is an unfair basis for assigning grades because it fails to take other factors into consideration. Fortunately, given appropriate instruction, student reasoning/learning ability will increase during the year. Hence, student performance will improve, and taking such improvement into account is fair and is encouraged. For example, given consistent improvement, early test scores can be disregarded—see point 11 page 226.

5. Summative, not formative, assessments should be used for grading. Reason: Frequent summative assessments give the most reliable measure of student progress and achievement.

6. Pencil-paper exams can provide valid and reliable means of summative assessment. Reason: They permit written and reproducible assessments and records of a variety of learning outcomes.

7. Oral exams should be used sparingly. Reason: They have questionable validity and reliability.

8. Data should be collected frequently in concise units. Reason: Doing so increases reliability and reduces student anxiety.

9. Grades should not be awarded solely on the normal curve (so-called norm-referenced assessment). Reason: Although classroom performance typically distributes itself normally, grading strictly on the normal curve is inherently unfair because, at least in theory, it is possible for all students to acquire the desired knowledge and skills; hence it should be possible for all students to receive high grades. Nevertheless, this seldom, if ever, happens. Hence reality dictates that the highest-performing students should receive the best grades and the lowest-performing students should receive the worst grades.

10. Grades should be assigned based on the extent to which predetermined objectives have been met. Reason: Although doing so is recommended (i.e., so-called criterion-referenced assessment), in practice it is extremely difficult to develop assessments in which reasonable percentages of students fall into fixed categories. For example, you may unintentionally develop and administer a test in which the highest score is 85%. This does not mean that your test was faulty or unfair or that the higher-scoring students should not be awarded grades of A. It simply means that grades should typically be assigned based on a combination of norm- and criterion-referenced methods. For example, suppose the class average on an exam was 65% instead of the expected 75%. All you have to do to correct this deviation is to add 10% to each student's score and then grade the resulting scores based on your categories of 90%–100%, 80%–89%, and so on.

11. Borderline cases should be reviewed in light of additional achievement information and/or extenuating circumstances. Reason: Although we seek to develop and use the most rational, valid, and reliable assessments possible, grading nonetheless is an inexact practice with somewhat arbitrary cutoff points. Hence it makes sense to review borderline cases and give the benefit of the doubt when warranted (e.g., consistent improvement allows one to drop an early poor exam score and thus award a higher grade). However, a note of caution is in order. If students learn that they are "on the borderline," they may pressure teachers for better grades. Students may even volunteer to do "extra credit" to get the better grade. Although "the squeaky wheel often gets the grease," you should resist this sort of pressure because giving in is unfair to other students who do not apply such pressure. What borderline students seldom realize is that the good and bad breaks tend to average out in the long run. I have yet to have a borderline student argue with me that he or she should receive the lower grade because he or she made a lucky guess on an exam item!

DEVELOPING EFFECTIVE EXAMS

Exploring Exam Items

Let's start our look at developing effective exams by exploring some typical exam items. Below are several example items. Read the items from your discipline(s) and think about how you would respond. Even if you do not know the answers (that is not important), think about what information you would need and/or what reasoning patterns you would need to answer each item. On the basis of what you have learned to this point, classify the items as requiring

1. only the recall of specific facts,
2. concept understanding and concrete reasoning patterns, or
3. concept understanding and formal or postformal reasoning patterns.

Recall that concrete reasoning patterns include

C1. classify observations; relate systems to subsystems, classes to subclasses;

C2. apply conservation reasoning to objects;

C3. establish one-to-one correspondences or serially order a set of observations;

C4. understand and apply descriptive concepts (i.e., concepts defined in terms of familiar objects, events, or situations);

C5. apply a memorized algorithm or formula.

Formal and/or postformal reasoning patterns include

F1. understand and apply theoretical concepts (i.e., concepts that derive their meaning from inferences rather than from direct experience); use theories and idealized models to interpret data;

F2. use combinatorial reasoning;

F3. identify functional relationships and apply proportional reasoning;

F4. understand the general necessity for the control of variables and recognize hidden assumptions;

F5. recognize the implications of probability for experimental design and data analysis;

F6. use hypothetical-predictive reasoning in causal contexts.

Item 1. The stages in the life cycle of a housefly are, in order,

        a. larva—egg—pupa—adult
        b. pupa—larva—egg—adult
        c. pupa—egg—larva—adult

    d. egg—larva—adult—pupa

    e. egg—larva—pupa—adult

Item 2. Fifty pieces of plant parts were placed in each of five sealed containers of equal size. At the start of the experiment each jar contained 250 units of CO_2. The amount of CO_2 in each jar at the end of 2 days is shown in the table.

Container	Plant	Plant Part	Light Color	Temperature °C	CO_2 Remaining
1	Willow	Leaf	Blue	10	200
2	Maple	Leaf	Purple	23	50
3	Willow	Root	Red	18	300
4	Maple	Stem	Red	23	400
5	Willow	Leaf	Blue	23	150

On the basis of these data, which jars should be compared to find out if temperature affects the amount of CO_2 used per day? Please explain why you chose those jars.

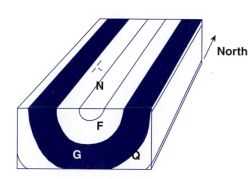

Item 3. Of the labeled beds of the block diagram at left, the correct order from oldest to youngest is:

    a. NFGQ

    b. FQGN

    c. QGFN

    d. GNFQ

Please explain your choice.

Item 4. Use the diagram and data below to answer the next question.

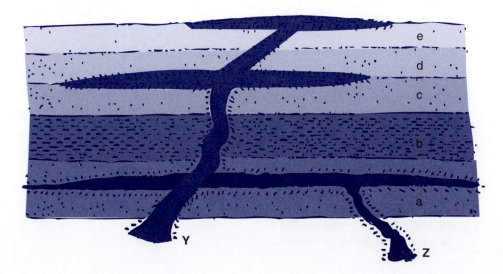

Data:

- a, b, c, d, and e are sedimentary beds.
- Y and Z are igneous rocks.
- All rocks adjacent to Y and Z appear to be chemically altered.
- Y contains radioactive material dated at 40 million years.
- b contains igneous rock material, which has been dated at 200 million years.

    a. Rock c is younger than b and older than Z.
    b. Rock b is younger than Z and older than a.
    c. Rock a is older than Z and younger than Y.
    d. Rock c is older than b and older than Z.
    e. Rock Z is younger than a and older than Y.

Please explain your choice.

_____

Item 5. A geologist finds a sandstone bed 1,000 feet in thickness. She notes the size of the sand particles and by studying the patterns of deposition determines that the sandstone bed was deposited by stream action. She then finds a stream that carries and deposits particles of the same size in the same patterns. This stream deposits 1 foot of sand every 10 years on the average. From this, she concludes that the sandstone bed was deposited over a period of at least 10,000 years. Which of the following are valid assumptions made by the geologist?

    a. Streams carried particles in the past as they do today.
    b. Particles deposited today are similar to particles deposited in the past.
    c. The deposition of the sandstone bed was continuous and constant.
    d. Gravity and climate acted on streams in the past as they do today.
    e. Three of the above are probably valid.

Please explain your choice.

_____

Item 6. The relative rates of diffusion of two gases under ideal conditions are inversely proportional to the square roots of their molecular weights. In a test comparing diffusion of onion vapor (molecular weight 720) and perfume vapor (molecular weight 360), the onion vapor is detected about 6 seconds after its release. About how long after release would you expect to detect perfume vapor?

    a. 3 seconds
    b. 4 seconds
    c. 5 seconds
    d. 9 seconds
    e. 12 seconds

_____

Item 7. How many atoms are in one molecule of a substance with the following molecular formula?

$(NH_4)_2TiO(C_4O_4) \cdot H_2O$

Item 8. Balance the following equation involving the new elements X and Z:

$$2\ H_2XO_3 + (A)\ H_3ZO_3 \rightarrow (B)\ HX + (C)\ H_3ZO_4 + (D)\ H_2O$$

The coefficient (C) is

a. 1

b. 2

c. 3

d. 4

e. 5

Item 9. An object falling from rest near the surface of the Earth moves through the distance s in the time t. These variables are related by the equation $s = 1/2gt^2$, where g is the acceleration of gravity. Circle the points where the particle will be at $t = 2$ sec and at $t = 3$ sec, given the marked points at $t = 0$ sec and $t = 1$ sec.

- $t = 0$ sec
- $t = 1$ sec

Spring balance

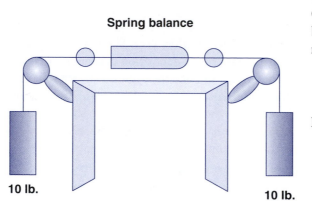

10 lb.   10 lb.

Item 10. The diagram to the left shows two weights connected to a scale by strings passing over two pulleys. What is the scale reading?

Classifying Exam Items

Item 1 involves only knowledge and thus falls into category 1. Students either know or do not know the proper sequence. Reasoning is not required. Item 2 was classified as formal because it requires students to recognize ambiguous and unambiguous experimental conditions—that is, to understand controlled experiments (F4). Item 3 was classified as concrete because it requires students to recall the fact that older layers of sediment are deposited first (C1) and to serially order the observations (C3) and (C4). Item 4 also involves serial ordering (C3). Although the problem involves a much more complicated application of reasoning, it does not demand formal reasoning. The item is classified as concrete. If, however, the alternatives given the students were not so directive, the item could require formal thought because a careful analysis of combinations of layers and ages (F2) would be required. Item 5 was classified as formal because it requires students to recognize hidden assumptions (F4) and understand the geologist's use of an incorrect assumption (F1 and F4). Item 6 requires students to apply an inverse square-root relationship and a formal reasoning pattern (F1). Item 7 was classified as concrete because the correct response requires applying certain facts and well-defined rules regarding chemical formulas and using them to manipulate symbols (F5). Item 8 was classified as formal because it requires a systematic overall approach to analysis and comparison of the various combinations and possibilities (F2). It also requires hypothetical-predictive reasoning (F6) as in "B has to be 2 because there are two atoms of X, A = C because of conservation of Z atoms," and so on. Item 9 was classified as formal because it requires the application of an algebraic formula to an unusual graphical representation of the motion (F3). Item 10 is formal. Students must suppress the impulse toward using vector addition of forces and apply the action-reaction principle instead (F1). Justifying how the correct answer of 10 lb is derived can be difficult even for a physics teacher.

You may recall the two items presented at the start of the chapter. The first item should be classified in the no-reasoning category (1) because it requires only knowledge of a sequence. However, the second item requires postformal thought essentially for two reasons. First, the presumed causal agents are unseen (i.e., theoretical) molecules, which are presumably diffusing from the notochord cells to the ectoderm cells. And second, the reasoning needed to identify the correct answer choice (i.e., choice a) is hypothetical-predictive in form:

If . . . notochord cells under the dorsal ectoderm induce the ectoderm cells to differentiate into a neural tube (hypothesis I)

and . . . notochord cells are removed,

then . . . the ectoderm cells should not differentiate into a neural tube (prediction).

But . . . according to choice a, they do differentiate into a neural tube.

Therefore . . . hypothesis I is contradicted.

You may have noticed that some of the example items asked students to explain their answers. Asking students to justify their answers can be an important part of a test because it emphasizes the use of reasoning patterns in identifiable ways. Thus, if selection of the correct answer is only partially justified, student reasoning can be probed further to find if the correct answer was in part a lucky guess or was the result of effective thinking. Conversely, although some items require only concrete reasoning for success, an analysis of student responses might indicate the use of formal reasoning. In view of these advantages, teachers are urged to include a few test items that require justification and for which more time is allowed. But don't use too many such items because they may take too long to answer and may create a severe grading problem.

BLOOM'S TAXONOMY OF EDUCATIONAL OBJECTIVES

Bloom's (1956) taxonomy of educational objectives (L. W. Anderson & Krathwohl, 2001) is a widely used method of classifying test items. The relationship between Bloom's taxonomy and the above classification scheme is of interest. Bloom's taxonomy consists of the following six levels:

1. *Knowledge:* Exam items written at the knowledge level require students to recall specific bits of information.

2. *Comprehension:* Comprehension items require an understanding of what is being communicated, but students do not need to relate it to other knowledge or discuss its implications.

3. *Application:* These items require students to apply concepts, procedures, and/or reasoning patterns in specific situations.

4. *Analysis:* Analysis items require students to break down a statement, statements, or a data set into parts so that a hierarchy of ideas is made clear and/or the relationships among ideas are made explicit; students must also recognize unstated assumptions, distinguish facts from hypotheses, and check the consistency of hypotheses with given information.

5. *Synthesis:* Synthesis items require students to put together parts to form a whole, to arrange and combine the parts to reveal a pattern or structure not present in the individual parts, to formulate appropriate hypotheses based upon an analysis of factors involved, and to modify such hypotheses in light of new considerations.

6. *Evaluation:* Here students must make judgments about the value of given materials and/or methods for specific purposes; they must compare major theories and find logical fallacies in arguments.

In general, any exam item at the knowledge level requires no reasoning (the previous category 1) or only concrete reasoning for successful response. Although items on this level may involve abstract theories or idealized models, students need only to *recall* the names of such theories. They do not need to use them in a way that would imply that the theories were understood. Items classified at the comprehension and application levels may require either concrete or formal reasoning depending upon the nature of the concepts being assessed. Test items on the analysis, synthesis, and evaluation levels, which require elements such as recognizing unstated assumptions, checking consistency of hypotheses with given information and assumptions, comprehending interrelationships among ideas, and comparing major theories and generalizations, all require formal or postformal reasoning.

USING EXAMS TO ENCOURAGE SELF-REGULATION

How can knowledge of the reasoning patterns and Bloom levels involved in responding to exam items help you develop and administer exams to encourage self-regulation? First, it should be clear that if your stated goals are to teach science *and* provoke students to improve their reasoning skills, then you should not only present students with activities that require reasoning, but you should also assess reasoning on tests. Students quickly learn that test items reveal what a teacher really believes is important. Thus, it is imperative for tests to include some items that challenge students' reasoning skills. However, such tests present a fundamental problem. Because some students initially reason only at the concrete level, such a test will include items that these students will almost certainly miss. The wrong thing to do, however, would be to eliminate this type of item completely. A line of attack more conducive to self-regulation and to intellectual growth would be to (a) include a few higher-level items, (b) discuss the reasoning needed to answer these items after the test, (c) discuss the reasoning involved in similar items during class time, (d) use some as thought-provoking homework assignments (see next section), and (e) award grades at least partially on the basis of improvement.

For example, suppose that laboratory and classroom activities invite the use of reasoning patterns required to understand controlled experimentation. The subsequent test should include a number of items that evaluate the extent to which students have become able to reason in this way. Not only should test items be included that refer to the materials used in the laboratory activities, but items involving new and unfamiliar materials should also be included. These allow for an evaluation of the extent to which the developing reasoning patterns can be generalized to new situations. Recall that advanced reasoning patterns become generally useful only after students have gradually thought through a wide variety of specific situations that invite the use of such reasoning patterns. Test items, if used properly, can aid in this process.

Although most of the example test items are of the multiple-choice type, you should also consider other types of items. For example, you could provide a paragraph or two on an examination that contains partially true or partially false statements. Have students argue for the statements (or even parts of the statements) they believe to be accurate and refute statements that they believe are inaccurate. Or you could provide data on examinations. Ask students to generate alternative hypotheses about the data. Then in light of their current knowledge and understanding, have them describe how they would go about testing their hypotheses. Also allowing students to work in small groups on exam items of the type just discussed can be effective. Groups of students or individual students might also be given paragraphs describing perplexing situations (e.g., current political, economic, and ecological issues), which do not allow for easy answers. They could then be asked to offer their assessment of the situation and perhaps propose a course of action to arrive at an optimum solution.

You can probably offer additional examples of appropriate assessment procedures. The point is that students can become motivated to inquire. After all, this is the behavior that governed a large part of their lives prior to the time they enrolled in school. However, if they are not at least partly assessed on the basis of their willingness and ability to inquire and their ability to think and instead are assessed solely on the amount of content they have stored, they will quickly learn that you value stored knowledge more than the intellectual processes needed to construct that knowledge. This will cause them to stop inquiring and thereby stop developing intellectually.

In summary, test items should not only assess specific knowledge; they should also assess descriptive and theoretical conceptual understanding, and they should assess the extent to which important reasoning patterns have developed. In this way tests will serve both as a means of assessment and as a valuable learning experience that will help provoke self-regulation and intellectual development.

DEVELOPING AND SCORING ESSAY EXAMS

Developing good multiple-choice items is difficult. But scoring them is relatively easy. On the other hand, developing good essay items is relatively easy. But scoring them in an unbiased, reliable, and valid way is not only difficult; it can be very time consuming. Having said this, essay testing has advantages over multiple-choice-type testing because essay tests can more effectively assess complex learning outcomes (e.g., explaining cause-effect relationships, generating and testing alternative hypotheses, graphing and interpreting data).

Not surprisingly, like multiple-choice items, essay items can be classified into Bloom's levels of recall, comprehension, application, analysis, synthesis, and evaluation. One advantage of using essay items is that it is easier to develop essay items that require higher-order Bloom levels. But how can teachers score essay items in an unbiased, reliable, and valid way—a way that accurately reflects what students know?

Suppose your class has just explored molecular motion. Suppose you have introduced the concept of diffusion and now you want to know if students understand the concept. Written responses to the following application-level essay item can be very revealing:

> A large container is full of clear water. Several drops of dark blue dye are dropped on the water's surface. The dye begins to spread throughout the water. Eventually the water in the container changes from clear to light blue. In a paragraph, explain why the dark blue dye spreads to change the water color to a uniform light blue. If possible, give your explanation in terms of interacting molecules.

Once you collect student paragraphs, your task is to read and develop a systematic means of ranking and scoring them—a scheme referred to as a scoring rubric (e.g., Arter & McTighe, 2001). Perhaps the best way to construct a good scoring rubric is to first sort the paragraphs into piles that represent different response categories. Next you will need to rank the response categories in terms of their quality and completeness. Finally, you will need to award points based on the ranking. When this procedure was used to score student responses to the dye question, researchers identified six response categories and awarded them scores from one point for the worst category to six points for the best (see Table 13.1).

When the rubric shown in Table 13.1 was used to compare the effectiveness of two instructional treatments, one treatment incorporating analogies such as shaking different-colored marbles and seeds in a jar and the other treatment lacking such analogies, the results shown in Figure 13.1 were obtained. As you can see, student responses in the analogy group were substantially better than those in the no-analogy control group. Although developing and validating a scoring rubric such as this one is often difficult and time consuming (e.g., for this study four raters independently scored each response using the above criteria and examples with an interrater agreement of 70% and with disagreements being resolved through discussion among the raters), the process can be very informative with regard to student difficulties and misconceptions. To that end Table 13.2 lists criteria for developing effective scoring rubrics.

TABLE 13.1   A Six-Point Rubric Used to Score Student Written Responses to the Dye Question

1. blank, irrelevant remarks or use of given terms without explanation (e.g., "Once you take away the water the cells get smaller. You put water in again and the cells will get back to normal size." "The molecules in the blue dye spread throughout the water. Therefore causing the water to turn blue." "The dye was diffused through the water.")

2. misconception, explanation based upon various concepts not related to the diffusion concept (e.g., "The molecules from both substances are small, uncharged and polar which allows them to pass." "The molecules of the dark blue dye were polar and took in clear water which made them expand and have a shade of light blue." "The dye is able to enter the water molecules.")

3. partially correct conception plus misconception: some notion of the diffusion process but combined with other causes and/or non-molecular level objects (e.g., "Diffusion: the movement of an organism from an area of high concentration to an area of low concentration." "This process is one type of diffusion. The molecules of dark blue dye spread out in the water and hook on to the molecules of water. The molecules of blue dye are distributed evenly throughout the water until the ratio of blue dye molecules to water molecules is equal in an area of the container.")

4. descriptive conception: some notion of the diffusion process but no mention of molecules (e.g., "Diffusion is the movement of a substance from an area of higher concentration to a lower concentration." "The dye will not stay concentrated in one spot. They will diffuse throughout the water. Just like if you sprayed perfume in a corner of a room, eventually the whole room would smell like perfume.")

5. partial theoretical conception: some notion of molecules moving from area of high molecular concentration to low (e.g., "Diffusion = movement of molecules from an area of higher concentration to the area of lower concentration." "Random movement of the molecules of dark blue dye. The molecules continually move through the water until they have dispersed themselves evenly." "The color appears to be relatively even light blue because the dye molecules disperse randomly throughout the water molecules. This is the same principle as shaking little marbles with big marbles.")

6. complete theoretical conception: molecules move from area of high molecular concentration to low due to collisions of randomly moving molecules (e.g., "Diffusion causes the water to turn blue. The dye is more concentrated and moves from that higher concentration to the lower concentration as the molecules randomly diffuse by bouncing off one another. This continues until the concentration equalizes throughout. Thus the lighter color." "When gases or liquids move randomly from an area of higher concentration to an area of lower concentration, such as perfume odor when someone enters a room. The diffusion continues until the concentrations equalize, if there are no other limitations. This random movement happens as the molecules mix by bouncing off one another.")

Source: From A. E. Lawson, Baker, DiDonato, Verdi, & Johnson, 1993.

Before leaving the issue of scoring rubrics, it should be pointed out that they can also be used to evaluate other important aspects of classroom performance. For example, Arter and McTighe (2001) offer the rubric (they call it a performance list) that appears in Table 13.3 to score the quality of student graphs. Note that both the student and the teacher can score the graph.

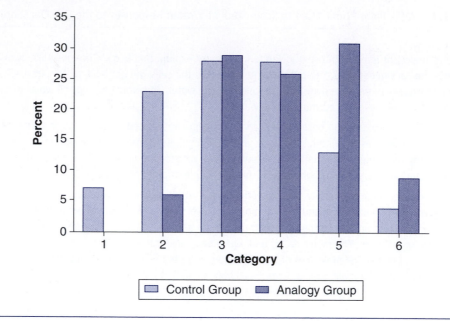

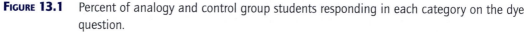

FIGURE 13.1 Percent of analogy and control group students responding in each category on the dye question.

TABLE 13.2 Criteria for Developing Effective Scoring Rubrics

1. The levels should be based on an absolute, rather than a relative, scale.
2. Include at least four levels to avoid being a measure of minimal competency.
3. The levels should cover the full range of concepts and skills involved reflecting least- to most-developed expertise.
4. Lower levels should not be written exclusively in terms of missing skills/concepts.
5. Include at least one level above the standard to identify "distinguished" performance.
6. Concepts and skills should vary consistently across the levels so that advancing to each higher level is of similar difficulty.
7. Describe the levels avoiding jargon and use of relative terms such as *below average, intermediate,* and *above average;* adjectives such as *minimum, inadequate, inconsistent,* and *excellent;* or value-laden constructs such as *creativity, elegance,* and *positive attitude.*
8. Provide responses exemplary of each level.

Arter and McTighe (2001) also offer a rubric that can be used to score the quality of a student's interaction within a group. Use of the rubric (shown in Table 13.4) allows teachers to quantify a very important but otherwise extremely difficult-to-assess aspect of student classroom performance. Making the rubric available to students also helps students better understand how to become effective group members.

TABLE 13.3 A Rubric to Evaluate and Score the Quality of Student Graphs

		Points Awarded By	
	Points Possible	Student	Teacher
Elements			
1. An appropriate type of graph is used.	3		
2. An appropriate title is given.	3		
3. Horizontal and vertical axes are labeled and spaced appropriately.	3		
4. Intervals of the axes are labeled and spaced appropriately.	3		
5. An appropriate key(s) for data is/are shown.	3		
6. Data are plotted accurately.	3		
7. The graph is neat and easy to interpret.	3		

TABLE 13.4 A Rubric for Scoring Group Interactions

High—*The student*

- initiates identifying group roles and accepts responsibility for fulfilling an assigned role.
- invites contributions from others.
- acknowledges the statements of others in a way that builds a consecutive interchange between participants.
- when disagreeing, does so respectfully.
- makes sure that all relevant points are heard.
- is aware of cultural differences in social interactions and behaves in an appropriate way.
- attempts to resolve conflicts when they arise.
- shares decision making.

Middle—*The student*

- participates in the development of the group process when initiated by others.
- attends to the discussion but doesn't participate very much.
- responds to the solicitation of opinions or ideas but doesn't volunteer them.
- doesn't detract from the functioning of the group.

Low—*The student*

- doesn't fulfill assigned roles.
- makes irrelevant or distracting statements.
- monopolizes the conversation.
- makes a personal attack.
- is uninvolved in the discussion, even when directly asked for an opinion.

USING HOMEWORK PROBLEMS TO ENCOURAGE SELF-REGULATION

Homework problems can also be used to provoke self-regulation provided that problems are chosen so students can partially but not completely understand them in terms of old ideas and that sufficient time is allowed for students to grapple with the new situation—possibly with appropriate "hints" to direct their thinking.

An important facet then in selecting homework problems that encourage self-regulation is obtaining a match between what students know and the kind of problems they are asked to work through. Ideally students should see the problems as challenging but solvable. Such problems place students in an initial state of disequilibrium. However, through their own efforts at bringing together what they have learned, they should be able to gradually organize their thinking and solve the problems. Success will then establish a new and more stable plain of equilibrium with increased understanding and problem-solving skill. Let's start by considering some deficiencies of typical homework problems.

What's Wrong With Typical Homework Problems?

Typical homework problems seldom require students to examine their thinking, make comparisons, and raise questions. Instead, most problems simply require students to apply a fact, an equation, or sometimes two or three equations to obtain a solution. Students quickly realize that the name of this game is "Can you recall the correct fact?" or "Can you discover the correct equation?" This is a game of recognition—a sort of matching process involving little thought or self-regulation. Typical homework problems do not require students to think about the following:

1. *The data of the problem.* Usually there is the right amount of information, no more and no less, whereas in real situations there is either a dearth or a superfluity of information and the problem is to discover what is relevant.

2. *The approach to the problem.* Usually this is determined by the chapter heading. If, for example, a mechanics problem can be solved either by Lagrange's equations, Newton's laws, or energy conservation, the choice is dictated by irrelevant considerations (e.g., the problem comes from the chapter on Lagrange's equations).

3. *The tacit assumptions of a problem-solving strategy*—for example, deciding between use of Boyle's law and use of the Van der Waals equation. This decision is usually made *for* the students, not *by* the students.

4. *The physical arguments involved in the problem as opposed to the mathematical ones.* Too often problems are only exercises in using mathematical tools without demanding that students try to either arrive at or qualitatively justify the mathematical result by physical arguments utilizing both principles and order-of-magnitude calculations. Indeed, in real research, the physical or intuitive argument often precedes the mathematical.

5. *The statement of the problem.* Problems are tailored to fit the text when, in fact, the real problem is doing the tailoring by conceptualizing a real situation in terms of a model. This involves all of the above points.

A few points should be kept in mind when designing, discussing, using, and scoring homework problems to encourage self-regulation:

1. Open-ended problems (problems with no single solution) are often excellent tools to encourage thinking.

2. Problems that present an apparent paradox produce disequilibrium and can initiate self-regulation. Paradox problems by their nature are generally short and incisive. Problems that are numerically or analytically simple yet incisive and illuminating in content are particularly useful.

3. To encourage self-regulation it is often helpful to ask students to record and hand in all the various ideas they tried and found unsuccessful as well as the ones that were successful in arriving at the problem solution. Discussions of these steps in an atmosphere in which these ideas are recognized not only as worthwhile but as necessary clue students in to the fact that "real" problems *should* and indeed *must* involve a certain amount of trial and error.

4. Have students search for necessary data so they examine their conceptualization of the problem. Either give superfluous data or omit necessary data. To account for the latter, students should have to make plausible assumptions or introduce suitable symbols for quantities that are needed to solve the problem.

5. Require students to draw a diagram of the situation. To do this students have to think deeply about the spatial relationships of the interacting objects and may find discrepancies as they compare their preconceptions with the diagram.

6. Provide a "problem clinic" or tutorial service where students can get help with problems while they are solving them and before they have to be turned in. If students are to conceptualize and then critically analyze their own thinking, interaction with others can be very helpful and is often even necessary.

7. When problems are intended to engage students over a period of, say, 2 weeks, the teacher should consult with students several times in order to
   a. discuss initial approaches. If the initial approach is reasonable but known in advance to be inappropriate, the teacher should *not* intervene at this point but rather should let the students discover for themselves why the approach will not work.
   b. discuss alternative approaches with students both when the initial approach is appropriate and when it is reasonable but not appropriate. In either case, let the students first discover which approach will work. *Then* discuss alternatives, *even* if the first approach worked. It may be that they will accept inappropriate alternatives as reasonable. They may then discover on their own why they are not.

c. discuss both semiquantitative (order or magnitude) and qualitative arguments anticipating the outcome of more rigorous approaches. Limiting cases should be used as a check when solutions to simpler problems are already known.

d. discuss alternatives to an inappropriate and *time-consuming* approach. Overall, students should get from the teacher a feeling for the general considerations appropriate to choosing and comparing strategies (e.g., a feeling for the process of inquiry).

8. Although solutions should be provided for all problems, students must understand that a premature glance at a solution will surely affect their conception of the problem and distort their problem-solving procedure. Knowledge of the solution can provide stimulating feedback *after* students have completed and carried through a formulation of a solution.

Some Effective Physical Science Homework Problems

Let's now take a look at some effective physical science problems. Comments follow each problem to help illustrate the points made above.

Spring balance

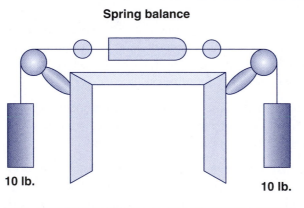

Spring balance and suspended weights.

Problem 1. Given that the net force on the spring scale shown in the diagram to the left is zero, how can the scale register a nonzero reading? What does the scale register? Why isn't it 20 since it is pulled down by 10 lb at each end?

Comment: This problem, which is especially useful when associated with a demonstration, illustrates how a little knowledge can go a wrong way. At first, concepts are only vaguely grasped and thus are overextended. Here we obviously have two forces whose sum is equal to zero, and yet the scale does not read zero. Or, we might think that each force contributes 10 lb of tension to the scale to give 20 lb. These two approaches use unrestricted (overextended) concepts that must be coordinated, via self-regulation, with other concepts (e.g., free-body diagrams and action-reaction) in order to resolve the discrepancy.

Problem 2. The gas temperature at one level of the upper atmosphere is about 1000°K. The temperature at the surface of a burning match is about the same. Yet a person would be very cold in the upper atmosphere. How can that be?

Comment: This problem presents a paradox because 1000°K is a very high temperature yet it is "cold up there." Resolution through self-regulation leads to a more scientific and less everyday notion of the relation between temperature and "cold" or "hot."

Problem 3. Everyone "knows" that to win a tug-of-war, a team has to pull harder than the other team. What everyone doesn't know is that, in fact, each team always pulls equally hard, even the winning team. Under these circumstances, how can one team ever win (short of the other team just letting go)?

Comment: One normally thinks that good teams pull harder than poor teams and this is why they win. This problem makes one apply the free-body diagram method and the action-reaction idea to resolve a problem already believed solved by common sense but now made to appear strange. This nonroutine use of physics concepts makes it more likely they will *not* be overlooked in the future.

Problem 4. A student measures her weight by climbing onto the large platform of a big spring scale. She takes a step to one side and notices that just as she started to do this, the scale registered less than her weight. Before she could puzzle this through, she noticed that just as she completed the step, the scale now registered more than her weight. If there is nothing wrong with the scale, then what was going on?

Comment: "Weight is weight is weight," a famous poet might have said. So how can the scale reading be less than one's weight? Worse, how can it also read more? Still worse, if it isn't the scale that must be fixed, then how am I, the student, to fix my ideas?

Problem 5. Assuming that the Earth is spherical and that the Sun is so far away that its rays strike the Earth parallel to each other and given the following information, Eratosthenes of Alexandria (273–192 BC) accurately computed the distance around the Earth. See if you can do what Eratosthenes did and figure out the distance around the Earth.

- The distance from the city of Alexandria to the city of Syene is 800 km.
- Alexandria is directly north of Syene.
- At noon on June 21st a post casts no shadow at Syene (note: the post is pointing toward the center of the Earth).
- At noon on June 21st a similar post casts a shadow at Alexandria (note: this post also points directly toward the center of the Earth).
- The angle at which lines drawn from the posts to the center of the Earth intersect = 7°.

Comment: This classic problem not only requires that students apply hypothetical-predictive reasoning, but it also involves proportional reasoning. Because of these complexities, the task should be seen not as one in which all students are expected to generate a "correct" solution but rather as one in which a variety of approaches are compared and constructed and their merits are explored.

Some Effective Biological Science Homework Problems

Problem 6. How long does mitosis take? The life span of a cell is the period of time from when it was formed to the time it completes division to form two new daughter cells. This time period is called the cell's *generation time*. By observing living cells, biologists have determined the generation time for a variety of cell types. If we know the generation time, we can determine how long a cell spends in mitosis. Given that 100 cells are observed in the field under a microscope and 50 of these cells are undergoing mitosis, and also knowing that the generation time is 2 hours, approximately how long does it take the cells to undergo mitosis? After you have arrived at an answer, reflect on your procedure. Try to write an equation expressing the numerical relationships using

No for total number of cells observed,

tm for time spent in mitosis,

Nm for number of cells observed in mitosis, and

Tgt for generation time.

Express the relationship below:

Comment: This problem, like the previous one, involves proportional relationships and hypothetical-predictive thought. Seldom are students in biology asked to think quantitatively and to generate general equations. Although the demands on student self-regulation may be great, the effort should pay off in terms of a better understanding of specific biological concepts and an increased understanding of the relationship between mathematics and science.

Problem 7. Evidence has been obtained to support the hypothesis that a gene is a segment of the DNA molecule that is capable of coding for the manufacture of protein molecules. How long a segment of DNA would be needed to code for any specific protein? (Hint: Assume that DNA consists of various sequences of just four different bases—A, T, G, and C. Assume also that protein molecules consist of chains of amino acid molecules and that there are 20 different kinds of amino acids. Hence protein molecules differ from each other in the number and sequence of their amino acids. This implies that the DNA code would have to be larger than a single base—a single letter. If the code consisted of a single letter [there are only four letters], then only four different amino acids could be coded for. Since there are 20 amino acids, the code must contain at least two bases [two letters]. Would a two-letter code work? How many different amino acids could a two-letter code specify? How about a three-letter code? And so on.)

Comment: Generating all possible combinations of code units requires use of combinatorial reasoning. Again the approach the teacher should take is to provide an opportunity for students to compare their problem approaches and argue for/against their alternatives. Let argumentation and self-regulation rather than the attainment of a single "correct" answer be the goal.

Problem 8. Carefully observe the illustration to the left and reflect on your previous laboratory work to answer the questions that follow.

a. What do you believe the function of the back teeth to be? Why?
b. What do you believe the function of the front teeth to be? Why?
c. Explain why you think this animal is an herbivore, a carnivore, or an omnivore.
d. Note the position of the eye orbits. How might this positioning be useful to this animal?
e. Can you think of any animals that also have this type of eye positioning?
f. Do you believe this animal to be terrestrial, aquatic, amphibious, or adapted for flight? Why?
g. The actual skull is really about 16 times larger in size than the illustration given. What animal do you think it is? Why?

Comment: This problem is primarily an opportunity for students to apply what they have learned about skull adaptations. However, the final question (g) requires a careful search through memory as well as an element of hypothetical-predictive reasoning. The problem is fun, especially if you choose not to tell students what the "real" answer is. What animal do *you* think it is? Why?

Problem 9.   Regions of relatively stable climax communities that cover many miles of land are sometimes referred to as biomes. Consult reference material and list the world's major terrestrial biomes and their primary locations. Most likely your reference source indicates that the state of Arizona is part of the desert biome. But in fact, all the world's major biomes, except for tropical rain forest, can be found in Arizona. How can this be? In other words, what conditions must exist in Arizona to allow for the existence of such a wide range of climax communities? Explain in general terms how these conditions influence the plants that dominate the various communities.

Comment: For students who live in mountainous regions this problem should cause little disequilibrium, but for those not accustomed to changes in elevation and their dramatic effect on community structure this problem provides an excellent opportunity to juxtapose the effects of elevation with those of latitude. It also provokes students to challenge the over-simplified biome diagrams found in most textbooks.

Problem 10. Eye color of the imaginary Grizzly Gronk population of the White Mountains varies. Some Gronks have purple eyes, some have white eyes, and some have orange eyes. Professor Greengenes has discovered that whenever two purple-eyed Gronks mate, they always produce purple-eyed offspring. Likewise, whenever two orange-eyed Gronks mate, they always produce orange-eyed Gronks. But when white-eyed Gronks mate, they are able to produce offspring with three colors of eyes.

a. Use aspects of Mendelian theory to explain how eye color is determined among Gronks (i.e., what is the genotype of the white-eyed Gronks, and how can they mate to reproduce offspring of all three colors of eyes?).
b. Use your theory to predict the phenotypic ratio of offspring if purple-eyed and white-eyed Gronks were mated.

Comment: This problem involves several elements of scientific reasoning, such as hypothetical-predictive reasoning, proportional reasoning, and probabilistic reasoning.

You may need to provide some students with the hypothetical-predictive "hint" to start by generating a number of ideas of what the genotype might be and then to proceed from these to the empirical reality stated in the problem. This idea of starting from the hypothetical and reasoning to the "real" is precisely the opposite of the way many students are accustomed to reasoning. Thus the problem will require a considerable amount of self-regulation. As with most problems of this type, giving students the opportunity to share ideas and discuss their thinking is an excellent way to help students acquire more advanced reasoning patterns.

USING WRITTEN ASSIGNMENTS TO ENCOURAGE SELF-REGULATION

Written Lab Reports

In addition to test items and homework problems, students should submit written reports. Writing forces students to reflect on past experiences and on partially understood concepts and synthesize them into coherent wholes. Thus, a written report provides an excellent impetus for self-regulation.

Perhaps the most common written report in the sciences is the lab report. The lab report is the classroom equivalent of the scientific research paper that scientists prepare and publish in scientific journals. The lab report should be structured in the same way as a scientific research paper. It should include sections devoted to the causal question raised, the alternative explanations proposed, the experimental procedures, the predicted results, the observed results, and a discussion of the results including a statement of the conclusion(s) drawn. Students can be required to submit such a report based upon specific labs conducted in class that included these elements, or they can be required to design and conduct research at home that includes these elements.

Preparing such a report will be particularly challenging for students who start the year as concrete thinkers. The disequilibrium and self-regulation that result can go a long way in helping these students improve their thinking skills. What follows are more specific guidelines for preparing lab reports in which students have raised and attempted to answer a specific causal question.

The One-Page Lab Report

Although lab reports are an excellent way to provoke students to reflect on the process of doing science, you will probably not want to require lengthy reports for all of the labs that students conduct. However, a much shorter one-page lab report that includes all of the major elements of scientific thought can be prepared and graded with relative ease. Because the one-page version (shown as Figure 13.2) includes the major elements of scientific thought, it can serve as a prod to get students to think in a hypothetical-predictive manner.

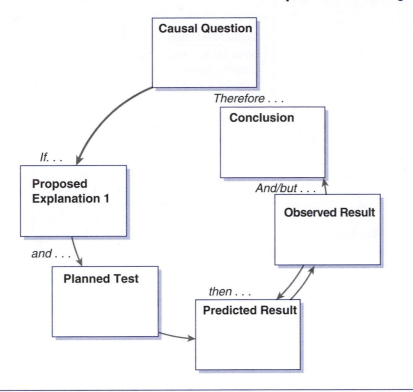

Figure 13.2   The one-page lab report.

All students need to do to complete the lab report is to fill in the boxes with the appropriate sentences. Figure 13.3 provides an example.

Science Fair Projects

The inquiry classroom is devoted to doing science. Puzzling observations are made, questions are raised, alternative hypotheses are freely generated, experiments are conducted, and so on. The beauty of teaching science in this way is that students are working like a team of scientists who share, discuss, and debate ideas. Consequently, no single student must shoulder all of the responsibility for the progress made by the team. In a very real sense, the total of the classroom activity is much greater than the sum of its parts.

The potential downside of this team approach is that some students may not fully participate in the process; or they may be able to follow along with the classroom investigations fairly well, but when left on their own to carry out an investigation, they may discover that they don't understand the process as well as they thought they did. For this reason having students prepare their own lab reports is a good idea even when teams of students conduct the labs. An even more demanding task is to have individual students derive their own questions, create their own alternative hypotheses, and conduct their own investigations. This is

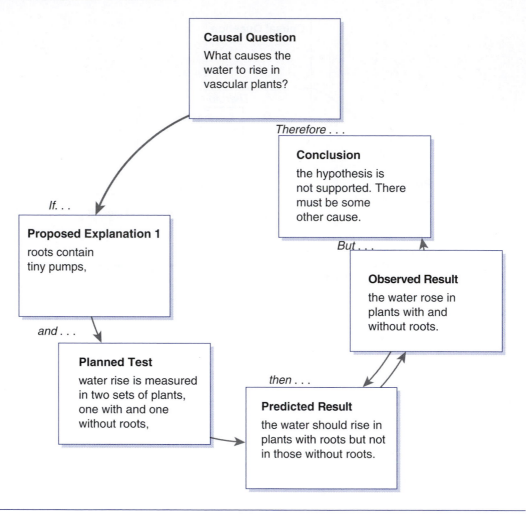

Causal Question
What causes the water to rise in vascular plants?

If. . .

Proposed Explanation 1
roots contain tiny pumps,

and . . .

Planned Test
water rise is measured in two sets of plants, one with and one without roots,

then . . .

Predicted Result
the water should rise in plants with roots but not in those without roots.

Therefore . . .

Conclusion
the hypothesis is not supported. There must be some other cause.

But . . .

Observed Result
the water rose in plants with and without roots.

FIGURE 13.3   A one-page lab report on an experiment on the cause of water rise in plants.

the role of individual investigations, such as science fair projects. However, one does not need to run a science fair to have students conduct and report on their own investigations. Indeed a wonderful activity would be to have students report their findings to the class in much the same way scientists present findings to their peers at scientific conventions. The key point, whether a science fair is actually held or not, is to make certain that students are challenged to conduct their own investigations to the extent possible and report their results.

In keeping with the nature of science, projects can be one of three types: descriptive, empirical-abductive, or hypothetical-predictive. The descriptive project investigates an aspect of nature and reports what patterns, if any, were found. The empirical-abductive project not only includes a descriptive element but also includes the student's subsequent explanations (hypotheses/theories) for the patterns found. For example, if the student asks, "What factors affect the role of breakdown of dead organisms?" and discovers that organisms break down best in hot and wet conditions, he or she should then generate (abduct) one or more possible explanations for this result. Finally the hypothetical-predictive project requires the student to raise a causal question, propose a number of alternative hypotheses, plan tests that involve the deduction of predicted results, and then carry out his or her tests to discover which hypotheses, if any, are supported. This type of project places greater demands on student reasoning skills than does either of the other two types.

Picking a reasonable question to investigate is not easy. Consider the following possibilities:

A. How does the number of coils of wire in an electromagnet affect the number of paper clips it can attract?

B. How do giraffes sleep?

C. How do different kinds of light affect the growth of a lima bean plant?

D. What elements react best in a nuclear fusion reactor?

E. Does age affect a person's reaction time?

F. What are the travel patterns of an ant colony?

G. How are locations for oil exploration determined?

H. Do mealworms react to sounds?

I. How do galaxies move?

J. What room designs provide the best musical sounds?

K. What causes water to rise in plant stems?

Questions B, D, G, and I are inappropriate because students cannot personally investigate them. The purpose of the project should *not* be to look up information in the library. Nevertheless, questions A, C, E, F, H, and J could form the basis of a descriptive project or an empirical-abductive project. Finally, because question K is a causal one, it lends itself best to a hypothetical-predictive project. This is the most demanding type of project but the one with the greatest payoff in terms of encouraging self-regulation and development of reasoning skills.

A problem that many students have in conducting hypothetical-predictive projects is that they confuse hypotheses with predictions. This problem often stems from a lack of hypothetical-predictive reasoning skills. However, it may sometimes also stem from confusion due to poor instruction. Consider, for example, Figure 13.4, which has been reproduced from a set of guidelines on science fair projects given to students. Look closely at the example hypothesis: Plants grow best in potting soil. Is this a hypothesis (a tentative explanation)? No, it is not. Instead it is a prediction, and the project that is suggested is not a hypothetical-predictive one. Instead it is a descriptive project or possibly an empirical-abductive one if in fact the predicted result occurs and a legitimate reason (hypothesis) is proposed. A legitimate reason, however, can't be that the student has observed plants in the past that grew best in potting soils and therefore, by extrapolation, these new plants should do as well. Notice that this reasoning merely extrapolates from past experience but no insight into *why* potting soil is best is proposed. What follows is a legitimate hypothesis to be tested: Potting soil contains more nutrients needed for plant growth than sand. To test this "nutrient hypothesis" we can do one or both of these two things. Either we take nutrients out of the potting soil, or we add nutrients to the sand. The reasoning would then look like this:

If . . . the nutrient hypothesis is correct,

and . . . we take nutrients out of the potting soil and add nutrients to the sand (planned test),

then . . . the plants should grow worse in nutrient-deficient potting soil, and the plants should grow better in nutrient-enriched sand (predictions).

How would you test the hypothesis that potting soil retains moisture needed for plant growth better than sand? Keep in mind that to test this hypothesis you must vary water retention ability while holding all other independent variables (possible causes/hypotheses) constant.

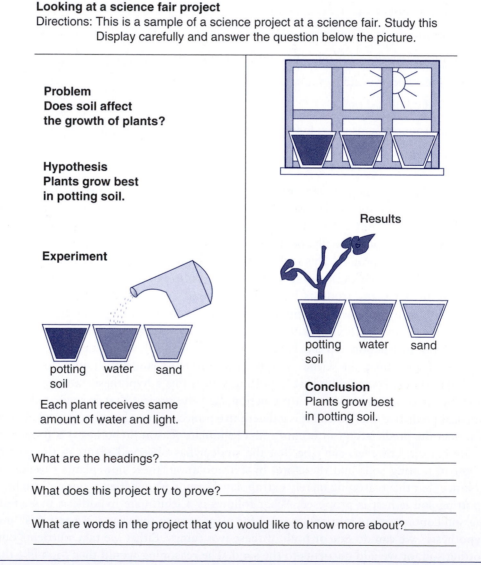

Looking at a science fair project
Directions: This is a sample of a science project at a science fair. Study this
Display carefully and answer the question below the picture.

Problem
Does soil affect
the growth of plants?

Hypothesis
Plants grow best
in potting soil.

Experiment

potting   water   sand
soil

Each plant receives same
amount of water and light.

Results

potting   water   sand
soil

Conclusion
Plants grow best
in potting soil.

What are the headings?_____

What does this project try to prove?_____

What are words in the project that you would like to know more about?_____

FIGURE 13.4   An example science fair project that confuses hypotheses with predictions.

In summary, the key point regarding science fair projects is that most teachers and even science fair judges, although well intentioned, do not understand the process of alternative hypothesis testing and experimental design well enough to encourage and/or reward students to actually generate and test alternative hypotheses. Most science fair projects are tired descriptions/demonstrations of some scientific principles rather than real science. How many more times will we see the exploding volcano at the science fair? Science fairs can be worthwhile, but to be of most value they should include all of the essential elements of doing hypothetical-predictive science.

Portfolios

Having students collect and file their course work in a notebook or folder is a common assessment strategy that has been employed by various teachers probably ever since teachers began looking for ways to assess student progress. These collections of assembled papers, lab reports, quizzes, class notes, and exams are called portfolios (e.g., Collins, 1990). Portfolios can be collected periodically and evaluated in one or more of several ways by the teacher. Portfolio assessment is a multifaceted process characterized by three qualities: (1) It provides both ongoing and cumulative monitoring of students' progress; (2) it is multidimensional (i.e., reflecting a wide variety of artifacts and processes reflecting various aspects of students' learning); and (3) it allows for collaborative reflection, including ways for students to reflect about their own thinking processes. A perceived advantage of portfolio assessment is that it may enable the teacher to better assess student progress over time. A possible disadvantage of its use in awarding grades is that the teacher may place too much emphasis on neatness and organization skills and not enough emphasis on real enthusiasm toward and understanding of the science. Table 13.5 (after Payne, 2003) summarizes these and several other possible advantages and disadvantages of using portfolios.

TABLE 13.5   What Are Some Possible Advantages and Disadvantages of Portfolio Assessment?

Possible Advantages

- Encourages self-directed learning
- Enlarges the view of what is learned
- Provides a way of presenting relevant achievements
- Stimulates communication among students, teachers, and parents
- Enhances student evaluative skills
- Represents realistic academic and real-world tasks
- Provides tangible evidence of accomplishment and progress toward identified outcomes

Possible Disadvantages

- Collecting and storing documents can become cumbersome
- Some students, teachers, and parents may be resistant
- Difficult to obtain acceptable scoring/grading reliability (i.e., lack of good scoring rubric)
- Required teacher training in use may strain resources
- Inappropriate selection of included materials may limit generalization

Summary

- Teachers should strive to assess the extent to which student learning can be applied in "real-world" contexts—a form of assessment known as authentic assessment. Teachers should also strive to eliminate gender and cultural bias in their assessments.

- Assigning grades must be carried out thoughtfully and fairly. Several ways exist to ensure that this is accomplished.

- Exam items require either concrete thought, formal thought, or postformal thought based on the reasoning patterns required to successfully respond without guessing.

- Exam items at Bloom's knowledge level require no reasoning or only concrete reasoning for successful response. Comprehension- and application-level items require either concrete or formal reasoning depending on the concepts assessed. Items on the analysis, synthesis, and evaluation levels require formal and/or postformal reasoning.

- Exams designed to encourage self-regulation and intellectual growth should include some challenging "higher-level" test items. When using such exams, you should discuss the reasoning needed to answer these items after the test, discuss the reasoning involved in similar items during class time, use some items as thought-provoking homework assignments, and award grades partially on the basis of improvement.

- Homework problems that are open ended present apparent paradoxes that can be effective at provoking self-regulation.

- Report writing forces students to reflect on past experiences and partially understood concepts. Thus, written reports provide an excellent impetus for self-regulation.

- Science fair projects can be one of three types: descriptive, empirical-abductive, or hypothetical-predictive. A value of science fair projects is that students work independently; thus each student must independently "come to grips" with key aspects of the scientific process.

- Portfolio assessment has advantages as well as disadvantages. Thus, like other means of assessment, portfolios can help but should not be a major aspect of assessment.

Key Terms

authentic assessment

formative assessment

summative assessment

Application Questions/Activities

1. Concrete thinkers experience disequilibrium when confronted with test items and written assignments that require formal or postformal thought. What strategies will assist such students on tests and quizzes? On written assignments?

2. Obtain a test that has recently been administered to middle school or high school students and analyze the test items in terms of the stages of required reasoning.

3. Construct a test item at each level of Bloom's taxonomy. Discuss each item in terms of the stage of required reasoning.

4. Construct two homework problems that will provoke self-regulation. Discuss how you will evaluate student responses.

PART V

Professional Induction and Development

Chapter 14

HELPING MORE TEACHERS USE INQUIRY

What do you think about inquiry teaching? Please respond to each of the following five items as *true* or *false*. If possible, discuss your responses with your classmates and/or the instructor.

1. Inquiry teaching is too slow to cover district and/or state standards.

2. Students are too immature to use inquiry, so they will waste too much time and not learn enough.

3. Inquiry teachers are not in control of the classroom, so they feel uncomfortable.

4. Students don't want to inquire. They just want to be told what to learn.

5. Most classrooms are not equipped for inquiry.

Why doesn't this teacher use inquiry?

In spite of how you may have responded to these items, educational research has repeatedly found that inquiry-based teaching methods are far superior to other methods for achieving our nation's educational goals. Consequently, a question is raised that has perplexed leaders of organizations such as the American Association for the Advancement of Science, the National Science Foundation, and the National Research Council for decades: *Why don't more teachers use inquiry?*

APPLICABLE NSES STANDARDS

Standard C Science teachers engage in ongoing assessment of their teaching and of student learning. In doing so, they

■ Use student data, teaching observations, and interactions with colleagues to reflect on and improve teaching practice.

To try to find out, interviews were conducted with several experienced science teachers—some who clearly preferred didactic teaching and some who at least professed to use inquiry. Table 14.1 lists the top 10 reasons the teachers gave for not using inquiry, with the most common numbered 1. Are these valid reasons? Or can the presumed difficulties be overcome? And, if so, how? The primary purpose of this chapter is to carefully consider each claim in turn.

TABLE 14.1 Why Don't More Teachers Use Inquiry?

1.	*Time and Energy*	Too much time must be devoted to developing good lessons.
		Too much energy must be expended to maintain a level of enthusiasm through five classes each day.
2.	*Too Slow*	We have district/state curricula and testing, so we must cover all the material.
		The class will not cover all students need to know.
3.	*Reading Too Difficult*	Students cannot read the inquiry book.
4.	*Risk Too High*	The administration will not understand what is going on and think I am doing a poor job. I am not sure how each unit will turn out.
5.	*Tracking*	There are no good thinkers left in regular biology.
6.	*Student Immaturity*	Students are too immature. They waste too much time; therefore, they will not learn enough.
7.	*Teaching Habits*	I have been teaching another way for 15 years and cannot change now.
8.	*Sequential Text*	Inquiry textbooks lock you into the order of the book. I cannot skip labs because there is sequential material in each lab.
9.	*Discomfort*	I feel uncomfortable not being in control of what is going on in my classroom. Students also feel too much discomfort.
10.	*Too Expensive*	My lab is not equipped for inquiry. My district will not buy materials needed to maintain an inquiry approach.

Source: From Costenson & Lawson, 1986.

INQUIRY DOESN'T TAKE TOO MUCH TIME AND ENERGY

Claim: Too much time must be devoted to developing good inquiry lessons, and too much energy is needed to remain enthusiastic through five classes each day.

Reply: Many teachers rely on the text and accompanying materials. This makes the day-to-day preparation relatively easy. The preparation for inquiry would initially be more time consuming. However, if you are a member of a large staff, this can be accomplished with little increase in overall time. Through the development of a central filing system and teaming, the effort needed to create inquiry materials could be minimized. Unfortunately, if you are not part of a large staff, the process would be more time consuming. As with other teaching approaches, once the initial development has been accomplished, time commitments decrease significantly each year. However, it would be extremely helpful if curriculum developers and publishers made more inquiry books and lab materials available. At the present time, fact-laden texts and verification lab programs still dominate the list of published materials.

The criticism that inquiry teaching requires too much energy seems odd. Granted, energy is required to prepare inquiry labs but certainly no more than for traditional verification labs. Inquiry labs can actually require less energy to teach than either lectures or verification labs. This is because students, once convinced that their data form the basis for classroom conclusions, become very motivated and involved and thus require little supervision beyond an occasional suggestion of ways to get started.

INQUIRY CAN "COVER" ENOUGH MATERIAL

Claim: Inquiry is too slow. We have district and/or state curricula and testing, so we must cover all the topics.

Reply: The question is, Too slow for whom? The teachers interviewed were all concerned about existing districtwide curricula and/or district and statewide testing. All felt that both would require strict adherence to an inflexible timetable and teaching massive amounts of facts. However, to "cover" the typical fact-laden text in 1 year forces one to instruct at a shallow and superficial level and forces students to memorize. As mentioned in Chapter 7, *Modern Biology* (Towle, 2002) contains 53 chapters, and the typical school year contains only 36 weeks. This means that about a chapter and a half would have to be covered every week to complete the book—clearly an impossible task if one is concerned about student motivation, understanding, and retention.

You may also recall from Chapter 7 that Mazzolini (1993) found that achievement in chemistry classes was highest when teachers introduced an intermediate number of topics and lowest in classes where teachers introduced the most topics. And Adamson et al. (2003) found that student achievement in high school biology classes was positively correlated with the use of inquiry teaching methods. Using inquiry may mean that the topics "covered" will be less, but the scientific concepts "uncovered" will be more. Not surprisingly the Third International Mathematics and Science Study (U.S. Department of Education, National Center for Education Statistics, 1998) found that teachers in higher-performing countries such as Canada, Japan, and Singapore attempt to teach much less content than teachers in lower-performing countries such as the United States.

American schools need help in developing narrower and deeper curricula. As we have seen, the central purpose of American education is to help students develop the ability to think. In the words of the Educational Policies Commission (1961),

> The ability to think cannot be developed or applied without subject matter. There are two bases for choosing the substantive knowledge that pupils should learn. One is the knowledge's potential for rational power development; the other is the knowledge's importance for the pupil's life and for society. (p. 19)

Table 14.2 What Are Some Embedded Theories in Biology?

Basic Theories of Inheritance, Development, and Growth

- Cell Theory
- Chromosome Theory of Inheritance
- Mendel's Theory of Inheritance
- Cell Differentiation Theory

Theories of Evolution and Speciation

- Darwin's Evolution Theory
- The Darwin/Wallace Theory of Natural Selection
- Synthetic Evolution Theory
- Biological Classification Theory
- Chemosynthesis Theory

Behavioral and Ecological Theories

- Ecosystem Dynamics Theory
- Population Growth Theory
- Competitive Exclusion Theory
- Cropping Theory
- Succession Theory

Theories of Plant Structure and Function

- Osmosis-Pull Theory of Water Rise in Vascular Plants
- Theory of Stomata Opening and Closing
- Phototropism Theory
- Flowering Theory

Theories of Animal Structure and Function

- Harvey's Circulation Theory
- Theory of Animal Heat
- Digestion Theory
- Excretion Theory
- Theory of Heart-Rate Regulation
- Nerve Impulse Theory
- Synaptic Transmission Theory
- Sliding-Filament Theory
- Sensory-Processing Theory

Atomic and Molecular Level Theories

- Kinetic-Molecular Theory
- Photosynthesis Theory
- Theory of Fermentation and Cellular Respiration
- Watson and Crick's Theory of DNA Structure and Replication
- Protein Synthesis Theory

Therefore, if the phase names of mitosis or a list of digestive enzymes produced by the small intestine does not meet these requirements, why emphasize them and why test for them?

Given limited time, what substantive (i.e., declarative) knowledge should be emphasized? According to most experts, emphasis should be placed upon unifying themes that reflect the structure of disciplines, which serve as frameworks to integrate information. The structure of a scientific discipline is reflected by its embedded theories. For example, Table 14.2 lists embedded theories that could be introduced in a biology course. As discussed in Chapter 2, each theory is composed of a small set of postulates (i.e., basic claims) that taken together serve to explain a set of related phenomena. For example, the osmosis-pull theory explains how water rises in vascular plants using these five postulates:

1. Water molecules evaporate from leaf cells and escape to the outside though tiny holes called stomata. This process (transpiration) increases the osmotic concentration inside leaf cells.

2. Due to this increased osmotic concentration, water molecules from the leaf xylem move into the leaf cells via osmosis.

3. This movement then pulls on the water column, which is held together by molecular adhesion, in the leaf xylem.

4. The leaf xylem water column then pulls upward on the stem water column, which then pulls on the root water column.

5. Water moves into the roots and root xylem primarily due to osmosis.

So osmosis-pull theory is a conceptual system consisting of concepts such as evaporation, transpiration, osmosis, xylem, osmotic concentration, and so on. Such a postulate list, if given to or constructed by students at the appropriate time (e.g., as a summary after the inquiries have taken place), serves to focus attention on the important ideas, thus reducing the need to introduce huge numbers of unrelated facts.

Consistent with the goal of improving reasoning skills, a university Board of Regents Task Force in Arizona identified major objectives of secondary school science. Its report lists 18 skills that every student should master. Importantly, these skills, listed in Table 14.3, do not involve any discipline-specific declarative knowledge. Rather, what the task force is saying to secondary teachers is that it does not matter what content you use; just have students inquire into some content to help them develop these skills.

READING INQUIRY TEXTBOOKS CAN BE EASIER

Claim: Students cannot read the inquiry textbook.

Reply: Although teachers were not able to articulate precisely why they felt their students had difficulty reading inquiry textbooks, the perceived difficulty may be due in part to the greater demands inquiry textbooks place on reasoning skills. Many secondary students are concrete or transitional thinkers while today's scientific inquiry is guided by formal and postformal reasoning skills. Therefore, reading about scientific inquiry can be difficult. Expository, fact-laden texts place no such demands on student reasoning. Rather, they place demands on memorization. However, it is far better to challenge students' reasoning skills than their ability to memorize because reasoning skills can improve and are of general use, whereas the rote recall of isolated facts has little value.

Importantly, reading difficulties are not confined to inquiry texts. Textbook publishers are concerned with book readability. Likewise, districts spend considerable time developing programs for below-grade-level readers. With the emphasis on lower reading

TABLE 14.3   What Are the Major Objectives for High School Laboratory Science Courses?

After completing 2 years of high school laboratory science, the student should be able to:

1. Describe the nature of science.
2. Describe the characteristics of a scientific theory.
3. Use the metric system and scientific notation.
4. Use mathematical relationships to describe observational and experimental results.
5. Determine the reasonableness of results through estimation, approximation, and order of magnitude.
6. Identify common variables and name specific values for these variables in dynamic and static systems.
7. Identify, measure, and conserve key characteristics of objects and substances including solid and liquid amount, length, area, weight, volume, and density.
8. Construct and use theoretical models.
9. Generate predictions based upon the assumed truth of hypotheses and imagined experimental situations.
10. Design and conduct controlled experiments to test hypotheses. Recognize information needed to establish the correlation between two variables and the additional information needed to establish cause and effect.
11. Demonstrate an ability to categorize or classify objects or data in an organized, logical manner.
12. Utilize appropriate instruments and tools to gather scientific information in a lab, field, or library setting.
13. Demonstrate a basic understanding of experimental error and its analysis.
14. Distinguish between observations and inferences.
15. Evaluate evidence in light of the probabilistic nature of phenomena.
16. Interpret data and observations for relationships and trends.
17. Organize and communicate results obtained by observation and experimentation, both quantitatively through the use of relationships and qualitatively in clear, concise spoken or written language.
18. Function with ambiguity and acceptance of divergent methods of problem solving.

Source: Task Force on Laboratory Science, 1985.

levels, many expository texts have created their own brand of problems. Sentences must be added to explain terms, which often creates additional difficulties. Further, expository textbooks frequently contain linguistic flaws, including a lack of unity, cohesion, and semantic elaboration. A primary characteristic of these texts is presentation of detailed facts with few cohesive ties either among the details or between the facts and the main point they intend to clarify.

Expository texts often make the problem worse by including an enormous number of terms. Biology texts are typically the biggest offenders. Although the 1981 edition of *Modern Biology* kept the reading level low, it included 17,130 special biological terms, with an average of 23 per page (Yager, 1983). The most recent edition is little better. Therefore, a low reading level does not mean better comprehension as the reader is so overwhelmed by the vast number of terms that comprehension is nearly impossible. Another part of the problem is that the terms are typically introduced *before* examples and definitions and thus come with no context in which to place them. Still another problem is that abstract superordinate terms come before the less abstract subordinate terms. This compounds the comprehension problem even further. In short, expository texts, particularly biology texts, quickly overwhelm students. No doubt you have dozed off a few times while trying to read such texts.

On the other hand, hands-on classroom inquiries can stimulate students to read the text to find answers to their own questions. This in turn gives the reader an internal locus of control. Students using the inquiry approach have fewer reading problems. Hill (1967) stated, "There is solid evidence to confirm that the content area textbook, as traditionally used, is less help and possibly more hindrance to the student than commonly assumed" (p. 412). The textbook should support class activities rather than be the ultimate source of all that is right or wrong. Thelen (1979) echoed this theme: "The textbook should be used to reinforce, confirm or enrich those concepts that the teacher is responsible for developing. The reader, when provided with sufficient background concerning the new material, should find the textbook easier to read" (p. 463). In other words, text reading should be assigned *after* the inquiry lessons on those topics that have been investigated—*not* before. In this way, text reading becomes part of the concept application phase of learning cycles and serves to reinforce and enlarge the already introduced concepts.

Risk Is Not Too High

Claim: The administration will not understand what is going on and will think I'm doing a poor job. When using inquiry, I'm not sure how each unit will turn out.

Reply: Perceived risk may be high whenever one deviates from the norm. Individual failures tend to be blamed on the method of instruction, and unsympathetic administrators will often agree. Therefore, it takes some courage to be different. Yet, can our society continue to let teachers risk losing students by boring them day after day with expository teaching? Can teachers continue to risk the trade-off of memorizing unnecessary facts in exchange for good reasoning and problem-solving skills? What then is really at risk? Surely the modest personal risk is less than that to society if our schools fail to provide students with an education in thinking. Contrary to what many preservice teachers suspect, a recent study of a biology faculty at one high school and a mathematics faculty at another found that the inquiry teachers were much more likely to be sought out for instructional advice than their more expository peers. Indeed, the inquiry teachers were by no means isolated. Instead, they were the faculty leaders (Judson & Lawson, 2007).

Do some teachers feel at risk when they do not know where the inquiry lesson will lead? Yes, but a good inquiry teacher is still leading, just not in the traditional sense. The good inquiry teacher is skilled at dealing with the unexpected because he or she knows the subject matter well and how to utilize the unexpected to provoke further thinking and inquiry. Teachers should not be afraid to say "I do not know"—even when they do!

The roles of the expository teacher as teller and the inquiry teacher as facilitator are at opposite poles. Traditional teaching, no matter how disguised, is based on the "mug and jug" theory (Rogers, 1983). The teller asks, "How can I make the mug stay still long enough to fill it from my jug of knowledge that I regard as being important?" The facilitator is concerned mostly with climate and asks, "How can I create an atmosphere that will allow my students to be curious, feel free to make mistakes, and feel free to learn from the environment as well as from their fellow students and me?" The Chinese philosopher Lao-Tse (Brynner, 1962) describes the proper attitude:

A leader is best

When people barely know he exists,

Not so good when people obey and acclaim him,

Worst when they despise him.

But of a good leader, who talks little,

When his work is done, his aim fulfilled,

They will all say, "We did this ourselves."

Do teachers risk anything when their administration does not support the inquiry method? Perhaps, but if your administration does not understand, then it is your job to instruct them in the proper use of inquiry in the classroom, to acquaint them with the data that show it to be a superior approach to teaching, and to show them its pervasiveness as part of the national agenda for science teaching. You might start by handing them a copy of *Inquiry and the National Science Education Standards: A Guide for Teaching and Learning* written by the National Research Council (2000a) and published by the National Academy Press in Washington, DC.

CONCRETE THINKERS CAN INQUIRE

Claim: Students can't inquire because there are no good thinkers left in regular biology.

Reply: Another teacher concern was the effects of a tracking system on inquiry. The better students, typically the formal thinkers, are sometimes placed in the upper track, leaving the concrete thinkers in the regular classes. Thus, some teachers ask, "How can my class use the inquiry approach?" The answer can be found in their own district if their elementary schools are using inquiry programs such as the Elementary Science Study (ESS), the Science Curriculum Improvement Study (SCIS), or the Full Option Science System (FOSS). Elementary school teachers are dealing with preoperational and concrete operational students every day, yet they still use inquiry to develop important science concepts and reasoning skills.

However, expectations for the lower tracks cannot initially be set too high, and teachers cannot expect the average student to initially function at the formal or postformal levels.

Knowing that a substantial portion of adolescents and adults do not presently reach these levels of thought, it becomes important that lower-track students be given the opportunity to develop their reasoning skills. A good program should start with descriptive lessons and group experiments and gradually and independently deal with more causal and theoretical issues. Teachers should make sure that students are personally engaged with each lesson so that confidence grows. With gains in confidence, students will be more willing to experience cognitive "discomfort" while attempting to construct more abstract concepts and develop higher-level reasoning skills.

Needless to say, if tracking inhibits the proper atmosphere for inquiry, then the same people (teachers) who created tracking can also discard it. Nontracked inquiry programs can and do work in many secondary schools. Inquiry eliminates many of the problems that tracking is supposed to solve. For example, classroom tests for measuring reasoning can be used for pairing concrete and formal reasoners in laboratory groups, thus letting the learning experiences develop through peer teaching and group dynamics. This gives concrete operational students an increased opportunity to achieve course goals. These same students in an expository classroom would have only their text to rely on.

STUDENTS DON'T WASTE TOO MUCH TIME

Claim: Inquiry can't be used because students are too immature and waste too much time.

Reply: If students are wasting time, then that is a classroom management problem—not a problem of the teaching method. If inquiries are at an appropriate level, interest should be high and participation widespread. There is always an opportunity for students to waste time with any teaching method. However, when using the lecture method, if the students keep their mouths shut, many teachers don't notice!

The nature of an inquiry class does give some students an opportunity to be nonproductive. Consequently, teachers need to develop techniques that will maintain participation. Leonard (1980, 1989) also provides many good suggestions. Using his Extended Discretion Approach, students begin with fairly structured inquiries requiring little student autonomy. Only gradually is structure decreased and autonomy increased. Inquiry surely means more noise and more mobility. However, the argument that secondary students are too immature to inquire cannot be taken seriously. Elementary school students are surely more immature yet are fully able to participate in inquiry lessons when properly designed and carried out. Again, the skeptical secondary school teacher is urged to consult an experienced ESS or SCIS elementary school teacher in his or her own or in a nearby district.

OLD "DOGS" CAN LEARN NEW "TRICKS"

Claim: I've been teaching this way for 15 years, and I cannot change now.

Reply: When people get stuck in old ruts, change becomes difficult but presumably still possible. When confronted with the considerable evidence that expository methods are less effective at improving student attitudes, interest, learning, and intellectual development, teachers should respond accordingly. Most teachers get very little outside help in the development of their teaching skills and just have not been exposed to proper inquiry lessons; therefore, they can hardly be expected to teach that way. However, all the blame cannot be deferred. These same teachers should be members of professional organizations that have communicated the effectiveness of inquiry in the past. It is almost unimaginable that any science teacher has not at least read about inquiry and wondered if it would work for him or her.

With federal or state support, many teachers have experienced inquiry firsthand. Yet, if no in-service program is available, then these teachers should consider seeking out an inquiry teacher and let him or her help develop an inquiry program. Old dogs can learn new tricks—and probably will once they become convinced that the goals and methods of inquiry are more effective and that inquiry teaching is more fun, for both students and teachers. Nevertheless, a crucial point must be made. Teachers tend to teach as they have been taught. Many secondary school teachers have been taught science in colleges and universities by professors who lecture and by labs that verify. And even when professors do attempt to reform their courses, they often run into difficulties due to their own pedagogical shortcomings and differences of opinion about the nature of inquiry (e.g., Southerland, Gess-Newsome, & Johnston, 2003). Consequently, the typical college professor serves as a very poor role model and must shoulder a major portion of the blame for poor teaching practice in secondary schools. Efforts to improve instructional methods in secondary schools should be accompanied by improvements in college teaching. This argument is brought out more fully in a wonderful book by Morris Kline (1977) titled *Why the Professor Can't Teach*. Although Kline's major thesis refers to mathematics instruction, many of his points are applicable to science teaching.

INQUIRY IS FLEXIBLE

Claim: Inquiry textbooks lock you into the order of the book. I cannot skip labs because there is too much new material in each.

Reply: Several teachers were concerned about perceived inflexibility of inquiry-oriented programs. They felt that because of their central themes and the constant referral to previous material, it became difficult to change the order of presentation, and, in too many cases, laboratory investigations could not be deleted, if the situation warranted, without losing valuable information. These disadvantages seem highly questionable when compared to the alternative of a disjointed chapter-by-chapter presentation of scientific facts. Without central themes, students are given the impression that the material in each chapter in no way relates to that in other chapters. The study of science becomes an exercise in memorization.

Many teachers fail to appreciate central themes themselves and fail to see the relationships among concepts. Some biology teachers, for example, require students to memorize steps in the Krebs cycle. Even more require memorization of the phase names of mitosis and meiosis. What possible purpose can this serve? Such teachers and districts should develop their own sound curricula independent of any text. In short, the teacher has three responsibilities before classes begin:

1. Isolate those theories that provide an accurate and adequate understanding of the discipline.

2. While using an inquiry framework, find laboratory investigations that help develop understanding of those theories.

3. Make sure that the investigations are carried out using inquiry.

Once this process is complete, readings (but not necessarily the textbook) should be selected that best meet the goals of the curriculum. This process would develop a better curriculum.

INQUIRY INCREASES COMFORT

Claim: I do not feel comfortable not being in control of what is going on in my classroom. Students also feel too much discomfort.

Reply: First it should be made clear that a good inquiry teacher *is* in control of the classroom! Inquiry teaching by no means implies a lack of classroom control. All teachers, inquiry or otherwise, want and need classroom control. The main point is this: When using inquiry, teachers and students are working together toward a common goal of exploring and explaining nature. The inquiry teacher is working with, not against, the students. Thus, there is no need to force students to remain silent and in their seats, and achieving classroom control becomes much easier and classroom comfort increases.

Perhaps teachers who experience discomfort with inquiry have limited training in its use or have had training, but their enthusiasm for the approach waned after returning to their own district. Much of this loss could be due to the lack of support both internally (district) and externally (workshop). Peer "coaching" and clinical supervision by supervisors may possibly furnish the needed support. If such support and gratification are not forthcoming, the enthusiasm required for inquiry could soon falter, letting the teacher fall back to the expository style.

There does seem to be a third possibility. Teachers are more comfortable when they can clearly demonstrate that students know what they are expected to know. Likewise administrators appreciate objectives that are clearly stated and evaluated. Unfortunately the objectives most easily spelled out, taught, and evaluated are typically of the least value to students and society. The objectives of inquiry cannot be so easily spelled out, taught, and evaluated and thus may produce discomfort. Thus, an important task is helping teachers learn how to evaluate higher-order cognitive outcomes.

Usually students feel discomfort not because inquiry is so difficult but because in many cases they have not been previously allowed to think for themselves and follow their own interests. As a former student remarked, "The discomfort students might feel could be the pain in their brains finally getting started. It's like having braces. They hurt when they are being tightened, but the final product is a straight brain." Being an active participant creates unfamiliarity for some—thus the discomfort. However, when students are led to believe that their ideas and results are important and not judged right or wrong by the teacher or by the text, this discomfort soon fades.

Importantly for students taught using an inquiry approach in elementary school, no such discomfort exists when faced with inquiry in secondary schools. In fact, just the opposite occurs when inquiry-oriented students meet expository teachers. The reaction is most certainly discomfort. More telling, students respond that they are no longer doing science in their "science" class! Teachers should not give up inquiry just because expository schooling typically makes up most of the students' past experience. Going along with this crowd does not create a better educational atmosphere.

INQUIRY IS NOT TOO EXPENSIVE

Claim: My lab is not equipped for inquiry. My district will not buy the materials needed to maintain an inquiry approach.

Reply: In many cases, science is being taught in classrooms that are not equipped for laboratory work. Hurd, Bybee, Kahle, and Yager (1980) found that 40% of science classes are taught in non-laboratory-designed classrooms. Yet only 25% of the teachers in those classrooms felt that the room was inadequate for lab work. Thus poorly equipped rooms may not be as limiting as some might think. Inquiry does not happen because of furniture. It happens because students' minds are at work.

Many of the interviewed teachers felt that materials needed to run an inquiry approach would be inhibiting both from a startup and from a maintenance cost standpoint. This objection appears valid. The problem may have to be taken to the district level for satisfactory results. Most districts have some funds available. However, administrators often need better directions in how to spend those funds. Nevertheless, teachers should know that inquiry often occurs without fancy equipment. This may require some creativity on the teachers' part to find alternative materials. Much inquiry can be achieved with materials just outside your classroom, purchased at local stores, or brought from students' homes. The outdoors and the world of living things are available, and bags of seeds from the grocery store work just as well as those from supply companies at a fraction of the cost. A former student remarked that while in the Peace Corps in Africa, she saw two young boys in the dust in their ragged, dirty clothes dissecting a lizard with a rusty razor blade found in the trash. One really cannot stop kids from inquiring on their own. It costs little and pays a lot when you allow it to occur in the classroom as well.

In conclusion, all 10 of the previous reasons for not using the inquiry method are insufficient to prevent its use. In fact, most likely the reasons are simply rationalizations for the most likely reason that many teachers do not use inquiry, which is that they simply don't know how. To successfully implement inquiry, teachers need to (a) understand and believe in the modern goals of science teaching; (b) understand the nature of scientific inquiry;

(c) understand the central concepts and theories of their particular disciplines; and (d) be skilled in classroom management and inquiry teaching techniques.

Unfortunately, lacking such knowledge and skills, many teachers may have little choice but to teach dry, boring facts in the less effective expository way. And, teachers also need to know how to integrate all of this into specific lessons designed to teach specific concepts to specific students (e.g., Roehrig & Luft, 2004; Schwartz & Lederman, 2002). Such knowledge, sometimes referred to as content pedagogical knowledge, must be gained largely though on-the-job experiences. In short, the job of the beginning inquiry teacher can be daunting indeed. Small wonder that it generally takes a few years before inquiry teaching expertise is attained, if it is attained at all (Berliner, 1994).

USING THE RTOP TO MEASURE AND IMPROVE INQUIRY TEACHING

Recently a classroom observational instrument called the Reformed Teaching Observation Protocol (RTOP) has been developed to quantitatively assess the extent to which elements of inquiry are embedded in lessons (Piburn et al., 2000). The RTOP consists of 25 statements (see Table 14.4). Each statement is scored on a 0–4 "Never Occurred" to "Very Descriptive" scale. Thus, the RTOP allows observers to rate instruction on a 0–100 scale reflective of the extent to which reformed/inquiry instructional practices are used.

Importantly, RTOP scores and student achievement have been found to be correlated positively in a wide variety of science and mathematics courses (e.g., A. E. Lawson et al., 2002). In other words, in classes that score high on the RTOP, student achievement tends to be high, whereas in classes with low RTOP scores, the classroom averages tend to be low. Good teaching practices improve student achievement. So take a good look at the RTOP items and use them to evaluate your future efforts at incorporating inquiry in your classroom. Over time, your RTOP scores should improve until you consistently score in the 90s. When you do, you will be having a great time teaching, and your students will be having a great time learning!

TABLE 14.4   What Does an Inquiry Classroom Look Like? The Reformed Teaching Observation Protocol

LESSON DESIGN AND IMPLEMENTATION

1. The instructional strategies and activities respected students' prior knowledge and the preconceptions inherent therein.
2. The lesson was designed to engage students as members of a learning community.
3. In this lesson, student exploration preceded formal presentation.
4. The lesson encouraged students to seek and value alternative modes of investigation or problem solving.
5. The focus and direction of the lesson were often determined by ideas originating with students.

(Continued)

TABLE 14.4   (Continued)

CONTENT

Propositional Knowledge

6. The lesson involved fundamental concepts of the subject.

7. The lesson promoted strongly coherent conceptual understanding.

8. The teacher had a solid grasp of the subject matter content inherent in the lesson.

9. Elements of abstraction (i.e., symbolic representations, theory building) were encouraged when it was important to do so.

10. Connections with other content disciplines and/or real-world phenomena were explored and valued.

Procedural Knowledge

11. Students used a variety of means (models, drawings, graphs, concrete materials, etc.) to represent phenomena.

12. Students made predictions, estimations, and/or hypotheses and devised means for testing them.

13. Students were actively engaged in thought-provoking activity that often involved critical assessment of procedures.

14. Students were reflective about their learning.

15. Intellectual rigor, constructive criticism, and the challenging of ideas were valued.

CLASSROOM CULTURE

Communicative Interactions

16. Students were involved in the communication of their ideas to others using a variety of means and media.

17. The teacher's questions triggered divergent modes of thinking.

18. There was a high proportion of student talk, and a significant amount of it occurred between and among students.

19. Student questions and comments often determined the focus and direction of classroom discourse.

20. There was a climate of respect for what others had to say.

Student/Teacher Relationships

21. Active participation of students was encouraged and valued.

22. Students were encouraged to generate conjectures, alternative solution strategies, and ways of interpreting evidence.

23. In general, the teacher was patient with students.

24. The teacher acted as a resource person, working to support and enhance student investigations.

25. The metaphor "teacher as listener" was very characteristic of this classroom.

Note. Each item is scored on a 0–4 "Never Occurred" to "Very Descriptive" scale.

Summary

- Interviews conducted with several experienced teachers identified 10 potential reasons why many teachers do not teach via inquiry.

- The development of inquiry lessons takes time and energy. However, once they are developed, the required time and energy are typically less than for traditional instruction.

- Some teachers think that inquiry is too slow and cannot "cover" enough content. Yet science curricula in high-achieving countries introduce less content than in relatively low-achieving countries such as the United States.

- Students may have difficulty reading inquiry texts. However, if reading assignments are made following classroom inquiries, difficulties can be reduced.

- Teachers who think that inquiry teaching is too risky should know that inquiry teachers often become team leaders. They also become more popular with students.

- Concrete reasoners can inquire. Initial inquiries should be descriptive or include group work and additional teacher guidance. Subsequent inquiries can deal with more theoretical issues and require more independent work. If students are wasting time, it is generally due to poor classroom management, not to inquiry.

- Old dogs can learn new tricks. Nevertheless, teachers tend to teach as they have been taught, and college professors often serve as poor role models. Efforts to improve secondary school instruction should be accompanied by improvements in college teaching.

- Teachers should realize that without central themes, sequential investigations, and links to previous material, instruction is less effective.

- Inquiry teachers are in control of their classroom. Nevertheless, it takes time and experience to become a good inquiry teacher. Continued teacher support and development are crucial.

- Many materials needed for inquiry can be purchased at local stores, collected from outdoors, or brought from students' homes at a fraction of the cost of purchasing them from supply companies.

- The Reformed Teaching Observation Protocol assesses the extent to which elements of inquiry instruction are used in the classroom. RTOP scores and student achievement are highly correlated. Repeated use of the RTOP will help you become a skilled inquiry teacher.

Application Questions/Activities

1. Visit one or more middle school or high school classrooms and evaluate the lesson(s) presented in terms of the 25 criteria of the Reformed Teaching Observation Protocol. If the teachers score relatively low, think about what they could or should have done to improve their score. Make a list of such changes. If the teachers score relatively high based on the criteria, interview them to find out what experience(s) helped them become inquiry-oriented teachers.

Chapter 15

PROFESSIONAL DEVELOPMENT

The bottom line from educational research is that you can't teach much, if anything, of lasting value by simply giving students answers. Effective teaching is *not* telling. Rather, meaningful learning is an internally mediated constructive process, a process embedded in the following four firm research findings (as reviewed by Lambert & McCombs, 1998):

1. Learning is a natural self-regulative process in which students are inherently curious and motivated to understand their world.

2. Students have distinctive experiences, interests, beliefs, emotional states, stages of development, talents, and goals that must be taken into account.

3. Learning occurs best when what is being learned is relevant and when students are

New teachers need expert mentoring to develop good inquiry-based lessons and effective teaching skills.

APPLICABLE NSES STANDARDS

Standard F Science teachers actively participate in the ongoing planning and development of the school science program. In doing so, they

- Plan and develop the school science program.

- Participate in decisions concerning the allocation of time and other resources to the science program.

- Participate fully in planning and implementing professional growth and development strategies for themselves and their colleagues.

actively engaged in constructing new understandings and making new connections with prior knowledge.

4. Learning occurs best in positive environments in which students' ideas and efforts are appreciated and respected.

In other words, effective teaching takes teachers off center stage and places student-generated questions, hypotheses, tests, evidence, arguments, and conclusions on center stage. Orchestrating this sort of student-centered inquiry instruction is by no means easy for beginning teachers. I can still recall my first feeble attempts at getting students actively involved in learning. I had no clue. Worse yet, I was amazed at what was going on in the teacher's class across the hall. We both kept our doors open, and whenever I checked out his class, the students always seemed totally engaged in some sort of interesting activity. Even more amazingly, whenever the teacher was in front of the class, the students were actually paying attention! What was his secret? Fortunately with his help, with the help of a wise mentor from the local university, and with the use of some excellent inquiry-based lessons developed by a National Science Foundation–funded project, I was able to put all of the pieces together and finally get inquiry going.

With this in mind, this final chapter will first consider important national standards for continuing professional development and ways in which you can become a more effective inquiry teacher. It will then consider relatively recent research on teacher effectiveness that will hopefully convince you that good teaching really does matter. The chapter will conclude by discussing some research questions that you can tackle in your own classroom. Becoming an active researcher may in fact be the best way for you to continue to develop professionally and contribute to your profession.

PROFESSIONAL DEVELOPMENT STANDARDS

The Committee on Science and Mathematics Teacher Preparation

Given that becoming a good teacher takes time and experience, continuing professional development is crucial (e.g., Berliner, 1994; Roehrig & Luft, 2004). Recently, the Committee on Science and Mathematics Teacher Preparation (2001) listed the following standards for science teacher professional development:

Standard A: Essential science content should be learned through inquiry and should

- actively involve teachers in investigating phenomena.
- address issues of scientific significance and of interest to teachers.
- introduce teachers to scientific literature, media, and technology.
- build on teachers' current science understandings, abilities, and attitudes.
- encourage reflection on the processes and outcomes of inquiry.
- encourage teacher collaboration.

Standard B: Professional development requires integrating science content and pedagogy and should

- occur within a variety of instructional contexts.
- build on teachers' current understandings of teaching and learning.
- use inquiry, reflection, and current research in science education and guided teaching practice.

Standard C: Professional development requires building for lifelong learning and should provide

- regular and frequent individual and collegial examination and reflection on teaching practice.
- regular feedback about teaching practice to improve that practice via mentors, teacher advisors, coaches, lead teachers, or resource teachers.
- opportunities to learn about and use techniques such as collegial reflection, peer coaching, portfolios, and journals.
- opportunities to learn about and use research skills to generate new knowledge about science teaching and learning.

Standard D: Professional development programs should be coherent and integrated and should be characterized by

- clear and shared goals that are consistent with the *National Science Education Standards*.
- integrated and coordinated components so that understanding and skill can develop over time.
- options that recognize teacher diversity.
- collaboration among teachers, teacher educators, teacher unions, scientists, school administrators, policymakers, professional organizations, businesspeople, and parents.
- recognition of the history, culture, and organization of schools.
- continuous assessment using a variety of strategies that leads to program improvement.

The National Board for Professional Teaching Standards

The National Board for Professional Teaching Standards is another organization concerned with teacher professional development. Formed in the 1980s, the National Board is an independent organization governed by a board of directors, many of whom are classroom teachers. The National Board's initial task was to identify what it means to be an excellent teacher. Its answer is contained in a policy statement listing five core propositions of teaching excellence (see Table 15.1). Based on these five propositions, the National Board has published sets of standards that further detail what constitutes accomplished teaching in every subject and for students at all stages of intellectual development (see http://www.nbpts.org). For practicing teachers, the National Board Standards provide a career-long learning curriculum for teaching excellence. Teachers can seek National Board Certification through an extensive series of performance-based assessments, which include teaching portfolios, student work samples, videotapes, and thorough analyses of classroom teaching and student learning. Teachers also complete written exercises probing their subject-matter knowledge, as well as their knowledge of how to teach those subjects (so-called content pedagogical knowledge). National Board Certification is voluntary and open to all teachers with a baccalaureate degree and 3 years of classroom experience.

TABLE 15.1   The National Board for Professional Teaching Standards' Five Components of Teaching Excellence—Abridged Version

1. *Teachers are committed to students and their learning.*

   Accomplished teachers understand how students develop and learn. They incorporate the prevailing theories of cognition and intelligence in their practice. They are aware of the influence of context and culture on behavior. They develop students' cognitive capacity and their respect for learning.

2. *Teachers know the subjects they teach and how to teach those subjects to students.*

   Accomplished teachers have a rich understanding of the subject(s) they teach and appreciate how knowledge in their subject is created, organized, linked to other disciplines and applied to real-world settings. While faithfully representing the collective wisdom of our culture and upholding the value of disciplinary knowledge, they also develop the critical and analytical capacities of their students.

3. *Teachers are responsible for managing and monitoring student learning.*

   Accomplished teachers know how to engage groups of students to ensure a disciplined learning environment, and how to organize instruction to allow the schools' goals for students to be met. They are adept at setting norms for social interaction among students and between students and teachers. They understand how to motivate students to learn and how to maintain their interest even in the face of temporary failure.

4. *Teachers think systematically about their practice and learn from experience.*

   Accomplished teachers are models of educated persons, exemplifying the virtues they seek to inspire in students—curiosity, tolerance, honesty, fairness, respect for diversity and appreciation of cultural differences—and the capacities that are prerequisites for intellectual growth: the ability to reason and take multiple perspectives, to be creative and take risks, and to adopt an experimental and problem-solving orientation.

5. *Teachers are members of learning communities.*

   Accomplished teachers contribute to the effectiveness of the school by working collaboratively with other professionals on instructional policy, curriculum development and staff development.

Professional Organizations

In addition to enrolling in inquiry-based in-service programs and perhaps working toward National Board Certification, you can improve your teaching skills and keep abreast of current research and development in your field by becoming a member of one or more of the professional organizations listed below. Each organization publishes a journal, has a Web site, and holds annual meetings. The journals and meetings are excellent sources of current ideas and research. You should become an active participant in one or more of these associations as well as state and local organizations also devoted to continuing professional development.

1. American Association for the Advancement of Science (AAAS)—*Science*—www.aaas.org

2. American Association of Physics Teachers—*American Journal of Physics* and *The Physics Teacher*—www.aapt.org

3. American Chemical Society—*Journal of Chemical Education* and *ChemMatters*—www.acs.org

4. Association for Science Teacher Education (ASTE)—*Journal of Science Teacher Education*—www.theaste.org

5. National Association of Biology Teachers—*The American Biology Teacher*—www.nabt.org

6. National Association of Geoscience Teachers—*Journal of Geoscience Education*—www.nagt.org

7. National Association for Research in Science Teaching—*Journal of Research in Science Teaching*—www.narst.org

8. National Science Teachers Association—*The Science Teacher, Science and Children,* and *Journal of College Science Teaching*—www.nsta.org

GOOD TEACHING REALLY MATTERS

Hopefully by this time you are convinced that good teaching really does matter. But perhaps you still need some convincing. After all, you have probably talked to lots of people who believe that students are either smart or dumb and the smart ones will learn pretty much on their own, while the dumb ones won't learn no matter what teachers do. So let's briefly review just what the research is telling us, starting with some large-scale studies.

Large-Scale Studies

Several large-scale studies have found positive and substantial relationships between teacher qualifications and student achievement. For example, a comprehensive study of some

150,000 teachers from over 900 Texas school districts found that teacher qualifications, as reflected by scores on a statewide teacher licensing exam, correlated highly with student reading and math achievement (R. F. Ferguson, 1991). Basic literacy skills, years of teaching experience, and presence of a master's degree accounted for more interdistrict variation in student reading and math achievement than did student socioeconomic status. The effects were so strong that after controlling for socioeconomic status, the large differences between Black and White students were almost completely accounted for by teacher qualifications.

In another Texas study, E. J. Fuller (1999) found that students in districts with a greater frequency of fully licensed teachers were significantly more likely to pass the state achievement tests after controlling for socioeconomic status, school wealth, and teacher experience. Similarly, Strauss and Sawyer (1986) found that North Carolina teachers' scores on the National Teacher Examinations had a substantial effect on students' pass rates on the state competency exams. A 1% increase in teacher quality was associated with a 3% to 5% increase in pass rate. Darling-Hammond (2000) reviewed data from a 50-state policy survey, case studies, the 1993–94 Schools and Staffing Surveys, and results of the National Assessment of Educational Progress (NAEP) testing program and found that the effects of well-prepared teachers on student achievement can be stronger than student background factors such as poverty, language background, and minority status. Being well prepared meant having sufficient (a) subject-matter knowledge, (b) pedagogical knowledge, and (c) years of teaching experience. Several studies have found that inexperienced teachers (those with fewer than 3 years of experience) are less effective than their more experienced peers (reviewed in Darling-Hammond). Perhaps not surprisingly, the benefits of experience tend to level off after about 5 years.

Wenglinsky (2000) reported results of a nationwide survey of math and science achievement of 7,146 eighth graders who took the 1996 National Assessment of Educational Progress math assessment and the 7,776 eighth graders who took the corresponding science assessment. Students whose teachers reported conducting hands-on learning outperformed their peers by about 70% of a grade level in math and 40% of a grade level in science. Further, students whose teachers reportedly emphasized higher-order reasoning skills outperformed their peers by about 40% of a grade level in math. In science, students whose teachers received professional development on hands-on inquiry learning did better by 40% of a grade level. In math, students whose teachers received professional development in teaching higher-order reasoning skills also did better by about 40% of a grade level.

Adamson et al. (2003) found that enrollment of preservice biology teachers in one or more inquiry-based science courses while they were undergraduates was linked to the way they taught after they graduated and became in-service biology teachers. Compared to "control" teachers who had not enrolled in inquiry-based courses as undergraduates, the "experimental" group biology teachers obtained significantly higher scores on a measure of inquiry instruction (i.e., the Reformed Teaching Observation Protocol). Further, their students demonstrated significantly higher achievement in terms of scientific reasoning, nature of science, and biology concepts. In short, it would seem that good teaching really does matter—a lot!

One more study deserves mention. Many preservice teachers learn about inquiry teaching in their undergraduate education courses and wonder if they will be supported in their efforts to become good inquiry teachers. After all, they know that many of their own secondary school and college science teachers did not use inquiry, and they will find peer teachers who do not. Will they become outcasts if they embark down the inquiry road? Or will they become school leaders—leaders who will help their more experienced but more "traditional" peers change their ways?

Judson and Lawson (2007) tried to answer this question by exploring communication patterns among teachers in two high schools. Using the biology faculty of one high school and the mathematics faculty of another, they pitted the hypothesis that inquiry teachers operate alone and cut off from communication with colleagues (the isolationist hypothesis) against the alternative that inquiry teachers are team leaders who are actively sought out by their colleagues (the team-leader hypothesis). The study plotted two types of communication patterns within the two faculties. One type concerned communications about teaching issues while the other concerned social issues. Using the Reformed Teaching Observation Protocol (RTOP), trained raters assessed the extent to which the teachers employed inquiry in their classrooms. Importantly, positive relationships were found between inquiry teaching (i.e., high RTOP scores) and the frequency and significance of communication links within both groups of teachers—more so for teaching issues than for social issues. In other words, teachers sought out their inquiry-oriented peers more often than they did their traditional peers for advice regarding teaching issues. This result supports the team-leader hypothesis and implies that preservice teachers need not fear becoming isolated from their peers when they adopt inquiry-teaching practices. Instead, they are more likely to become team leaders!

CONDUCTING ACTION RESEARCH IN YOUR CLASSROOM

In addition to joining one or more of the previously mentioned professional organizations and reading their journals to keep up with new research and curriculum developments efforts, you might want to consider conducting some classroom research of your own—so-called action research. After all, in Thomas Kuhn's sense (1970), inquiry represents a paradigm for instruction. Thus, a considerable amount of "normal" science remains to test the limits of its effectiveness and fine-tune its use with different topics, students, and materials. In that spirit let's take a brief look at a variety of issues that you can research in your classroom.

Student Misconceptions

In recent years, a highly productive research field has emerged that aims to learn more about the concepts students bring to the classroom (e.g., Anamvah-Mensah, 1987; Clark & Jorde, 2004; Committee on Undergraduate Science Education, 1997; Guzzetti, Snyder, Glass, & Gamas, 1993; Hewson & Hewson, 1984; Kikas, 2004; She, 2004; Smith & Anderson, 1987; Wandersee, Mintzes, & Novak, 1994; Weaver, 1998). Much of this research has centered on identifying concepts that students hold that are inconsistent with, or even contradictory to, modern scientific views. Some of these so-called misconceptions are deeply rooted and quite instruction resistant.

In the context of inquiry instruction, misconceptions (or alternative conceptions) are alternative hypotheses that should be tested. Recall that the process of hypothesis generation involves the use of analogical reasoning (abduction). So alternative hypothesis generation and test is about finding out whose analogy is the best explanation for the puzzling observation under current consideration. Thus when tested and contradicted by evidence, alternative conceptions—alternative analogies—play an integral role in prompting disequilibrium, argumentation, inquiry, and conceptual change (e.g., C. W. Anderson & Smith, 1986; Chi & Roscoe, 2002; Pintrich, Marx, & Boyle, 1993; Yerrick, Doster, Nugent, Parke, & Crawley, 2003). Clearly, misconceptions should be openly discussed and tested rather than avoided. Therefore, a fertile area of research is the identification of alternative conceptions in different areas of science and the identification of explicit ways in which they can be tested (e.g., D. L. Anderson, Fisher, & Norman, 2002). Teachers need to know ahead of time what alternative hypotheses students are likely to generate, what tests they can conduct, and what specific predictions follow from the hypotheses and planned tests. Clearly at this time too few published instructional guides contain this sort of information.

Developing taxonomic systems of alternative conceptions should also be useful. Taxonomies would presumably be based in part on the origins of the alternatives. For example, the special creation concept has its origin in religion. Alternatively, the ideas that gravity pulls heavy objects down faster than light objects and that we are capable of pulling/sucking liquids up through straws have their origins in personal experience. Other misconceptions may have their origins in defective classroom instruction. Such taxonomies have potential value because an obvious goal of instruction is to help students construct more appropriate conceptions, and the way to do this may depend in large part on the misconception's source. Once such taxonomies have been developed, a next step is to develop corresponding assessment instruments. Such instruments differ from typical tests because their item distracters consist of common student misconceptions. For example, a misconceptions test called the Force Concept Inventory (FCI) (Hestenes, Wells, & Swackhammer, 1992) contains items such as the following:

Two metal balls are the same size, but one weighs twice as much as the other. The balls are dropped from the roof of a single-story building at the same instant of time. The time it takes the balls to reach the ground will be

a. about half as long for the heavier ball as for the lighter one.

b. about half as long for the lighter ball as for the heavier one.

c. about the same for both balls.

d. considerably less for the heavier ball, but not necessarily half as long.

e. considerably less for the lighter ball, but not necessarily half as long.

Importantly, when students are taught physics with traditional methods, their performance on the FCI improves very little from the start of the school year to the end. However, improvements are considerable when inquiry methods that directly deal with alternative conceptions are employed (Hake, 2000). In fact, this approach is so successful that average high school physics students have made greater gains on the FCI than first-year physics students at Harvard (Hestenes et al., 1992).

In addition to tests like the FCI, concept mapping (e.g., Lehman, Carter, & Kahle, 1985; Mintzes, Wandersee, & Novak, 1998; Novak, Gowin, & Johansen, 1983) is potentially a productive tool to identify particular students' misconceptions. Regardless of the specific misconception, reasoning skills appear to play a major role in their eventual elimination. For example, with respect to genetics and natural selection, A. E. Lawson and Thompson (1988) found that concrete operational seventh graders held more misconceptions than their formal operational peers. A. E. Lawson and Weser (1990) found the same result with college students. Further, the concrete operational college students were less likely to give up their misconceptions than their more developmentally advanced classmates, suggesting that the concrete students lacked the reasoning skills needed to adequately consider the evidence and arguments favoring the scientific conceptions. Thus, they were less likely to modify or reject prior misconceptions. More recently, Dodick and Orion (2003) found that thinking skills, including spatial-visual thinking, influenced students' understanding of geological time and related geological processes.

Think of it this way. During the course of instruction, teachers introduce lots of new terms. Whenever a new term is introduced, students have to figure out what it means. To do this they must subconsciously generate and test alternative ideas concerning its possible meaning. In other words, they have to link the term to the correct mental representation—that is if they have already constructed such a representation. And if they have not, they must do so. Either way, cycles of hypothetical-predictive reasoning are involved. The implication is that in order for students to reject misconceptions and construct scientific conceptions, they must first develop the reasoning skills needed to do so.

In summary, future research on student misconceptions and conceptual change should be designed to answer four general questions: (1) What alternative conceptions do students bring with them to the classroom? (2) What are the sources of these alternatives, their generality, and their stability? (3) What factors play a role in their modification and/or elimination? And (4) How can instruction best modify and/or replace them among different types of students?

Motivation and Mastery Learning

Inquiry instruction relies on intrinsic motivation to fuel learning. Events occur, puzzling observations are made, and questions are raised, all designed to provoke disequilibrium, arouse student curiosity, and initiate self-regulation. The goal is to satisfy one's curiosity, rather than obtain an extrinsic reward such as a good grade. Learning activities that relate to personal interests, needs, and goals have been found to be most conducive to learning (McCombs, 1998). In fact, in a now classic study, researchers found that students who were given extrinsic rewards for performing an initially interesting activity actually lost interest in the activity while nonrewarded students retained their interest (Lepper, Greene, & Nisbett, 1973). Thus, inquiry instruction is designed to properly rely on intrinsic motivation. But schools typically require student evaluation and grading. How can this best be accomplished without damaging intrinsic motivation?

One evaluation method that takes student motivation into consideration is called "mastery" learning. A notion behind mastery learning is that all students can acquire key ideas/skills and should do so (i.e., master them) before going on to the next topic. Presumably students succeed and remain intrinsically motivated to learn more. A mastery approach called Hunter's Essential Elements of Instruction (EEI) correctly argues that good instruction includes a few essential elements. However, Hunter's (1982, 1995) elements include teaching to one objective at a time and telling students beforehand precisely what they are supposed to learn. Unfortunately, because students are unable to easily master higher-order reasoning skills or acquire complex concepts in a short time, attempts at mastery are often dropped. So the EEI approach and similar mastery approaches often degenerate into teaching only the simplest facts. EEI even seems to deny the dualistic goal of inquiry instruction, which is to teach concepts *and* improve reasoning skills. Further, telling students precisely what they are supposed to learn beforehand robs the lesson of its inquiry nature and, therefore, reduces or eliminates intrinsic motivation. EEI also appears to directly contradict the notion that students actively construct knowledge. Nevertheless, it may be possible to synthesize mastery and inquiry approaches in some way. Perhaps a closer look is in order as it may be possible to go beyond these apparent contradictions to find some common ground to strengthen both approaches.

Group Learning

Inquiry instruction includes many opportunities for students to work together in small groups—a mode of instruction that students prefer (e.g., Johnson & Johnson, 1979, 1994). But what are the best ways to form and utilize student groups during inquiry? In an early study, a physical science course was taught with lab groups based upon level of reasoning skills in three ways—homogeneously grouped, heterogeneously grouped, and student choice (Lawrenz & Munch, 1985). The homogeneous groups did the best in terms of reasoning gains and concepts achievement. In other words, students learned best when they interacted with others at or near their developmental level. This finding contradicts the notion that advanced peers can serve as effective peer tutors. Perhaps, instead of assisting other group members, the advanced students merely take over and tell others what to do. More recently, Jensen (2008) found a similar result in inquiry-based classrooms but not in traditional classrooms where the grouping method did not seem to matter.

Clearly, additional research should explore the complexities of group dynamics and student argumentation during inquiry so that appropriate guidelines can be suggested (e.g., Keys, 1994; Kittleson & Southerland, 2004; Roth & Duit, 2003; Wellington & Osborne, 2001). Certainly for the teacher's point of view, heterogeneous groups make classroom activities run more smoothly because each group has a built-in leader. However, in terms of learning, it is probably better to eliminate higher-level students and let the lower groups struggle and eventually self-regulate.

Selecting and Sequencing Concepts

Because concepts build upon one another to form conceptual systems, some concepts should be taught prior to others. Also some concepts are more abstract than others and hence require more advanced reasoning skills for their construction. However, the learning cycle method does not specifically address these larger curriculum development issues—issues discussed in some detail in Chapter 12. For example, in what order should related concepts be taught in contexts that were not discussed in Chapter 12? And how can the complexity and abstractness of concepts best match students' developmental stages to promote optimal concept learning and continued intellectual development?

As mentioned, some research has identified appropriate concepts for students of various ages and developmental stages. Thus your curriculum needs to articulate concepts with developmental stages so that students first take a descriptive look at objects and their properties and only later explore theoretical issues. This progression from descriptive to theoretical science mirrors children's intellectual development as they progress from the concrete to the formal and perhaps to the postformal stage.

There may be an additional way to articulate content with students' developmental stages. Recall that the three types of learning cycles place differing demands on student reasoning. Descriptive cycles generally require concrete reasoning, while hypothetical-predictive cycles require more advanced formal or postformal reasoning skills. Empirical-abductive cycles require intermediate skills. This has led some researchers to suggest that instruction in the elementary grades should employ only descriptive and empirical-abductive cycles while the secondary grades should employ empirical-abductive and hypothetical-predictive learning cycles.

Although developers of the K–6 Science Curriculum Improvement Study (SCIS) program did not identify the three types of learning cycles, they clearly exist in the program. Interestingly, a variety of types are used at each grade. For example, the first-grade *Organisms* unit includes a learning cycle in the causal question: What caused the black stuff on the bottom of the aquarium? After this question is raised, students generate several alternative hypotheses. Student hypotheses include the aquarium's organisms—fish, plants, snails, and so on. Students then design and conduct experiments to test their hypotheses. To do this, the fish, plants, and snails are isolated in new aquariums to see in which aquarium the black stuff appears—for example,

If . . . "pooping" fish caused the black stuff (fish hypothesis),

and . . . a new aquarium is set up that contains only fish (planned test),

then . . . the black stuff should appear in this aquarium but not in other aquariums that lack fish (prediction).

Thus, the first graders are proposing and testing alternative hypotheses. Furthermore, their attempts to do so are generally quite successful. It should be noted, however, that student hypotheses are based upon observable objects and direct experiences and do not involve the postulation of unseen theoretical entities. Also, another key element is involved in the lesson—the teacher. The teacher is guiding the students as they work as one large group to generate hypotheses and design experiments. Thus, it would seem that the key instructional variable is not the type of learning cycle employed but the nature of the hypothesized entities under consideration and the extent to which students work individually without much teacher guidance or work together with much teacher guidance. In other words, the SCIS curriculum is designed to gradually move from the observable to the theoretical and gradually increase the burden placed on students to carry out their own inquiries.

Given the importance of matching concepts with developmental stages, it is unfortunate that many textbooks introduce theoretical entities such as atoms and energy to young elementary school children. Indeed, if a postformal stage really exists, if it does not develop until after age 18, and if postformal thought is needed to really understand theoretical concepts, then it follows that introducing such concepts to elementary school and even to secondary school students is largely a waste of time. In other words, a significant portion of some elementary school programs, a significant portion of the typical high school biology curriculum (e.g., the molecular aspects of biology), virtually all of high school chemistry, and much of the physics curriculum may be beyond the typical student's developmental grasp! Perhaps this is why many college professors claim that most freshmen know very little science when they enroll. More research into the best ways of articulating the intellectual demands of the curriculum with the intellectual capabilities of the students is needed.

The Development and Transfer of Reasoning Skills

Factors such as high motivation, multiple learning contexts, making connections with prior knowledge, and consciously monitoring one's learning (i.e., so-called metacognition) all contribute to successful transfer (e.g., Baron, 1998; Bransford, Brown, & Cockling, 1999). One increasingly popular way to engage students in motivating inquiries is through the use of socially relevant issues such as cloning, stem cell research, global warming, the energy crisis, and alternative energy sources. As mentioned in Chapter 12, Arwood (2004) developed and taught a cell biology course in which students learned how to use fingerprinting and DNA typing and then held a mock murder trial in which these and other techniques were used to gather key evidence. The highly motivating course significantly increased both student reasoning skills and their attitudes toward science. Sadler's (2004) study was also mentioned as it similarly found that such Science-Technology-Society (i.e., STS) instructional approaches can boost students' reasoning/argumentation skills, their understanding of the nature of science, and their understanding of key science concepts.

In general, research has made it clear that diverse, long-term inquiry instruction is slower to achieve specific reasoning gains than short-term efforts to teach specific reasoning skills. However, the slowly acquired gains seem to be of more general use as they involve a greater variety of skills applicable to a greater variety of contexts. This result seems reasonable given that more diverse and longer-term instruction more closely approximates the out-of-school experiences that contribute to intellectual development. Importantly, the relatively few long-term studies conducted in the sciences have found transfer to academic areas as diverse as mathematics, social studies, reading, and English (e.g., J. W. Renner, Stafford, Coffia, Kellogg, & Weber, 1973; Shayer & Adey, 1993). For example, the Shayer and Adey study mentioned in Chapter 5 evaluated the effects of a middle school inquiry program called *Thinking Science* aimed at improved formal reasoning. Interestingly, some of the positive and general effects did not show up immediately at the end of the 2-year program. Instead, they showed up some 4 years later as significant gains in science, in mathematics, and in

English as measured by the British National Examinations. These "delayed" gains are interesting and important because they support Piagetian theory. As you may recall, Piaget (1964) argued that gains in reasoning come about only when children and adolescents have sufficient time for equilibration (i.e., self-regulation).

It should be noted that improvements in subsequent academic performance due to programs such as *Thinking Science* are expected only when that academic performance requires reasoning skills. Many advanced courses are not really advanced at all as they simply require the memorization of more facts and place very little, if any, demand on higher-order reasoning skills. One might well predict that the more able reasoners would be turned off by such courses and do more poorly. All of this is not to say that research cannot be carried out to further investigate these issues. It merely says that such research is difficult, particularly because appropriate measures of long-term success are often difficult to develop and use. The suggested research study that has yet to be conducted is one in which students are raised on a diet of learning cycles in all disciplines, in, say, Grades K–12, and are then compared to those raised by more traditional means.

In summary, the development and transfer issue is complex and difficult to research. In general, it has been attacked in steps. First, we would like to know if inquiry is better than other approaches at teaching reasoning skills that are the explicit focus of instruction. Research strongly suggests that this is so. Second, we would like to know if inquiry is better at teaching reasoning skills that are *not* the explicit focus of instruction. Research suggests that this is so. Third, do improved reasoning skills transfer to other academic subjects? The answer to this question appears to be yes. Fourth, do such improvements translate into improved performance in "real" life? The jury is still out on this question. Nevertheless, at least several former students have volunteered enthusiastic responses in the affirmative.

Standardized Testing

Standardized tests such as the SAT, the Iowa Tests of Educational Development, and the ACT Critical Thinking Test attempt to assess general knowledge and general reasoning skills. For example, the ACT Critical Thinking Test includes items in four main categories: recognition of the elements of an argument, analyzing the structure of an argument, evaluation of an argument, and extension of an argument (American College Testing Program, 1988). Similarly, the Science Research Associates (1970, pp. 1–2), makers of the Iowa Tests, had this to say about the skills required for success on their tests: ". . . the student must interpret and analyze material that is new to him, and apply broad concepts and generalized skills to situations not previously encountered in the classroom."

In other words, most national-level standardized tests assess broad concepts and general reasoning skills. More recently, many state and local districts have set up committees to develop state- and district-level tests in specific disciplines. Typically, these tests are less thoughtful. In some cases the tests almost exclusively require the rote recall of isolated facts. Such tests are counterproductive to efforts at developing, disseminating, and teaching science programs based on inquiry/constructivist methods. Nevertheless, as mentioned previously, some learning cycle teachers have found that their students outperform those of traditional teachers on locally developed fact-oriented tests—even on topics that were not directly taught. This is what one would expect if learning cycle instruction improves general reasoning skills that manifest themselves in terms of better test-taking skills.

In short, the recent trend in many states and districts to develop so-called high-stakes tests poses a threat to quality teaching and learning. As Paris (1998) points out, such testing programs, if not developed with care and thoughtfulness, can undermine effective education in several ways including (a) misdirected motivation and learning, (b) distorted curricula and instruction, (c) cheating, (d) a misinformed and misguided public, and (e) runaway costs. Consequently, teachers must work hand in hand with test developers and policymakers to make sure that high-quality tests are developed. It would be wonderful if *all* students knew *everything* there is to know about *all* the sciences. But this is not possible. Therefore, we must be selective about what we teach, how we teach it, and how we assess what students learn. Low-level teaching and testing programs used in many classrooms, in many districts, and even in some states create many of the same problems that arise from mastery instruction. It is difficult to teach and assess higher-order reasoning skills and complex concepts while it is relatively easy to teach and assess educational trivia. Consequently, teaching and testing is often reduced to the trivial. This trend must be fought.

Concluding Remarks

In conclusion, a considerable amount of research has found that classroom inquiry is the most effective way of achieving the educational system's central objectives. Additional research remains to be done to explore various facets of inquiry instruction and to extend and test its effectiveness to new areas and for longer periods of time. Also, future theoretical work in the field of neuroscience and new technologies will no doubt aid our understanding and ability to teach effectively. Although these improvements will help fine-tune the inquiry approach, they will not alter its fundamental role and importance. This is because inquiry instruction follows the way in which humans spontaneously construct knowledge. Educational theorists and researchers may improve on this pattern of instruction, but the pattern will not change unless humans evolve a new means of constructing knowledge.

Summary

- In addition to finding an experienced and expert mentor, standards for professional development exist as do professional organizations and journals that can help you learn about current research findings, learn about new curriculum developments, and develop teaching expertise.

- Good teaching matters in terms of student achievement. Observational instruments such as the Reformed Teaching Observation Protocol (RTOP) can reliably measure good teaching and should be repeatedly used to help you monitor your progress.

- Developing teaching expertise can be facilitated by generating and testing your own hypotheses about effective instruction in your own classroom. Several issues remain open for continued research.

- Although theoretical and empirical issues remain, research has found that classroom inquiry is the most effective way of achieving the educational system's central objectives. This is presumably because inquiry follows the pattern in which humans spontaneously construct knowledge. Future research will surely improve instruction, but the instructional pattern itself should not change unless humans evolve a new way of constructing knowledge.

Application Questions/Activities

1. What role(s) should student misconceptions play in hypothetical-predictive learning cycles?

2. Select a scientific concept or set of related concepts with important implications and applications to societal issues and design a learning cycle in which these social issues are addressed.

3. In what ways might new technologies improve science instruction? In what ways might they actually make instruction less effective?

4. Design a research study to test alternative hypotheses about the most effective ways to establish classroom groups. Conduct the study when you have an opportunity to do so in the future. Consider submitting a written report of your research to a journal devoted to science education research.

5. Design a second research study to test alternative hypotheses about another aspect of science instruction. Conduct and consider reporting this research as well.

Glossary

accommodation   The modification of a mental structure in response to a mismatch between expectations (based on use of that structure) and subsequent observations.

analogy   An agreement, a likeness, a similarity, or a correspondence between things; reasoning in which such similarities are used as a source of hypotheses.

applied research   Research aimed at answering questions that have practical human applications (e.g., determining the causes of diseases so that cures might be found).

assimilation   The act of taking in, absorbing. Cognitively, automatically and subconsciously taking in external stimuli by already acquired mental structures. In theory no act of assimilation can be completely independent of accommodation because no two external stimuli are identical. Consequently, every instance of assimilation involves some accommodation of prior mental structures.

authentic assessment   An assessment composed of performance tasks/activities that simulate real-world challenges with genuine purposes, audiences, and situational attributes.

basic research   Research designed to describe or explain nature to satisfy one's curiosity (compare with *applied research*).

bias   A tendency or inclination in favor of one idea or belief that prevents unprejudiced consideration of alternatives.

causal question   A question—that is, a "why" or "how" question but not a "who," "what," "when," or "where" question—inquiring into the cause or causes of some phenomenon; for example, Why do spiders have eight legs? Why do gazelles stott?

chunking   The mental process in which previously unrelated pieces of information held in working memory are combined/integrated into one piece of information, the process of forming new higher-order concepts; conceptualization; concept construction.

circumstantial evidence   Evidence that can test an explanation by observing other events or circumstances that according to common experience are usually linked to the cause (e.g., a wet street is usually caused by rain; therefore seeing a wet street in the morning supports the hypothesis that the pitter patter you heard on your roof last night was caused by rain). However, circumstantial evidence does not necessarily rule out alternatives (e.g., a burst fire hydrant may have sprayed the street).

class inclusion   A concrete operational reasoning pattern in which an individual understands simple classifications and generalizations (e.g., all dogs are animals; only some animals are dogs).

combinatorial reasoning   A formal operational reasoning pattern in which an individual systematically considers all possible relations of experimental conditions, even though some may not be realized in nature (recall in Chapter 1 how we generated all possible combinations of hypotheses to explain salmon navigation).

comparison group   Individuals in an experiment who either differ from the experimental group in only one way or are treated differently from the experimental group in only one way; used as a comparison with the experimental group; sometimes called the control group.

concept   A mental construction representing an object, an event, or a situation plus the associated term; a mental picture; an idea; a notion.

concept application   The third phase of inquiry instruction in which students attempt to apply newly introduced concepts and/or reasoning patterns to new contexts.

concept by apprehension   A type of concept that derives meaning directly from internal or external sensory stimuli.

conceptual system   A group of related concepts that derive meaning from one another and from analogies.

conclusion   A statement or statements that summarize the extent to which tentative generalizations or explanations have been supported or contradicted by observed results (evidence).

concrete operational stage   The stage of intellectual development that typically begins at 7 years of age. Concrete reasoning patterns allow children to generate and test descriptive hypotheses and thus accurately order and describe perceptible objects, events, and situations. Causal hypotheses are generated but not tested.

conservation reasoning   A concrete operational reasoning pattern in which an individual "conserves" certain properties of perceptible objects (e.g., if nothing is added or taken away, the amount, number, length, weight, etc., remains the same—is "conserved"—even though the appearance differs).

controlled experiment   A "fair" test. An experiment in which the values of only one independent variable differ; the values of other independent variables are the same—that is, they are held constant or "controlled." An experiment with experimental and control groups that differ in only one way or are treated differently in only one way.

convergent question   A question with only one correct answer.

cooperative learning   A collection of teaching strategies in which small groups, each with students of different ability levels, use a variety of activities to improve their understanding of a subject. Each group member is responsible for his or her own learning *and* for helping other group members learn.

correlation   Mutual relation of two or more things, parts, or variables.

correlational evidence Evidence that tests tentative explanations by determining the extent to which the values of two or more variables, which have been predicted to be correlated, are in fact correlated.

correlational reasoning A formal operational reasoning pattern in which, in spite of random fluctuations, an individual recognizes causes or relations in the phenomenon under study by comparing the relative number of confirming to disconfirming cases (e.g., to test the hypothesis that breast implants cause connective tissue disease, one compares the ratio of women with implants and the disease to the ratio of nonimplant women with the disease).

creativity The process of finding questions and/or problems and answering/solving them by generating and testing possible answers/solutions. The creative process is a four-step process involving preparation, incubation, illumination, and verification.

declarative knowledge Knowledge about objects, events, and situations; for example, cars usually have four tires, Paris is in France, evolution occurs due to natural selection, and atoms are the basic building blocks of matter; figurative knowledge; conceptual knowledge; the products of science.

deduction An *If/and/then* pattern of reasoning in which an assumed-to-be-correct statement and an imagined test condition together allow the derivation of an expected (i.e., potentially observable) consequence.

dependent variable The variable in an experiment whose values may vary in response to changes in the values of some independent variable; outcome variable; the effect.

descriptive concept A type of concept that derives meaning from postulation and test; has directly perceptible properties.

descriptive learning cycle A type of learning cycle in which students raise and answer one or more descriptive questions (i.e., "who," "what," "when," and/or "where" questions). Causal questions are not raised.

disequilibrium The cognitive state (sometimes called cognitive dissonance) resulting from a mismatch between expectations and observations.

disprove To establish as false beyond any possible doubt; not possible in science.

divergent question A question with several possibly correct answers.

empirical-abductive learning cycle A type of learning cycle that begins with one or more descriptive questions and then raises a causal question. Students then generate one or more causal hypotheses, which are initially tested with the previously gathered data.

expected result A statement of an expected (future) outcome of a planned test assuming that the hypothesis being tested is correct; to be compared with observed result to test the hypothesis (also see *prediction*).

experiment A set of manipulations of nature designed to test a tentative explanation.

experimental evidence Evidence that tests tentative explanations using experiments.

experimental group   Individuals in an experiment who either differ from the control group in only one way or are treated differently from the control group in only one way.

exploration   The initial phase of inquiry instruction in which students investigate new phenomena based in large part on their own background knowledge and interests.

faculty theory   Theory claiming that human mental behavior is compartmentalized into several "faculties" or abilities such as logic, memorization, and observation; that "exercising" the faculties enhances their development; and that the faculties, when developed, are of general use.

formal operational stage   The stage of intellectual development that, given the proper environmental stimuli, normally begins at 12 years of age. Formal reasoning patterns allow the adolescent to systematically generate and test alternative causal claims provided the possible causes are perceptible and can be manipulated.

formative assessment   The use of procedures and data to develop, modify, revise, and improve a curriculum during its inception and developmental phases.

hypothesis   A statement intended as a tentative explanation for an observed phenomenon; a possible cause for a specific observation.

hypothetical-predictive learning cycle   A type of learning cycle in which students generate and test alternative causal hypotheses based on their own planned tests, predictions, and results.

identification and the control of variables   In testing hypotheses, a formal operational reasoning pattern in which an individual recognizes the need to consider all the possible causal variables and design a test that controls all but the variable being investigated (e.g., in the Mealworm Puzzle, he or she recognizes the inadequacy of the setup in Box 1).

independent variable   The variable in a controlled experiment whose values vary to see if that variation causes a change in the outcome of the experiment; the input, manipulated, or causal variable.

inquiry instruction   An instructional approach consisting of three sequential phases of instruction called exploration, term introduction, and concept application; a method in which students construct new concepts and improve their reasoning skills; also known as learning cycle instruction.

intelligence   The capacity for understanding, for answering questions, for solving problems, and for making reasonable decisions.

law   A statement that summarizes a pattern of regularity detected in nature (i.e., the manner or order in which a set of natural phenomena occurs under certain conditions). Note: A satisfactory explanation for the detected pattern may not exist.

learning   The process of acquiring new behaviors largely as a consequence of experience; noninnate behavior.

learning cycle   An instructional approach consisting of three sequential phases of instruction called exploration, term introduction, and concept application; a method in which students construct new concepts and improve their reasoning skills; also known as inquiry instruction.

model   A representation, generally in miniature, to show the structure or serve as a copy of something.

phlogiston   The name given to fire by 18th-century chemists who believed that fire was one of four basic materials of all matter (i.e., earth, air, water, and fire).

planned test   Imagined conditions that when carried out test a hypothesis.

postformal operational stage   A stage of intellectual development, which, given the proper environmental stimuli, may begin at about 18 years of age. Postformal reasoning is characterized as hypothetico-deductive in contexts where the proposed causal agents are nonperceptible and thus must be tested by indirect means.

prediction   A statement of an expected (future) outcome of a planned test assuming that the hypothesis being tested is correct; to be compared with observed result to test the hypothesis (also see *expected result*).

probabilistic reasoning   A formal operational reasoning pattern in which an individual recognizes that natural phenomena are probabilistic in character and that conclusions and explanations must involve probabilistic considerations (e.g., in the Mealworm Puzzle the ability to disregard the few mealworms in the "wrong" ends of Boxes 1, 2, and 3; in the Frog Puzzle the ability to assess the probability of certain assumptions holding true such as the banded and unbanded frogs mingled thoroughly, no new frogs were born, and the bands did not increase death or predation rate).

procedural knowledge   Knowledge of how to do something such as drive a car, speak Spanish, test a hypothesis, or construct a frequency graph; operative knowledge; the processes of science.

proportional reasoning   A formal operational reasoning pattern in which an individual recognizes and interprets relationships between relationships described by observable variables (e.g., for every 12 banded frogs there are 72 total frogs; therefore, for every 55 banded frogs there must be 330 total frogs).

prove   To establish as true beyond any possible doubt; not possible in science.

self-regulation   The cognitive process that results from disequilibrium and restores equilibrium by the search for new mental structures or the accommodation of prior mental structures. Equilibrium is restored when new or accommodated mental structures drive noncontradicted behaviors (also called equilibration).

serial ordering   A concrete operational reasoning pattern in which an individual arranges a set of objects or data in serial order and establishes a one-to-one correspondence (e.g., the youngest plants have the smallest leaves).

summative assessment   The use of procedures and data to determine the extent to which students have attained course goals as well as determine the effectiveness of a unit, course, or program after it has been completed.

term introduction   The second phase of inquiry instruction in which a new term or terms are introduced to the students. The term(s) must relate to the phenomena and/or ideas embedded in the exploration.

theoretical concept   A type of concept that derives meaning from analogy and from its position within a complex conceptual system; verified through postulation and test; lacks directly perceptible properties.

theory   A collection of statements (conditions, components, claims, postulates, propositions) that when taken together attempt to explain a broad class of related phenomena. A theory whose statements have been tested and supported repeatedly becomes a well-accepted theory.

undifferentiated whole   A mental event that spontaneously results from an interaction of the mind with new sensory input. The undifferentiated whole becomes differentiated, and its resulting parts become integrated as a result of continued interaction with the experience that produced the initial sensory input.

wait-time I   The period of time the questioner waits after posing a question before making an additional remark or posing an additional question—the period of silence following a question.

wait-time II   The period of time the questioner waits after receiving a response to a question before making an additional remark—the period of silence following a response.

References

Adamson, S. L., Burtch, M., Cox, F., III, Judson, E., Turley, J. B., Benford, R., et al. (2003). Reformed undergraduate instruction and its subsequent impact on secondary school teaching practice and student achievement. *Journal of Research in Science Teaching, 40*(10), 939–957.

Alexander, P. A., & Murphy, P. K. (1999). The research base for APA's learner-centered psychological principles. In N. M. Lambert & B. L. McCombs (Eds.), *How students learn: Reforming schools through learner-centered education*. Washington, DC: American Psychological Association.

American Association for the Advancement of Science (1989). *Project 2061: Science for all Americans*. Washington, DC: Author.

American Association for the Advancement of Science. (1990). *The liberal art of science: Agenda for action*. Washington, DC: Author.

American College Testing Program. (1988). *Item writer's guide for the collegiate assessment of academic proficiency critical thinking test*. Iowa City, IA: Author.

American Psychiatric Association. (1987). *Diagnostic and statistical manual of mental disorders* (3rd ed., rev.). Washington, DC: Author.

Anamvah-Mensah, J. (1987). Comments on plants as producers: A case study of elementary science teaching. *Journal of Research in Science Teaching, 24*(8), 769–770.

Anderson, C. W., & Smith, E. R. (1986). Teaching science. In V. Koehler (Ed.), *The educator's handbook: A research perspective*. New York: Longman.

Anderson, D. L., Fisher, K. M., & Norman, G. J. (2002). Development and evaluation of the conceptual inventory of natural selection. *Journal of Research in Science Teaching, 39*(10), 952–978.

Anderson, L. W., & Krathwohl, D. R. (2001). *A taxonomy for learning, teaching and assessing*. New York: Longman.

Anderson, R. D., DeVito, A., Dyris, O. E., Kellogg, M., Kochendorfer, L., & Weigand, J. (1970). *Developing children's thinking through science*. Englewood Cliffs, NJ: Prentice-Hall.

Arredondo, M. A., Busch, E., Douglas, H. O., & Petrelli, N. J. (1994). The use of videotaped lectures in surgical oncology. *Journal of Cancer Education, 9*(2), 86–89.

Arter, J., & McTighe, J. (2001). *Scoring rubrics in the classroom*. Thousand Oaks, CA: Corwin Press.

Arwood, L. (2004). Teaching cell biology to nonscience majors through forensics, or how to design a killer course. *Journal of Cell Biology Education, 3*, 131–138.

Association for Supervision and Curriculum Development. (1994). *Challenging the gifted in the regular classroom: Facilitator's guide*. Alexandria, VA: Author.

Atkin, J. M., & Karplus, R. (1962). Discovery or invention? *Science Teacher, 29*(5), 45.

Atwater, M. M. (1994). Research on cultural diversity in the classroom. In D. L. Gabel (Ed.), *Handbook of research on science teaching and learning*. New York: Macmillan.

Ausubel, D. P., Novak, J. D., & Hanesian, H. (1978). *Educational psychology: A cognitive view* (2nd ed.). New York: Holt, Rinehart, & Winston.

Baker, D., & Leary, R. (1995). Letting girls speak out about science. *Journal of Research in Science Teaching, 32*(1), 3–28.

Baker, D. R., & Piburn, M. D. (1997). *Constructing science in middle and secondary classrooms*. Boston: Allyn & Bacon.

Baron, J. B. (1998). Using learner-centered assessment on a large scale. In N. M. Lambert & B. L. McCombs (Eds.), *How students learn: Reforming schools through learner-centered education*. Washington, DC: American Psychological Association.

Barrett, C. (2006). *Panel says U.S. is losing ground in math, science* (News Brief No. 3685 Category: Role of Education in Business). Washington, DC: National Alliance of State Science and Mathematics Coalitions.

Bell, R. L., Gess-Newsome, J., & Luft, J. (Eds). (2007). *Technology in the secondary science classroom*. Arlington, VA: NSTA Press.

Berger, C. F., Lu, C. R., Belzer, S. J., & Voss, B. E. (1994). Research on the uses of technology in education. In D. L. Gabel (Ed.), *Handbook of research on science teaching and learning*. New York: Macmillan.

Berliner, D. C. (1994). Expertise: The wonder of exemplary performances. In J. N. Mangieri & C. C. Block (Eds.), *Creating powerful thinking in teachers and students*. Fort Worth, TX: Holt, Rinehart, & Winston.

Bloom, B. S. (Ed.). (1956). *Taxonomy of educational objectives: Cognitive domain*. New York: Longmans, Green, & Co.

Bransford, J. D., Brown, A. L., & Cockling, R. R. (1999). *How people learn: Brain, mind, experience, and school*. Washington, DC: National Academy Press.

Brickhouse, N. W. (2001). Embodying science: A feminist perspective. *Journal of Research in Science Teaching, 38*(3), 282–295.

Brynner, W. (Trans.) (1962). *From the way of life according to Lao-Tse*. New York: Capricorn Books.

Bybee, R. W., & DeBoer, G. E. (1994). Research on goals for the science curriculum. In D. L. Gabel (Ed.), *Handbook of research on science teaching and learning*. New York: Macmillan.

Cajas, F. (2001). The science/technology interaction: Implications for science literacy. *Journal of Research in Science Teaching, 38*(7), 715–729.

Carin, A. A., & Sund, R. B. (1980). *Teaching modern science* (3rd ed.). Columbus, OH: Charles E. Merrill.

Cavanaugh, C. (2001). *Guide to classroom discussions*. Retrieved May 13, 2009, from http://drscavanauh.org/discussions/inclass/index.htm

Chi, M. T. H., & Roscoe, R. D. (2002). The processes and challenges of conceptual change. In M. Limon & L. Mason (Eds.), *Reconsidering conceptual change: Issues in theory and practice*. Dordrecht, The Netherlands: Kluwer.

Chiappetta, E. L., & Koballa, T. R. (2002). *Science instruction in the middle and secondary schools* (5th ed.). Upper Saddle River, NJ: Merrill Prentice Hall.

Chiras, D. D. (1999). *Human biology* (3rd ed.). Boston: Jones & Bartlett Publishers.

Chown, M. (2001). *The magic furnace: The search for the origin of atoms*. New York: Oxford University Press.

Clark, D. C., & Jorde, D. (2004). Helping students revise disruptive experientially supported ideas about thermodynamics: Computer visualizations and tactile models. *Journal of Research in Science Teaching, 41*(1), 1–23.

Collea, F. P, Fuller, R. G., Karplus, R., Paldy, L. G., & Renner, J. W. (1975). *Workshop on physics teaching and the development of reasoning.* Stony Brook, NY: American Association of Physics Teachers.

Collette, A. T., & Chiappetta, E. L. (1986). *Science instruction in the middle and secondary schools.* Columbus, OH: Charles E. Merrill.

Collins, A. (1990). Portfolios for assessing student learning in science: A new name for a familiar idea? In A. B. Champagne, B. E. Lovitts, & B. J. Calinger (Eds.), *Assessment in the service of instruction.* Washington, DC: American Association for the Advancement of Science.

Committee on Science and Mathematics Teacher Preparation (2001). *Educating teachers of science, mathematics, and technology.* Washington, DC: National Research Council.

Committee on Undergraduate Science Education. (1997). *Science teaching reconsidered: A handbook.* Washington, DC: National Academy Press.

Costenson, K., & Lawson, A. E. (1986). Why isn't inquiry used in more classrooms? *American Biology Teacher, 48*(3), 150–158.

Council of State Science Supervisors. (n.d.). *Science & safety: Making the connection.* Retrieved May 13, 2009, from http://www.csss-science.org/downloads/scisafe.pdf

Crouch, C. H., Fagen, A. P., Callen, J. P., & Mazur, E. (2004). Classroom demonstrations: Learning tools or entertainment? *The American Journal of Physics, 72*(6), 835–838.

Darling-Hammond, L. (2000, January 1). Teacher quality and student achievement: A review of state policy evidence. *Education Policy Analysis Archives, 8*(1). Retrieved October 16, 2001, from http://epaa.asu.edu/epaa/v8n1/

Dewey, J. (1916). Method in science teaching. *General Science Quarterly, 1, 3.*

Diller, J. V., & Moule, J. (2005). *Cultural competence: A primer for educators.* Belmont, CA: Thomson Wadsworth.

Division of Undergraduate Science, Engineering, and Mathematics Education. (1989). *Report of the National Science Foundation Workshop on Undergraduate Laboratory Development.* Washington, DC: National Science Foundation.

Dodick, J., & Orion, N. (2003). Cognitive factors affecting student understanding of geologic time. *Journal of Research in Science Teaching, 40*(4), 415–442.

Duncan, J., Seitz, R. J., Kolodny, J., Bor, D., Herzog, H., Ahmed, A., et al. (2000). A neural basis for general intelligence. *Science, 289,* 457–460.

Echevarria, J., Vogt, M., & Short, D. J. (2004). *Making content comprehensible for English learners.* Boston: Pearson Education.

Edelson, D. C. (2001). A framework for the design of technology-supported inquiry activities. *Journal of Research in Science Teaching, 38*(3), 355–385.

Edlich, R. F. (1993). My last lecture. *Journal of Emergency Medicine, 11*(6), 771–774.

Educational Policies Commission. (1961). *The central purpose of American education.* Washington, DC: National Education Association of the United States.

Educational Policies Commission. (1966). *Education and the spirit of science.* Washington, DC: National Education Association of the United States.

Elementary Science Study. (1974). *Teachers' guide for attribute games and problems.* New York: McGraw-Hill.

Ferguson, R. F. (1991). Paying for public education: New evidence on how and why money matters. *Harvard Journal on Education, 28*(2), 465–498.

Flick, L., & Bell, R. (2000). Preparing tomorrow's science teachers to use technology: Guidelines for science educators. *Contemporary Issues in Technology and Teacher Education, 1*(1). Retrieved January 23, 2002, from http://www.citejournal.org/achives.cfm

Fuller, E. J. (1999). *Does teacher certification matter? A comparison of TAAS performance in 1997 between schools with low and high percentages of certified teachers.* Austin: Charles A. Dana Center, University of Texas.

Fuller, R. G. (2002). *A love of discovery: Science education—the second career of Robert Karplus.* New York: Kluwer Academic/Plenum.

Galloway, T. W. (1910). Report of the committee on fundamentals of the Central Association of Science and Mathematics Teachers. *School Science and Mathematics, 10,* 801–813.

Grove, P. B., & the Merriam-Webster Editorial Staff. (Eds.). (1986). *Webster's third new international dictionary.* Springfield, MA: Merriam-Webster.

Gruber, H. E., & Barrett, P. H. (1974). *Darwin on man.* New York: E. P. Dutton & Co.

Guzzetti, B. J., Snyder, T. E., Glass, G. V., & Gamas, W. S. (1993). Promoting conceptual change in science: A comparative meta-analysis of instructional interventions from reading education and science education. *Reading Research Quarterly, 28*(2), 117–155.

Hake, R. R. (2000). Interactive-engagement vs. traditional methods: A six-thousand student survey of mechanics test data for introductory physics courses. *American Journal of Physics, 66,* 67–74.

Hall, E. H., & Committee (1898). Memorandum concerning report of committee of sixty. *Addresses and proceedings* (Vol. 37, pp. 964–965). Washington, DC: National Education Association.

Heiss, E. D., Obourn, E. S., & Hoffman, C. W. (1950). *Modern science teaching.* New York: Macmillan.

Hestenes, D., Wells, M., & Swackhammer, G. (1992). Force concept inventory. *The Physics Teacher, 30*(3), 141–151.

Hewson, P. W., & Hewson, M. G. A. (1984). The role of conceptual conflict in conceptual change and the design of science instruction. *Instructional Science, 13,* 1–13.

Hiebert, J. C. (1999). Relationships between research and the NCTM standards. *Journal for Research in Mathematics Education, 30,* 3–19.

Hill, W. (1967). Content textbook: Help or hindrance? *Journal of Reading, 10,* 40.

Hunt, E. (1974). Quote the raven? Nevermore! In L. W. Gregg (Ed.), *Knowledge and cognition.* Potomac, MD: Lawrence Erlbaum Associates.

Hunter, M. (1982). *Mastery teaching.* El Segundo, CA: TIP Publications.

Hunter, M. C. (1995). *Teach more—faster.* Thousand Oaks, CA: Corwin Press.

Hurd, P. D. (1961). *Biological education in American secondary school, 1890–1960.* Washington, DC: American Institute of Biological Sciences.

Hurd, P. D., Bybee, R. W., Kahle, J. B., & Yager, R. E. (1980). Biology education in secondary schools of the United States. *American Biology Teacher, 42*(7), 388.

Inhelder, B., & Piaget, J. (1958). *The growth of logical thinking from childhood to adolescence.* New York: Basic Books.

Isen, A. M., Means, B., Patrick, R., & Nowicki, G. (1982). Some factors influencing decision-making and risk-taking. In M. S. Clark & S. T. Fiske (Eds.), *Affect and cognition.* Hillsdale, NJ: Erlbaum.

Jacobson, W., & Kondo, A. (1968). *SCIS elementary science sourcebook.* Berkeley, CA: Science Curriculum Improvement Study.

Jensen, J. L. (2008). *The effects of collaboration and inquiry on reasoning and achievement in biology.* Unpublished doctoral dissertation, Arizona State University–Tempe.

Johnson, D. W., & Johnson, R. T. (1979). Cooperation, competition and individualization. In H. J. Walberg (Ed.), *Educational environments and effects.* Berkeley, CA: McCutchen.

Johnson, D. W., & Johnson, R. T. (1994). *Learning together and alone: Cooperative, competitive, and individualistic learning* (4th ed.). Edina, MN: Interaction Book Co.

Johnson, D. W., & Johnson, R. T. (2003). *Assessing students in groups: Promoting group responsibility and individual accountability.* Thousand Oaks, CA: Corwin Press.

Judson, E., & Lawson, A. E. (2007). What is the role of constructivist teachers within faculty communication networks? *Journal of Research in Science Teaching, 44*(3), 490–505.

Kahle, J. B., & Meece, J. (1994). Research on gender differences in the classroom. In D. L. Gabel (Ed.), *Handbook of research on science teaching and learning.* New York: Macmillan.

Karplus, R., Lawson, A. E., Wollman, W., Appel, M., Bernoff, R., Howe, A., et al. (1977). *Science teaching and the development of reasoning: A workshop.* Berkeley: Regents of the University of California.

Karplus, R., & Thier, H. D. (1967). *A new look at elementary school science.* Chicago: Rand McNally.

Keller, E. (2005). *Strategies for teaching students with disabilities.* Retrieved September 15, 2008, from http://www.as.wvu.edu/~scidis/learning.html

Keys, C. W. (1994). The development of scientific reasoning skills in conjunction with collaborative assignments: An interpretive study of six ninth-grade students. *Journal of Research in Science Teaching, 31*(9), 1003–1022.

Kikas, E. (2004). Teachers' conceptions and misconceptions concerning three natural phenomena. *Journal of Research in Science Teaching, 41*(5), 432–448.

Kittleson, J. M., & Southerland, S. A. (2004). The role of discourse in group knowledge construction: A case study of engineering students. *Journal of Research in Science Teaching, 41*(3), 267–293.

Kline, M. (1977). *Why the professor can't teach.* New York: St. Martins Press.

Koestler, A. (1964). *The act of creation.* London: Hutchinson.

Kuhn, T. S. (1970). *The structure of scientific revolutions.* Chicago: The University of Chicago Press.

Kuslan, L. I., & Stone, A. H. (1968). *Teaching children science: An inquiry approach.* Belmont, CA: Wadsworth.

Lambert, N. M., & McCombs, B. L. (1998). Learner-centered schools and classrooms as a direction for school reform. In N. M. Lambert & B. L. McCombs (Eds.), *How students learn: Reforming schools through learner-centered education.* Washington, DC: American Psychological Association.

Lawrenz, F., & Munch, T. W. (1985). Aptitude treatment effects of laboratory grouping method for students of differing reasoning ability. *Journal of Research in Science Teaching, 22*(3), 279–287.

Lawson, A. E. (2004). *Biology: An inquiry approach.* Dubuque, IA: Kendall/Hunt.

Lawson, A. E. (2008). *Biology: An inquiry approach* (2nd ed.). Dubuque, IA: Kendall/Hunt.

Lawson, A. E., Abraham, M. R., & Renner, J. W. (1989). *A theory of instruction: Using the learning cycle to teach science concepts and thinking skills.* Cincinnati, OH: National Association for Research in Science Teaching.

Lawson, A. E., Baker, W. P., DiDonato, L., Verdi, M. P., & Johnson, M. A. (1993). The role of physical analogies of molecular interactions and hypothetico-deductive reasoning in conceptual change. *Journal of Research in Science Teaching, 30*(9), 1073–1086.

Lawson, A. E., Benford, R., Bloom, I., Carlson, M. P., Falconer, K., Hestenes, D., et al. (2002). Evaluating college science and mathematics instruction. *Journal of College Science Teaching, 36*(6), 388–393.

Lawson, A. E., Drake, N., Johnson, J., Kwon, Y., & Scarpone, C. (2000). How good are students at testing alternative hypotheses involving unseen entities? *American Biology Teacher, 62*(4), 249–255.

Lawson, A. E., & Renner, J. W. (1975). Relationship of science subject matter and the developmental level of the learner. *Journal of Research in Science Teaching, 12*(4), 347–358.

Lawson, A. E., & Thompson, L. D. (1988). Formal reasoning ability and misconceptions concerning genetics and natural selection. *Journal of Research in Science Teaching, 25*(9), 733–746.

Lawson, A. E., & Weser, J. (1990). The rejection of nonscientific beliefs about life: Effects of instruction and reasoning skills. *Journal of Research in Science Teaching, 27*(6), 589–606.

Lawson, C. A. (1958). *Language, thought, and the human mind.* East Lansing: Michigan State University Press.

Lawson, C. A. (1967). *Brain mechanisms and human learning.* Boston: Houghton Mifflin.

Lawson, C. A., & Paulson, R. E. (Eds.). (1958). *Laboratory and field studies in biology: A source book for secondary schools.* New York: Holt, Rinehart, & Winston.

Lehman, J. D., Carter, C., & Kahle, J. B. (1985). Concept mapping, vee mapping, and achievement: Result of a field study with black high school students. *Journal of Research in Science Teaching, 22*(7), 663–673.

Leonard, W. H. (1980). Using the extended discretion approach to biology laboratory investigation. *American Biology Teacher, 42*(7), 338.

Leonard, W. H. (1989). An experimental test of an extended discretion laboratory approach for university level biology. *Journal of Research in Science Teaching, 26*, 79–91.

Lepper, M. R., Greene, D., & Nisbett, R. E. (1973). Undermining children's intrinsic interest with extrinsic reward: A test of the "overjustification" hypothesis. *Journal of Personality and Social Psychology, 28*(1), 129–137.

Linn, M. C., Davis, E. A., & Bell, P. (2004). Inquiry and technology. In M. C. Linn, E. A. Davis, & P. Bell (Eds.), *Internet environments for science education.* Mahwah, NJ: Erlbaum.

Lott, G. W. (1983). The effect of inquiry teaching and advanced organizers upon student outcomes in science education. *Journal of Research in Science Teaching, 20*(5), 437–451.

Luria, A. R. (1961). *The role of speech in the regulation of normal and abnormal behavior.* New York: Irvington.

Marek, E. A., & Cavallo, A. M. L. (1997). *The learning cycle: Elementary school science and beyond.* Portsmouth, NH: Heinemann.

Marshall, P. L. (2002). *Cultural diversity in our schools.* Belmont, CA: Wadsworth/Thomson.

Matsumoto-Grah, K. (1992). Diversity in the classroom: A checklist. In D. A. Byrnes & G. Kiger (Eds.), *Common bonds—anti-bias teaching in diverse society.* Wheaton, MD: Association for Childhood Education International.

Mayer, W. V., & Barufaldi, J. P. (1988). *The textbook chooser's guide.* Berkeley, CA: National Center for Science Education.

Mazzolini, A. (1993). *Learning cycles in high school chemistry.* Unpublished manuscript, Department of Chemistry, Arizona State University.

McCombs, B. L. (1998). Integrating metacognition, affect, and motivation in improving teacher education. In N. M. Lambert & B. L. McCombs (Eds.), *How students learn: Reforming schools through learner-centered education.* Washington, DC: American Psychological Association.

McIntosh, N. (1996). *Why do we lecture?* (JHPIEGO Strategy Paper No. 2). Baltimore: JHPIEGO Corp.

Miller, G. A. (1956). The magical number seven, plus or minus two: Some limits on our capacity for processing information. *Psychological Review, 63*(2), 81–97.

Minstrell, J., & van Zee, E. H. (Eds.). (2000). *Inquiring into inquiry teaching.* Washington, DC: American Association for the Advancement of Science.

Mintzes, J., Wandersee, J., & Novak, J. (1998). *Teaching science for understanding.* San Diego, CA: Academic Press.

Musheno, B. V., & Lawson, A. E. (1999). Effects of learning cycle and traditional text on comprehension of science concepts by students at differing reasoning levels. *Journal of Research in Science Teaching, 36*(1), 23–37.

National Research Council (1990). *Fulfilling the promise: Biology education in the nation's schools.* Washington, DC: National Academy Press.

National Research Council. (1996). *Inquiry and the* National Science Education Standards: *A guide for teaching and learning.* Washington, DC: National Academy Press.

National Research Council. (2000a). *Inquiry and the National Science Education Standards: A guide for teaching and learning.* Washington, DC: National Academy Press.

National Research Council. (2000b). *Knowing and learning mathematics for teaching: Proceedings of a workshop.* Washington, DC: National Academy Press.

National Research Council. (2001). *Educating teachers of science, mathematics, and technology.* Washington, DC: National Academy Press.

New Jersey Department of Education. (1998). *New Jersey science curriculum framework.* Retrieved May 8, 2009, from www.state.nj.us/njded/frameworks/science/chap9c.pdf

Novak, J. D., Gowin, D. W., & Johansen, G. T. (1983). The use of concept mapping and knowledge vee mapping with junior high school science students. *Science Education, 67*(5), 625–645.

Papanastasiou, E., Zemblyas, M., & Vrasidas, C. (2003). Can computer use hurt science achievement? *Journal of Science Education and Technology, 12*(3), 325–332.

Paris, S. G. (1998). Why learner-centered assessment is better than high-stakes testing. In N. M. Lambert & B. L. McCombs (Eds.), *How students learn: Reforming schools through learner-centered education.* Washington, DC: American Psychological Association.

Payne, D. A. (2003). *Applied educational assessment* (2nd ed.). Belmont, CA: Wadsworth.

Piaget, J. (1962). The stages of the intellectual development of the child. *Bulletin of the Menninger Clinic, 26*(3), 120–145.

Piaget, J. (1964). Cognitive development in children: Development and learning. *Journal of Research in Science Teaching, 2*(2), 176–186.

Piaget, J. (1965). *The child's conception of number.* New York: Norton.

Piaget, J. (1976). Piaget's theory. In B. Inhelder & H. H. Chipman (Eds.), *Piaget and his school.* New York: Springer-Verlag.

Piburn, M., Sawada, D., Turley, J., Falconer, K., Benford, R., Bloom, I., et al. (2000). Reformed Teaching Observation Protocol (RTOP) reference manual (ACEPT Technical Report No. IN00–3). Tempe: Arizona Board of Regents. Retrieved May 19, 2009, from http://cresmet.asu.edu/instruments/RTOP/index.shtml

Pintrich, P. R., Marx, R. W., & Boyle, R. A. (1993). Beyond cold conceptual change: The role of motivational beliefs and classroom contextual factors in the process of conceptual change. *Review of Educational Research, 63*(2), 167–199.

Raven, J. C. (1940). *Matrix tests.* London: Mental Health.

Reis, S. M., Burns, D. E., & Renzulli, J. S. (1992). *Curriculum compacting: The complete guide to modifying the regular curriculum for high ability students.* Mansfield Center, CT: Creative Learning Press.

Renner, J. W., Stafford, D. G., Coffia, W. J., Kellogg, D. H., & Weber, M. C. (1973). An evaluation of the Science Curriculum Improvement Study. *School Science and Mathematics, 73*(4), 291–318.

Renner, P. (1993). *The art of teaching adults.* Vancouver, British Columbia, Canada: Training Associates.

Roehrig, G. H., & Luft, J. A. (2004). Constraints experienced by beginning secondary science teachers in implementing scientific lessons. *International Journal of Science Education, 26*(1), 3–24.

Rogers, C. (1983). *Freedom to learn for the 80s.* Columbus, OH: Charles E. Merrill.

Roschelle, J. M., Pea, R. D., Hoadley, C. M., Gordin, D. N., & Means, B. M. (2000). Changing how and what children learn in school with computer-based technologies. *Future of Children, 10*(2), 76–101.

Roth, W., & Duit, R. (2003). Emergence, flexibility, and stabilization of language in a physics classroom. *Journal of Research in Science Teaching, 40*(9), 689–697.

Rowe, M. B. (1973). *Teaching science as continuous inquiry.* New York: McGraw-Hill.

Rowe, M. B. (2003). Wait-time and rewards as instructional variables, their influence on language, logic, and fate control. *Journal of Research in Science teaching, 40*(Suppl.), 19–32.

Sadler, T. D. (2004). Informal reasoning regarding socioscientific issues: A critical review. *Journal of Research in Science Teaching, 41*(5), 513–536.

Sandholtz, J. H., Ringstaff, C., & Dwyer, D. C. (1997). *Teaching with technology: Creating student-centered classrooms.* New York: Teachers College Press.

Schwartz, R. S., & Lederman, N. G. (2002). "It's the nature of the beast": The influence of knowledge and intentions on learning and teaching nature of science. *Journal of Research in Science Teaching, 39*(3), 205–236.

Science Curriculum Improvement Study. (1970). *Subsystems and variables: Teacher's guide.* Chicago: Rand McNally.

Science Curriculum Improvement Study. (1973). *SCIS omnibus.* Berkeley, CA: Lawrence Hall of Science.

Science Research Associates. (1970). *Iowa Tests of Educational Development*, Grades 9–12, Form X5. Iowa City: College of Education, University of Iowa.

Semken, S. C. (2001). An indigenous physical geology course for Navajo undergraduates. *Geological Society of America Abstracts With Programs, 33*(5), A3.

Shayer, M., & Adey, P. S. (1993). Accelerating the development of formal thinking in middle and high school students IV: Three years after a two-year intervention. *Journal of Research in Science Teaching, 30*(4), 351–366.

She, H. C. (2004). Fostering radical conceptual change through dual-situated learning models. *Journal of Research in Science Teaching, 41*(2), 142–164.

Shymansky, J. A., Kyle, W. C., and Alport, J. M. (1983). The effects of new science curricula on student performance. *Journal of Research in Science Teaching, 20*(5), 387–404.

Simanek, D. (2003). Physics lecture demonstrations, with some problems and puzzles, too. Retrieved October 15, 2008, from http://www.lhup.edu/~dsimanek/scenario/demos.htm

Smith, E. L., & Anderson, C. W. (1987). Response to comments and criticism of "Plants as producers: A case study of elementary science teaching." *Journal of Research in Science Teaching, 24*(8), 771–772.

Southerland, S. A., Gess-Newsome, J., & Johnston, A. (2003). Portraying science in the classroom: Manifestation of scientists' beliefs in classroom practice. *Journal of Research in Science Teaching, 40*(7), 669–691.

Spearman, C., & Wynn-Jones, L. (1951). *Human ability.* London: Macmillan.

Sprick, R. S., & Howard, L. M. (1995). *The teacher's encyclopedia of behavior management: 100 problems, 500 plans.* Longmont, CO: Sopris West.

Stern, L., & Roseman, J. E. (2004). Can middle-school science textbooks help students learn important ideas? *Journal of Research in Science Teaching, 41*(6), 538–568.

Stiggins, R. J., Frisbie, D. A., & Griswold, P. A. (1989). Inside high school grading practices: Building a research agenda. *Educational Measurement: Issues and Practice, 8*(2), 5–14.

Strauss, R. P., & Sawyer, E. A. (1986). Some new evidence on teacher and student competencies. *Economics of Education Review, 5*(1), 41–48.

Sullivan, R. L., & McIntosh, N. (1996). Delivering effective lectures (JHPIEGO Strategy Paper). Retrieved October 20, 2008, from http://www.reproline.jhu.edu/english/6read/6training/lecture/delivering_lecture.htm

Sullivan, R. L., & Wircenski, J. L. (1996). *Technical presentation workbook*. New York: ASME Press.

Takemura, S., Matsubara, M., Manzno, V. U., Tadokoro, Y., & Nakayama, G. (1985). *A comparison of reasoning skills of Japanese and American middle school students*. Unpublished manuscript, The Japan-U.S. Cooperative Science Program, Hiroshima University.

Task Force on Laboratory Science. (1985). *Final report*. Phoenix: Arizona Board of Regents.

Thelen, J. N. (1979). Just because kids can't read doesn't mean they can't learn! *School Science and Mathematics, 79*(6), 457.

Thomas, R., & Hooper, E. (1991). Simulations: An opportunity we are missing. *Journal of Research on Computing in Education, 23*(4), 497–513.

Torrance, E. P. (1967). Scientific views of creativity and factors affecting its growth. In J. Kagan (Ed.), *Creativity and learning*. Boston: Beacon Press.

Towle, A. (2002). *Modern biology*. New York: Holt, Rinehart, & Winston.

Tufte, E. R. (2003). *The cognitive style of PowerPoint*. Cheshire, CT: Graphics Press.

U.S. Department of Education, National Center for Education Statistics. (1998). *Pursuing excellence: A study of U.S. twelfth-grade mathematics and science achievement in international context* (NCES 98–049). Washington, DC: U.S. Government Printing Office.

Van Deventer, W. C. (1958). A simplified approach to the problem of scientific methodology. *School Science and Mathematics, 58*, 90–95.

Victor, E. (1989). *Science for the elementary school* (6th ed.). New York: Macmillan.

Vygotsky, L. S. (1962). *Thought and language*. Cambridge, MA: The MIT Press.

Wallas, G. (1970). The art of thought. In P. E. Vernon (Ed.), *Creativity*. Middlesex, England: Penguin Education. (Original work published 1926)

Wandersee, J. H., Mintzes, J. J., & Novak, J. D. (1994). Research on alternative conceptions in science. In D. L. Gabel (Ed.), *Handbook of research on science teaching and learning*. New York: Macmillan.

Washton, N. S. (1967). *Teaching science creatively in the secondary schools*. Philadelphia: Saunders.

Watson, G. (1998). *Classroom discipline problem solver*. West Nyack, NY: The Center for Applied Research in Education.

Weaver, C. G. (1998). Strategies in K–12 science instruction to promote conceptual change. *Science Education, 82*(4), 455–472.

Wellington, J., & Osborne, J. (2001). *Language and literacy in science education*. Buckingham, England: Open University Press.

Wells, M., Hestenes, D., & Swackhammer, G. (1995). A modeling method for high school physics instruction. *American Journal of Physics, 63*(7), 606–619.

Wenglinsky, H. (1998). *Does it compute? The relationship between educational technology and student achievement in mathematics*. Princeton, NJ: ETS Policy Information Center.

Wenglinsky, H. (2000). *How teaching matters: Bringing the classroom back into discussions of teacher quality.* Princeton, NJ: The Educational Testing Service.

Wiggins, G., & McTighe, J. (2005). *Understanding by design* (2nd ed.). Alexandria, VA: Association for Supervision and Curriculum Development.

Yager, R. E. (1983). The importance of terminology in teaching K–12 science. *Journal of Research in Science Teaching, 20*(6), 577.

Yerrick, R. K., Doster, E., Nugent, J. S, Parke, H. M., & Crawley, F. E. (2003). Social interaction and the use of analogy: An analysis of preservice teachers' talk during physics inquiry lessons. *Journal of Research in Science Teaching, 40*(5), 443–463.

Yezierski, E. J., & Birk, J. P. (2006). Misconceptions about the particulate nature of matter: Using animations to close the gender gap. *Journal of Chemical Education, 83*(6), 954–960.

Credits

Chapter 1

Chapter Opening Photo: © 2009 Jupiterimages Corporation.

Figure 1.1: Jesus Solano/Getty Images.

Figure 1.2: © Karl Ammann/Getty Images.

Chapter 2

Chapter Opening Photo: © 2009 Jupiterimages Corporation.

Figure 2.1: Courtesy of David Smith Arizona State University.

Table 2.1: American Association for the Advancement of Science, 1989.

Chapter 3

Chapter Opening Photo: © Photo Artville Education High School CD.

Figure 3.6. From A. E. Lawson & Renner, 1975.

Chapter 4

Chapter Opening Photo: Photo by author.

Figure 4.5 Elementary Science Study, 1974.

Chapter 5

Chapter Opening Photo: Photo courtesy of Gerry Foster, Desert Vista High School, Phoenix, Arizona.

Chapter 6

Chapter Opening Photo: Photo courtesy of Gerry Foster, Desert Vista High School, Phoenix, Arizona.

Chapter 7

Chapter Opening Photo: © 2009 Jupiterimages Corporation.

Chapter 8

Chapter Opening Photo: Photo courtesy of Gerry Foster, Desert Vista High School, Phoenix, Arizona.

Table 8.1: *Source:* From *Science & Safety: Making the Connection,* by the Council of State Science Supervisors (n.d.), available at http://www.csss-science.org/downloads/scisafe.pdf.

Table 8.2: *Source:* From *Science & Safety: Making the Connection,* by the Council of State Science Supervisors (n.d.), available at http://www.csss-science.org/downloads/scisafe.pdf.

Table 8.3: *Source:* From *Science & Safety: Making the Connection,* by the Council of State Science Supervisors (n.d.), available at http://www.csss-science.org/downloads/scisafe.pdf.

Chapter 9

Chapter Opening Photo: © Photo Artville Education High School CD.

Table 9.1: From Sullivan, R.L., & McIntosh, N. (1996). Delivering effective lectures. JHPIEGO Strategy Paper. Online at http://www.reproline.jhu.edu/ english/6read/6training/lecture/delivering_lecture.htm.

Table 9.3: From *Science & Safety: Making the Connection,* by the Council of State Science Supervisors (n.d.), available at http://www.csss-science.org/downloads/scisafe.pdf.

Table 9.2: Chiappetta & Koballa, 2002.

Chapter 10

Chapter Opening Photo: © Banana Stock Teen Education CD.

Chapter 11

Chapter Opening Photo: © 2009 Jupiterimages Corporation.

Table 11.1: From Echevarria, Vogt, & Short, 2004.

Table 11.2: From Keller, E. (2005). Online at http://www.as.wvu.edu/~scidis/learning.html.

Chapter 12

Chapter Opening Photo: © 2009 Jupiterimages Corporation.

Figure 12.1: From A. E. Lawson, 2008.

Figure 12.3: From Semken, 2001.

Table 12.2: National Research Council, 1996, pp. 157–158, 186.

Chapter 13

Chapter Opening Photo: © Banana Stock Teen Education CD.

Table 13.1: From A. E. Lawson, Baker, DiDonato, Verdi, & Johnson, 1993.

Figure 13.1: From A. E. Lawson, Baker, DiDonato, Verdi, & Johnson, 1993.

Table 13.3: From *Performance Assessment Tasks, V. 9* © Maryland Assessment Consortium.

Table 13.4: From Arter & McTighe, 2001.

Table 13.5: From Payne, 2003.

Chapter 14

Chapter Opening Photo: © Photo Artville Education High School CD.

Chapter 15

Chapter Opening Photo:© 2009 Jupiterimages Corporation.

Table 15.1: Reprinted with permission from the National Board for Professional Teaching Standards. www.nbpts.org. All rights reserved.

Index

Note: In page references, f indicates figures and t indicates tables.

About the Author

Dr. Anton Lawson's career in science education began in the late 1960s in California where he taught middle school science and mathematics for 3 years before completing his PhD at the University of Oklahoma and moving to Purdue University in 1973. Lawson continued his research career at the University of California–Berkeley in 1974 and then moved to Arizona State University in 1977, where he currently conducts research and teaches courses in biology, in biology teaching methods, and in research methods. Lawson has directed over 150 workshops for teachers, mostly on inquiry teaching methods, and has published over 200 articles and over 20 books including *Science Teaching and the Development of Thinking* (1995), *Biology: A Critical Thinking Approach* (1994), and *The Neurological Basis of Learning, Development and Discovery* (2003). Lawson's most recent book is an introductory biology text called *Biology: An Inquiry Approach* (2008, 2nd ed.). Lawson is perhaps best known for his research articles in science education, which have three times been judged to be the most significant articles of the year by the National Association for Research in Science Teaching (NARST). He has also received NARST's career award for Distinguished Contributions to Science Education Through Research as well as the Outstanding Science Educator of the Year Award from the Association for the Education of Teachers in Science.

Supporting researchers for more than 40 years

Research methods have always been at the core of SAGE's publishing program. Founder Sara Miller McCune published SAGE's first methods book, *Public Policy Evaluation*, in 1970. Soon after, she launched the *Quantitative Applications in the Social Sciences* series—affectionately known as the "little green books."

Always at the forefront of developing and supporting new approaches in methods, SAGE published early groundbreaking texts and journals in the fields of qualitative methods and evaluation.

Today, more than 40 years and two million little green books later, SAGE continues to push the boundaries with a growing list of more than 1,200 research methods books, journals, and reference works across the social, behavioral, and health sciences. Its imprints—Pine Forge Press, home of innovative textbooks in sociology, and Corwin, publisher of PreK–12 resources for teachers and administrators—broaden SAGE's range of offerings in methods. SAGE further extended its impact in 2008 when it acquired CQ Press and its best-selling and highly respected political science research methods list.

From qualitative, quantitative, and mixed methods to evaluation, SAGE is the essential resource for academics and practitioners looking for the latest methods by leading scholars.

For more information, visit **www.sagepub.com**.